T0350387

Global Perspectives on Information Security Regulations:

Compliance, Controls, and Assurance

Guillermo A. Francia III
University of West Florida, USA

Jeffrey S. Zanzig
Jacksonville State University, USA

A volume in the Advances in
Information Security, Privacy, and
Ethics (AISPE) Book Series

Published in the United States of America by
   IGI Global
   Information Science Reference (an imprint of IGI Global)
   701 E. Chocolate Avenue
   Hershey PA, USA 17033
   Tel: 717-533-8845
   Fax: 717-533-8661
   E-mail: cust@igi-global.com
   Web site: http://www.igi-global.com

Copyright © 2022 by IGI Global. All rights reserved. No part of this publication may be reproduced, stored or distributed in any form or by any means, electronic or mechanical, including photocopying, without written permission from the publisher.
Product or company names used in this set are for identification purposes only. Inclusion of the names of the products or companies does not indicate a claim of ownership by IGI Global of the trademark or registered trademark.

Library of Congress Cataloging-in-Publication Data

Names: Francia, Guillermo, editor. | Zanzig, Jeffrey Scott, DATE editor.
Title: Global perspectives on information security regulations :
   compliance, controls, and assurance / Guillermo Francia III, and Jeffrey
   Zanzig, editor.
Description: Hershey PA : Information Science Reference, [2022] | Includes
   bibliographical references and index. | Summary: "This book summarizes
   current cybersecurity guidance and provides a compendium of innovative
   and state-of-the-art compliance and assurance practices and tools that
   can function both as a reference and pedagogical source for
   practitioners and educators"-- Provided by publisher.
Identifiers: LCCN 2021050104 (print) | LCCN 2021050105 (ebook) | ISBN
   9781799883906 (hardcover) | ISBN 9781799883913 (paperback) | ISBN
   9781799883920 (ebook)
Subjects: LCSH: Computer security. | Data protection. | Computer
   security--Law and legislation. | Data protection--Law and legislation.
Classification: LCC QA76.9.A25 G565 2022 (print) | LCC QA76.9.A25 (ebook)
   | DDC 005.8--dc23/eng/20211130
LC record available at https://lccn.loc.gov/2021050104
LC ebook record available at https://lccn.loc.gov/2021050105

This book is published in the IGI Global book series Advances in Information Security, Privacy, and Ethics (AISPE) (ISSN: 1948-9730; eISSN: 1948-9749)

British Cataloguing in Publication Data
A Cataloguing in Publication record for this book is available from the British Library.

All work contributed to this book is new, previously-unpublished material.
The views expressed in this book are those of the authors, but not necessarily of the publisher.

For electronic access to this publication, please contact: eresources@igi-global.com.

Advances in Information Security, Privacy, and Ethics (AISPE) Book Series

ISSN:1948-9730
EISSN:1948-9749

Editor-in-Chief: **Manish Gupta**, State University of New York, USA

MISSION

As digital technologies become more pervasive in everyday life and the Internet is utilized in ever increasing ways by both private and public entities, concern over digital threats becomes more prevalent.

The **Advances in Information Security, Privacy, & Ethics (AISPE) Book Series** provides cutting-edge research on the protection and misuse of information and technology across various industries and settings. Comprised of scholarly research on topics such as identity management, cryptography, system security, authentication, and data protection, this book series is ideal for reference by IT professionals, academicians, and upper-level students.

COVERAGE

- Global Privacy Concerns
- Cookies
- Telecommunications Regulations
- Tracking Cookies
- IT Risk
- Computer ethics
- Internet Governance
- Cyberethics
- Privacy Issues of Social Networking
- Device Fingerprinting

IGI Global is currently accepting manuscripts for publication within this series. To submit a proposal for a volume in this series, please contact our Acquisition Editors at Acquisitions@igi-global.com or visit: http://www.igi-global.com/publish/.

The Advances in Information Security, Privacy, and Ethics (AISPE) Book Series (ISSN 1948-9730) is published by IGI Global, 701 E. Chocolate Avenue, Hershey, PA 17033-1240, USA, www.igi-global.com. This series is composed of titles available for purchase individually; each title is edited to be contextually exclusive from any other title within the series. For pricing and ordering information please visit http://www.igi-global.com/book-series/advances-information-security-privacy-ethics/37157. Postmaster: Send all address changes to above address. Copyright © 2022 IGI Global. All rights, including translation in other languages reserved by the publisher. No part of this series may be reproduced or used in any form or by any means – graphics, electronic, or mechanical, including photocopying, recording, taping, or information and retrieval systems – without written permission from the publisher, except for non commercial, educational use, including classroom teaching purposes. The views expressed in this series are those of the authors, but not necessarily of IGI Global.

Titles in this Series

For a list of additional titles in this series, please visit:
https://www.igi-global.com/book-series/advances-information-security-privacy-ethics/37157#titles

For an entire list of titles in this series, please visit:
https://www.igi-global.com/book-series/advances-information-security-privacy-ethics/37157#titles

701 East Chocolate Avenue, Hershey, PA 17033, USA
Tel: 717-533-8845 x100 • Fax: 717-533-8661
E-Mail: cust@igi-global.com • www.igi-global.com

To my wife, Nimfa, for her boundless love, patience, and support. To my children, Jima and Xavier, for inspiring me to work harder and continue learning. Above all, to almighty God for all the blessings.
Guillermo A. Francia III

To my father and mother along with others including my siblings, teachers, and friends who have all been instrumental in helping me to grow as a person.
Jeffrey S. Zanzig

Table of Contents

Section 3
Cybersecurity Consulting and Assurance

Section 4
Other Information Security Concerns

Detailed Table of Contents

Section 1
Legislation and the Cybersecurity Environment

Chapter 1

    Miloslava Plachkinova, Kennesaw State University, USA

This study presents a historic overview of laws and regulations pertaining to cybersecurity issues in the United States. Cybersecurity is a relatively new field and has presented some unique challenges to law enforcement agencies in the last few decades. The author investigates the current state of legal frameworks to provide decision makers with mitigation steps when moving forward. More specifically, this study presents a possible approach to develop and evaluate policies to combat cybercrime. The theoretical lens used to explain offender motivation integrates rational choice, deterrence, and routine activity theories. The current work identifies trends and deficiencies in the existing cybersecurity laws and regulations. Exploring such problems can be a valuable tool to better understand this complex and rapidly developing field in which cybercriminals often rely on loopholes and lack of resources of law enforcement agencies to avoid prosecution.

Chapter 2

    Jeffrey S. Zanzig, Jacksonville State University, USA
    Guillermo A. Francia III, University of West Florida, USA

The rapid advancement of automotive vehicle communication technology ushered in the expansion of the cyber-attack surface on this type of transport system. A recent study projects that there will be 200 million vehicles on the road worldwide with embedded connectivity by 2025. The security and safety of these vehicles and, most importantly, their occupants are paramount. Recognizing this need, organizations consisting of entities from governments, manufacturers, service providers, professionals, and/or trade groups are constantly introducing, revising, and updating automotive vehicle security standards and regulations. This chapter examines the state of automotive vehicle communication, their vulnerabilities and security issues, the existing security standards and regulations that apply to this type of transport, and the compliance and auditing issues related to these directives. The chapter concludes with reflections and directions for continuous improvements and future research.

Section 2
Approaches to Cybersecurity Training

Chapter 3
Guillermo A. Francia III, University of West Florida, USA
Eman El-Sheikh, University of West Florida, USA

The critical infrastructure protection (CIP) set of standards is developed by the North American Electric Reliability Corporation (NERC) to ensure the protection of assets used to operate North America's bulk electric systems (BES). Any entity that owns or operates any type of BES in the United States and Canada must be compliant with the requirements of the NERC CIP standards. The purpose of this chapter is to provide an ample overview of the NERC CIP standards, to describe its relevance to the protection electric utility entities, to establish its harmonizing relation with the NIST cyber security framework, to provide a glimpse of its compliance requirements, and to investigate the gaps and prospects for workforce development training in this area of critical need. This chapter lays the foundation for opportunities in the design of automated NERC CIP standards compliance processes and toolkit, the feasibility study of adopting the CIP standards in other sectors, and the development of training materials in NERC CIP standards for workforce development.

Chapter 4
David Thornton, Jacksonville State University, USA

In this chapter, the author discusses the need for appropriate training to improve information security compliance and some of the human factors that lead to non-compliance. Following is a section on theories that attempt to model and predict compliance. The author discusses the use of serious games, games-based learning, and gamification as educational tools, and their strengths in providing some of the major training needs, including emotional engagement, intrinsic motivation, repetition, discussion, reflection, and self-efficacy. This is followed by a list of some prominent games and gamification tools in the field of information security. Finally, the author concludes with guidelines and considerations for information security professionals who may be considering the use of serious games and gamification to enhance their information security awareness training.

Section 3
Cybersecurity Consulting and Assurance

Chapter 5
    Jeffrey S. Zanzig, Jacksonville State University, USA

Information processing in a cyber environment offers tremendous benefits but is also accompanied by inevitable dangers including compromised confidentiality and malware such as ransomware that can shut down major segments of a country's operations. A variety of forms of guidance and regulation have been developed to deal with these cybersecurity issues. The professions of public accounting and internal audit have long worked with organizations to protect the integrity of their information systems. Both of these professions are working diligently to guide organization management in the area of cybersecurity. An important aspect of such services is an appropriate framework to use as a basis for advisement and assurance. One such framework is the Framework for Improving Critical Infrastructure Cybersecurity issued by the National Institute of Standards and Technology.

Chapter 6
    Thomas Tribunella, State University of New York at Oswego, USA
    Heidi Tribunella, University of Rochester, USA

Many organizations outsource their business processes to service providers. The service providers must be audited by certified public accountants (CPA) to check the design and operation of their security procedures and internal controls (IC). These reports are called service organization control (SOC) reports. Through these reports, a CPA can express an opinion on the ICs of the services provider. SOC reports come in several different formats depending on the circumstance. As outsourcing becomes more popular and computer crimes increase, SOC reports will be more important. The objective of this chapter is to explain SOC reports, how they are compiled, and how they are used. Accordingly, this chapter gives a technical description of SOC reports so that professionals in the areas of accounting, auditing, and risk management can understand the purpose, application, and value of SOC reports. The authors conclude that as managers put more information on the cloud, SOC reports will fill an important need since they inform managers about risk management issues such as internal controls.

Section 4
Other Information Security Concerns

Chapter 7

 Kátia Lemos, Research Centre on Accounting and Taxation, Polytechnic Institute of Cávado and Ave, Portugal
 Sara Serra, Research Centre on Accounting and Taxation, Polytechnic Institute of Cávado and Ave, Portugal
 Filipa Pacheco, Management School, Polytechnic Institute of Cávado and Ave, Portugal
 Maria Sofia Martins, Management School, Polytechnic Institute of Cávado and Ave, Portugal

The aim of this study is to analyze the influence of certain characteristics associated with the corporate governance model on the level of disclosure of financial risks in non-financial entities listed in Euronext Lisbon. For this purpose, a content analysis of the reports and accounts of those companies was conducted for the periods 2017 to 2019 through a disclosure index based on the disclosure requirements contained in international financial reporting standards. Subsequently, in order to assess the influence of the corporate governance model on the level of risk disclosure, several simple linear regression models were estimated, which correlate the disclosure index with certain characteristics associated with the board of directors and the auditor. The results obtained show that larger boards of directors with greater gender diversity and auditors belonging to the Big 4 positively influence the level of disclosure of financial risks.

Chapter 8

 Adamkolo Mohammed Ibrahim, University of Maiduguri, Nigeria
 Bukar Jamri, Yobe State University, Damaturu, Nigeria
 Abubakar Zakari, Federal Polytechnic, Damaturu, Nigeria

The first quarter of the 21st century has barely passed, but a barrage of 'disrupting' surprises emerged – from the proliferation of information and communication technologies (ICT) to the weaponisation of ICT itself. Hence, cyberfakes or cyber deceptions (e.g., deepfakes, fake news, and even hate speech) have the potential to cause monumental problems related to cybersecurity and other online information management for organisations, nations, and individuals. Because literature and theories related the novel cyber deceptions may be scanty, this chapter attempted to close this research and theoretical gaps by deriving concepts leading to the development of a 'modelled framework' for the study of deepfakes and other related cyber deceptions and violence in social, organisational, or national contexts. Performing brainstorming reviews of extant literature, several theoretical concepts were derived leading to the development of the unified model of digital deception and online hate pronouncement. Policy recommendations were offered at the end.

Chapter 9

This study aims to assess the effect of the Protection of Personal Information Act No. 4 of 2013 on research data ethics in South Africa. The Protection of Personal information Act No 4 of 2013 includes a clause on protection of confidentiality and privacy during the collection of data. This research recommends universities to develop privacy data policy and records management policy to improve compliance with the legislation. Furthermore, training and awareness of staff on data ethics is necessary in universities. The research ethics committees are to be established to provide advice on conducting of research in South African universities.

Preface

The pervasiveness of the Internet and society's unquenchable thirst for connectivity present security challenges that are constantly evolving in conjunction with rapid advances in technology. The mobile devices that are in the market today are twice as powerful and faster than those that were sold just two years ago. The new frontier, called cyberspace, presents both opportunities and challenges that must be controlled through the proper development of security mechanisms. Controls need to be established and maintained to protect the confidentiality, integrity, and availability of information; the privacy of consumers; the continuity of business activity; and world security. Indeed, a cyberwar between competing nations could easily escalate to a much larger conflict that could involve many countries.

Recognizing the need for cybersecurity directives and controls, government regulations are continuously being enacted and industry standards are being established. Compliance with these regulations or standards does not necessarily translate to achieving a full measure cybersecurity. Everyone must realize that cybersecurity is a process and not a goal. Technology appears to introduce vulnerabilities as rapidly as it evolves.

This compendium of works detailing regulations, standards, compliance, auditing, and assessment illustrates the multifaceted nature of cybersecurity that cuts across national boundaries, industry sectors, societies, and cultures.

ORGANIZATION OF THE BOOK

The book is organized into nine chapters. The abstract of each of the chapters follows:

Chapter 1: This study presents a historic overview of laws and regulations pertaining to cybersecurity issues in the United States. Cybersecurity is a relatively new field and has presented some unique challenges to law enforcement agencies in the last few decades. The author investigates the current state of legal frameworks to provide decision makers with mitigation steps when moving forward. More specifically, this study presents a possible approach to develop and evaluate policies to combat cybercrime. The theoretical lens used to explain offender motivation integrates rational choice, deterrence, and routine activity theories. The current work identifies trends and deficiencies in the existing cybersecurity laws and regulations. Exploring such problems can be a valuable tool to better understand this complex and rapidly developing field, in which cybercriminals often rely on loopholes and lack of resources of law enforcement agencies to avoid prosecution.

Chapter 2: The rapid advancement of automotive vehicle communication technology ushered in the expansion of the cyber-attack surface on this type of transport system. A recent study projects that there will be 200 million vehicles on the road worldwide with embedded connectivity by 2025. The security and safety of these vehicles and, most importantly, their occupants are paramount. Recognizing this need, organizations consisting of entities from governments, manufacturers, service providers, professionals, and/or trade groups are constantly introducing, revising, and updating automotive vehicle security standards and regulations. This chapter examines the state of automotive vehicle communication, their vulnerabilities and security issues, the existing security standards and regulations that apply to this type of transport, and the compliance and auditing issues related to these directives. The chapter concludes with reflections and directions for continuous improvements and future research.

Chapter 3: The Critical Infrastructure Protection (CIP) set of standards is developed by the North American Electric Reliability Corporation (NERC) to ensure the protection of assets used to operate North America's Bulk Electric Systems (BES). Any entity that owns or operates any type of BES in the United States and Canada must be compliant with the requirements of the NERC CIP Standards. The purpose of this chapter is to provide an ample overview of the NERC CIP Standards, to describe its relevance to the protection electric utility entities, to establish its harmonizing relation with the NIST Cyber Security Framework, to provide a glimpse of its compliance requirements, and to investigate the gaps and prospects for workforce development training in this area of critical need. This chapter lays the foundation for opportunities in the design of automated NERC CIP Standards compliance processes and toolkit, the feasibility study of adopting the CIP Standards in other sectors, and the development of training materials in NERC CIP Standards for workforce development.

Chapter 4: In this chapter, the author discusses the need for appropriate training to improve information security compliance and some of the human factors that lead to non-compliance. Following is a section on theories that attempt to model and predict compliance. The author discusses the use of serious games, games-based learning, and gamification as educational tools, and their strengths in providing some of the major training needs, including emotional engagement, intrinsic motivation, repetition, discussion, reflection, and self-efficacy. This is followed by a list of some prominent games and gamification tools in the field of information security. Finally, the author concludes with guidelines and considerations for information security professionals who may be considering the use of serious games and gamification to enhance their information security awareness training.

Chapter 5: Information processing in a cyber environment offers tremendous benefits but is also accompanied by inevitable dangers including compromised confidentiality and malware such as ransomware that can shut down major segments of a country's operations. A variety of forms of guidance and regulation have been developed to deal with these cybersecurity issues. The professions of public accounting and internal audit have long worked with organizations to protect the integrity of their information systems. Both of these professions are working diligently to guide organization management in the area of cybersecurity. An important aspect of such services is an appropriate framework to use as a basis for advisement and assurance. One such framework is the Framework for Improving Critical Infrastructure Cybersecurity issued by the National Institute of Standards and Technology.

Chapter 6: Many organizations outsource their business processes to service providers. The service providers must be audited by Certified Public Accountants (CPA) to check the design and operation of their security procedures and internal controls (IC). These reports are called Service Organization Control (SOC) reports. Through these reports a CPA can express an opinion on the ICs of the services provider. SOC reports come in several different formats depending on the circumstance. As outsourcing becomes more popular and computer crimes increase, SOC reports will be more important. The objective of this chapter is to explain SOC reports, how they are compiled, and how they are used. Accordingly, this chapter gives a technical description of SOC reports so that professionals in the areas of accounting, auditing and risk management can understand the purpose, application, and value of SOC reports. The authors conclude that as managers put more information on the cloud, SOC reports will fill an important need since they inform managers about risk management issues such as internal controls.

Chapter 7: The aim of this study is to analyze the influence of certain characteristics associated with the corporate governance model on the level of disclosure of financial risks in non-financial entities, listed in Euronext Lisbon. For this purpose, a content analysis of the reports and accounts of those companies was conducted, for the periods 2017 to 2019, through a disclosure index, based on the disclosure requirements contained in International Financial Reporting Standards. Subsequently, in order to assess the influence of the corporate governance model on the level of risk disclosure, several simple linear regression models were estimated, which correlate the disclosure index with certain characteristics associated with the board of directors and the auditor. The results obtained show that larger boards of directors, with greater gender diversity and auditors belonging to the Big 4 positively influence the level of disclosure of financial risks.

Chapter 8: The first quarter of the 21st-century has barely passed than a barrage of 'disrupting' surprises emerged – from the proliferation of information and communication technologies (ICT) and to the weaponisation of ICT itself. Hence, cyberfakes or cyber deceptions (e.g., deepfakes, fake news, and even hate speech) have the potential to cause monumental problems related to cybersecurity and other online information management for organisations, nations, and individuals. Because literature and theories related the novel cyber deceptions may be scanty, this chapter attempted to close this research and theoretical gaps by deriving concepts leading to the development of a 'modelled framework' for the study of deepfakes and other related cyber deceptions and violence in social, organisational, or national contexts. Performing brainstorming reviews of extant literature, several theoretical concepts were derived leading to the development of the Unified Model of Digital Deception and Online Hate Pronouncement. Policy recommendations were offered at the end.

Chapter 9: This study aim to assess the effect of the Protection of Personal Information Act No. 4 of 2013 on research data ethics in South Africa. The Protection of Personal information Act No 4 of 2013 includes clause on protection of confidentiality and privacy during the collection of data. This research recommend universities to develop privacy data policy and records management policy to improve compliance with the legislation. Furthermore training and awareness of staff on data ethics is necessary in universities. The research ethics committees are to be established to provide advice on conducting of research in South Africa universities.

Acknowledgment

The editors would like to acknowledge the help of all the people involved in this project and, more specifically, to the authors and reviewers that took part in the review process. Without their support, this book would not have become a reality.

First, the editors would like to thank each one of the authors for their contributions. Our sincere gratitude goes to the chapter's authors who contributed their time and expertise to this book.

Second, the editors wish to acknowledge the valuable contributions of the reviewers regarding the improvement of quality, coherence, and content presentation of chapters. Most of the authors also served as referees; we highly appreciate their double task. Special mention goes to Dr. Orlando Catuiran, University of Bahrain, Bahrain, Dr. Garg Anchal, University of Bolton, UK, Dr. Srinivasarao Krishnaprasad, Jacksonville State University, USA, and Dr. Imane Lamrani, Arizona State University, USA, for their invaluable contributions in providing additional and insightful reviews of the manuscript.

Finally, we want to express our gratitude to Ms. Angelina Olivas, Assistant Development Editor at IGI-Global for her guidance, patience, and encouragement during the entire development process.

Guillermo A. Francia
University of West Florida, USA

Jeffrey S. Zanzig
Jacksonville State University, USA

Introduction

In today's world, practically all our lives depend on computers and the Internet. Problems arise when hackers attempt to take advantage of vulnerabilities in software and computer systems. The motives of a hacker can range from just performing some mischief to harmful activities such as theft, altering information content, or even destroying information. Cybersecurity is the process of shielding data, devices, and networks from unapproved access or illegal use, and the exercise of safeguarding the availability, confidentiality, and integrity of information (Cybersecurity & Infrastructure Security Agency, 2019). To better understand how society came to this point, it should be considered how it all began with the best of intentions to establish a reliable communications network for research and defense.

HOW IT ALL BEGAN

The history of cybersecurity began with the birth of the Internet, which can be initially traced to the 1970s with the creation of the Advanced Research Projects Agency Network (ARPANET). At first, ARPANET expanded with little public knowledge of its existence. On January 1, 1975, it was placed under the explicit control of the Defense Communication Agency (DCA) who became concerned about the lack of control of the network. The DCA warned against unauthorized persons accessing and using the network, hoping to limit its use to military persons or validated persons working on government contracts. However, by the early 1980s the network was pretty much open access to users regardless of whether they were authorized. The access situation got even more out of control when there was a significant drop in computer prices giving more persons the ability to access the network (The Conversation, 2016).

To deal with the situation, ARPANET was split into two distinct networks. The one part kept the name ARPANET and was primarily devoted to research. The other part known as MILNET served as a military operational network shielded by strong security measures involving limited access control and the use of encryption.

By the middle of the 1980s, many researchers and developers began using the network. In 1984, the National Science Foundation (NSF) began using ARPANET as the backbone for its own network NSFNET. Under the guidance of the NSF, the use of the network was guided into the development of private and long-haul networks. "The ARPANET was officially decommissioned in 1990, whilst in 1995 the NSFNET was shut down and the Internet effectively privatized. By then the network – no longer the private enclave of computer scientists or militaries – had become the Internet" (The Conversation, 2016). Few would argue that the growth Internet has expanded the ability of society to obtain valuable knowledge and engage in electronic commerce. However, the issue of lack of control expressed by the DCA has only gotten worse as the Internet becomes a greater part of our everyday lives.

With the Internet becoming publicly available in the 1990, more and more persons started to put personal information online. Organized crime quickly recognized this as an opportunity to generate revenue by using the web to steal data of both people and the government. With the tremendous increase in network security threats, there was a strong demand for both antivirus programs and network firewalls to provide protection from hackers. After the turn of the century, organized crime stepped up their attacks by funding professional cyberattacks. The role of information security began to increase significantly, and governments began handing down more serious penalties against hackers (Davies, 2021).

INFORMATION SECURITY

Information Security entails the protection of information and information systems from unauthorized access, use, disclosure, disruption, modification, or destruction in order to provide confidentiality, integrity, and availability (National Institute of Standards and Technology, 2006).

Information security encompasses several domains: application security, cloud security, Information Technology (IT) risk management, vulnerability management, network and infrastructure security, incident response, intrusion detection and prevention, personnel security, data protection and cryptography, and privacy, legal, and ethical issues. Application security is focused on the security of software that is used to process the information that is pushed or pulled by the user or other system applications. Cloud security refers to the protection of services that are provided by a third party. Most of the applications available on the Internet are hosted by cloud service infrastructures. IT risk management entails the prevention, mitigation, and assessment of risks. It also covers threat detection and control. Vulnerability management is focused on the identification, assessment, and remediation of vulnerabilities. Network and infrastructure security deals with the protection of network and infrastructure systems and devices that are used to conduct effective and efficient business operations. Incident response refers to the planning and handling of unwanted security incidents and the business recovery mechanisms. Intrusion detection and prevention refers to the technologies and techniques for the prevention, detection, reaction, and remediation from security intrusions. Personnel security includes programs such as awareness training, physical and system access controls, and human resource policies and procedures on security. Data protection and cryptography safeguards information, whether in transit or at rest, using a reasonably strong encryption mechanism. Privacy, legal, and ethical issues are implicitly affected by information security via personal identification protection, regulatory constraints and compliance, and ethical standards that must be upheld.

THE GROWTH OF REGULATION

Due to growing concerns over information security, recent years have seen a proliferation of cybersecurity guidance in the form of government regulations and standards with which organizations must comply. As society becomes more heavily dependent on cyberspace, increasing levels of security measures will need to be established and maintained to protect the confidentiality, integrity, and availability of information; the privacy of consumers; and the continuity of economic activity.

There is no doubt that cyberattacks are increasing in size, sophistication, and volume. However, increases in regulation are unlikely to solve the problem if they are implemented in an uncoordinated and piecemeal approach that just makes it more difficult to manage cyber risks. Coordination in the development of cybersecurity standards is imperative to achieve long-term success in implementing appropriate guidance and regulations (Fitch Ratings, 2021). A primary component in achieving such coordination is to ensure that such regulations draw upon common frameworks of information security that are continually updated to reflect the growth of technology and the accompanying vulnerabilities that are bound to arise.

This book summarizes current cybersecurity guidance and provides a compendium of innovative and state-of-the-art compliance and assurance practices and tools that can function both as a reference and pedagogical source for practitioners and educators. It also provides a synopsis of current cybersecurity guidance that organizations should consider in establishing and updating their cybersecurity systems. This book provides company management, practitioners, and academics with a good summary of current guidance and how to conduct assurance of compliance.

The target audience of this book is composed of professionals, researchers, students and faculty working in the field of information security; and knowledge management in various disciplines, (e.g., library, information and communication sciences, administrative sciences and management, education, law, sociology, computer science, and information technology). Moreover, the book provides insights to support executives concerned with regulatory compliance, controls, and assessment practices.

ORGANIZATION OF THE BOOK

The following summarizes some of the content of this book:

Chapter 1 takes note of the fact that the constantly changing environment of technology makes it very difficult for legislation in the United States and elsewhere to keep pace with various cybersecurity issues. The chapter reviews a variety of federal and state laws and proposes a model to address the problem. It presents important insights in cybercrime and cyber deterrence. These insights are based on three theoretical frameworks: rational choice theory, deterrence theory, and routine activity theory. Cybersecurity policy makers and legislative bodies may be able to utilize such frameworks in developing new laws and regulations.

Chapter 2 considers that although advances in vehicle communication technologies have brought in a variety of automotive features from automated braking to the development of autonomous vehicles, these same technologies also provide an entry point for cybersecurity attacks. The chapter considers a variety of vehicle security standards and regulations. In addition, it illustrates how best practices suggested by the National Highway Traffic Safety Administration (NHTSA) are linked to the National Institute of Standards and Technology (NIST) Cybersecurity Framework and COBIT 2019. The chapter raises the issue of the lag of the enactment of regulations with the development of new technologies. These regulations affect the lives and limbs of both vehicle occupants and pedestrians. It is imperative that security and safety regulations be in lock-step with new technologies.

Chapter 3 points out that both implementers and auditors of systems of cybersecurity need training regarding cybersecurity standards. The North American Electric Reliability Corporation (NERC) has developed a set of Critical Infrastructure Protection (CIP) Standards. The chapter describes 12 of those standards and provides a mapping of them to the National Institute of Standards and Technology (NIST) Cybersecurity Framework. It also describes the development of a course on NERC-CIP compliance. With the renewed and urgent concern on Critical Infrastructure protection due to the current events in Europe, the chapter is of great interest to practitioners, educators, and government officials. Although the NERC-CIP standards address a small segment of the US critical infrastructure—the electric utility sector, they have a far-reaching influence in deterring cyberattacks that could devastate the entire country.

Chapter 4 points out that the human element is often the weakest link regarding information security. Current approaches to training personnel are often not effective in achieving an appropriate level of security compliance. The chapter considers theories that attempt to model and predict compliance and proposes an approach to security training known as gamification, which incorporates game mechanics into a non-game context. It argues that gamification is an effective and innovative way of achieving regulatory compliance on information security awareness training. The arguments for game-based learning are supported by solid pedagogical theories. With this chapter, the long-sought solution to the weakest chain in cybersecurity may be within reach.

Chapter 5 considers the cybersecurity consulting and assurance services offered by certified public accountants and internal auditors. Such engagements should have a framework that is both comprehensive and regularly updated. The chapter describes how the Framework for Improving Critical Infrastructure Cybersecurity as issued by the National Institute of Standards and Technology offers such a framework that is grounded in recognized guidance including COBIT 2019. The chapter illustrates the manner with which other professionals could have a significant impact in improving an organization's cybersecurity posture. Certified public accountants and internal auditors are major players in regulatory compliance assessment and, consequently, security confidence builders.

Chapter 6 points out that many organizations in today's world outsource some of their business processes. The chapter considers the role of Service Organization Control (SOC) reports to meet the needs of certified public accountants in obtaining an evaluation of internal controls over outsourced business processes. Further, the chapter refers to the fact that many processes are being outsourced to external service organizations and it is prudent to require these organizations to produce the relevant SOC reports. By highlighting this requirement, the chapter provides awareness of a best practice in promoting information security.

Chapter 7 considers organization governance by weighing if certain characteristics influence the level of an organization's financial risk disclosure. Specific items evaluated include characteristics regarding the board of directors and the external auditor. The chapter describes an empirical study on the influence of the make-up of the board of directors on risk disclosure. The results provide insights into financial risk disclosures and governance mechanisms that could influence future regulatory enhancements and enforcement mechanisms.

Chapter 8 addresses the use of deepfakes in creating misinformation. To mislead the viewer, the creation of a deepfake involves the fabrication of images or videos that portray events that are false but are represented in a manner that makes the occurrence appear as real as possible. The chapter correctly posits that the gap between emerging technologies and systems to regulate them exists and that the complex legislative processes are too slow to respond and adapt. This observation is a major take-away from this book. It would be fitting and proper to recognize this global phenomenon because the rapid development of technology across the globe will only exacerbate the problem.

Chapter 9 considers the environment of research in South African universities and how it is influenced by the Protection of Personal Information Act of 2013. The chapter points out that universities need to improve polices over privacy and records management to better comply with the legislation. Although this issue is not as prevalent in the US due to the existence of Institutional Review Boards (IRBs) in most research institutions, the chapter highlights an issue that could easily get out of control. This can happen especially when research collaborations cross campus boundaries. Indeed, with a weak information security posture, personal data can be compromised when improperly handled.

The chapters described above present problems on information security along with current legislation, frameworks, and a variety of approaches to address those problems. Compliance is a measure of the extent to which a current state is in conformance with a desired state. A global phenomenon that is worth repeating is the fact that legislations and standards are barely keeping up with advancing technologies. The desired state will only be achieved through a collaborative effort involving research, proactive and appropriate legislation, and assurance services.

REFERENCES

Cybersecurity & Infrastructure Security Agency. (2019, November 19). Retrieved March 6, 2022, from What is Cybersecurity?: https://www.cisa.gov/uscert/ncas/tips/ST04-001

Davies, V. (2021, October 4). *Cyber*. Retrieved 03 6, 2022, from The History of Cybersecurity: https://cybermagazine.com/cyber-security/history-cybersecurity

Fitch Ratings. (2021, May 25). *Evolving US Regulation a Positive Step in Addressing Cyber Risks*. Retrieved March 6, 2022, from https://www.fitchratings.com/research/insurance/evolving-us-regulation-positive-step-in-addressing-cyber-risks-25-05-2021

National Institute of Standards and Technology (NIST). (2006). FIPS Pub 200: Minimum Security Requirements for Federal Information and Information Systems. U.S. Department of Commerce. Gaithersburg, MD: NIST.

The Conversation. (2016, November 2). Retrieved March 6, 2022, from How the Internet was born: from the ARPANET to the Internet: https://theconversation.com/how-the-internet-was-born-from-the-arpanet-to-the-internet-68072

Section 1

Legislation and the Cybersecurity Environment

Chapter 1
US Cybersecurity Laws and Regulations:
Current Trends and Recommendations for Improvement

Miloslava Plachkinova
Kennesaw State University, USA

ABSTRACT

This study presents a historic overview of laws and regulations pertaining to cybersecurity issues in the United States. Cybersecurity is a relatively new field and has presented some unique challenges to law enforcement agencies in the last few decades. The author investigates the current state of legal frameworks to provide decision makers with mitigation steps when moving forward. More specifically, this study presents a possible approach to develop and evaluate policies to combat cybercrime. The theoretical lens used to explain offender motivation integrates rational choice, deterrence, and routine activity theories. The current work identifies trends and deficiencies in the existing cybersecurity laws and regulations. Exploring such problems can be a valuable tool to better understand this complex and rapidly developing field in which cybercriminals often rely on loopholes and lack of resources of law enforcement agencies to avoid prosecution.

DOI: 10.4018/978-1-7998-8390-6.ch001

Copyright © 2022, IGI Global. Copying or distributing in print or electronic forms without written permission of IGI Global is prohibited.

INTRODUCTION

Cybersecurity is a rapidly growing field that has already presented numerous challenges and opportunities. For instance, in the last few decades technology has radically changed the way we communicate and do business. It has impacted every aspect of our lives and while many of those changes have been positive, certain individuals have taken advantage of technology to commit crime in cyberspace. These crimes vary greatly – data breaches, ransomware, money laundering, hacking, identity theft, and child pornography, just to name a few. According to Vailshery (2021), 50 billion devices are expected to be connected to the Internet by 2030. The growing number of such devices demonstrates the need to proactively address the issue of their exploitation by cybercriminals. Identifying the gaps in current laws and regulations in the US is a great first step in raising awareness about cybercrime and the challenges associated with prosecuting the individuals who commit those crimes.

Cybersecurity has become a matter of global interest and importance. Already more than 50 nations have officially published some form of strategy document outlining their official stance on cyberspace, cybercrime, and/or cybersecurity (Klimburg, 2012). The Whitehouse (2011) outlined a cyber strategy that provides the stance of the US government on cyber-related issues and developed a unified approach to the country's engagement with other countries on cyber issues. While this is a more recent attempt at addressing the issue, it is important to review other pieces of legislation to better understand how the US is approaching the issue on a federal and state level.

One of the biggest challenges of developing adequate legal frameworks is the fact that technology changes so rapidly, while the process of creating, reviewing, approving, and passing any piece of legislation takes significantly long time. To further complicate the issue, often lobbyists and politicians want to push forward their own agendas, which does not always align with societal needs. Thus, moving forward, it is necessary to think of ways how this problem can be resolved, so that cybercriminals are not able to avoid prosecution. From a criminological standpoint, currently, there is little deterrence to commit cybercrime. Thus, assuming that attackers make logical decisions, rational choice theory posits that they will continue to offend given there is minimal risk of being caught (Cornish & Clarke, 1986). Another significant issue is related to the multiple jurisdictions when it comes to cybercrime, so figuring how to secure the cooperation of multiple agencies on a local, state, national, and international level is imperative. While reviewing international legislation is beyond the focus of the current study, it is necessary to put the problem into perspective and also consider the big picture when making recommendations to policy makers in the US.

BACKGROUND

Cybersecurity

Definition

In most literature, cybersecurity is used as an all-inclusive term. Definitions of this term vary. For example the International Telecommunications Union (ITU) (2008) defines cyber security as follows:

Cybersecurity is the collection of tools, policies, security concepts, security safeguards, guidelines, risk management approaches, actions, training, best practices, assurance and technologies that can be used to protect the cyber environment and organization and user's assets. Organization and user's assets include connected computing devices, personnel, infrastructure, applications, services, telecommunications systems, and the totality of transmitted and/or stored information in the cyber environment. Cybersecurity strives to ensure the attainment and maintenance of the security properties of the organization and user's assets against relevant security risks in the cyber environment. The general security objectives comprise the following: availability, integrity, which may include authenticity and nonrepudiation, and confidentiality. (ITU, 2008)

This definition showcases the complexity of the problem and its impact on a variety of aspects – not only devices, but also individuals, processes, and data. Such complexity makes it challenging to develop legal frameworks that can encompass the entirety of cybersecurity as a field. Von Solms and Van Niekerk (2013) have done an extensive review of other terms, such as "information security" or "data security", to describe this phenomenon. For the purposes of the current study, the author will use the term "cybersecurity" as it best reflects the focus of the work.

Trends

While cybersecurity is a relatively new field, it has been growing with an astonishing pace. For instance, the World Wide Web (WWW) became publicly available in 1991 (Bryant, 2011) and just 30 years later, there are more Internet-connected devices than people (Vailshery, 2021). This rapid growth was also noted by criminals who started using technology as a new arena to commit crime. For more than a decade, cybersecurity has been a concern for the government and the private sector alike. The increasing number of cybercrimes have caused a huge loss to the US government and its people.

Data breaches are one example of these relatively new crimes. They have gained more attention due to the impact of digitization on financial, healthcare, small and medium enterprises, and other industries. Even though data breaches occurred before digitization became popular, but the popularity of the digital platforms gave a new dimension to these breaches as the importance, volume, and cost of the data breaches have increased considerably. The number of data breaches in the U.S. increased from 157 million in 2005 to 781 million in 2015, while the number of exposed records jumped from around 67 million to 169 million during the same time frame. In 2016, the number of data breaches in the United States amounted to 1,093 with close to 36.6 million records exposed (Clement, 2019). These are just some examples of the growing trend of reliance on technology and the new opportunities this provides to criminals.

The year 2016 witnessed the largest data breach till date in US history as online platform Yahoo revealed that hackers stole user data and information related to at least 500 million accounts back in 2014. In December 2016, the company announced another hack dating back to 2013 that affected over 1 billion user records (Clement, 2019). Privacy Rights Clearinghouse (2010) has been keeping track of data breaches involving personal information such as Social Security numbers, account numbers, and driver's license numbers that can be used by identity thieves. These concerning trends indicate the need to proactively address the issue of cybersecurity and protection not on a case-by-case basis but on a state and federal level and provide law enforcement agencies with the tools and resources they need to do investigate and prosecute cybercriminals.

US Cybersecurity Laws and Regulations

The US cybersecurity laws and privacy system is among the oldest, most robust, and effective in the world. Unlike the European Union, the US privacy system relies more on post hoc government enforcement and private litigation. Currently, cyber security regulation comprises of directives from the Executive Branch and legislation from Congress that safeguards information technology and computer systems. The purpose of cyber security regulation is to force companies and organizations to protect their systems and information from cyber-attacks such as viruses, trojan horses, phishing, denial of service (DOS) attacks, unauthorized access (stealing intellectual property or confidential information) and control system attacks.

Overview

While legislature addressing certain technical concerns has existed for a while, laws and regulations specifically referring to cybersecurity in the USA are relatively recent. For instance, in 2011 the Department of Defense (DoD) released a Strategy for Operating in Cyberspace, which included five main initiatives: to treat cyberspace as an operational domain, to employ new defensive concepts to protect DoD networks and systems, to partner with other agencies and the private sector in pursuit of a "whole-of-government cybersecurity Strategy", to work with international allies in support of collective cybersecurity and to support the development of a cyber workforce capable of rapid technological innovation (DoD, 2011). Schooner & Berteau (2012) point out that systems protecting critical infrastructure, called cyber critical infrastructure protection (CIO) of cyber have also been included by the DoD. In fact, in 2018 The Cybersecurity and Infrastructure Security Agency (CISA) became a standalone US federal agency, under the Department of Homeland Security (DHS). According to Cimpanu (2018), its purpose was "to improve cybersecurity across all levels of government, coordinate cybersecurity programs with U.S. states, and improve the government's cybersecurity protections against private and nation-state hackers." These actions demonstrate the government's strategy to consolidate its efforts to combat cybercrime on a federal level.

In November 2013, the DoD put forward the new cybersecurity rule (78 Fed. Reg. 69373), which described certain obligations for contractors including compliance with certain NIST IT (National Institute of Standards and Technology Information Technology) standards, mandatory reporting of cybersecurity incidents to the DoD, and a "flow-down" clause that applies the same requirements to subcontractors (Schooner & Berteau, 2014). A Congressional report from June 2013 found there were over 50 statutes relevant to cybersecurity compliance. The Federal Information Security Management Act of 2002 (FISMA) is one of the key statutes governing federal cybersecurity regulations (Schooner & Berteau, 2014). FISMA together with the Federal Risk and Authorization Management Program (FedRAMP) have also been used to assist to standardize cloud auditing and compliance practices not only for the federal government, but for the private sector as well (Gupta, 2020).

Federal Government Regulations

There are very few federal cybersecurity regulations and they are mostly focused on specific industries. The three main cybersecurity regulations are the Health Insurance Portability and Accountability Act (HIPAA) of 1996, the Gramm-Leach-Bliley Act of 1999, and the Homeland Security Act of 2002, which includes FISMA. These three regulations describe that healthcare organizations, financial institutions and federal agencies, respectively, should protect their systems and information.

However, they only require a "reasonable" level of security without describing any specifics and without providing much guidance to security professionals how to exactly implement these regulations. To illustrate, FISMA, which applies to every government agency, "requires the development and implementation of mandatory policies, principles, standards, and guidelines on information security" (Aliyev et al., 2020). Another issue with existing policies is that they do not address other technological organizations, such as Internet Service Providers (ISPs), hardware, software, and data mining companies, car manufacturers, etc. Furthermore, the vague language of regulations leaves much room for interpretation and ambiguity when cases are filed in court. An implication stemming from defining only the basic security standards in current legislation is the fact that technological companies are not incentivized to spend more time and resources to go above and beyond the bare minimum.

Cybersecurity Information Sharing Act (CISA)

The objective of the Cybersecurity Information Sharing Act (CISA) is to detect, prevent, or mitigate cybersecurity threats through enhanced information sharing. The law allows the sharing of Internet traffic information between the US government and technology and manufacturing companies. In addition, CISA emphasizes that federal agencies must identify and mitigate skill shortages in federal workforce positions requiring the performance of cybersecurity functions. Through discovering such talent gaps, the government can be better prepared to build a more skilled workforce and address the existing knowledge gaps.

Bill S.754

Bill S.754 is called "To improve cybersecurity in the United States through enhanced sharing of information about cybersecurity threats, and for other purposes". It was first introduced in the U.S. Senate on July 10, 2014 and passed as a bill on October 27, 2015. The purpose of the bill is to require the Director of National Intelligence and the Departments of Homeland Security, Defense, and Justice to proactively share cybersecurity threat information with private entities and organizations from outside of their respective agencies. Bill S.754 aims to increase collaboration between the government and industry in an effort to combat cybercrime.

Cybersecurity Enhancement Act of 2014

Cybersecurity Enhancement Act of 2014 or S.1353, was signed into law on December 18, 2014. Its purpose is to provide for an ongoing, voluntary public-private partnership to improve cybersecurity, and to strengthen cybersecurity research and development, workforce development and education, and public awareness and preparedness, and for other purposes.

The Cybersecurity Enhancement Act of 2014 also requires the Director of NIST to facilitate the development of a "voluntary, industry-led, consensus-based" set of cybersecurity standards and best practices for "critical infrastructure." The bill calls for the Director of NIST to coordinate closely with the private sector in developing these standards, which should incorporate industry best practices and align with voluntary international cybersecurity standards "to the fullest extent possible." In addition, federal, state, and local governments are forbidden from using information shared by a private entity to develop such standards for the purpose of regulating that entity (Cybersecurity Enhancement Act, 2014).

Data Security and Breach Notification Act of 2015

H.R.1770 - Data Security and Breach Notification Act of 2015 was first introduced in 2015 and was amended by the Committee on Energy and Commerce in 2017. This bill requires a health insurance exchange to notify everyone whose personal information is known to have been acquired or accessed as a result of a breach of security of any system maintained by the exchange as soon as possible but not later than 60 days after discovery of the breach. The purpose of the Data Security and Breach Notification Act of 2015 is (1) to protect consumers from identity theft, economic loss or economic harm, and financial fraud by establishing strong and uniform national data security and breach notification standards for electronic data in interstate commerce while minimizing State law burdens that may substantially affect interstate commerce; and (2) expressly preempt any related State laws to ensure uniformity of this Act's standards and the consistency of their application across jurisdictions. A violation of this requirement is an unfair or deceptive act or practice under the Federal Trade Commission Act.

National Cybersecurity Protection Advancement Act of 2015

H.R.1731 - National Cybersecurity Protection Advancement Act was introduced and passed in April 2015. This law amends the Homeland Security Act of 2002 to allow the DHS's national cyber security and communications integration center (NCCIC) to include tribal governments, information sharing, and analysis centers, and private entities among its non-federal representatives. Such a change was needed to make the law more encompassing and to ensure that all entities are explicitly required to follow it.

Overall, these laws demonstrate that in the past two decades there have been a lot of efforts on a federal level to address the increasing threat of cybercrime. However, it is important to acknowledge that, unlike physical crime, cybercrime does not require the victim and the offender to be in the same location at the same time. In fact, very often cybercrime crosses national borders, so a more comprehensive view to it is needed to better protect citizens, their data, and any other valuable assets.

State Laws

In addition to federal efforts to keep up with cybercrimes, state governments have also taken a step forward to update their legislation and reflect the rapid changes in technology and the novel ways offenders come up with to commit crime in cyberspace. Most noticeably, state governments have focused on making public the organizations that have failed to provide sufficient security measures. Following are examples of legislation from California and New York who have been some of the pioneers in this domain.

California

One such example of cybersecurity laws is the State of California. In 2003, California passed the Notice of Security Breach Act, which requires that any company that maintains personal information of California citizens and has a security breach, must disclose the details of the event. The security breach regulation punishes firms for their cybersecurity weaknesses, while giving them the opportunity to decide how to secure their systems. This regulation creates an incentive for companies to proactively invest in cybersecurity to avoid potential loss of reputation and economic loss. This approach worked well for California and later several other states have implemented similar security breach notification regulations.

Another law that was recently passed in the state is the California Consumer Privacy Act (CCPA) of 2018. It came as a response to the European Union' General Data Protection Regulation (GDPR) of 2018 and Japan's Act on the Protection of Personal Information (2003). They are concerned with users' privacy rights and protection of consumers' data. CCPA went into effect on January 1, 2020, and any company operating in the State of California needs to understand its implications and be able to demonstrate compliance with it. More specifically, the new CCPA data protections give Californians the right to:

- Know what personal information is being collected.
- Access the personal information that is collected, and request it be deleted.
- Know whether their personal information is being shared, and if so, with whom.
- Opt-out of the sale of their personal information.
- Have equal service and price, whether or not they choose to exercise their privacy rights.

Businesses are also be prohibited from selling the personal information of consumers ages 13–16 (unless the consumer opts-in). For consumers under the age of 13, consent from a parent or guardian is required. These new protections not only affect California consumers, but also California businesses. Under the CCPA, California citizens will have the ability to bring a civil action lawsuit against companies that do not abide by the law. The state can also bring these charges to a company directly — charging a $7,500 fine for any violation that is not addressed within 30 days (Hospelhorn, 2018). While currently this regulation only applies to California, it is highly likely that other states will soon address the issue of consumer privacy rights and develop similar legislation.

New York

The New York Cyber Security regulation has been effective since March 1, 2017. Covered Entities have been required to annually prepare and submit to the superintendent a Certification of Compliance with New York State Department of Financial Services Cybersecurity Regulations since February 15, 2018.

The financial services industry is a significant target of cybersecurity threats. The New York State Department of Financial Services (DFS) has recently started monitoring the ever-growing threat posed to information and financial systems by nation-state actors such as China, Russia, or North Korea, terrorist organizations like ISIS, and independent criminal actors whose reasoning may vary from just proving their abilities to socio-economic or political motivation (Gandhi, Sharma, Mahoney, Sousan, Zhu, & Laplante, 2011). These efforts demonstrate the need to proactively address cybercrime not only on a federal level, but also on a state and local level, so that such threats are acted upon in a more comprehensive manner.

The cost of cybercrime has been growing significantly. A recent report done by Lewis (2018) of McAfee shows a potential estimate of cybercrime losses in 2017 that almost reach 1% of the world's gross domestic product (GDP) or over $75 trillion in one year alone. These numbers indicate the magnitude of the problem and highlight the need to address it on a global level, as it is not just a US concern. In addition to the financial losses, cybercriminals can exploit technological vulnerabilities to gain access to sensitive electronic data. These criminals can cause significant financial losses for DFS regulated entities as well as for New York consumers whose private information may be revealed and/or stolen for illicit purposes. Since New York is a hub for most major global financial companies, such strict regulations are highly needed.

Given the seriousness of the issue and the risk to all regulated entities, certain regulatory minimum standards are required but they should allow some flexibility. There are so many threats specific to different attack vectors and targets, so companies should be able to focus on those that are relevant to them, without necessarily spending extra resources for risks that are not pertinent to them. The current regulation in

New York is designed to promote the protection of customer information as well as the information technology systems of regulated entities. The law requires each company to assess its specific risk profile and design a program that addresses its risks in a robust fashion.

Issues, Controversies, Problems

While there have been growing efforts to address cybersecurity in terms of laws and regulations on a federal and state level, a lot more work needs to be done. Schwartz (2015) have identified some of the biggest challenges and barriers to the development of such frameworks. He discusses the current state of laws and regulations, the disconnect between local, state, federal, and international legislation, the impossible balance between civil liberties and security, the difficulty of information sharing on various levels, and the lack of standards and definitions for cybercrime.

Outdated Laws and Regulations

Most of the existing regulations are based on issues surrounding telephones or antiquated systems of communication that are from 20 to 30 years ago (Wiretap Act of 1968, The Electronic Communications Privacy Act of 1986, and The Privacy Act of 1974 to name a few). Regulations that were made in pre-smartphone times cannot be expected to handle today's sophisticated threats and challenges (Sivan-Sevilla, 2017; Srinivas et al., 2019). They have not kept pace with the forms of digital communications we have today or the diverse threat environment that we are facing — and they need to catch up as soon as possible, because right now courts are making decisions based on interpretations of these outdated laws. In addition, such laws significantly hinder law enforcement officers' ability to investigate and prosecute cybercrimes.

Multiple Jurisdictions

In addition to the outdated laws, companies also are experiencing confusion and frustration when dealing with multiple jurisdictions. Currently, organizations must deal with a mix of state, federal, and international legislation that often combine outdated viewpoints and conflicting goals and objectives relative to cybersecurity and data privacy. Furthermore, determining the jurisdictions of cybercrimes has been another significant challenge and there is not a unified approach to addressing this issue. One particularly important implication of this is related to cloud computing where data may reside in multiple jurisdictions and its dynamic nature further complicates digital forensic investigations (Hooper et al., 2013). Overall, cybersecurity truly seems to be a bipartisan issue and having the federal government step in and create a uniform approach to breach reporting could benefit both companies and consumers.

Civil Liberties

While cybersecurity regulations are really needed, some worry that attempts to protect individuals and organizations from cyberattacks will prevent attempts to protect civil liberties. Unfortunately, the current regulations do not offer much protection of civil liberties so any future legal framework that are developed need to take that concern seriously and offer means to adequately address it. One example of this is how less than two months after 9/11, Congress passed the USA PATRIOT Act, which many argued restricted individual privacy rights in the name of public safety (Deflem & McDonough, 2015; Hamm, 2016). As a result of these controversies, the US FREEDOM Act of 2015 was enacted and its main tenets were to limit the bulk collection of telecommunication metadata on US citizens by American intelligence agencies and to restore authorization for wiretapping (Forsyth, 2015). As society changes, we need to be able to also change legislation to align with the citizens' needs and to keep up with technological advancements. Achieving strong balance between security and privacy is necessary if we want to avoid even bigger issues in the future, especially with the massive amounts of data being collected about us on a daily basis.

SOLUTIONS AND RECOMMENDATIONS

Improving Definitions of Cybercrime

Currently, there are too many definitions of cybercrime and, at the same time, the existing US penal code focuses predominantly on physical crimes. One reason for this is the lack of adequate classifications of cybercrime that legislators and businesses can agree upon. It is imperative that the government lays the foundations for such a taxonomy that can immensely benefit law enforcement officers who are currently struggling to investigate and prosecute cybercriminals. Furthermore, governments have to agree on a global level what the cybersecurity norms and responsibilities are and define when hacking by a country is inappropriate. Countries need to come together to work on this issue because otherwise cybercriminals will continue to take advantage of the disjointed efforts and patched legislation in individual countries.

Information Sharing

Stronger cybersecurity laws can also provide better information and intelligence sharing between companies and agencies. Such an approach can also address the problem of multiple jurisdictions and can help to provide a solid foundation for cooperation on local, state, and federal level. This strategy brings certain concerns related to potential liability issues for companies that share information with the government or each other (Koepke, 2017). Such liability issues can potentially hinder organizations from coming together against a common adversary. Thus, to facilitate information sharing, it will be necessary to reduce those liabilities or ensure exclusion from liability. There has been legislation on the table in the past that would have reduced those liabilities, but that legislation has never made it past the houses of Congress. There is a significant amount of data being collected every minute of every hour. It is entirely possible that information to be shared and used for good and beyond its current application building capital, but this requires a strong political impact and decision makers who truly understand and care about this issue.

Policy Development and Evaluation

Policy development to reduce cybercrime is clearly challenging and there needs to be a comprehensive approach to address this problem. From a practical perspective, it will be more feasible and prudent to focus on developing resources and establishing cybersecurity best practices rather than relying on any possible agreements signed by other countries, such as the 2015 Obama-Xi Cyber Espionage Agreement, as those have proven to be unreliable and inapplicable. Even though the US and Chinese presidents agreed to limit cyberespionage for commercial gains, there was not really any action being taken (Lewis, 2018). Thus, engaging top consultants in the field as well as the FBI and NSA would be a good starting point to deter crime rather than relying solely on international treaties and agreements.

The current study presents an approach to address this issue grounded in Routine Activity Theory (Cohen & Felson, 2003). While there is not much that we can do about other countries' cyber armies (the likely offenders), we can focus our efforts on not being a suitable target by improving our security measures and implementing controls that function properly to prevent crime. We can study other examples of cyberattacks and learn from them so we can fix any security holes that our systems may be experiencing. And finally, by employing capable and skilled cybersecurity professionals, we can ensure that there are capable guardians to protect our most valuable resources and national security as a whole.

In order to develop and evaluate this new policy, the author employs the seven stage approach developed by Welsh and Harris (2016). This methodology is appropriate because it is comprehensive and offers a broad perspective to the problem. At the same time, it is not specific enough and could be applied to a number of issues, including cybercrime. Using the Welsh and Harris (2016) systematic approach to program and policy development, following is list of proposed actions for each of the seven stages using critical infrastructure attacks as an example to illustrate the process.

Stage 1: Analyzing the Problem

In this initial stage, the main activities that take place are documenting the need for change and describing the history of the problem by demonstrating relevant evidence from prior cybercrimes in the US and globally. Since cybercrime is an umbrella term that encompasses multiple different crimes, the author recommends that the focus be narrowed in this stage. For example, one possible direction could be cyber-attacks against critical infrastructure. In terms of examining the potential causes, things to be considered could be how these attacks are developed, what resources are required for the advanced persistent threats (APT) and analyzing how supervisory control and data acquisition (SCADA) systems have been previously protected from a policy perspective. Due to the growing number of cyber threats, it is important to be proactive and assume the worst-case scenarios. Relevant stakeholders such as various government agencies and security professionals from the industry should be identified in order to obtain their input and determine the best course of action for developing policies to protect critical infrastructure. As part of conducting the systems analysis, it is recommended to perform penetration tests to identify vulnerabilities in the systems. With regards to the barriers to change, the author proposes demonstrating the growing concern for these systems and the impact previous security breaches have made to government agencies and private sector organizations. One way to appeal to these various agents is by showing the impact of cybercrime in terms of financial losses, lack of trust, and reputational crises.

Stage 2: Setting Goals and Objectives

In this second stage, the goal statements of the program are defined. They should show overall reduction in number of potential vulnerabilities in the systems. To further define these goals, specific outcomes for each goal can be provided. These could include performing independent security audits by a third party at least once a year, getting certified through the National Institute of Standards and Technology (NIST) or the International Standards Organization (ISO), and providing regular security training for employees. Consultations with the stakeholders can be used to specifically identify the relevant goals and impact model. That can lead to developing a list of goals that may be incompatible or outside of the scope of the proposed policy. Since this type of project would demand the need for interagency collaborations, it is recommended that the FBI, NSA, DHS, CISA, and other key players are involved in the policy development process.

Stage 3: Policy Design

In this next stage, different intervention options are considered. Since the proposed policy is based on Routine Activities Theory, the intervention options would affect mostly internal systems and employees. They would go through rigorous training to ensure that the policy is properly implemented. Interventions would also include technological enhancements, upgrading hardware and software to ensure the latest security patches are installed. With regards to the policy design, the exact target population of the policy should be defined in this stage. In this case, it would be mostly internal employees, which could help design it in a way that is very specific and relevant to the audience. The general population in the US would not be directly affected, which makes it easier to create a policy for the specific, since there would be exact knowledge of their job descriptions and the systems they are running. These considerations would also apply to the responsible authorities and the provisions and procedures of the policies. The proposed changes could be mandated by the government in a more generic form, so that no sensitive information on national security is released to the public and the specifics of the policy would be made available only to the individuals who are responsible for maintaining and securing critical infrastructures.

Stage 4: Action planning

The action planning stage would start with identifying the resources needed and a plan how to acquire or relocate resources that may be needed to implement the policy. These may be disclosed only on a need-to-know basis due to the sensitivity of the policy. In this stage, the author recommends focusing extensively on the project management portion because it is crucial to specify dates to complete implementation tasks and to develop mechanisms for self-regulation. By having a concrete plan for the entire project, it would be easier to identify possible gaps and request support or additional resources if needed. It is necessary to carefully plan the implementation of this policy because if the threats are exploited, this could have a devastating effect on the US as a country and could impact the lives of thousands, if not millions, of people.

Stage 5: Policy Implementation

If the newly proposed policy is implemented, the next step should be a pilot study to test it on a smaller scale. For instance, that may include several critical infrastructure facilities. They would first be evaluated, similar to a pre-test. The audit would be performed by specially trained government employees who have the necessary security clearance and knowledge on SCADA systems. This pre-test would establish the baselines and would evaluate the preparedness of the systems (hardware and software) and the employees to stop potential attacks. As part of the preliminary evaluation, establishing these baselines would serve to later compare the security of critical infrastructure after the policy is implemented.

It is critical to also design instruments to collect monitoring data and to designate responsibility of individuals who would collect, store, and analyze it. It is important to keep in mind the sensitivity of the data and to ensure that only those with the highest security clearance are authorized to handle the data. As part of this stage, information system capacities need to be developed, because once the pilot test is over and the policy is implemented on a large scale, there would be a lot more data to collect and analyze. Furthermore, developing mechanisms to provide feedback to stakeholders and informing them on the progress of the policy implementation is essential to the success of the initiative. As for the general public, it is not advisable that any of this would be shared since it concerns matters of national security.

Stage 6: Evaluating Outcomes

In this stage, outcome measures would be developed based on the preliminary defined objectives. This would help identify whether the proposed policy is adequate and effective. Next, it is important to specify the research design to be implemented. Ideally, scientists with relevant backgrounds in statistics, data mining, and research methods would be tasked with this activity. That would provide an applied approach grounded in theory, to identify potential cofounding factors, and to expand the use of the evaluation results. Since this policy would concern a small subset of government facilities, it would be a little easier to identify the cofounding factors compared to a general population where there is a lot less control over external factors. Once all these activities are completed, the next step would be to reassess the entire policy plan and ensure there are no gaps or issues. If this is performed during the pilot test, it would be much easier and cheaper to calibrate the policy due to the much smaller scale.

Stage 7: Reassessment and Review

In this final stage of the process, a number of activities would be performed to reassess the policy and ensure its effectiveness in the long run. First, a back-up plan should be developed in case anything goes terribly wrong. If the policy is successful, ongoing assessments would be performed and the policy would be revised if necessary. Since the world of cybercrime changes so quickly, it is crucial to be able to adapt to any changes in the environment and address new emerging threats. If that is the case and changes to the proposed policy need to be made, then the process will continue again from stage three. Once sufficient data is collected and feedback is provided to the stakeholders, the final step would be to reassess the entire policy plan and make any necessary modifications to increase its fit with the always changing world of cyber threats.

These actions outlined in stages one to seven demonstrate how a cybersecurity policy focused on critical infrastructure protection could be developed and evaluated. The author emphasizes that this is just one approach to address the issue of outdated regulations in this field and it is not the only solution. However, the purpose of this section is to provide policy makers with some tangible outcomes by combing academic rigor with the practical need to address the increasing cybercrimes.

FUTURE RESEARCH DIRECTIONS

As technology changes so rapidly, it is difficult for policy makers to keep up and address the ever-growing threats. This study presents an overview of the current state of laws and regulations in the US and outlines one possible approach to implement new policies. Thus, the author encourages others to further investigate this problem and add more information to this relatively new domain. In addition, researchers can consider a comparison of various state laws and/or different national regulations. Due to its nature, cybercrime is a global problem, so exploring how national governments can collaborate and exchange information in a safe and secure manner, could be another possible angle to consider. Legislation takes time to be developed and approved. However, an equally important part of the process is the policy evaluation. Thus, others can also examine whether existing policies and regulations are effective and, if not, to come up with recommendations for improvement.

CONCLUSION

The current state of cybersecurity laws and regulations in the US is discouraging due to the extremely outdated frameworks that exist. This prevents not only the court to convict, but also law enforcement officers to investigate cybercrimes. This rapidly developing new field has been neglected for a while, but it is obvious that it is not going away any time soon. Thus, decision makers need to shift their attention from street crime to cybercrime. First, we need better definitions and classification of cybercrimes so we can more adequately investigate and prosecute cybercriminals. Second, coordination between agencies on local, state, federal, and international level is necessary to come up with a more comprehensive solution. Third, only by taking a rigorous and global approach, we can ensure that civil liberties and individual rights are not sacrificed for public safety.

REFERENCES

Aliyev, A. I., Ibrahimova, A. N., & Rzayeva, G. A. (2020). Information security: Legal regulations in Azerbaijan and abroad. *Journal of Information Science*, 1–14. doi:10.1177/0165551520981813

Beccaria, C., Newman, G. R., & Marongiu, P. (2017). *On crimes and punishments*. Routledge. doi:10.4324/9781315125527

Cimpanu, C. (2018). *Trump signs bill that creates the Cybersecurity and Infrastructure Security Agency*. Retrieved from https://www.zdnet.com/article/trump-signs-bill-that-creates-the-cybersecurity-and-infrastructure-security-agency/

Cohen, L. E., & Felson, M. (2003). Routine activity theory. In F. Cullen & R. Agnew (Eds.), Criminological theory: Past to present (essential readings) (pp. 70–79). Academic Press.

Cornish, D., & Clarke, R. (1986). *The reasoning criminal*. Springer-Verlag. doi:10.1007/978-1-4613-8625-4

Deflem, M., & McDonough, S. (2015). The fear of counterterrorism: Surveillance and civil liberties since 9/11. *Society*, *52*(1), 70–79. doi:10.100712115-014-9855-1

Forsyth, B. (2015). Banning bulk: Passage of the USA FREEDOM Act and ending bulk collection. *Washington and Lee Law Review*, *72*, 1307.

Glahe, F. R. (Ed.). (1993). *Adam Smith's an inquiry into the nature and causes of the wealth of nations: A concordance*. Rowman & Littlefield Pub Incorporated.

Goldman, Z. K., & McCoy, D. (2016). Deterring Financially Motivated Cybercrime. *Journal of National Security Law & Policy, 8*(3), 1.

Granger, D. (2017). *Karmen Ransomware Variant Introduced by Russian Hacker.* Retrieved from https://www.recordedfuture.com/karmen-ransomware-variant/

Gupta, S. (2020). Assuring compliance with government certification and accreditation regulations. In *Cloud computing security* (2nd ed., pp. 387–394). CRC Press. doi:10.1201/9780429055126-32

Hamm, M. S. (2016). The USA patriot act and the politics of fear. In *Cultural criminology unleashed* (pp. 301–314). Routledge-Cavendish.

Hooper, C., Martini, B., & Choo, K.-K. R. (2013). Cloud computing and its implications for cybercrime investigations in Australia. *Computer Law & Security Review, 29*(2), 152–163. doi:10.1016/j.clsr.2013.01.006

Hui, K. L., Kim, S. H., & Wang, Q. H. (2017). Cybercrime deterrence and international legislation: Evidence from distributed denial of service attacks. *Management Information Systems Quarterly, 41*(2), 497–523. doi:10.25300/MISQ/2017/41.2.08

International Telecommunications Union (ITU). (2008). *ITU-TX.1205: Sries X: Data networks, open system communications and security: Telecommunication security: Overview of cybersecurity 2008.* Retrieved from https://www.itu.int/rec/dologin_pub.asp?lang=s&id=T-REC-X.1205-200804-I!!PDF-E&type=items

Jeffery, L., & Ramachandran, V. (2021). *Why ransomware attacks are on the rise — and what can be done to stop them.* https://www.pbs.org/newshour/nation/why-ransomware-attacks-are-on-the-rise-and-what-can-be-done-to-stop-them

Klimburg, A. (2012). *National cyber security framework manual.* NATO Cooperative Cyber Defense Center of Excellence.

Koepke, P. (2017). *Cybersecurity information sharing incentives and barriers.* Sloan School of Management at MIT University. Working Paper CISL# 2017-13.

Leeper Piquero, N., Lyn Exum, M., & Simpson, S. S. (2005). Integrating the desire–for–control and rational choice in a corporate crime context. *Justice Quarterly, 22*(2), 252–280. doi:10.1080/07418820500089034

Lévesque, F. L., Fernandez, J. M., & Batchelder, D. (2017). Age and gender as independent risk factors for malware victimisation. *Proceedings of the 31st British Computer Society Human Computer Interaction Conference.* 10.14236/ewic/HCI2017.48

Lewis, J. (2018). *Economic impact of cybercrime-No slowing down*. Santa Clara: McAfee & CSI (Center for Strategic and International Studies). Retrieved from https://www.csis.org/analysis/economic-impact-cybercrime

Llinares, F. M. (2015). *That Cyber Routine, That Cyber Victimization: Profiling Victims of Cybercrime. In Cybercrime Risks and Responses*. Springer. doi:10.1057/9781137474162.0011

Mandelcorn, S., Modarres, M., & Mosleh, A. (2013). An explanatory model of cyberattacks drawn from rational choice theory. *Transactions of the American Nuclear Society*, 109.

Muncaster, P. (2021). *One Ransomware Victim Every 10 Seconds in 2020*. Retrieved from https://www.infosecurity-magazine.com/news/one-ransomware-victim-every-10/

Paternoster, R., Jaynes, C. M., & Wilson, T. (2017). Rational choice theory and interest in the "fortune of others". *Journal of Research in Crime and Delinquency*, *54*(6), 847–868. doi:10.1177/0022427817707240

Paternoster, R., & Simpson, S. (1993). Rational Choice Theory of Corporate Crime. In Routine Activity and Rational Choice: Advances in Criminological Theory (vol. 5, pp. 37-58). Academic Press.

Ransbotham, S., & Mitra, S. (2009). Choice and chance: A conceptual model of paths to information security compromise. *Information Systems Research*, *20*(1), 121–139. doi:10.1287/isre.1080.0174

Robinson, M. (2014). Why do people commit crime? An integrated systems perspective. Applying Complexity Theory: Whole Systems Approaches to Criminal Justice and Social Work, *59*.

Sales, N. A. (2012). Regulating cyber-security. *Northwestern University Law Review*, *107*, 1503.

Sivan-Sevilla, I. (2017). Trading privacy for security in cyberspace: A study across the dynamics of US federal laws and regulations between 1967 and 2016. *9th International Conference on Cyber Conflict (CyCon)*.

Srinivas, J., Das, A. K., & Kumar, N. (2019). Government regulations in cyber security: Framework, standards and recommendations. *Future Generation Computer Systems*, *92*, 178–188. doi:10.1016/j.future.2018.09.063

Vailshery, L. S. (2021). *Number of internet of things (IoT) connected devices worldwide in 2018, 2025 and 2030*. Retrieved from https://www.statista.com/statistics/802690/worldwide-connected-devices-by-access-technology/

Von Solms, R., & Van Niekerk, J. (2013). From information security to cyber security. *Computers & Security, 38*, 97–102. doi:10.1016/j.cose.2013.04.004

Welsh, W. N., & Harris, P. W. (2016). *Criminal justice policy and planning: Planned change*. Routledge. doi:10.4324/9781315638614

Whitehouse. (2011). *International strategy for cyberspace: prosperity, security, and openness in a networked world*. Retrieved from https://obamawhitehouse.archives.gov/sites/default/files/rss_viewer/international_strategy_for_cyberspace.pdf

Willison, R., & Siponen, M. (2009). Overcoming the insider: Reducing employee computer crime through Situational Crime Prevention. *Communications of the ACM, 52*(9), 133–137. doi:10.1145/1562164.1562198

Wright, V. (2010). *Deterrence in criminal justice: Evaluating certainty vs. severity of punishment*. Sentencing Project.

ADDITIONAL READING

Delaney, D. G. (2013). Cybersecurity and the Administrative National Security State: Framing the Issues for Federal Legislation. *Journal of Legislation, 40*, 251.

Flowers, A., Zeadally, S., & Murray, A. (2013). Cybersecurity and US legislative efforts to address cybercrime. *Journal of Homeland Security and Emergency Management, 10*(1), 29–55. doi:10.1515/jhsem-2012-0007

Kosseff, J. (2017). Defining cybersecurity law. *Iowa Law Review, 103*, 985.

Kosseff, J. (2018). Developing collaborative and cohesive cybersecurity legal principles. In *Proceedings of 2018 10th International Conference on Cyber Conflict (CyCon)* (pp. 283-298). IEEE. 10.23919/CYCON.2018.8405022

Kshetri, N. (2015). Recent US cybersecurity policy initiatives: Challenges and implications. *Computer, 48*(7), 64–69. doi:10.1109/MC.2015.188

Margulies, P. (2013). Sovereignty and cyber-attacks: Technology's challenge to the law of state responsibility. *Melbourne Journal of International Law, 14*, 496.

Nolan, A. (2015). *Cybersecurity and information sharing: Legal challenges and solutions* (Vol. 5). Congressional Research Service.

Sales, N. A. (2012). Regulating cyber-security. *Northwestern University Law Review*, *107*, 1503.

Thaw, D. (2013). The efficacy of cybersecurity regulation. *Georgia State University Law Review*, *30*, 287.

Trautman, L. J. (2015). Cybersecurity: What about US policy. *University of Illinois Journal of Law, Technology & Policy, 341*.

KEY TERMS AND DEFINITIONS

Critical Infrastructure: Physical and cyber systems and assets that are so vital to the United States that their incapacity or destruction would have a debilitating impact on the physical or economic security or public health or safety.

Cybercrime: Criminal activities carried out by means of computers and technology and/or targeting computers/technology.

Cybersecurity: A combination of tools, policies, controls, and best practices to protect an organization's assets such as people, data, technology, and processes.

Data Breach: An incident wherein information is stolen or taken from a system without the knowledge or authorization of the system's owner.

Jurisdiction: The official power to make legal decisions and judgments.

Law: System of rules in a particular country or community recognized as regulating the actions of its members and which may be enforced by imposing penalties.

Policy: A course or principle of action adopted or proposed by a government, party, business, or individual.

Chapter 2
Automotive Vehicle Security Standards, Regulations, and Compliance

Jeffrey S. Zanzig
Jacksonville State University, USA

Guillermo A. Francia III
ⓘD https://orcid.org/0000-0001-8088-2653
University of West Florida, USA

ABSTRACT

The rapid advancement of automotive vehicle communication technology ushered in the expansion of the cyber-attack surface on this type of transport system. A recent study projects that there will be 200 million vehicles on the road worldwide with embedded connectivity by 2025. The security and safety of these vehicles and, most importantly, their occupants are paramount. Recognizing this need, organizations consisting of entities from governments, manufacturers, service providers, professionals, and/or trade groups are constantly introducing, revising, and updating automotive vehicle security standards and regulations. This chapter examines the state of automotive vehicle communication, their vulnerabilities and security issues, the existing security standards and regulations that apply to this type of transport, and the compliance and auditing issues related to these directives. The chapter concludes with reflections and directions for continuous improvements and future research.

DOI: 10.4018/978-1-7998-8390-6.ch002

Copyright © 2022, IGI Global. Copying or distributing in print or electronic forms without written permission of IGI Global is prohibited.

INTRODUCTION

The future of the automotive industry looks very promising with technology adding many conveniences such as Internet access, automated parking, and automated braking being applied using sensors that observe a crash situation before a driver would have time to react. In the foreseeable future, it is quite possible that consumers will even be able to purchase completely autonomous vehicles offering tremendous advantages for persons who are not able to drive but would still like to have the independence of being able to get around on their own.

However, the automation of vehicles does carry risks that society is currently trying to address in terms of cybersecurity. Taub (2021) makes the point that although consumers love the many automated features that are being included in today's automobiles, hackers likely see this trend as an upcoming opportunity to eventually hijack vehicles. He states that probably "the best-known vehicle takeover occurred in 2015 when security researchers on a laptop 10 miles away caused a Jeep Cherokee to lose power, change its radio station, turn on the windshield wipers and blast cold air." This incident resulted in Jeep's parent company recalling 1.4 million vehicles to fix the vulnerability. The ability to breach a vehicle's security could range in severity from being annoying like turning on the windshield wipers to something disastrous like making a vehicle unexpectedly speed up or lose its ability to apply braking.

The semi- or full-automation of vehicles requires a dependable and robust connectivity. A study (Juniper Research, 2020) by Juniper Research reports that the number of vehicles with embedded connectivity will reach 200 million globally by 2025. This is a significant increase from the 110 million in 2020. Consequently, this Machine-to-Machine (M2M) connectivity provides both conveniences as well as additional safety and security issues to manufacturers, consumers, and service providers.

The demand for increased safety and security measures due to the technological advancements of connected and autonomous vehicles prompted the creation of new and additional vehicle standards and regulations. These efforts are made to produce secure, reliable, effective, and safe vehicles.

The remainder of this chapter is conceptually divided into four major topics:

1. The first is some background describing vehicle communications and communication protocols.
2. The main focus of the chapter considers some guidance regarding vehicle security and related guidelines, standards and regulations.
3. The section on Solutions and Recommendations begins by discussing compliance with IS 21434 along with describing cybersecurity assessments and audits.

It then presents illustrations regarding how key elements of a cybersecurity framework are addressed by the NIST Framework Core in a way that links them to COBIT 2019. It closes with a consideration of reasons why fuzz testing should be a part of a system development life cycle.

4.   Concluding sections are then presented to describe some future research directions and a conclusion.

BACKGROUND

The automobiles of today offer several driver assistance technologies including "forward collision warning, automatic emergency braking, and vehicle safety communications." The future of this trend has the potential to drastically reduce the number of crashes. This is particularly true regarding accidents attributable to errors in human judgment (National Highway Traffic Safety Administration (NHTSA), 2020) Unfortunately, the automation of automobiles is subject to dangers associated with cybersecurity challenges. The connectivity of vehicle communication provides an entry point for a variety of cyber-attacks. In order to familiarize the uninitiated, this section describes categories of vehicle communication and types of communication protocols.

Vehicle Communications

The advancement of vehicular communication technologies has expanded the reach of automotive devices from the localized in-vehicle arrangement to a globalized outreach that is facilitated by the Internet and broadband cellular systems.

Modern automotive vehicle communication can be classified into four main categories: in-vehicle communication, vehicle-to-device (V2D) communication, vehicle-to-vehicle communication (V2V) and vehicle-to-infrastructure (V2I or V2X) communication (Francia, 2020). In-vehicle communications include those in which information and control signals are dispatched among electronic control units (ECUs) and sensors in the local vehicle network. A V2D communication system includes Bluetooth transmission between devices such as a smartphone and the vehicle infotainment system. Connected vehicles communicate through V2V communication through some form of ad-hoc wireless network. This vehicular ad-hoc network (VANET), first introduced at the turn of century, is an extension of the mobile ad-hoc network (MANET). For the V2I or V2X communication category, a good example is the scenario wherein a vehicle captures and sends real-time data about the traffic conditions to the highway infrastructure management system or

Roadside Units (RSUs) via broadband communication technology. These captured data are then fed into an intelligent traffic system that manages and optimizes traffic control in that locality.

Vehicle Communication Protocols

Vehicle communication protocols can be either intra-vehicle (local scope) or inter-vehicle (global scope).

Intra-Vehicle Communication Protocols

The modern intra-vehicle network communication protocol group consists of the five predominant communication protocols. These are the Controller Area Network (CAN), Local Interconnect Network (LIN), Media Oriented System Transport (MOST), FlexRay, and Automotive Ethernet.

The CAN communication protocol (SAE International, 1998) works on a two wired half duplex high speed serial network bus topology using the Carrier Sense Multiple Access (CSMA)/Collision Detection (CD) protocol (Francia III & El-Sheikh, Applied Machine Learning to Vehicle Security, 2021). Most of the functions of the lower two layers of the International Standards Organization (ISO) Reference Model is implemented in the CAN protocol. The typical network topology for the CAN protocol is point to point. There are 4 different types of CAN frames: Data, Remote, Error, and Overload. The Data frame is the most common message type and utilizes the arbitration ID field to enforce bus arbitration.

Local Interconnect Network (LIN) (CSS Electronics, 2019) is an in-vehicle serial communication protocol that delivers a low-cost alternative to CAN and FlexRay (National Instruments, 2019) for vehicle network applications. However, it delivers a lower performance and less reliability. A LIN bus uses a single 12V line and has a node that acts as a Master gateway for other LIN nodes. Up to 16 of these slave nodes can be connected to the LIN bus (Francia, 2020).

MOST is a serial communication system for transmitting audio, video, and control data via fiber-optic cables (Vector Informatik GmbH, 2020). The MOST specification covers all seven layers of the ISO/OSI Reference model for data communication. For example, low level system services are implemented on Layer 2; MOST transceivers are on the Physical layer; network system services are on Layers 3, 4 and 5; and finally, application socket and Application Program Interfaces (APIs) are in layers 6 and 7, respectively. The network topology for the MOST protocol is a ring configuration of up to 64 devices.

FlexRay (National Instruments, 2019) is an in-vehicle communication bus whose purpose is to meet the need for a fast, reliable, and greater bandwidth data communication system. National Instruments correctly pointed out that the optimization of cost and reduction of transition challenges can be accomplished by using FlexRay for high-end applications, CAN for powertrain communications, and LIN for low-cost body electronics. The FlexRay protocol topology can be either a single or dual channel. Automotive Ethernet is an adaptation of the standard ethernet but works on 2-wire instead of the 4-wire configuration. It is standardized by IEEE with 802.3bw expanded with 802.3bp (Keysight, 2019). It is designed to meet the needs of the automotive market, including meeting electrical requirements and emissions, bandwidth requirements, latency requirements, synchronization, and network management requirements (Francia III, Vehicle Network Security Metrics, 2021).

Inter-Vehicle Communication Protocols

The inter-vehicle network communication protocols enable short- and long-range communication capabilities.

Dedicated Short Range Communications (DSRC), a variation of the Institute of Electrical and Electronics Engineers (IEEE) 802.11 Wi-Fi standard, is primarily intended for the automotive environment. It uses the IEEE 802.11p standard in the 5.9 GHz band. Additionally, this standard is a companion for the proposed IEEE 1609 Family of Standards for Wireless access in Vehicular Environments (WAVE).

Another inter-vehicle communication protocol is the IEEE 802.11a standard. It operates on both the 2.4 GHz and 5.2 GHz Industrial, Scientific, and Medical (ISM) bands. It delivers a data rate of 6 to 54 Mbps on an operating bandwidth of 20 MHz and operates on a limited distance of approximately 100 meters, which is suitable for V2V communication.

Vehicular Ad-Hoc Network (VANET) is a form of a Mobile Ad-Hoc Network (MANET) that utilizes the Wi-Fi (802.11 a/b/g), the Worldwide Interoperability for Microwave Access (WiMAX), a family of wireless broadband communication standards based on IEEE 802.16, or the Wireless Access in Vehicular Environments (WAVE) based on the IEEE 1609-12 standards. WAVE is a layered protocol architecture that includes the security of message exchange and operates on the Dedicated Short-Range Communication (DSRC) band *(Francia III, Vehicle Network Security Metrics, 2021)*.

MAIN FOCUS OF THE CHAPTER

This section describes cyber vulnerabilities in vehicle security and various forms of guidelines, standards, and regulations that attempt to address the problem.

Vehicle Security

Despite the benefits offered by the advancement of vehicular communication technologies, it introduces a myriad of unintended vulnerabilities and threats to this type of transport system.

A myriad of vulnerabilities has been discovered and reported in several areas of the vehicle digital ecosystem (Burkacky, Deichmann, Klein, Pototzky, & Scherf, 2020). In 2018, researchers have exploited the vulnerabilities of some infotainment systems, vehicle data were exposed during registration in Original Equipment Manufacturer (OEM) back-end services, security issues were discovered in car-sharing apps in 2018, the vulnerability of a cloud services provider exposing password, API keys, and tokens was exposed in 2019, and a malware infection at a car parts manufacturing floor caused a significant downtime in production. We highlighted these security vulnerabilities as a segue to discussions on the sources and causes of vehicle security issues.

The most common protocol used in vehicle communication is the CAN protocol. It was designed for functionality and not for security. Thus, it has an inherent vulnerability, found in the arbitration scheme, that can easily be exploited. The Arbitration ID field determines who gets preferential treatment in the CAN bus. By simply setting the Arbitration ID to the lowest possible value, a node can perpetually take over the bus and thus, enabling a denial-of-service attack on other nodes in the network.

There are other security and mitigation issues concerning the CAN protocol. Some of those issues and proposed solutions are described in the following. Zhou, Li and Shen used a deep neural network (DNN) method to detect anomalies on CAN bus messages for autonomous vehicles (Zhou, Li, & Shen, 2019). The system imports three CAN bus data packets, represented as independent feature vectors, and is composed of a deep network and triplet loss network, which are trainable in an end-to-end fashion. The results demonstrated that the proposed DNN architecture can make real-time responses to anomalies and attacks to the CAN bus and significantly improve the detection ratio (Francia III & El-Sheikh, 2021). A three-pronged approach to detect anomalies in the Controller Area Network was first proposed by Vasistha (Vasistha, 2017). To improve the data integrity of CAN bus message, anomalies are detected using the order of messages from the Electronic Control Unit (ECU) and using a timing-based detector to observe and detect changes in the timing behavior through deterministic and statistical techniques (Francia III & El-Sheikh, Applied Machine Learning to Vehicle Security, 2021). The drawback of this approach is the prohibitive length of detection latency.

Security issues are not isolated in the intra-vehicle networks. The consequence of the advancements in vehicle communication technologies is the expansion of the attack surfaces on connected vehicles. These attack surfaces include the following (Francia, 2020):

- The accessibility of telematics servers. These servers act as remote command and controls, which not only collect data for insurance, fleet management, location tracking, and performance monitoring. They can also be used to send remote commands such as locking and unlocking doors, switching engines on and off, etc.
- The physical access to Onboard Diagnostic (OBD) Ports. These ports can be locally accessed through a physical port underneath the steering wheel. It can also be remotely reached through OBD devices that are configured for Wi-Fi or cellular communications.
- The built-in Mobile Device Apps that are increasingly used to communicate with connected vehicles via centralized application servers that can be remotely compromised.
- The built-in Wi-Fi access points which car manufacturers provide for convenient access to the Internet. If these devices are left unsecured, they can easily become entry points for a malicious intrusion.

Vehicle Datasets and Privacy

Information collected on operating vehicles, specifically those from Roadside Units (RSUs), Telematics systems, fleet management, subscription-based services, insurance, etc. are governed by privacy regulations such the General Data Protection Regulation (GDPR), the California Consumer Privacy Act (CCPA), and others. Awareness and compliance with these regulations are imperative. The V2X Communication Message Set Dictionary (SAE J2735_202007) standard specifies a message set and its data frames and data elements (SAE International, 2020). The data elements, in SAE J2735 message format, include, among others, the following: BasicSafetyMessage (BSM), PersonalSafetyMessage (PSM), SignalPhaseAndTiming (SPAT), SignalRequestMessage (SRM), SignalStatusMessage (SSM), and TravelerInformationMessage (TIM). In using and disseminating this dataset, due care and diligence is crucial for the purpose of privacy protection that is required by existing regulations and standards.

Vehicle System Software

Dechand puts it best in stating that "in software development, there is a distinction between safety and security. Safe software describes a system that is generally free of defects or crashes - or simply put "does not fail". Secure software means that a system is immune to external interference or ungranted access" (Dechand, 2020). There are two major regulations that address the security of system software in automotive vehicles: the UNECE R156 and the ISO/SAE 21434 standard. The United

Nations Economic Commission for Europe (UNECE) Regulation R156 is focused on securing vehicle system software update. ISO/SAE 21434 standard sets forth a new framework for secure software development in the automotive vehicle sector,

Vehicle Security Guidelines, Standards, and Regulations

Vehicle Security Standards and Regulations have long been established and continuously revised and updated. Emerging technologies prompted the creation of new directives to address issues that developed.

SAE J3061 SAE J3061 *Cybersecurity Guidebook for Cyber-Physical Vehicle Systems* provides a complete guide to cybersecurity implementation on cyber-physical vehicle systems throughout the entire development life cycle process. In essence, it is complementary to ISO 26262 which lacks the much-needed cybersecurity guidance (Argus Cyber Security, 2016).

ISO/SAE 21434

The ISO/SAE 21434 came about when standards from two organizations: the ISO 26262 and the SAE J3061 were merged to address a common goal: the automotive safety and security related standards. The two groups together with Original Equipment Manufacturers (OEMs), ECU suppliers, cybersecurity vendors, and governing organizations established a working group to put together an effective global standard for automotive cybersecurity (Upstream Security Ltd., 2020). The Joint Working Group (JWG) is divided into four working groups: PG1: Risk Management, PG2: Product Development, PG3: Operation, Maintenance, and other Processes, and PG4: Process Overview and Interdependencies (Schmittner, Griessnig, & Ma, 2018).

Macher, et al. (Macher, Schmittner, Veledar, & Brenner, 2020) provide an initial review of the ISO/SAE 21434 draft standard. The authors conclude that the standard does not prescribe specific technology or solutions related to cybersecurity and, as a result, the descriptions of processes and approaches become more ambiguous. Given this opinion, it may also be worth pointing out that Standards and Guidelines are better assembled by being not prescriptive on technologies and solutions. Afterall, prescribing specific technologies or solutions may limit the flexibility of the user and create unintended compliance issues.

UNECE Regulation R156

The United Nations Economic Commission for Europe (UNECE) Regulation R156 (United Nations Economic Commission for Europe (UNECE), 2021) is focused on securing vehicle system software update. The regulation applies to certain categories of vehicles as defined in WP.29 (United Nations Economic Commission for Europe (UNECE), 2021).

UNECE WP.29 Cybersecurity Regulation

In June 2020, the UNECE World Forum for Harmonization of Vehicle Regulations adopted two new WP.29 automotive cybersecurity regulations. The regulations require the implementation of measures in the following distinct areas related to automotive vehicles (Goldstein, 2020):

- Cyber risk management on vehicles
- Value chain risk mitigation for secure vehicle design
- Incident detection and response, and
- Provision for secure and safe software updates

NHSTA Cybersecurity Best Practices

In 2020, the National Highway Traffic Safety Administration (NHTSA) updated the document entitled *Cybersecurity Best Practices for the Safety of Modern Veh*icles. Recognizing the fact that vehicles are cyber-physical systems and that any cyber intrusion could have a negative impact on safety, NHTSA started advocating the adoption of proactive measures such as guidance and standards (National Highway Traffic Safety Administration (NHTSA), 2020).

The National Highway Traffic Safety Administration (NHTSA) supports a multi-layered style to cybersecurity issues by concentrating on both wireless and wired entry points that are possibly susceptible to a cyberattack. They state that an all-inclusive and methodical method of obtaining a layered cybersecurity defense should include the following **(National Highway Traffic Safety Administration (NHTSA), n.d.)**:

- Safety-critical vehicle control systems should follow a "risk-based prioritized identification and protection process." The NHTSA recognizes that it is not feasible to address all safety-critical vulnerabilities simultaneously. Therefore, those involving the greatest risk to safety should be identified and prioritized.
- Potential automotive cybersecurity occurrences in America should be detected in a timely manner and receive a swift response.
- Automobiles should be designed in a way that has cyber resiliency and enable quick recovery from instances when they happen.
- Intelligence and information sharing within the automotive industry should facilitate the communication of lessons learned throughout the industry.

In fact, the NHTSA would like to see the start of an Auto-ISAC. It would function in a manner like the Information Technology-Information Sharing and Analysis Center (IT-ISAC), "a one-of-its kind forum which assembles some of the brightest minds from the world's leading IT companies to minimize threats, manage risk, and respond to cyber incidents impacting the IT Sector **(Information Technology-Information Sharing and Analysis Center, 2022)**."

SOLUTIONS AND RECOMMENDATIONS

The prior discussion describes a variety of forms of guidance and regulation that have been recommended and/or enacted. The future of a quality form of automotive cybersecurity strongly relies on ensuring compliance through a process of evaluation. In addition, it is also imperative that the evaluation of automotive cybersecurity be grounded in common best practices of cybersecurity and testing.

In today's world, cybersecurity issues arise in many aspects of our lives and the automotive industry is no exception. As automobiles become more sophisticated in their use of technology to control both critical and noncritical functions within vehicles, cybersecurity standards are being developed to address automotive cybersecurity risks. In addition to original equipment manufacturers, a wide range of stakeholders involved in the automotive life cycles will be affected (UL, 2022). Cybersecurity concerns involve the complete lifecycle of a vehicle including formation of the idea, design, production, use, upkeep, resale, and retirement (McKinsey & Company, 2020).

Compliance with ISO 21434

A major component of the ISO 21434, *Road Vehicles-Cybersecurity Engineering*, is the due diligence requirement with respect to system software security. Dechand (Dechand, 2020) proposes the following six tips for achieving compliance with ISO 21434, specifically that on software security:

- Make security culture a priority in the software development lifecycle. This can be achieved through education and awareness training on basic security protocols and best practices. Further security controls should be employed throughout all the stages of the software development lifecycle.
- Use a secure language for software development. To meet the requirements of ISO 21434, it is imperative that the chosen language should be able to promote secure design and coding techniques.

- Use a language subset that can help mitigate security risks. ISO 21434 explicitly requires compliance with coding standards such as the MISRA C:2021 revisions 1 and 3 CERT C guidelines for C/C++.
- Enforce strong typing rules. Again, this is in compliant with ISO 21434 requirement to use coding standards such as the MISRA C:2021 revisions 1 and 3 CERT C guidelines.
- Implement defensive guards in software. This ensures that the software can handle unpredictable results and exceptions. The implementations are found in recognized coding guidelines such as the MISRA C:2012 revision 1.
- Implement fuzz testing. ISO 21434 recommends fuzz testing as a method to cope with its increased testing requirements. This testing method can be partially automated to speed up the development process. Software testing should be done as early as possible in the development process. The early detection and correction of bugs promotes the cost effectiveness of the entire software development process. A detailed discussion on fuzz testing is provided in a subsequent section.

Section 5 of ISO 21434, *Management of Cybersecurity*, calls for a periodic organizational cybersecurity audit. This activity should be performed by an independent party to objectively assess the cybersecurity posture of the organization. The following section describes cybersecurity assessment and audit processes in detail.

Cybersecurity Assessments and Audits

Organizations associated with automobile manufacturing and maintenance should conduct routine cybersecurity audits to isolate gaps in their cybersecurity infrastructure. These audits can also aid in ensuring that a variety of laws and regulations are being complied with. To avoid potential conflicts of interest, it is important that the independence of the audits be preserved by either having third party vendors perform the audit or ensuring that in-house audits are conducted by a team that acts independently of the parent organization (SecurityScorecard, 2020).

It is crucial to understand that both audits and assessments play important roles in evaluating cybersecurity. SecurityScorecard (SecurityScorecard, 2020) points out that an audit will evaluate if certain controls are in place while an assessment considers how well each of the controls manage risk. In addition, they point out that there are five best practices that organizations can follow to prepare for a cybersecurity audit:

1. Review your data security policy
   a. An organization's information security policy sets out guidance for managing confidential employee and customer information. The policy should appropriately address the availability, confidentiality, and integrity of data. Availability sets out the terms of when authorized users can access data. Confidentiality addresses which employees can access data and who they are permitted to disclose it to. Integrity is concerned with whether controls can preserve the accuracy of data. Data security is crucial to maintaining regulatory compliance. Therefore, auditors need good information regarding it so they can effectively evaluate compliance strengths.
2. Centralize your cybersecurity policies
   a. Providing auditors with a consolidated listing of an organizations cybersecurity policies can increase the proficiency of the audit process by giving auditors a better understanding security practices that they can use to pinpoint probable gaps. Significant policies should include:
   b. Network access controls in place setting out who can access specific data.
   c. Disaster recovery and business continuity plans to keep a company running should a disaster occur.
   d. Remote work policies regarding the maintenance of security for employees working outside of the business.
   e. Acceptable use policy setting out the conditions that employees must accept before being permitted to obtain access to information technology assets.
3. Detail your network structure
   a. An auditor should be provided with a network diagram which sets out an organization's network assets along with a description of how they work together. Such diagrams provide a top-down picture that can be used to recognize possible weaknesses and edges more clearly.
4. Review relevant compliance standards
   a. An organization should identify applicable compliance standards and review their requirements. Sharing these requirements with the audit team allows them to ensure that their assessments will appropriately address what is needed to ensure regulatory compliance.
5. Create a list of security personnel and their responsibilities
   a. A principal part of cybersecurity audits is to interview security personnel so that auditors can obtain a sounder grasp of an organization's security architecture. Savings in time and improved audit efficiency can be achieved by ensuring that auditors have a listing of the individual responsibilities of members of the security team.

Cybersecurity Best Practices and the NIST

The National Highway Traffic Safety Administration (NHTSA) states that the automotive industry should follow the five principal functions of the National Institute of Standards and Technology's (NIST's) Cybersecurity Framework: Identify, Protect, Detect, Respond, and Recover (National Highway Traffic Safety Administration (NHTSA), 2020). This section considers how best practices for cybersecurity as suggested by the NHTSA fit within the five principal functions. For each of these functions, tables provide examples of guidance from both the NIST framework (National Institute of Standards and Technology, 2018) and COBIT 2019 (ISACA, 2019).

Identify

The NHTSA states that a risk assessment process should contain an assessment of cybersecurity risk that exhibits risk mitigation over the complete life cycle of the vehicle. The safety of persons both within the vehicle and others on the road should be a prime consideration in the risk assessment process (National Highway Traffic Safety Administration (NHTSA), 2020). Some examples of concerns regarding to the possible exploitation of vehicle sensor data include GPS spoofing and road sign modification. GPS spoofing occurs when an illegitimate signal from a radio transmitter overrides a legitimate satellite signal that is not as strong as the radio signal (McAfee, 2020). Regarding road sign modification,

Table 1. Risk Identification – Assesment

Framework Function: Identify (ID) Develop an organizational understanding to manage cybersecurity risk to systems, people, assets, data, and capabilities.	
Framework Category: Risk Assessment (ID.RA) The organization understands the cybersecurity risk to organizational operations (including mission, functions, image, or reputation), organizational assets, and individuals.	**Informative Reference from COBIT 2019 (APO12.02 – Analyze Risk)** Develop a substantiated view on actual I&T (information and technology) risk, in support of risk decisions.
Framework Subcategory: (ID.RA-5) Threats, vulnerabilities, likelihoods, and impacts are used to determine risk.	**Suggested Activity from COBIT 2019** Build and regularly update I&T risk scenarios; I&T-related loss exposures; and scenarios regarding reputational risk, including compound scenarios of cascading and/or coincidental threat types and events. Develop expectations for specific control activities and capabilities to detect. **Suggested Metric from COBIT 2019** Number of identified I&T risk scenarios

automobiles equipped with machine-learning algorithms for interpreting signs can be tricked into thinking a sign says something completely different by applying slight modifications to the sign that are often invisible to humans (Ackerman, 2017). Obviously, such practices can have severe consequences for autonomous vehicles. Table 1 illustrates how the NIST Framework and COBIT 2019 can be employed to a process of risk identification.

Protect

The NHTSA makes it clear that any unwarranted risk to safety-critical systems should be eliminated or lessened to an acceptable risk level through the application of proper design of the system. In addition, any functionality that shows an obvious and preventable risk needs to be removed whenever possible (National Highway Traffic Safety Administration (NHTSA), 2020). Once this has been achieved, layers of protection should be created and employed to address remaining risks and functionality.

In addition, it is recommended that automotive manufactures maintain a database of operational software components that are associated with each vehicle over its lifetime. The database should allow newly identified vulnerabilities in software to be traced to the engine control units of specific vehicles that are making use of the software component (National Highway Traffic Safety Administration (NHTSA), 2020).

The multi-talented Leonardo Da Vinci is credited for having made the statement that "simplicity is the ultimate sophistication." The concept known as the principle of least functionality can be thought of as the application of Da Vinci's clever observation to the realm of computer systems design. It "means that systems are to only have mission-essential software installed, only essential ports open and essential services on." The most prominent benefit of this approach is that a system configured in this manner has inherently fewer avenues open to a cybersecurity attack (Cub Cyber, 2021). Table 2 describes how protection can be approached in the NIST Framework and COBIT 2019 by minimizing the complexity of software design to achieve the desired functionality of an automotive system.

Detect

The NHTSA indicates that automotive "manufacturers should evaluate all commercial off-the-shelf and open-source software components used in vehicle engine control units (ECUs) against known vulnerabilities" (National Highway Traffic Safety Administration (NHTSA), 2020). In conducting testing, the independence of the process should be ensured by employing competent personnel that have not

Table 2. Simplicity as a form of protective techology

Framework Function: Protect (PR) Develop and implement appropriate safeguards to ensure delivery of critical services.	
Framework Category: Protective Technology (PR.PT) Technical security solutions are managed to ensure the security and resilience of systems and assets, consistent with related policies, procedures, and agreements.	**Informative Reference from COBIT 2019 (DSS05.02 – Manage Network and Connectivity Security)** Use security measures and related management procedures to protect information over all methods of connectivity.
Framework Subcategory: (PR.PT-3) The principle of least functionality is incorporated by configuring systems to provide only essential capabilities	**Suggested Activity from COBIT 2019** Configure network equipment in a secure manner. **Suggested Metric from COBIT 2019** Percent of time network and systems not available due to security incident.

been members of the development team. The testers should be well compensated based on their ability to identify software vulnerabilities. In the software development process, it is important that product cybersecurity testing include approved simulated cyberattacks on the computer system, commonly known as a penetration test.

It is also imperative to properly document system vulnerabilities. This documentation should include a vulnerability analysis for each assessed known vulnerability or newly identified vulnerability that arises during cybersecurity testing. Properly documentation should also describe how vulnerabilities have been either removed or how an organization plans to manage them (National Highway Traffic Safety Administration (NHTSA), 2020).

Table 3 describes how detection of vulnerabilities is addressed in the NIST Framework and COBIT 2019 through testing for vulnerabilities.

Respond

The NHTSA points out that since it is impossible to anticipate all prospective attacks, the automotive industry should create a plan for cybersecurity incident response (National Highway Traffic Safety Administration (NHTSA), 2020). The plan should include:

- A standard incident response plan that clearly identifies appropriate procedures.
- Clearly identified roles and responsibilities of members of the response team.
- Specific communication channels within the organization and who should be contacted outside the organization.

Table 3. Monitoring for cybersecurity incidents

Framework Function: Detect (DE) **Develop and implement appropriate activities to identify the occurrence of a cybersecurity event.**	
Framework Category: Security Continuous Monitoring **(DE.CM)** The information system and assets are monitored to identify cybersecurity events and verify the effectiveness of protective measures.	**Informative Reference from COBIT 2019** **(DSS05.07 – Manage Vulnerabilities and Monitor the Infrastructure for Security-Related Events)** Using a portfolio of tools and technologies (e.g., intrusion detection tools), manage vulnerabilities and monitor the infrastructure for unauthorized access. Ensure the security tools, technologies, and detection are integrated with general event monitoring and incident management.
Framework Subcategory: **(DE.CM-1)** The network is monitored to detect potential cybersecurity events.	**Suggested Activity from COBIT 2019** Continually use a portfolio of supported technologies, services and assets (e.g., vulnerability scanners, fuzzers and sniffers, protocol analyzers) to identify information security vulnerabilities. **Suggested Metric from COBIT 2019** Number of vulnerabilities discovered during testing.

Table 4. Responding to cybersecurity incidents

Framework Function: Respond (RS) **Develop and implement appropriate activities to take action regarding a detected cybersecurity incident.**	
Framework Category: Response Planning **(RS.RP)** Response processes and procedures are executed and maintained, to ensure response to detected cybersecurity incidents.	**Informative Reference from COBIT 2019** **(APO12.06 – Respond to Risk)** Respond in a timely manner to materialized risk events with effective measures to limit the magnitude of loss.
Framework Subcategory: **(RS.RP-1)** Response plan is executed during or after an incident.	**Suggested Activity from COBIT 2019** Apply the appropriate response plan to minimize the impact when risk incidents occur. **Suggested Metric from COBIT 2019** Percent of information and technology (I&T) risk action plans executed as designed.

It is also imperative that organizations develop metrics which regularly allow them to evaluate how effectively the response process is functioning. Table 4 illustrates how the NIST Framework and COBIT 2019 consider an incident response plan.

Recover

The NHTSA states that "the automotive industry should establish rapid vehicle cybersecurity incident detection and remediation capabilities" (National Highway

Table 5. Recovery

Framework Function: Recover (RC) Develop and implement appropriate activities to maintain plans for resilience and to restore any capabilities or services that were impaired due to a cybersecurity incident.	
Framework Category: Recovery Planning (RC.RP) Recovery processes and procedures are executed and maintained to ensure restoration of systems or assets affected by cybersecurity events.	**Informative Reference from COBIT 2019 (DSS03.04 – Resolve and Close Problem)** Identify and initiate sustainable solutions addressing the root cause. Raise change requests via the established change management process, if required, to resolve errors. Ensure that the personnel affected are aware of the actions taken and the plans developed to prevent future incidents from occurring.
Framework Subcategory: RC.RP-1 Recovery plan is executed during or after a cybersecurity incident.	**Suggested Activity from COBIT 2019:** Throughout the resolution process, obtain regular reports from IT change management on progress in resolving problems and errors. **Suggested Metric from COBIT 2019:** Decrease in number of recurring incidents caused by unresolved problems.

Traffic Safety Administration (NHTSA), 2020). These capabilities should minimize the risk to both persons within the vehicle and surrounding road users. Upon detection of a cyber-attack, the vehicle should move to a least risk condition that is suitable for the known risk situation. Table 5 considers the importance of having recovery capabilities in the NIST Framework and COBIT 2019.

Fuzz Testing in the System Development Life Cycle

In the realm of cybersecurity, fuzz testing is an approach to performing automated software testing that inputs inacceptable and unanticipated data into computer programs for the purpose of identifying coding errors and loopholes in software security. It is accomplished by feeding large amounts of random data (fuzz) into the computer program in effort to either make it crash or find a break in its defenses. Once vulnerabilities are identified, a software tool known as a fuzzer can be used to determine potential probable causes (Contrast Security, n.d.).

Beyond Security points out that even is NIST recognizes that the software development life cycle (SDLC) of many organizations does not specifically consider a detailed level of software security (Beyond Security, 2020). They then go on to discuss eight reasons for including Fuzz Testing as part of an organization's SDLC:

1. Test your application with real-world attacks. Incorporating fuzz testing in different part of the SDLC helps developers to think like a hacker and possibly halt attacks before they have a chance to get started.

2. Eliminate zero-day attacks. Wikipedia defines a zero-day attack as one involving a software vulnerability that the software vendor has zero days to correct in that the vulnerability has already allowed the system to be hacked (Wikipedia, 2022). Fuzz testing applied to either the implementation or verification phase of an organization's software development life cycle can help to expose security vulnerabilities before hackers have a chance to discover them.

3. Create more efficient code. Applying fuzz testing can help discover bugs that were not found in a manual audit. This results in code that is more in that it contains fewer weaknesses.

4. Detect software vulnerabilities before deployment. Smart fuzzing evaluates the security of a greater number of attack entry points than many other application security practices.

5. Save time and money. Once fuzz testing is up and running it can search for vulnerabilities for extended periods of time. Smart fuzzers that possess auto-learn capabilities can easily test over 250,000 attacks per second and will likely be even faster in the future.

6. Test applications without knowing the source code. Source code is generally not available for commercial applications. Blackbox fuzzers possess the ability to evaluate applications when the source code is unavailable.

7. Test all protocols. Fuzzers are often transferrable meaning that they allow testing over an extensive selection of protocols, reducing the need to rely on different testing tools.

8. Reduce false alerts. Smart fuzzers allow the creation of "enterprise-oriented rules" that are centered around the in-house frameworks of an organization.

FUTURE RESEARCH DIRECTIONS

The development of cybersecurity in the automotive industry is just recently becoming a primary issue as vehicles are equipped with more automation moving toward the goal eventually becoming an autonomous driving machine. Future research in the following areas could be helpful as automotive cybersecurity matures:

- The development of specific measures to determine when regulatory requirements have been met.
- Auditing standards for the conduct of an automotive cybersecurity evaluation and report.

- The development of cybersecurity metrics for automotive vehicles.
- The enhancement of a robust, secure, and safe vehicle communication system using blockchain technology.
- The development of cybersecurity guidelines that can be applied throughout the complete life cycle of a vehicle.

CONCLUSION

The idea of applying cybersecurity to protect the technology components of organizational information systems has existed for some time. However, cybersecurity is in its relative infancy regarding the increasing level of technology that is being employed to manufacture and maintain the automobiles of today and in the future.

The development of regulations over automotive cybersecurity helps to ensure that a proper level of safety accompanies the advances in automotive technology. This growth in regulation is accompanied by an increase in the need to ensure compliance. Fortunately, existing cybersecurity frameworks such as those provided by National Institute of Standards and Technology and COBIT offer common guidance that can be applied to automotive cybersecurity.

Great strides in the development and enhancement of automotive vehicle security regulations and standards have been recently made. However, with the introduction of Electric Vehicles (EVs) and their supporting technologies along the periphery, there are new challenges that loom in the horizon. Existing regulations and standards need to be continuously improved; cybersecurity tools need to be implemented that will protect the national power grid from the vulnerabilities created by EVs; and a Cybersecurity Maturity Model Certification, similar to that being required on the Defense Industrial Base entities, must be developed specifically for automotive vehicle manufacturers.

REFERENCES

Ackerman, E. (2017, August 4). *Slight Street Sign Modifications Can Completely Fool Machine Learning Algorithms.* Retrieved February 19, 2022, from IEEE Spectrum: https://spectrum.ieee.org/slight-street-sign-modifications-can-fool-machine-learning-algorithms

Argus Cyber Security. (2016, January). *SAE J3061 Cyber Security Guidebook for Cyber-Physical Vehicle Systems.* Retrieved February 2022, from Argus Cyber Security: https://argus-sec.com/sae-j3061-cyber-security-guidebook-for-cyber-physical-vehicle-systems/

Burkacky, O., Deichmann, J., Klein, B., Pototzky, K., & Scherf, G. (2020, March). *Cybersecurity in Automotive.* Retrieved February 2022, from McKinsensy.com: https://www.mckinsey.com/~/media/mckinsey/industries/automotive%20and%20 assembly/our%20insights/cybersecurity%20in%20automotive%20mastering%20 the%20challenge/cybersecurity-in-automotive-mastering-the-challenge.pdf

Cyber, C. (2021, February 15). *The Principle of Least Functionality, Simplicity is the Ultimate Sophistication.* Retrieved February 19, 2022, from Cub Cyber: https://www.cubcyber.com/the-principle-of-least-functionality-simplicity-is-the-ultimate-sophistication

Dechand, S. (2020, October 8). *Automotive Software: 6 Tips to Comply With ISO 21434 Cheat Sheet).* Retrieved February 2022, from Code Intelligence: https://www.code-intelligence.com/blog/iso-21434-compliance?utm_term=automotive%20 software&utm_campaign=&utm_source=adwords&utm_medium=ppc&hsa_ acc=1156374742&hsa_cam=14540066791&hsa_grp=121993923530&hsa_ ad=544093176460&hsa_src=g&hsa_tgt=kwd-10652700&hsa_k

Electronics, C. S. S. (2019). *A Simple Intro to LIN bus.* Retrieved October 2019, from CSS Electrnoics: https://www.csselectronics.com/screen/page/lin-bus-protocol-intro-basics/language/en

Francia, G. A. (2020). Connected Vehicle Security. *15th International Conference on Cyber Warfare and Security (ICCWS 2020)*, 173-181.

Francia, G. A. III. (2021). Vehicle Network Security Metrics. In K. Daimi & C. Peoples (Eds.), *Advances in Cybersecurity Management* (pp. 55–73). Springer Nature. doi:10.1007/978-3-030-71381-2_4

Francia, G. A. III, & El-Sheikh, E. (2021). Applied Machine Learning to Vehicle Security. In Y. Maleh, M. Shojafar, M. Alazab, & Y. Baddi (Eds.), *Machine Intelligence and Big Data Analytics for Cybersecurity Applications* (pp. 423–442). Springer Nature Switzerland AG. doi:10.1007/978-3-030-57024-8_19

Goldstein, F. (2020). *Understanding the UNECE WP.29.* Retrieved February 2022, from Upstream: https://upstream.auto/blog/understanding-the-unece-wp-29-cybersecurity-regulation

Information Technology-Information Sharing and Analysis Center. (2022). Retrieved February 22, 2022, from About Us: https://www.it-isac.org/about

International, S. A. E. (1998, August 1). *CAN Specification 2.0: Protocol and Implementations.* Retrieved October 13, 2019, from SAE Mobilus: https://www.sae.org/publications/technical-papers/content/921603/

International, S. A. E. (2020, July 23). *V2X Communications Message Set Dictionary*. Retrieved February 2022, from SAE Mobilus: https://www.sae.org/standards/content/j2735_202007/

ISACA. (2019). *COBIT 2019 Framework: Governance and Management Objectives*. ISACA.

Juniper Research. (2020, September). *Cars With Embedded Connectivity To Reach 200 Million by 2025, With 5G Adoption Set to Soar*. Retrieved February 2022, from Juniper Research: https://www.juniperresearch.com/press/cars-with-embedded-connectivity-to-reach-200

Keysight. (2019, February 28). *From Standard Ethernet to Automotive Ethernet*. Retrieved November 6, 2020, from Keysight: https://www.keysight.com/us/en/assets/7018-06530/flyers/5992-3742.pdf

Macher, G., Schmittner, C., Veledar, O., & Brenner, E. (2020). ISO/SAE DIS 21434 Automotive Cybersecurity Standard - In a Nutshell. In A. Casimiro, F. Ortmeier, E. Schoitsch, F. Bitsch, & P. Ferreira (Eds.), Lecture Notes in Computer Science: Vol. 12235. *Computer Safety, Reliability, and Security. SAFECOMP 2020 Workshops. SAFECOMP 2020*. Springer. doi:10.1007/978-3-030-55583-2_9

McAfee. (2020, August 25). *What is GPS Spoofing?* Retrieved February 19, 2022, from McAfee: https://www.mcafee.com/blogs/internet-security/what-is-gps-spoofing/

McKinsey & Company. (2020, March). *Cybersecurity in automotive*. Retrieved February 22, 2022, from https://www.mckinsey.com/~/media/mckinsey/industries/automotive%20and%20assembly/our%20insights/cybersecurity%20in%20automotive%20mastering%20the%20challenge/cybersecurity-in-automotive-mastering-the-challenge.pdf

National Highway Traffic Safety Administration (NHTSA). (2020). *Cybersecurity Best Practices for the Safety of Modern Vehicles*. Retrieved February 13, 2022, from UD Department of Transportation National Highway Traffic Safety Administration: https://www.nhtsa.gov/sites/nhtsa.gov/files/documents/vehicle_cybersecurity_best_practices_01072021.pdf

National Highway Traffic Safety Administration (NHTSA). (n.d.). *Vehicle Cybersecurity*. Retrieved February 22, 2022, from U.S. Department of Transportation NHTSA: https://www.nhtsa.gov/technology-innovation/vehicle-cybersecurity

National Institute of Standards and Technology. (2018, April 16). *Framework for Improving Critical Infrastructure Security*. Retrieved February 17, 2022, from https://nvlpubs.nist.gov/nistpubs/cswp/nist.cswp.04162018.pdf

National Instruments. (2019, May 28). *FlexRay Automotive Communication Bus Overview.* Retrieved October 13, 2019, from National Instruments: https://www.ni.com/en-us/innovations/white-papers/06/flexray-automotive-communication-bus-overview.html

Schmittner, C., Griessnig, G., & Ma, Z. (2018). Status of the Development of ISO/SAE 21434. *Proc of the 25th European Conference, EuroSPI 2018.* 10.1007/978-3-319-97925-0_43

Security, B. (2020, August 4). *To Fuzz or Not to Fuzz: 8 Reasons to Include Fuzz Testing in Your SDLC.* Retrieved February 19, 2022, from Beyond Security: https://blog.beyondsecurity.com/fuzz-testing-sdlc/

Security, C. (n.d.). *Contrast Security.* Retrieved February 20, 2022, from Fuzz Testing: https://www.contrastsecurity.com/knowledge-hub/glossary/fuzz-testing

SecurityScorecard. (2020, August 17). *Best Practices for Cybersecurity Auditing [A Step-by-step Checklist].* Retrieved February 13, 2022, from SecurityScorecard: https://securityscorecard.com/blog/best-practices-for-a-cybersecurity-audit

Taub, E. (2021, March 18). *Carmakers Strive to Stay Ahead of Hackers.* Retrieved February 24, 2022, from New York Times: https://www.nytimes.com/2021/03/18/business/hacking-cars-cybersecurity.html#:~:text=The%20effects%20of%20a%20breach,and%20a%20lot%20of%20firewalls.&text=In%20your%20garage%20or%20driveway,than%20a%20modern%20passenger%20jet

UL. (2022). *Automotive Cybersecurity Auditing and Testing.* Retrieved February 13, 2022, from https://www.ul.com/services/automotive-cybersecurity-auditing-and-testing

United Nations Economic Commission for Europe (UNECE). (2021, April 3). *UN Regulation No. 156.* Retrieved February 2022, from Uniform Provisions Concerning the Approval of Vehicles with Regards to Software Update and Software Updates Management System: https://unece.org/sites/default/files/2021-03/R156e.pdf

United Nations Economic Commission for Europe (UNECE). (2021, May 27). *World Forum for Harmonization of Vehicle Regulations (WP.29) Terms of Reference and Rules of Procedure--Revision 2.* Retrieved February 2022, from UNECE: https://unece.org/transport/documents/2021/05/standards/world-forum-harmonization-vehicle-regulations-wp29-terms-0

Upstream Security Ltd. (2020). *ISO/SAE 21434: Setting the Standard for Automotive Cybersecurity.* Retrieved November 5, 2020, from Upstream: https://info.upstream.auto/hubfs/White_papers/Upstream_Security_Setting_the_Standard_for_Automotive_Cybersecurity_WP.pdf?_hsmi=87208721&_hsenc=p2ANqtz-8ke_6RWU7hkISDBzRoHFeUhfbaRRQ7E9-Z2bvc4YMlP3JNvc42_oh1ZxJ5jtWQOUlTehUaSmp7MfNDcwzbzUWoZjrGHw

Vasistha, D. K. (2017, August). *Detecting Anomalies in Controller Area Network (CAN) for Automobiles.* Retrieved April 13, 2020, from http://cesg.tamu.edu/wp-content/uploads/2012/01/VASISTHA-THESIS-2017.pdf

Vector Informatik Gmb, H. (2020). *Media Oriented Systems Transport (MOST).* Retrieved November 5, 2020, from Vector: https://www.vector.com/int/en/know-how/technologies/networks/most/#c21313

Wikipedia. (2022, February). Retrieved February 21, 2022, from Zero-day (computing): https://en.wikipedia.org/wiki/Zero-day_(computing)

Zhou, A., Li, Z., & Shen, Y. (2019). Anomaly Detection of CAN Bus Messages Using A Deep Neural Network for Autonomous Vehicles. *Applied Sciences (Basel, Switzerland), 9*(3174), 3174. doi:10.3390/app9153174

ADDITIONAL READING

El Sadany, M., Schmittner, C., & Kastner, W. (2019). Assuring compliance with protection profiles with threatget. In A. Romanovsky, E. Troubitsyna, I. Gashi, E. Schoitsch, & F. Bitsch (Eds.), *Computer Safety. Reliability, and Security* (pp. 62–73). Springer. doi:10.1007/978-3-030-26250-1_5

Heinemann, H. (2018, August). *Fending Off Cyber Attacks – Hardening ECUs by Fuzz Testing.* Retrieved February 28, 2022, from: https://cdn.vector.com/cms/content/know-how/_technical-articles/Security_FuzzTesting_HanserAutomotive_201808_PressArticle_EN.pdf

Lee, Y., Woo, S., Song, Y., Lee, J., & Lee, D. H. (2020). Practical Vulnerability-Information-Sharing Architecture for Automotive Security-Risk Analysis. IEEE Access. *Access, IEEE, 8*(January), 120009–120018. doi:10.1109/ACCESS.2020.3004661

Leveson, N. (2019). *CAST HANDBOOK: How to Learn More from Incidents and Accidents*. Accessed March 11, 2022. Retrieved from: http://sunnyday.mit.edu/CAST-Handbook.pdf

Marksteiner, S., Bronfman, S., Wolf, M. & Lazebnik, E. (2021). *Using Cyber Digital Twins for Automated Automotive Cybersecurity Testing*. . doi:10.1109/EuroSPW54576.2021.00020

Schmittner, C., & Macher, G. (2019). Automotive cybersecurity standards - relation and overview. In A. Romanovsky, E. Troubitsyna, I. Gashi, E. Schoitsch, & F. Bitsch (Eds.), *Computer Safety. Reliability, and Security* (pp. 153–165). Springer. doi:10.1007/978-3-030-26250-1_12

Teuchert, D. (2021, April 23). *Roadmap to Successful Fuzz Testing (for Automotive Software)*. Retrieved February 28, 2022, from: https://www.code-intelligence.com/blog/roadmap-to-successful-fuzz-testing

KEY TERMS AND DEFINITIONS

Cybersecurity: A set of processes, practices, and technologies designed to protect, in the realm of cyberspace, the three tenets of information security: confidentiality, integrity, and availability.

Cybersecurity Audit: Involves an evaluation of information technology for the purpose of identifying vulnerabilities that could be exploited to interfere with the proper functioning a critical components of system functioning.

Engine Control Unit: A principal component of a vehicle that controls one or more electrical systems in a car.

Framework: A grouping of rules and related concepts into a logical approach that can be used to identify complex problems and decide upon appropriate courses of action to address them.

Fuzz Testing: A form of automated software testing that can comprehensively test for vulnerabilities to identify coding errors and loopholes that could compromise software security.

Regulatory Compliance: The state of being in conformance to the requirements of a relevant law, policy, or regulation.

Standards: A set of rules that can be monitored for compliance by a specialized field's authoritative bodies and related professionals.

Vehicle-to-Infrastructure (V2X or V2I) Communication: A type of communication link between an automotive vehicle with the cyber-infrastructure.

Vehicle-to-Vehicle (V2V) Communication: A type of communication link between two or more automotive vehicles.

Zero-Day Attack: A software vulnerability that has already been hacked meaning that the time for the developer to respond to prevent the attack has already passed.

Section 2
Approaches to Cybersecurity Training

Chapter 3
NERC CIP Standards:
Review, Compliance, and Training

Guillermo A. Francia III

https://orcid.org/0000-0001-8088-2653
University of West Florida, USA

Eman El-Sheikh
University of West Florida, USA

ABSTRACT

The critical infrastructure protection (CIP) set of standards is developed by the North American Electric Reliability Corporation (NERC) to ensure the protection of assets used to operate North America's bulk electric systems (BES). Any entity that owns or operates any type of BES in the United States and Canada must be compliant with the requirements of the NERC CIP standards. The purpose of this chapter is to provide an ample overview of the NERC CIP standards, to describe its relevance to the protection electric utility entities, to establish its harmonizing relation with the NIST cyber security framework, to provide a glimpse of its compliance requirements, and to investigate the gaps and prospects for workforce development training in this area of critical need. This chapter lays the foundation for opportunities in the design of automated NERC CIP standards compliance processes and toolkit, the feasibility study of adopting the CIP standards in other sectors, and the development of training materials in NERC CIP standards for workforce development.

DOI: 10.4018/978-1-7998-8390-6.ch003

Copyright © 2022, IGI Global. Copying or distributing in print or electronic forms without written permission of IGI Global is prohibited.

INTRODUCTION

Industrial Control Systems (ICS) have been widely employed to supervise and control critical infrastructures in various sectors such energy, defense industrial base manufacturing, water treatment, transportation, nuclear, chemical, health, and maritime, just to name a few. This chapter is focused on one prominent application of ICS: the electric utility sector. ICS are originally designed to operate on air-gapped networks, but due to expanded operational requirements, the interconnectivity between Information Technology (IT) and Operational Technology (OT) became inevitable. Such interfacing augmented the attack surfaces on ICS and prompted the increased incidence of cyberattacks. These cyberattacks on ICS can have devastating effects, which may include:

- Personal safety
- Damage to assets
- Damage to the environment
- Financial loss
- Compliance issues with legal and regulatory standards
- Loss of trust
- Loss of proprietary data

The serious consequences of a cyberattack prompted the development and implementation of standards and regulations to protect our nation's critical infrastructures. Standards provide a set of rules that can be monitored for compliance by a specialized field's authoritative bodies and related professionals. The grouping of rules and related concepts into appropriate frameworks furnishes the basic building blocks to identify and decide upon appropriate courses of action to address complex problems. Although the enumeration of an exhaustive set of standards and frameworks appropriate for a cybersecurity audit is beyond the scope of this article, we focus our attention to the standards created by the North American Electric Reliability Corporation—the CIP Standards.

This chapter highlights the NERC CIP Standards significance for the protection electric utility entities, and its mapping to the NIST Cyber Security Framework. We illustrate the compliance requirements, including a case study, and investigate the gaps and prospects for workforce development training in this crucial area. This work lays the foundation for the development of automated NERC CIP Standards compliance processes and toolkit, the feasibility of adopting the CIP Standards in other sectors, and the development of training materials in NERC CIP Standards for workforce development.

BACKGROUND

The Critical Infrastructure Protection (CIP) set of standards is developed by the North American Electric Reliability Corporation (NERC) to ensure the protection of assets used to operate North America's Bulk Electric Systems (BES). Any entity that owns or operates any type of BES in the United States and Canada must be compliant with the requirements of the NERC CIP Standards.

A closely related set of standards is the International Society of Automation/ International Electrotechnical Commission (ISA/IEC) 62443 Standards (ISA/IEC, 2020), which addresses the Security of Industrial Automation and Control Systems (IACS). These standards were initially intended for the industrial sector but evolved and applied to building automation, medical device, and transportation sectors.

An early study on the viability and significance of the NERC CIP standards is made in (Zhang Z., 2011). The study focused on CIP-002 (Critical Cyber Asset Identification), which is the predecessor of the currently enforced CIP-002-5.1a (BES Cyber System Categorization) and concluded that the mandatory cybersecurity standards are beneficial and promoted an increase in technological products, better security management, personnel training, and public trust in the industry.

Design challenges on substation equipment upgrades in light of cybersecurity requirements by the NERC CIP standards are described in (Cole, 2016). The challenges are based mainly on the discovery of legacy and obsolete equipment to be replaced and exacerbated by the lack of up-to-date design and configuration documents. The contingencies that must be included in resource plans, budgets and schedules of equipment upgrades as required by the standards further the burden on the process.

A review of the NERC CIP standards and arguments in favor of the implementation of security plans and adherence to the mandates are presented in (Proctor & Smith, 2017). The review presents how the NERC CIP standards can be applied to the cybersecurity of industrial sectors as well.

In (Mukherjee, 2015), the physical security of Transmission stations and substations as specified in CIP-014-1, later supplanted by CIP-014-2, is taken into consideration in recognizing innovative techniques for power restoration during unplanned outages. With the emerging distributed energy resources such as microgrids and the application of this standard, the risk of re-energizing the power grid after a blackout may be safely and securely mitigated. Along the same goal of protecting transmission substations, Nakao, Loo and Melville (Nakao, Loo, & Melville, 2015) described a substation automation system managed by an enterprise system that supports the security, operations, testing, and maintenance of automation components. This is an emerging model of an Information Technology (IT) – Operational Technology (OT) convergence. In this setup, managed and centralized syslog monitoring solutions were implemented to ensure the integrity of substation equipment.

The benefits of utilizing keyless signature infrastructure blockchain technology in enabling distributed data validation is explored in (Mylrea, Bishop, Johnson, & Gupta Gourisetti, 2018). This provides entity verification and promotes a community of trust and partly satisfies the security requirements of the NERC CIP standards.

In (Hyder & Govindarasu, 2020), game-theoretic approach is applied the problem of optimizing investment strategies on cybersecurity infrastructure of a smart grid. The adversary is modeled using various attacker profiles while the defender is modeled with various pragmatic characteristics which include the NERC CIP standards. The results of the study include optimal strategies for resource allocation and a validation of the feasibility of the work using a case study.

Physical security requirements call for the protection of transmission stations and substations that may result in cascading effect in power system interconnection. Ramanathan, et al. (Ramanathan, Popat, Papic, & Ciniglio, 2017) presented a practical approach for performing steady-state cascading analysis of a power system as a node/breaker model using real-time State Estimator cases. In their approach, actual switch statuses are modeled allowing the accurate simulation of power outages and contingencies.

The impacts of Intelligent Electronic Device (IED) management systems in securing power utility infrastructures are explored in the works of Mack (Mack, 2017), Weerathunga & Cioraca (Weerathunga & Cioraca, 2016), and Salvador, Mack & Carnegie (Salvador, Mack, & Carnegie, 2016).

Information protection is specifically addressed in one of the NERC-CIP standards. A study by Sriharsha et al. (Etigowni, Tian, Hernandez, Zonouz, & Butler, 2016) described CPAC, a cyber-physical access control implementation for the protection of industrial control systems against operational mistakes and insider attacks. The application utilizes a physical system model, information flow tracking, and logic-based context-aware policies to mitigate damage to the system and prevent the leakage of sensitive information to malicious insiders.

System security management which includes, among others, the protection of control devices such as Programmable Logic Controllers (PLCs) is also addressed in the NER-CIP Standards. These devices, mostly the legacy types, are designed with security as an afterthought. Thus, the urgent need to develop extenuating techniques and tools is paramount. One attempt to fill this gap is presented in (Salehi & Bayat-Sarmadi, 2021). The work proposes a mitigation method that combines hybrid remote attestation technique with a physics-based model to preserve the integrity of the control behavior of an industrial control system. The implementation of such combined technique is reported to attain an accuracy of 98% in modeling the physical behavior a PLC and accurately detect a wide range of attack scenarios on PLCs.

Vulnerability assessment is required by the NERC-CIP 010-3 standard. The ever-increasing trend of cyber threats in utility systems prods the development of vulnerability assessment mechanisms. To this end, a probabilistic Multi-Attribute Vulnerability Criticality Analysis (MAVCA) model is proposed in (Ani, He, & Tiwari, 2020). The model combines three attributes for impact estimation and prioritization: the severity of vulnerability as influenced by environmental factors, the attack probability on that vulnerability, and the functional dependency attributed to host component vulnerability. Similar published works on vulnerability assessments exist on smart grids (Woo & Kim, 2020), ICS system based on zero-day attack graphs (Wang, et al., 2020), and SCADA for a waste water treatment plant (Stanculescu, et al., 2019). In (Zhang & Li, 2018), a real-world case study on security vulnerability and patch management analysis was made on a dataset provided by an electric utility company. The study revealed that vulnerability distribution over software and asset was skewed indicating the issues reside in a small subset of the software and asset. This discovery provided a clear guide for remediation actions. Along the same vein, a study on ICS security assessment methodologies to identify appropriate vulnerability assessment method was conducted and reported in (Qais, Jamil, Daud, Patel, & Norhamadi, 2019). The review reported that most methodologies appear to concentrate on vulnerability identification and prioritization techniques. In addition, the study highlighted the fact that the patch management process in ICS is inadequate. This fact is well recognized in the community and is based on the fact that system patches are very difficult to apply in legacy systems and during operations.

A NERC-CIP compliance audit process, utilizing a Cyber-Physical Topology Language (CPTL), is described in (Weaver, Cheh, Rogers, Sanders, & Gammel, 2013). The language enabled the cyber-physical assets and operations to be logically represented through the aid of graph theory. With this representation, the auditors are afforded with a visual display of network and system architectures as well as the pertinent security controls.

MAIN FOCUS OF THE CHAPTER

NERC-CIP Standards

As of October 2021, the NERC-CIP Standards include 12 items that are enforceable, 4 subject to future enforcement, 1 pending to be inactive, and 78 are inactive (NERC CIP, 2021). Note that organizations that are found to be non-compliant incur heavy financial penalties among other consequences. Below is an overview of the 12 NERC-CIP Standards that are subject to enforcement.

CIP-002-5.1a Cyber Security - BES Cyber System Categorization

NERC-CIP states that the purpose of this standard is "to identify and categorize BES Cyber Systems and their associated BES Cyber Assets for the application of cyber security requirements commensurate with the adverse impact that loss, compromise, or misuse of those BES Cyber Systems could have on the reliable operation of the BES" (NERC CIP002-5.1a, 2021). In essence, the Responsible Entity should have a process that identifies and categorizes all cyber assets according to their respective degree of impact to the reliable operation of the BES.

CIP-003-8 Cyber Security - Security Management Controls

The purpose of this standard is "to specify consistent and sustainable security management controls that establish responsibility and accountability to protect BES Cyber Systems against compromise that could lead to misoperation or instability in the BES (NERC CIP 003-8, 2021). This standard requires management controls that include the identification of CIP senior manager and authority delegation and the establishment of cyber security plans and policies.

CIP-004-6 Cyber Security - Personnel and Training

The purpose of this standard is "to minimize the risk against compromise that could lead to mis-operation or instability in the Bulk Electric System (BES) from individuals accessing BES Cyber Systems by requiring an appropriate level of personnel risk assessment, training, and security awareness in support of protecting BES Cyber Systems" (NERC CIP 004-6, 2021). This standard simply calls for the implementation of a periodic cybersecurity awareness training program and the establishment of personnel risk assessment and access management programs.

CIP-005-6 Cyber Security - Electronic Security Perimeter(s)

The purpose of this standard is "to manage electronic access to BES Cyber Systems by specifying a controlled Electronic Security Perimeter (ESP) in support of protecting BES Cyber Systems against compromise that could lead to misoperation or instability in the BES" (NERC CIP 005-6, 2021). This standard requires that cyber assets on a network via routable protocol must reside within the ESP and that external routable connectivity must go through an identified Electronic Access Point (EAP). Further, there must be an established access control for inbound and outbound network traffic.

CIP-006-6 Cyber Security - Physical Security of BES Cyber Systems

The purpose of this standard is "to manage physical access to Bulk Electric System (BES) Cyber Systems by specifying a physical security plan in support of protecting BES Cyber Systems against compromise that could lead to misoperation or instability in the BES" (NERC CIP 006-6, 2021). This standard requires a documented and implemented physical security plan that includes operational and procedural controls for restricted access. The implementation may include, but not limited to, monitors, alarms, and entry logs. In addition, periodic maintenance and testing of the physical controls must be conducted.

CIP-007-6 Cyber Security - System Security Management

The purpose of this standard is "to manage system security by specifying select technical, operational, and procedural requirements in support of protecting BES Cyber Systems against compromise that could lead to misoperation or instability in the BES" (NERC CIP-007-6, 2021). This standard pertains to the requirement to securely manage ports and services, to develop, implement, and document a sound patch management process, to install and maintain methods to deter, detect, and prevent malicious code, to implement a security event monitoring system, and a robust system access control.

CIP-008-6 Cyber Security - Incident Reporting and Response Planning

The purpose of this standard is "to mitigate the risk to the reliable operation of the BES as the result of a Cyber Security Incident by specifying incident response requirements" (NERC CIP-008-6, 2021). In essence, this standard requires an incident response plan that includes the following:

- A process to identify, classify, and respond to a cybersecurity incident
- A process for determining whether a cybersecurity incident is a reportable incident and to notify the Electricity Sector Information Sharing and Analysis Center (ES-ISAC) as needed
- A clear delineation of responsibilities in conducting the incidence response
- A process for periodic review, update and/or revision of the cybersecurity incident plan
- A procedure for record keeping and retention
- Testing through tabletop exercises

CIP-009-6 Cyber Security - Recovery Plans for BES Cyber Systems

The purpose of this standard is "to recover reliability functions performed by BES Cyber Systems by specifying recovery plan requirements in support of the continued stability, operability, and reliability of the BES" (NERC CIP-009-6, 2021). This standard requires a documented recovery plan that includes the following:

- A clear delineation of roles and responsibilities of responders
- Specified conditions for the activation of the plan
- Processes for backup and restoration
- Periodic review and update
- Testing through tabletop exercises

CIP-010-3 Cyber Security - Configuration Change Management and Vulnerability Assessment

The purpose of this standard is "to prevent and detect unauthorized changes to BES Cyber Systems by specifying configuration change management and vulnerability assessment requirements in support of protecting BES Cyber Systems from compromise that could lead to mis-operation or instability in the BES" (NERC CIP-010-3, 2021). This standard calls for the design and implementation of a change management and vulnerability assessment processes that includes the following:

- Establishment of a baseline configuration
- A process for change authorization and documentation
- A process for verification of the required security controls after the change
- A process to detect unauthorized changes
- A process to undo the applied changes
- A process to perform and document an active vulnerability assessment
- An action plan to remediate or mitigate the discovered vulnerabilities

CIP-011-2 Cyber Security - Information Protection

The purpose of this standard is "to prevent unauthorized access to BES Cyber System Information by specifying information protection requirements in support of protecting BES Cyber Systems against compromise that could lead to mis-operation or instability in the BES" (NERC CIP-011-2, 2021). This standard requires that information, in transit or at rest, need to be protected through strong encryption techniques. During the disposal of cyber assets, proper actions must be executed to ensure that unauthorized retrieval of information from those assets is prevented.

CIP-013-1 Cyber Security - Supply Chain Risk Management

The purpose of this standard is "to mitigate cyber security risks to the reliable operation of the Bulk Electric System (BES) by implementing security controls for supply chain risk management of BES Cyber Systems" (NERC CIP-013-1, 2021). This standard requires the implementation of processes that will identify and assess cybersecurity risks from vendor products or services, verify software integrity and authenticity of all software and patches provided by the vendor, and the coordination of access controls for vendors.

CIP-014-2 Physical Security

The purpose of this standard is "to identify and protect Transmission stations and Transmission substations, and their associated primary control centers, that if rendered inoperable or damaged as a result of a physical attack could result in instability, uncontrolled separation, or cascading within an interconnection" (NERC CIP-014-2, 2021). This standard requires the utility operators to perform initial and follow-up risk assessments on Transmission stations and substations. It also requires an independent third party to perform verification review of the risk assessment conducted by the operator and recommend, as needed, actions that must be taken on the stations and/or substations involved in the review.

THE NERC-CIP STANDARDS AND THE NIST CYBERSECURITY FRAMEWORK

Marron, Gopstein & Bogle (Marron, Gopstein, & Bogle, 2021) write that the two approaches to cybersecurity, namely the NERC Standards and NIST Framework are complementary. Indeed, a combination of the standards-driven requirements of NERC-CIP with the NIST Framework for assessing and mitigating risk through sound management strategies would be highly beneficial.

The NIST Cybersecurity Framework

NIST published the original Cybersecurity Framework based on existing standards, guidelines, and practices for reducing cybersecurity risks in 2014. The Framework is comprised of three parts: Core, Profile, and Tiers. We will briefly cover the Core part in this work and refer the interested reader to the complete publication found in (NIST CSF, 2018). The so-called Core material is a set of cybersecurity activities, desired outcomes, and applicable references for the critical infrastructure sectors. It

Figure 1. NIST cybersecurity framework core structure

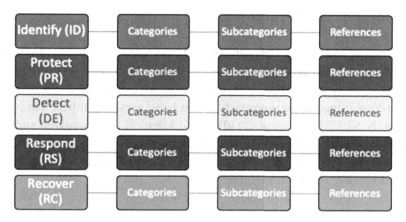

is organized into five functions, which are further sectioned into 23 categories. The categories are further divided into subcategories and references. The Framework structure is depicted in Figure 1.

The five functions are briefly described in the following.

- **Identify.** This function addresses the need to manage cybersecurity risks pertaining to systems, people, assets, data, and capabilities. Categories within this function include Asset Management, Business Environment, Governance, Risk Assessment, Risk Management Strategy, and Supply Chain Risk Management.
- **Protect.** This function addresses the need to implement appropriate safeguards to ensure delivery of critical services. Categories within this function include Access Control, Awareness and Training, Data Security, Information Protection Processes and Procedures, Maintenance, and Protective Technology.
- **Detect.** This function requires the development and implementation of appropriate measures to identify the occurrence of a cybersecurity event. Categories within this function include Anomalies and Events, Security Continuous Monitoring, and Detection Processes.
- **Respond.** This function requires the development and implementation of appropriate actions to take upon detection of a cybersecurity incident. Categories within this function include Response Planning, Communications, Analysis, Mitigation, and Improvements.
- **Recover.** This function requires the development and implementation of appropriate measures for the maintenance of the resiliency plan and restoration of capabilities or services that were affected by the cybersecurity incident.

Mapping the NERC CIP Standards to the NIST Cybersecurity Framework

In collaboration with NIST staff, NERC staff assessed and updated the reference document mapping NERC-CIP Reliability Standards to the NIST Cybersecurity Framework. This mapping underscores the complementary attribute and the benefits derived in combining the two approaches. The latest version published in June 2020 is found in (NIST CSF Mapping, 2020). Table 1 depicts a summarized and updated version of the mapping. We believe that the mapping provided in the latest version, particularly on CIP-014-2 (Physical Security), is lacking and, thus we offer our own augmented version as shown in Table 1.

COMPLIANCE WITH THE NERC-CIP STANDARDS

All too often, compliance with standards or regulations is burdensome, particularly the compilation of documents as evidentiary materials. This is further exacerbated by the need for additional personnel to handle the activities related to the compliance requirements. In Table 2, we attempt to provide a glimpse of the compliance requirements with a two-fold purpose: firstly, to create a springboard with which compliance actions can be initiated, and secondly, to provide a quick glance on what it entails to be in compliant with the NERC-CIP Standards. Further, we caution the reader that the table, depicting the compliance requirements, is not an exhaustive enumeration of the evidence, documents, and implementations required by the NERC-CIP Standards.

In addition, the reader should carefully note that compliance does not mean security. Compliance is basically accountability to meet certain standards or regulations. It does not ensure that trusted assets, people, systems, or devices, remain trustworthy. A compromise of a trusted account due to negligence can be a source of a cyber breach even though the organization is fully compliant.

TRAINING ON THE NERC-CIP STANDARDS

There is a great need for training on both sides of the standards: the implementers and the auditors. To address this need, we developed and introduced a course module on NERC CIP Compliance as part of an ICS Security course. The course was offered as part of workforce development training program with the aim of preparing military personnel and veterans for cybersecurity work roles. The course was delivered asynchronously online over a two-week duration. The module included The module

Table 1. Extended mapping of NERC-CIP standard to NIST cybersecurity framework

NERC CIP Standard	NIST Cybersecurity Framework
CIP-002-5.1a Cyber Security - BES Cyber System Categorization	Identify-Asset Management (ID-AM) Identify-Risk Assessment (ID-RA) Identify-Business Environment (ID-BE)
CIP-003-8 Cyber Security - Security Management Controls	Identify-Asset Management (ID-AM) Identify-Governance (ID-GV) Protect-Awareness and Training (PR-AT)
CIP-004-6 Cyber Security - Personnel & Training	Identify-Business Environment (ID-BE) Identify-Asset Management (ID-AM) Protect-Awareness and Training (PR-AT) Protect-Access Control (PR-AC) Protect-Data Security (PR-DS)
CIP-005-6 Cyber Security - Electronic Security Perimeter(s)	Identify-Asset Management (ID-AM) Protect-Access Control (PR-AC) Protect-Data Security (PR-DS) Protect-Maintenance (PR-MA) Protect-Protective Technology (PR-PT)
CIP-006-6 Cyber Security - Physical Security of BES Cyber Systems	Detect-Detection Processes (DE-DP) Protect-Access Control (PR-AC) Protect-Awareness & Training (PR-AT) Protect-Maintenance (PR-MA) Protect-Protective Technology (PR-PT)
CIP-007-6 Cyber Security - System Security Management	Protect-Access Control (PR-AC) Protect-Data Security (PR-DS) Detect-Anomalies and Events (DE-AE) Detect-Security Continuous Monitoring (DE-CM)
CIP-008-6 Cyber Security - Incident Reporting & Response Planning	Detect-Anomalies and Events (DE-AE) Detect-Data Protection (DE-DP) Identify-Business Environment (ID-BE) Identify-Risk Assessment (ID-RA) Respond-Communications (RS-CO) Respond-Analysis (RS-AN) Respond-Improvements (RS-IM) Respond-Mitigation (RS-MI)
CIP-009-6 Cyber Security - Recovery Plans for BES Cyber Systems	Protect-Information Protection Processes (PR-IP) Recover-Communications (RC-CO) Recover-Improvements (RC-IM)) Recover-Recovery Planning (RC-RP)
CIP-010-3 Cyber Security - Configuration Change Management & Vulnerability Assessment	Detect-Security Continuous Monitoring (DE-CM) Identify-Risk Assessment (ID-RA) Protect-Information Protection Processes (PR-IP) Respond-Analysis (RS-AN) Respond-Mitigation (RS-MI) Respond-Improvements (TS-IM)
CIP-011-2 Cyber Security - Information Protection	Protect-Data Security (PR-DS) Protect-Information Protection Processes (PR-IP) Respond-Information Protection Processes (RS-IP)

continued on following page

Table 1. Continued

NERC CIP Standard	NIST Cybersecurity Framework
CIP-013-1 Cyber Security - Supply Chain Risk Management	Identify-Risk Assessment (ID-RA) Identity-Business Environment (ID-BE) Identify-Risk Management (ID-RM) Identify-Supply Chain Management (ID-SC) Protect-Access Control (PR-AC) Protect-Awareness & Training (PR-AT) Protect-Maintenance (PR-MA) Respond-Analysis (RS-AN)
CIP-014-2 Physical Security	Identify-Asset Management (ID-AM) Identify-Risk Assessment (ID-RA) Identify-Risk Management (ID-RM) Protect-Access Control (PR-AC) Protect-Protective Technology (PR-PT) Detect-Security Continuous Monitoring (DE-CM) Respond-Improvements (RS-IM)

Table 2. NERC CIP standards compliance requirements

NERC CIP Standard	Compliance Requirements
CIP-002-5.1a Cyber Security - BES Cyber System Categorization	1. Evidence of process implementation for the identification and categorization of BES cyber systems and assets. 2. Retention of evidentiary materials on compliance, non-compliance, and audit records for a minimum duration as specified by the standard.
CIP-003-8 Cyber Security - Security Management Controls	1. One or more cyber security policy document reviewed and approved by a CIP Senior Manager at least once every 15 calendar months collectively addressing high, medium, and low impact BES cyber systems. These include, among others, personnel and training, electronic security perimeters, physical security, system security management, incident reporting and response planning, recovery plans, configuration change management, information protection, cyber security awareness, physical security controls, electronic access controls, cyber security incident response, and transient cyber assets.
CIP-004-6 Cyber Security - Personnel & Training	1. Evidence of quarterly reinforcement of cyber security practices and awareness. 2. Evidence of an implementation of one or more cyber security training program(s) appropriate to individual roles, functions, or responsibilities. 3. Evidence of a process to conduct a seven-year criminal history records check of each personnel. 4. Evidence of criteria or process to evaluate criminal history records check for authorizing access. 5. Evidence of verification, at least once every 15 months, of electronic access accounts and privileges are correct.

continued on following page

Table 2. Continued

NERC CIP Standard	Compliance Requirements
CIP-005-6 Cyber Security - Electronic Security Perimeter(s)	1. Evidence indicating that all applicable cyber assets connected to a network via a routable protocol reside within a defined Electronic Security Perimeter (ESP). 2. Evidence comprised of network diagrams showing all external routable communication paths and the identified Electronic Access Points (EAPs) 3. Evidence of a documented process describing the authenticated access authorization and a list of rules (firewall, access control list, etc.) 4. Evidence of multi-factor authentication for all interactive remote access.
CIP-006-6 Cyber Security - Physical Security of BES Cyber Systems	1. Evidence of the existence of operational and/or operational controls. 2. Evidence of the process of unescorted physical access control. 3. Evidence of a monitoring process for unauthorized access through a physical access point. 4. Evidence of the issuance of an alert or alarm in response to the detection of an unauthorized access through a physical access point. 5. Evidence of the logging and recording of physical entry into each Physical Security Perimeter.
CIP-007-6 Cyber Security - System Security Management	1. Documentation of the need for all enabled ports on all applicable cyber assets and configuration files of host-based firewalls that only allow needed ports. 2. Documentation of a patch management process. 3. Documentation of an evaluation of security-related patches every 35 calendar days. 4. Evidence of a mitigation plan for vulnerabilities addressed by the security patch. 5. Evidence of the deployment of methods to deter, detect, or prevent malicious code. 6. Evidence of the logging of events at the BES cyber system level for identification of, and after-the-fact investigations of, cyber security incidents.
CIP-008-6 Cyber Security - Incident Reporting & Response Planning	1. Evidence of a dated documentation of cybers security incident plan(s) including process to identify, classify, and respond to a cyber security incident. 2. Evidence of a dated documentation of cybers security incident plan(s) providing guidance for determining which cyber security incident is reportable and documented processes for notification. 3. Documentation of the roles and responsibilities of cyber security incident response groups or individuals. 4. Documentation of incident handling procedures. 5. Evidence of exercises to test each cyber security incident response plan at least once every 15 calendar months. 6. Dated documentation of records related to reportable cyber security incidents and cyber security incidents that attempted to compromise a system.

continued on following page

Table 2. Continued

NERC CIP Standard	Compliance Requirements
CIP-009-6 Cyber Security - Recovery Plans for BES Cyber Systems	1. Evidence of a plan identifying conditions for activation of the recovery plan(s). 2. Documentation of the roles and responsibilities of responders. 3. Documentation of specific processes for the backup and storage of information required for recovery. 4. Documentation of the successful backup and recovery processes. 5. Evidence of exercises to test the recovery plan(s) at least once every 15 calendar months.
CIP-010-3 Cyber Security - Configuration Change Management & Vulnerability Assessment	1. Evidence of a baseline configuration for each cyber asset. 2. Documentation of change request and authorization and the completion of the change according to requirements. 3. Documentation of updated baseline configuration after the completion of the change. 4. Evidence of verification of cyber security controls and dated test results. 5. Evidence of the verification of identity of the software source and integrity of the software. 6. Evidence of monitoring at least once every 35 calendar days for changes to the baseline configuration. 7. Evidence of a paper or active vulnerability assessment at least once every 15 calendar months including the results of the testing.
CIP-011-2 Cyber Security - Information Protection	1. Evidence of a method to identify BES cyber system information and training materials for personnel to recognize BES cyber system information. 2. Evidence of a repository for BES cyber system information in the organization's protection program. 3. Evidence of procedure(s) for protecting and securely handling BES cyber system information, including storage, transit, and use. 4. Documentation of process(es) for records tracking sanitization actions or encryption to prevent unauthorized retrieval of BES cyber system information. 5. Documentation of process(es) for records tracking for the destruction of storage media before disposal.
CIP-013-1 Cyber Security - Supply Chain Risk Management	Evidence of a documented supply chain cyber security risk management plan(s) to identify and assess cyber security risks from vendor products and services resulting from the procurement and installation of vendor equipment and software and the transitions from one vendor to another.

included the NERC CIP Standards and Compliance Requirements described above. The module and entire course were well received. Consequently, we plan to offer a complete training course for a workforce development cohort next summer. In that course, we plan to provide a detailed coverage of the standards and compliance complemented by tabletop exercises and hands-on laboratory projects. The projects will utilize tools that will automate the implementation of the requirements of the standards. The tabletop exercises will utilize case studies synthesized from real-world cyber security incidents. One such case study is presented in the following.

CASE STUDY IN NERC-CIP COMPLIANCE

To analyze our proposed model, a scenario-based case study on NERC-CIP compliance was conducted. The objectives of the case study are to

- identify the cybersecurity gaps found in a typical electric utility company,
- understand regulatory compliance,
- understand the relevance of being in compliant with cybersecurity regulations, and
- provide a hands-on experience in the implementation of the NERC-CIP standards and best practices on compliance.

The participants were required to review the NERC-CIP standards, peruse the scenario transcript, and provide a thorough response to the key issues and questions posed. The results of the survey completed by the participants illustrate the effectiveness of using a scenario-based case study in learning about NERC-CIP compliance.

The Scenario Transcript

ACME Power, an electric power company servicing the Northwest Florida, South Alabama, and South Mississippi geographical areas, is a publicly traded company with an annual revenue exceeding $750 million. The company is headquartered in downtown Pensacola, Florida and employs 1230 engineers and staff. Its main power generation station is located in Orange Beach, AL and has multiple substations scattered in the operating area.

The company experienced a major cyber-attack during the weekend. The incident shutdown the main power generation station for two days and rendered the service areas with no electricity during that period.

Precursor events during the week prior to the attack include an illegal entry of a non-employee in the Operations Center (OC), a terminated employee was allowed to work for an additional week to complete his assigned projects, the detection of several remote access to the HMI, the loss of a laptop computer which contains unencrypted customer data by the company auditor, and the discovery of an unlocked substation in Daphne, AL. In addition, an unusual volume of phishing email was experienced by IT and OT staff members three weeks prior to the incident.

The incident response (IR) plan was set into action immediately after the attack was detected. The IR team was convened but initially, there was confusion on who is responsible for some of the tasks assigned to three members who are currently on vacation.

The IT staff started with a check on the Human Machine Interface (HMI) and the Data Historian that may have been causing the issues. The security and system logs on the Historian provide preliminary indications that it is compromised. This is followed by a clean reboot of the server on the corporate LAN. In the OT side, the gas turbine was running at an excessive speed and three cooling pumps were discovered to intermittently turn off and on; the fail-safe systems then triggered a shutdown of the facility. This created a condition that requires reporting to local, state, and federal agencies. The news media was alerted by a third-party and reports on this incident started to circulate. Extortion emails were received by the company's financial controller and a Distributed Denial of Service (DDoS) attack was launched against the company's public website but was quickly restored with a live backup. The company incurred great expense due to the attack. The IT staff managed to create system images, capture network packets, and preserve memory forensics before IT operations were shutdown. On-going forensics and investigation are being conducted by law enforcement to identify and prosecute the perpetrators.

The after-action review required by the IR plan reveals the following:

1. The non-employee entered the OC premises by tailgating.
2. There is no documented process for employee termination.
3. Remote access to the OT equipment and systems is not secure.
4. Company equipment is allowed to be carried outside of company premises.
5. Some substations are not secured.
6. Security awareness training for employees is outdated and nonperiodic.
7. The IR plan has not been reviewed and updated for 5 years.
8. The access control mechanism on the Historian is extremely weak.
9. The HMI server has not been patched—missing at least 3 full patch versions.
10. The testing procedure for the Cybersecurity Recovery Plan is not documented.
11. Vulnerability assessment on both IT and OT systems is outdated.
12. There is no documented process on vetting equipment vendors.
13. Computing equipment and storage devices are being donated to non-profit organizations without data sanitization.
14. Some computing equipment and wireless access points are discovered to not appear on the company inventory.
15. The change management process is completely ad-hoc.
16. The transmission of data from the OT side to the corporate side is unencrypted.
17. There is no password policy in place.
18. Unnecessary network ports on the Historian and HMI are open.

Key Issues and Question

1. Name at least two lessons learned from the incident.
2. Name at least two best practices discovered.
3. For each of the items in the after-action review, identify the applicable NERC-CIP standard.
4. Could the security gaps that were identified in the after-action review have been mitigated or resolved had the company remained in compliant with NERC-CIP requirements?

ADDITIONAL CASE STUDIES IN NERC-CIP COMPLIANCE

Perhaps, the most prominent case of cyberattack on ICS is the Stuxnet (Kushner, 2013) intrusion. Stuxnet was disclosed in 2010 as the first cyber weapon causing havoc to a uranium enrichment facility in Iran. Until September 2010, Stuxnet infected approximately 100,000 hosts across over 155 countries.

A coordinated cyberattack on the Ukrainian power grid (Zetter, 2016) was conducted in 2015 and resulted in power outages for over 230,000 residents. It is known to be the first cyberattack on the power grid. The Ukrainian Power Grid cyber-attack demonstrated an adversary that is extremely capable and highly resourced. Several evidence materials indicate that the adversary had been conducting long-term planning and reconnaissance, lasting at least six months (Polityuk, 2016).

The attacks on small electricity providers in proximity to critical infrastructures have been investigated by the FBI in late 2019 (Smith & Barry, 2019). These attacks involved more a dozen U.S. utilities operating in 18 states from Maine to Washington. The main thrust of the attacks is to get malware installed on the victim computers through "phishing" emails.

These are just a few case studies that training scenarios could be built on. A quick perusal of the nature of the attacks will yield several instances in which the CIP Standards can be applied to at least mitigate or even prevent the attacks from occurring.

FUTURE RESEARCH DIRECTIONS

The NERC-CIP Standards continue to evolve and present challenges to practitioners and researchers. As such, the research and application frontiers in this area continue to expand. Recognizing this fact, we propose the following future directions for study:

- Development of an automated NERC-CIP Standards compliance toolkit; We are developing a pilot toolkit that could be used to develop compliance scenarios and enhance education and training in this area; and
- The application of a subset of the NERC-CIP Standards to related sectors such as manufacturing, transportation, defense industrial base, and health care.

The evolving nature of the field also creates a need for more agile education and training methods and resources that integrate updated CIP Standards and compliance requirements. To address this, we are developing a complete NERC-CIP course that will be offered next year and include the proposed alignment of the Standards with the NIST Framework and compliance requirements. A more exhaustive follow-up study will be conducted in conjunction with that course to evaluate the application of the NERC-CIP Standards and compliance requirements, and their alignment with the NIST Framework. This will help identify any gaps and further refine the mapping and proposed compliance activities.

CONCLUSION

This chapter highlights the NERC-CIP Standards and its significance for the protection electric utility entities. The chapter describes the Standards alignment with the NIST Cybersecurity Framework and presented an expanded mapping to the Framework.

There is a significant need and opportunities to expand education and workforce development training in this area. We describe the compliance requirements and present a case study to illustrate effective use of the NERC-CIP Standards and compliance requirements in a training course. By mapping the NIST Framework functions and categories to the NERC-CIP Standards, we highlight their complementary approaches to cybersecurity. We also illustrate what it entails to be compliant with the NERC-CIP Standards. Finally, we describe our ongoing efforts to provide training and expand the workforce in this area of urgent need.

The contributions of this chapter are enumerated as follow:

1. It provides multiple perspectives on the NERC-CIP Standards impact on the protection of electric utility entities, relationship to the NIST Framework, compliance requirements, and influence on the creation of a new training field for workforce development;
2. It lays the groundwork for initiating NERC-CIP Standards compliance activities;
3. It illustrates NERC-CIP compliance activities through a case study; and
4. It provides clear directions for research and application development opportunities in the field.

ACKNOWLEDGMENT

This work is partially supported by the National Security Agency under Grant Number H98230-20-1-0350, the Office of Naval Research (ONR) under grant number N00014-21-1-2025, and the National Security Agency under grant numbers H98230-20-1-0414 and H98230-21-1-0319. The United States Government is authorized to reproduce and distribute reprints notwithstanding any copyright notation herein.

REFERENCES

Ani, U. D., He, H., & Tiwari, A. (2020). Vulnerability-Based Impact Criticality Estimation for Industrial Control Systems. In *2020 International Conference on Cyber Security and Protection of Digital Services (Cyber Security)* (pp. 1-8). IEEE. 10.1109/CyberSecurity49315.2020.9138886

Cole, J. M. (2016). *Challenges of Implementing Substation Hardware Upgrades for NERC CIP version 5 Compliance to Enhance Cybersecurity. In 2016 IEEE/PES Transmission and Distribution Conference and Exposition (T&D).* IEEE.

Etigowni, S., Tian, D., Hernandez, G., Zonouz, S., & Butler, K. (2016). CPAC: Securing Critical Infrastructure with Cyber-Physical Access Control. In *32nd Annual Conference on Computer Security Applications*. Los Angeles, CA: ACM. 10.1145/2991079.2991126

Hyder, B., & Govindarasu, M. (2020). *Optimization of Cybersecurity Investment Strategies in the Smart Grid Using Game-Theory. In 2020 IEEE Power & Energy Society Innovative Smart Grid Technologies Conference (ISGT).* IEEE.

ISA/IEC. (2020, June). *Your Guide to Cybersecurity Standards.* Retrieved from Global Cybersecurity Alliance: https://gca.isa.org/ isagca-quick-start-guide-62443-standards?__hstc= 16245038. c309ffdf29b0a 2e310f4400349939d99. 1634749414522. 1634749414522. 1634749414522. 1&__hssc = 16245038. 1.1634749414522 &__hsfp= 970585634

Kushner, D. (2013, February 26). *The Real Story of Stuxnet.* Retrieved from IEEE Spectrum: https://spectrum.ieee.org/the-real-story-of-stuxnet#toggle-gdpr

Mack, D. (2017). Implementing a Modern, Secure Relay Integration Solution with Existing IEDs. In *2017 70th Annual Conference for Protective Relay Engineers (CPRE)* (pp. 1-3). IEEE.

Marron, J., Gopstein, A., & Bogle, D. (2021, September 29). *Benefits of an Updated Mapping between the NIST Cybersecurity Framework and the NERC Critical Infrastructure Protection Standards.* Retrieved October 2021, from National Institute of Standards and Technology: https://nvlpubs.nist.gov/nistpubs/CSWP/NIST.CSWP.09292021.pdf

Mukherjee, S. (2015). *Applying the Distribution System in Grid Restoration/NERC CIP-014 Risk Assessment. In 2015 IEEE Rural Electric Power Conference.* IEEE.

Mylrea, M., Bishop, R., Johnson, M., & Gupta Gourisetti, S. N. (2018). *Keyless Signature Blockchain Infrastructure: Facilitating NERC CIP Compliance and Responding to Evolving Cyber Threats and Vulnerabilities to Energy Infrastructure. In 2018 IEEE/PES Transmission and Distribution Conference and Exposition (T&D).* IEEE.

Nakao, M., Loo, S., & Melville, L. (2015). Integrating Modern Substation Automation Systems with Enterprise-level Management. In *2015 68th Annual Conference for Protective Relay Engineers* (pp. 557-562). IEEE.

NERC CIP002-5.1a. (2021, October 23). *CIP-002-5.1a.* Retrieved from North American Electric Reliability Corporation (NERC): https://www.nerc.com/_layouts/15/ Print Standard. aspx? standard number= CIP-002-5. 1a&title = Cyber %20 Security %20 — %20 BES %20 Cyber %20 System %20 Categorization & Jurisdiction = United %20 States

NERC CIP. (2021, October 23). *CIP Standards.* Retrieved from North American Electric Reliability Corporation (NERC): https://www.nerc.com/pa/Stand/Pages/CIPStandards.aspx

NERC CIP 003-8. (2021, October 23). *CIP-003-8.* Retrieved from North American Electric Reliability Corporation: https://www.nerc.com/_layouts/15/ Print Standard. aspx? standard number = CIP-003-8 & title = Cyber %20 Security %20 — %20 Security %20 Management %20 Controls & Jurisdiction = United %20 States

NERC CIP 004-6. (2021, October 23). *CIP-004-6.* Retrieved from North American Electric Reliability Corporation: https://www.nerc.com/_layouts/15/ Print Standard. aspx? standard number = CIP-004-6 & title = Cyber %20 Security %20 - %20 Personnel %20 & %20 Training & Jurisdiction = United %20 States

NERC CIP 005-6. (2021, October 23). *CIP-005-6.* Retrieved from North American Electric Reliability Corporation: https://www.nerc.com/pa/Stand/Reliability%20 Standards/CIP-005-6.pdf

NERC CIP 006-6. (2021, October 23). *CIP-006-6.* Retrieved from North American Electric Reliability Corporation: https://www.nerc.com/pa/Stand/Reliability%20 Standards/CIP-006-6.pdf

NERC CIP-007-6. (2021, October 23). *CIP 007-6.* Retrieved from North American Electric Reliability Corporation: https://www.nerc.com/pa/Stand/Reliability%20 Standards/CIP-007-6.pdf

NERC CIP-008-6. (2021, October 23). *CIP-008-6.* Retrieved from North American Electric Reliability Corporation: https://www.nerc.com/pa/Stand/Reliability%20 Standards/CIP-008-6.pdf

NERC CIP-009-6. (2021, October 23). *CIP 009-6.* Retrieved from North American Electric Reliability Corporation: https://www.nerc.com/pa/Stand/Reliability%20 Standards/CIP-009-6.pdf

NERC CIP-010-3. (2021, October 23). *CIP-010-3.* Retrieved from North American Electric Reliability Corporation: https://www.nerc.com/pa/Stand/Reliability%20 Standards/CIP-010-3.pdf

NERC CIP-011-2. (2021, October 23). *CIP-011-2.* Retrieved from North American Electric Reliability Corporation: https://www.nerc.com/pa/Stand/Reliability%20 Standards/CIP-011-2.pdf

NERC CIP-013-1. (2021, October 23). *CIP-013-1.* Retrieved from North American Electric Reliability Corporation: https://www.nerc.com/pa/Stand/Reliability%20 Standards/CIP-013-1.pdf

NERC CIP-014-2. (2021, October 23). *CIP-014-2.* Retrieved from North American Electric Reliability Corporation: https://www.nerc.com/pa/Stand/Reliability%20 Standards/CIP-014-2.pdf

NIST CSF. (2018, April 16). *Cybersecurity Framework versions 1.1.* Retrieved from National Institute of Standards and Technology: https://nvlpubs.nist.gov/nistpubs/ CSWP/NIST.CSWP.04162018.pdf

NIST CSF Mapping. (2020, June 8). *Mapping of NIST Cybersecurity Framework v1.1 to NERC CIP Reliability Standards.* Retrieved from National Institute of Standards and Technology: https://data.nist.gov/od/id/mds2-2348

Polityuk, P. (2016, February 12). *Ukraine sees Russian hand in cyber attacks on power grid.* Retrieved from REUTERS: https://www.reuters.com/article/idUSKCN0VL18E

Proctor, M., & Smith, T. (2017). Lessons Learned from NERC CIP Applied to the Industrial World. In *2017 70th Annual Conference for Protective Relay Engineers (CPRE)* (pp. 1-6). IEEE.

Qais, S. Q., Jamil, N., Daud, M., Patel, A., & Norhamadi, J. (2019). A Review of Security Assessment Metodologies in Industrial Control Systems. *Information and Computer Security, 27*(1), 47–61. doi:10.1108/ICS-04-2018-0048

Ramanathan, R., Popat, A., Papic, M., & Ciniglio, O. (2017). *Idaho Power Experience of Implementaing Cascade Analysis Study Using the Node/Breaker Model. In 2017 IEEE Power & Energy Society General Meeting*. IEEE.

Salehi, M., & Bayat-Sarmadi, S. (2021, May 1). PLCDefender: Improving Remote Attestation Techniques for PLCs Using Physical Model. *IEEE Internet of Things Journal, 8*(9), 7372–7379. doi:10.1109/JIOT.2020.3040237

Salvador, A., Mack, D., & Carnegie, C. (2016). Secure IED Management Case Studies. In *2016 IEEE International Conference on Power System Technologies (POWERCON)* (pp. 1-4). IEEE.

Smith, R., & Barry, R. (2019, November 24). *Utilities Targeted in Cyberattacks Identified*. Retrieved from The Wall Street Journal: https://www.wsj.com/articles/ utilities-targeted-in-cyberattacks-identified-11574611200

Stanculescu, M., Badea, C. A., Marinescu, I., Andrei, P., Drosu, O., & Andrei, H. (2019). Vulnerability of SCADA and Security Solutions for a Waste Water Treatment Plant. In *11th International Symposium on Advanced Topics in Electrical Engineering*. Bucharest, Romania: IEEE. 10.1109/ATEE.2019.8724889

Wang, W., Chen, L., Han, L., Zhou, Z., Xia, Z., & Chen, X. (2020). Vulnerability Assessment for ICS System Based on Zero-day Attack Graph. In *2020 International Conference on Intelligent Computing, Automation, and Systems (ICICAS)*. IEEE. 10.1109/ICICAS51530.2020.00009

Weaver, G. A., Cheh, C., Rogers, E. J., Sanders, W. H., & Gammel, D. (2013). Toward a Cyber-Physical Topolgy Language: Applications to NERC CIP Audit. *First ACM Workshop on Smart Energy Grid Security* (pp. 93-104). Berlin, Germany: ACM. 10.1145/2516930.2516934

Weerathunga, P. E., & Cioraca, A. (2016). The Importance of Testing Smart Grid IEDs Against Security Vulnerabilities. In *2016 59th Annual Conference for Protective Relay Engineers (CPRE)* (pp. 1-21). IEEE.

Woo, P.-S., & Kim, B. H. (2020). Contingency Analysis to Evaluate the Robustness in Large-Scale Smart Grids: Based on Information Security Objectives and Frequency Stability. *Energies*, *13*(6267), 6267. doi:10.3390/en13236267

Zetter, K. (2016, January 28). *Everything We Know About Ukraine's Power Plant Hack*. Retrieved from WIRED: https://www.wired.com/2016/01/everything-we-know-about-ukraines-power-plant-hack/

Zhang, F., & Li, Q. (2018). Security Vulnerability and Patch Management in Electric Utilities: A Data-driven Analysis. In *First Workshop on Radical and Experiential Security* (pp. 65-68). ACM. 10.1145/3203422.3203432

Zhang, Z. (2011). Environmental Review & Case Study: NERC's Cybersecurity Standards for the Electtric Grid: Fulfilling its Reliability Day Job and Moonlighting as a Cybersecurity Model. *Environmental Practice*, *13*(3), 250–264. doi:10.1017/S1466046611000275

KEY TERMS AND DEFINITIONS

Critical Infrastructures: Entities whose operations and assets, physical or virtual, are vital to a nation's interests.

Cybersecurity: A set of processes, practices, and technologies designed to protect, in the realm of cyberspace, the three tenets of information security: confidentiality, integrity, and availability.

Framework: A grouping of rules and related concepts into a logical approach that can be used to identify complex problems and decide upon appropriate courses of action to address them.

Information Technology: The utilization of hardware, software, and systems to monitor, control, and implement business processes and objectives.

Operational Technology: The utilization of hardware, software, and systems to monitor and drive industrial equipment, processes, and events.

Regulatory Compliance: The state of being in conformance to the requirements of a relevant law, policy, or regulation.

Scenario-Based Learning: A type of learning based on the theory that learning takes place in which the context is applied.

Standards: A set of rules that can be monitored for compliance by a specialized field's authoritative bodies and related professionals.

Supply Chain Risk: The risk associated with the system that supplies products and services to an organization.

Chapter 4
The Potential of Gaming to Ameliorate Human Factors in Information Security Compliance

David Thornton
Jacksonville State University, USA

ABSTRACT

In this chapter, the author discusses the need for appropriate training to improve information security compliance and some of the human factors that lead to non-compliance. Following is a section on theories that attempt to model and predict compliance. The author discusses the use of serious games, games-based learning, and gamification as educational tools, and their strengths in providing some of the major training needs, including emotional engagement, intrinsic motivation, repetition, discussion, reflection, and self-efficacy. This is followed by a list of some prominent games and gamification tools in the field of information security. Finally, the author concludes with guidelines and considerations for information security professionals who may be considering the use of serious games and gamification to enhance their information security awareness training.

INTRODUCTION

Information security professionals are always trying to manage risk. The four phases of security risk management are deterrence, prevention, detection, and recovery (Warkentin & Willison, 2009). A thorough, readable information security policy

DOI: 10.4018/978-1-7998-8390-6.ch004

Copyright © 2022, IGI Global. Copying or distributing in print or electronic forms without written permission of IGI Global is prohibited.

(ISP) can serve as both prevention and deterrence, and should include the following items (Sommestad et al., 2014):

- descriptions of acceptable use of resources
- security responsibilities
- consequences for violations of the policy
- required training types appropriate to each employee

However, the presence of a well-written ISP alone is not sufficient to prevent and deter security breaches caused by employee non-compliance, especially if they are written in a "technocratic" style (Vance et al., 2012).

Kirlappos et al. (2013) warn against long lists of prohibited actions and advocate for a higher-level set of awareness principles to support personal agency. Further, D'Arcy et al. (2014) found that security-related stress (SRS) caused by complex, ambiguous, and overlong ISPs can foster non-compliant behavior. Such policies must be paired with effective, engaging training that not only seeks to mitigate threats but to build a broader safety culture (Fagade & Tryfonas, 2016). Although the costs of recovery can be much higher than prevention, 75% of security awareness professionals reported spending less than half their time on awareness (SANS, 2021). Further, most report that time, not budget, is the limiting factor. It can be difficult to convince administration to commit more personnel, because it is much harder to estimate what security breaches were prevented versus those that actually occurred. Even so, more action must be taken to improve information security compliance, because the losses associated with security breaches are not only monetary, but reputational as well (Safa & Ismail, 2013).

BACKGROUND

Many scholars agree that the human element is the "weak link" in information security (Bulgurcu et al., 2010; Hu et al., 2012). According to the Verizon Data Breach Investigations Report, 85% of data breaches involved some form of human interaction, with the highest-ranking risks involving phishing and poor passwords (Verizon, 2021). IBM Security and the Ponemon Institute (2020) reported that 63% of security incidents in 2019 were related to negligence which cost companies over $300,000.

Other human factors that lead to non-compliance include ignorance, apathy, mischief, and resistance (Safa et al., 2016; Siponen et al., 2010). Combating these factors can be challenging because information security program leads tend to have a more technical background, and often lack the soft skills needed to communicate effectively with users about human factor risks. The aforementioned human factors leave employees vulnerable to a wide array of attacks, including phishing and social engineering. Credential phishing via email was by far the most common social engineering attack type of 2021, according to Proofpoint (2021). Social engineering attacks are especially effective because they exploit the abiding human vulnerabilities referred to by Scholl (2018) as "social gateways", including stress, helpfulness, and curiosity.

Information security risk can be mitigated through improved awareness (Arachchilage & Love, 2014), so most organization employ some form of information security awareness training. Traditionally, this often takes the form of PowerPoint presentations or videos followed by short quizzes. These training modules may be required as little as once a year. Julie Haney and Wayne Lutters advise against depending on this type of sparse training curriculum alone, but instead combining it with repetition and personal motivation. They state that such training should "move employees toward intrinsic motivation, where they see the value of security, develop the curiosity to learn more on their own, feel a sense of ownership and empowerment, want to do the right thing, and as a result, actually practice good behaviors" (Haney & Lutters, 2020, p. 92).

REASONS FOR NON-COMPLIANCE AND THE POTENTIAL OF GAMES

Issues, Controversies, Problems

As in the parable of the blind men holding different parts of an elephant, no single theory encompasses all the reasons for non-compliance, nor does any one solution present itself. However, general principles emerge from meta-analyses of such theories. Sommestad et al. (2014) found that emotional elements (such as normative belief and self-efficacy) seem to be stronger predictors of non-compliance than more technical factors (like cybersecurity knowledge and skill). As such, Scholl (2018) argues that training which includes emotionalizing elements will be more effective. This section surveys some of the theories that attempt to model and predict compliance.

Social Bond Theory

First described by Travis Hirschi in 1969, social bond theory is composed of the following four elements (Hirschi, 1969, p. 16):

- Attachment to the Group
- Commitment to Social Norms and Institutions
- Involvement in Conventional Activities
- Personal Norms

In Hirschi's view, each of these elements represents a check on a person's inherent tendency toward delinquency, or non-conforming behavior. Individuals with stronger social bonds would therefore be more likely to conform to the group and comply with their shared expectations. Safa et al. (2016) applied this theory into a larger framework focused on information security. In a study of the information security policies of four Malaysian companies, they explored which of Hirschi's social elements had the strongest effect on compliance. They concluded that commitment, involvement, and personal norms are salient indicators of compliance, while attachment does not have a positive effect on compliance. Next, they theorized that involvement, in the context of information security, is expressed by the following four activities:

- **Knowledge Sharing:** When employees share their technical knowledge with colleagues, they spread information security competence while forming stronger social bonds. This also reduces the need for outside training.
- **Collaboration:** When employees work together to solve a problem, they strengthen bonds while also developing novel solutions based on complementary skills and experience.
- **Intervention:** In information security, this takes the form of training, dialogue, discussion, and reflection. Participating in these activities allows employees to deeply internalize the hard and soft skills needed for success.
- **Experience:** Employees who are experienced in dealing with information security problems are more knowledgeable. Also, employees with a long history at an organization tend to have a deeper sense of allegiance to it.

General Deterrence Theory

Deterrence theory is a centuries-old explanation of criminal behavior as well as an attempt to control it. It postulates that individuals' criminal behavior can be decreased by increasing two factors: punishment severity and punishment certainty. According to the National Institute of Justice (2016), however, punishment severity suffers from diminishing returns, and punishment certainty is a much more important factor. Indeed, excessive punishment may lead to desensitization and recidivism. In a proposed theoretical model by Pahnila et al. (2007), they posited that the factors which most affect compliance are information quality, threat appraisal, and facilitating conditions, while rewards and punishments did not significantly affect behavior or intention. Even more surprising, a study from Herath & Rao (2009) found that while punishment certainty had a significant positive effect on compliance, punishment severity actually had a significant reverse effect of that desired.

Because punishment certainty is the more salient factor, the National Institute of Justice recommends committing resources to visibility and presence. Lastly, a well-written information security policy is toothless without detection of non-compliance and enforcement of the concomitant punishment.

Protection Motivation Theory

According to Boss et al. (2015), there has been a trend away from general deterrence theory and similar theories toward protection motivation theory (PMT). Rather than focusing on top-down command and control, PMT persuades users to comply through communicating the personal dangers of non-compliance paired with recommended protective behavior. According to Boss et al., researchers have not properly leveraged the use of fear appeals which can lead employees to the correct behavior, known as danger controls. In other words, by avoiding the emotionalizing recommend by Scholl (2018) and focusing on technical skills alone, information security professionals are neglecting a powerful motivator.

Persuasion and Social Engineering

In Robert Cialdini's book *Influence, New and Expanded: The Psychology of Persuasion*, he identifies seven principles which make humans vulnerable to social engineering attacks (Cialdini, 2021). They include the following:

1. **Reciprocation:** When given a gift, people tend to feel obligated to return the favor. A social engineer can exploit this by giving a small gift or favor to the intended victim.
2. **Commitment and Consistency:** People do not like to go back on a promise. Social engineers often convince victims to make a small commitment which is then amplified later.
3. **Social Proof:** People look to others for action cues. Social engineers may work in teams to exert peer pressure on the intended victim.
4. **Liking:** People are more likely to cooperate with people they find likable. Social engineers may begin an attack by exchanging "small talk" and personal details in order to charm victims.
5. **Authority:** If someone believes you are an authority figure, they are easier to influence. Social engineers often impersonate trusted sources to prevent victims from contradicting them.

6. **Scarcity:** People tend to want what they cannot have. Social engineers can use artificial scarcity and exclusivity to motivate victims.

7. **Unity:** Beyond likability, people are more easily influenced by people with whom they share identity. An adept social engineer will build a mosaic of real and fraudulent similarities to the victim. As in Kurt Vonnegut's concept of the *granfalloon* (Vonnegut, 2010), these similarities may have little to do with choice or meaningful association.

In addition to the factors above, lack of privacy awareness contributes to information security vulnerabilities. Many employees are unaware of the collective impact of information disclosure in public spaces like social media. Indeed, most social engineers depend on it. Most attacks begin with a research phase, in which the attacker learns about the intended victim and related information using open-source intelligence, or OSINT (Glassman & Kang, 2012). OSINT is simply the act of searching through publicly available Internet resources, such as social media and municipal records, in order to collect a rich set of facts that will support the social engineering attack. Social engineers often perform serial attacks, leveraging the information gained from a victim into subsequent attacks.

The Moderating Effect of Personality

Properly designed and delivered information security awareness training can improve an employee's intention to comply. However, even intention does not necessarily lead to desired behavior because of the effect of personality, especially two of the personality traits belonging to the so-called Big Five (Warkentin et al., 2012). The more important of the two, conscientiousness, is associated with organization, carefulness, reliability, self-discipline and achievement (McCrae and John, 1992). The second, agreeableness, is associated with rule following, altruism, modesty, sociability, and privacy (Brecht et al., 2012). High conscientiousness and agreeableness lead to a stronger connection between intent and actual behavior (Shropshire & Sharma, 2015). Security professionals must therefore have realistic expectations about their ability to change behavior. They may also wish to perform personality evaluations before placing employees into positions with high security privileges.

SOLUTIONS AND RECOMMENDATIONS

As discussed, scholars recommend information security awareness training that includes repetition, discussion, reflection, social elements, personal intrinsic motivation, curiosity, and empowerment. Following are arguments in favor of employing games, games-based learning, and gamification to achieve these goals.

Proponents of Games for Transformative Learning

Jane McGonigal, author of the book *Reality is Broken* (McGonigal, 2011), believes that games have the power to improve our real lives. She lists 14 qualities of games that she argues are "fixes" for our daily experience. They include the following:

1. **Unnecessary Obstacles:** People want to be challenged to encourage our best work and provide the satisfaction of accomplishment.
2. **Emotional Activation:** These include *fiero* (triumph over adversity), *naches* (vicarious pride), happy embarrassment, and *Flow* (see Flow section below).
3. **More Satisfying Work:** Because games are more organized and simplistic than the real world, they can provide clear, modular, bite-size goals. When paired with instant feedback, players can easily perceive their progress and plan for the future.
4. **Better Hope of Success:** The idea of fun failure is possible in games because they are designed artifacts with balanced challenge. Because players know that goals are attainable, they play with confidence and can withstand failure on up to 80% of attempts.
5. **Stronger Social Connectivity:** Because multiplayer games provide us opportunities to interact with others, they help us to become more sociable, even in situations where we are "playing together alone" (McGonigal, 2011, p. 89). They also give players more "pro-social emotions", akin to the aforementioned social bond theory.
6. **Epic Scale:** Games often provide a grand storyline with many players (synchronously or asynchronously) which often takes place over several years. Because of this, players can experience awe and feel that they are part of something bigger than themselves.
7. **Wholehearted Participation:** Players are never passive actors in a game, leading to intense interest. Further, because games can be played in a wide variety of settings, times, and formats, players learn to exert their best effort whenever and wherever they are.
8. **Meaningful rewards When Needed:** The mechanics of game progress (see the gamification section below) such as points and levels support a player's agency by reinforcing the idea that harder work leads directly to high achievement.
9. **Fun with Strangers:** Games give us the opportunity for empathy and a wider societal view by grouping strangers together via matchmaking.

10. **Happiness Hacks:** Games can help players to invent and adopt habits that bring them happiness, consistent with positive-psychology research. In games like *Life is Strange: True Colors*, for instance, the protagonist copes with a personal loss, and the player must consider appropriate choices to lead the character through their grief (Life is Strange, 2021).
11. **Sustainable Engagement Economy:** The power of crowdsourcing gives players the collective power to solve large, real-world problems. Also, games can provide us with nearly unlimited gratification throughout life.
12. **Epic Wins:** When players defeat difficult odds in a game, they become more confident to overcome even real-life obstacles.
13. **Collaboration:** Multiplayer games confer useful life skills related to teamwork and project planning.
14. **Massively Multiplayer Foresight:** Large multiplayer games that employ grand scale encourage players to think long-term and to tackle problems in a high-level, systematic way.

McGonigal cautions against excessive use of extrinsic motivators (McGonigal, 2011, p. 242) because they can lead to demotivation if removed. This is especially true if the activity being reinforced is one that the player already enjoys intrinsically. However, she argues that games offer inherently intrinsic rewards because their rewards (points, levels, badges, bragging rights, personal satisfaction) do not have extrinsic value. The behaviorist model in psychology asserts that consistent reinforcement, in the form of punishment or reward, will condition people towards certain behaviors (Werbach & Hunter, 2012).

Moreover, there is some evidence that extrinsic motivators may actually help to create intrinsic motivators (Silic & Lowry, 2020; Werbach & Hunter, 2012). Professors at the Rochester Institute of Technology (RIT) gamified a first-year course. One of the badges would be awarded to the whole course, provided that 90% of the students pass the course. This mechanic encouraged higher-performing students to mentor and tutor struggling students. The following term, these mechanics were removed. Even so, students continued the peer-to-peer assistance because they found them intrinsically rewarding. In this case, the extrinsic motivators encouraged new habits which persisted after their removal. Once the students discovered the inherent pleasure of helping others, the extrinsic motivators were no longer necessary.

Another early proponent of games-based learning and author of *Good Video Games and Good Learning*, James Paul Gee identifies sixteen principles that make games inherently powerful educational tools. They include the following (Gee, 2007, p. 31-43, 131):

1. **Identity:** Players form an identity during gameplay, sometimes through avatars. Playing the role of a character provides an opportunity for empathy and broader perspective. Players form a personal connection to the game/lesson, as in Scholl's aforementioned emotionalizing elements.

2. **Interaction:** The inherent interactivity of games makes them more engaging to the player than media which is passively received (ie, an instructional video or PowerPoint presentation).

3. **Production:** Similar to the educational theory of constructivism (Bíró, 2014), players take a role in creating meaning as they play.

4. **Risk Taking:** Games allow players a safe way to practice in a simulated environment, where failure is not costly. When free from fear, players are more confident to experiment with novel solutions.

5. **Customized:** Akin to the educational trends toward personalized learning and individualized instruction, games can be tuned to each player's abilities and preferences.

6. **Agency:** Games put the locus of control squarely with the player, satisfying their need for agency and autonomy (Deci & Ryan, 2012).

7. **Well-Ordered Problems:** Challenges in games are scaffolded appropriately to build skills hierarchically (Gibbons, 2002).

8. **Challenge and Consideration:** As in learning, good games support self-reflection on completed challenges in order to form competence and lasting behavior change.

9. **Just in Time or On Demand:** Concepts are associated with a challenge, not presented too early or divorced from practical application. This limits inefficiencies and reinforces the importance of the content beyond simply earning a grade or passing a training certification.

10. **Situated Meanings:** Players are exposed to new terminology naturally and gradually as they solve problems, rather than at the beginning in an overwhelming list.

11. **Pleasantly Frustrating:** The difficulty of the game is gracefully curved, and often dynamically adjusted, in order to support Flow (see Flow section below) and immersion. (Csíkszentmihályi, 1997).

12. **System Thinking:** Games help players form a high-level mental model through inductive reasoning (McDougall et al., 2001). Players learn to "see the forest, not the trees".

13. **Explore, Think Laterally, Rethink Goals:** Games encourage players to "think outside the box" to solve novel problems.

14. **Smart Tools and Distributed Knowledge:** As they become more competent, players teach others, leading to deeper, long-term understanding (Fiorella & Mayer, 2013).

15. **Cross-Functional Teams:** In multiplayer games, players work alongside teammates with complementary skills. This leads to an appreciation for other disciplines and satisfies the need for relatedness (Deci & Ryan, 2012).
16. **Performance before Competence:** Players often learn by doing. This ties multiple of the aforementioned principles together (Risk Taking, Just in Time or On Demand, and System Thinking). If players fail, they recognize the need for further instruction and are more receptive to it.

The former director of the Government-University-Industry Research Roundtable at The National Academies, Merrilea Mayo, posited that games-based learning may constitute a "bronze bullet" for STEM education, because of the following qualities (Mayo, 2007):

- Video games are widely played by all demographics.
- Video games can serve as an adjunct to the classroom by providing opportunity for recitation and reflection outside of school hours.
- Video games are compelling and engaging.
- Video games stimulate chemical changes in the brain that promote learning.
- Research supports the efficacy of games-based learning over the traditional lecture approach.

Additional Advantages of Games for Learning

This section discusses additional qualities of games that make them well-suited to learning.

Real-time Monitoring and Feedback. Digital games can easily monitor and record player actions in real-time for reflection afterwards. This data can even include biofeedback, using tools like low-cost electroencephalography (EEG) headsets.

Emotional engagement. Games are well suited to engaging the player emotionally, which can have lasting effects on behavior (Haucke & Pokoyski, 2018). As Darvasi (2016) of York University put it, "The potential to positively impact attitudes with digital games is not only rooted in their ability to grant perspective, but also in their potency as instruments of persuasion." In fact, there is a category of games whose main purpose is to challenge the player's understanding of a subject. They inform and persuade players regarding topics like segregation, ecology, and poverty (3rd World Farmer, 2022; A World Without Oil, 2022; Parable of the Polygons, 2022; Reality Drop, 2022; Spent, 2022).

Immersion and Flow. Games are capable of deeply engaging players. Indeed, game designers aim to put players in what psychologist Mihaly Csíkszentmihályi called *Flow*, a hyper-focused state of intense immersion. Achieving this state depends on optimizing challenge with ability. In his words:

The climber will feel it when the mountain demands all his strength, the singer when the song demands the full range of her vocal ability, the weaver when the design of the tapestry is more complex than anything attempted before, and the surgeon when the operation involves new procedures or requires an unexpected variation. (Csíkszentmihályi, 1997, p. 30)

Further, Csíkszentmihályi asserts that some of the most important attributes of a Flow experience are self-chosen goals, personally optimized obstacles, and continuous feedback. (McGonigal, p. 36). Games are uniquely suited to this because they can dynamically change the difficulty based on both player actions and biofeedback. Such an approach maintains Gee's aforementioned goal of "pleasant frustration". Figure 1 displays the relationship between challenge and ability. If the player's ability improves as the game difficulty remains the same, the player will feel control, followed by relaxation, and finally boredom and apathy. On the other hand, a game whose difficulty level grows faster than the player's ability will progressively lead to arousal, anxiety, and worry.

Versatility. Games can be delivered in a variety of formats to fit the setting. This includes digital gaming, board games, playing cards, and talking (or discussion) games. Scholl (2018), for instance, employed multiple formats, with single player digital games being the most portable and easy to schedule, and multiplayer discussion games providing the social and reflective aspects.

Figure 1. The relationship between challenge, skill level, and emotion in Flow
Source: Wikimedia, 2022

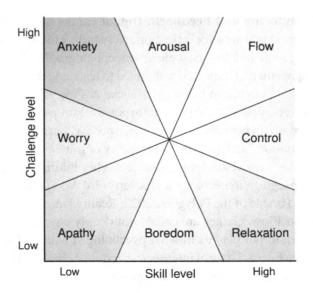

Availability. Games can be played in almost any place or time that is convenient for the player. Remember that security awareness professionals cited time constraints as the primary limiting factor in building awareness. Therefore, educational games can free up security professionals by providing interstitial training and reinforcement between more formal re-certifications.

Self-Paced Mastery. Mastery Learning is an instructional strategy first proposed by Benjamin Bloom in the 1960's and refined by James Block in the 1970's (Block & Burns, 1976). It bears strong similarities to Keller's Personalized System of Instruction (Eyre, 2007). These concepts took on new popularity and a new name in the 1980's, with the moniker Adaptive Learning. Figure 2 shows the progression of learning. The major ideas include the following:

- Students may progress at their own pace
- Once a student is ready, they may take an assessment
- Passing students move on to the next concept
- Failing students continue to learn

While this model may be taken to its logical extreme with unlimited assessment attempts and unlimited time to complete the curriculum, most educators use a hybrid that includes soft deadlines and limited attempts. Even so, self-pacing naturally leads to procrastination with some students. Games can help support Mastery Learning and mitigate these problems by motivating students and providing instant, automated feedback.

Incremental Progress. First defined by Lev Vygotsky in the 1970's, social development theory is based on the concepts of the zone of proximal development (ZPD) and mediation (Brown et al., 2003, p. 18). Vygotsky proposed that for every learner, there are certain concepts that are already mastered. Beyond that, there is a set of concepts that can be mastered with the help of a mediator. In order to locate

Figure 2. Mastery Learning progression

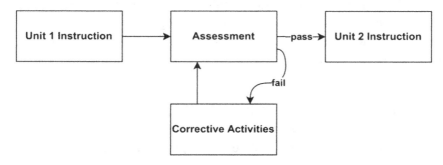

Figure 3. The zone of proximal development, a concept in Vygotsky's social development theory

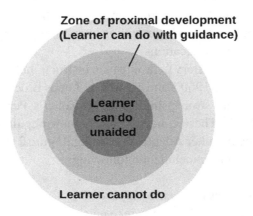

this zone, educators should employ learning potential assessments. Mediation consists of scaffolding, apprenticeship, socialization, and reciprocal teaching. Games support such proximal development through appropriate (and sometimes dynamic) challenge (as in Gee's pleasant frustration) and reciprocal teaching (as in McGonigal's distributed knowledge). Vygotsky's zone of proximal development is illustrated in Figure 3.

Gamification

Often confused with games-based learning and serious games, gamification is a distinct approach which incorporates game mechanics into a non-game context. These mechanics can be used to motivate the user in situations as widely varying as learning a new skill, improving diet and exercise, quitting bad habits, or encouraging domestic chores (Fitocracy, 2022; Habitica, 2022; Microsoft, 2022; Pop Sugar, 2022). Gamification has been widely adopted in fitness tracking, like that provided by Fitbit and Nike. The Nike+ running system employs leaderboards, real-time feedback, competition, and avatars to motivate runners (Huang et al., 2016).

Gamification leverages mechanics inherent to games to motivate users. Several of these mechanics are described in the table below, with a focus on educational application.

1. **Leaderboards:** This mechanic displays a ranking of user performance relative to their peers. Leaderboards encourage competitive engagement and take advantage of social factors. There may be multiple leaderboards per game,

based on different performance types or time periods. In a study by the author (Thornton & Francia, 2014), nearly all students who employed a leaderboard in their course requested it for subsequent courses.

2. **Levels:** As a user improves in competence and completes challenges, they graduate through multiple ordinal levels. These represent milestones in player progress.

3. **Titles:** Related to levels, users may attain nominal titles that correspond to their achievements and/or competence level.

4. **Points:** Numeric tallying of user performance. As with leaderboards, there may be more than one points category. Zichermann (2011, p. 38) defines the following types of points:

    a. Experience Points: Players earn these by completing challenges, and they represent the player's competence. This is by far the most common type.

    b. Redeemable Points: Players may earn these in a variety of ways. These points can be used as currency in a virtual marketplace to purchase items (see Items/Loot below).

    c. Skill Points: An adjunct to experience points, these are tied to a particular skill or competence category.

    d. Karma Points: These points are designed to be given away. They may be used to serve as votes in favor of an action or feature, or as a way to socialize with other players by awarding them as a type of trophy.

    e. Reputation Points: Similar to the above, these are awarded by other players as evidence of trustworthiness or competence.

5. **Badges:** Similar to titles, this mechanic represents a sort of microcredential. Often taking the form of graphical icons which may be embedded in web pages, frameworks to support educational badges are widespread (BadgeOS, 2022; Badgr, 2022; Credly, 2022).

6. **Avatars:** This is a visual representation of the player, ranging from cartoonish anthropomorphized caricatures to photorealistic 3D models. This element primarily supports Gee's aforementioned principle of identity. Players may personalize their avatar to suit personal style, or to display wearable badges. In an exercise study at Stanford University, they found that avatars motivated experiment participants to perform 8 times as many repetitions as the control group (Fox & Bailenson, 2009).

7. **Items/Loot:** As players complete challenges, they may earn special items, which allow them real-life privileges. These items may have instant, temporary, or permanent effects, depending on instructor goals. Examples in a curriculum would include an item which grants the player an extended due date, or an extra attempt on an exam. This mechanic can support personalized learning

if combined with a currency system (as in the redeemable points above) that allows players to purchase items as they choose.

8. **Non-linear Rewards:** Games often use exponential or logarithmic reward structures to control behavior. When building a new habit, an exponential reward may keep a player engaged by stimulating dopamine release (Kobayashi & Schultz, 2008), while a habit that needs less reinforcement may require only logarithmic rewards.

9. **Multiple Learning Paths:** The best educational games allow learners some degree of control in their learning journey. For the instructional designer, this requires careful scaffolding to ensure that learners are prepared for the next concept. It is noteworthy that the appearance of choice, even if it is ultimately an illusion, can motivate players (Stipek, 1996). Indeed, Felicia (2012) identified this characteristic as one of the most important to the success of educational games, along with matching difficulty to the learner's present skill level (see dynamic difficulty adjustment and Flow above).

10. **Random Chance (Luck):** This mechanic can excite players by adding an element of surprise and uncertainty. Educators must take care with this mechanic in the context of a course, however, because it can lead to arbitrary grades which are not directly tied to performance. If using random chance, it is important to tie the results to small, equally valuable rewards.

Figure 4. Various gamification mechanics are depicted, including a leaderboard (top left), loot/item marketplace (bottom left), and scaffolded learning map (right)

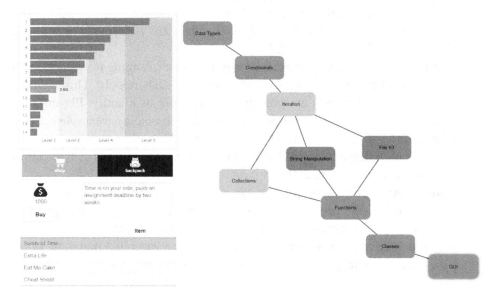

11. **Competition and Cooperation:** The element of competition incentivizes some players to do their best work, while cooperation provides social connectedness and pro-social emotions. When these elements are paired (as in team vs. team challenges), they provide an excellent balance of individual and group motivation.

12. **Reputation:** As in reputation points above, this mechanic can be used to reward pro-social habits, such as mentoring coworkers. This can lead to the creation of new intrinsic motivators, as in the aforementioned Rochester Institute of Technology experiment (Werbach & Hunter, 2012).

Figure 4 depicts some of the items described above via screenshots from author-developed gamification apps.

Case Studies Supporting the Use of Games

While the use of serious games, games-based learning, and gamification are still fairly new in the field of information security awareness training, there are promising results from a number of cases. In a field study of ~300 students by the author (Thornton & Francia, 2014), undergraduate students taking a gamified version of a computer programming course attended more often (30 days gamified, 26 days control), were more participatory in class meetings (8.2 interactions gamified, 5.7 control), and had a higher success rate (61% gamified, 54% control).

Baxter et al. (2016) studied the application of basic gamification elements to compliance training. Trainees reported a higher subjective satisfaction and had marginally better learning outcomes. People who identified as "gamers" experienced the greatest improvements in learning.

In a literature review of 24 peer-reviewed empirical studies of gamification, Hamari et al. (2014) found that a majority of studies yielded positive results. The authors posit that gamification may be less effective in contexts that call for strictly rational behavior, such as e-commerce sites. As discussed, many of the human factor weaknesses include emotional elements rather than pure reason.

Vail (2015) used the information security game CyberCIEGE (see next section) in a cybersecurity course. Students reported higher enjoyment and engagement, as well as a higher average assessment score, versus the control group.

Silic & Lowry (2020) conducted a six-month field study of over 400 employees with a gamified security training system. They found improvement in engagement, learning, self-efficacy, and actual behaviors. The authors hired a third-party firm to conduct realistic phishing attacks post-training, which confirmed a significant positive effect in trainees' ability to reject such attacks compared to control.

Serious Games and Gamification for Information Security

In a wide survey of serious games and gamified systems, El-Khuffash (2013) discovered that over half (54%) of the 79 systems studied were focused towards behavior change, as opposed to improving business processes or generating profit. Below are some prominent information security awareness games and gamification frameworks.

1. **CyberCIEGE:** First released in 2005, CyberCIEGE is a resource management simulation developed by the Naval Postgraduate School's Center for Information Systems Security Studies and Research. This high-quality gaming framework is highly configurable to a wide range of information security scenarios. The player takes the role of an IT security professional, attempting to optimize budget, security, and end user satisfaction. A well-designed scenario tuned to end users provides an opportunity for building technical skills, paired with empathy and reflection that comes from playing the perspective of the security professional. This tool, along with movies, manual, and starting scenarios are all available at no cost for educational and U.S. government use (Naval Postgraduate School, 2022) at https://nps.edu/web/c3o/downloads

2. **Cyber Awareness Challenge:** This high-quality free web-based game was developed by the Department of Defense (DoD). In the intriguing narrative, players are visited by a person from a dystopian future and must change the future by making wise security decisions and solving the mystery of what went wrong. This game emphasizes the broader impact of individual non-compliance. Available at https://dl.dod.cyber.mil/wp-content/uploads/trn/online/cyber-awareness-challenge/launchPage.htm

3. **CyberMission:** Another free web-based DoD game, players must design, defend, and attack systems. Each activity is an exploratory mini-lesson on a cybersecurity or computer science concept. Available at https://www.cybermission.tech/#!/page/home

4. **Cyber Threat Defender:** Available in digital and physical card formats, this free game is part of a suite of cyber awareness games developed in the Unity game engine by the University of Texas at San Antonio. Available at https://cias.utsa.edu/ctd.php

5. **Zero Threat:** This award-winning turn-based strategy game is designed for corporate employees. It is compatible with most learning management systems (LMS) for easy progress monitoring. Available at https://preloaded.com/work/preloadedeukleia-zero-threat/

6. **CyberEscape Online:** This online multiplayer escape game is designed to be played in small groups via videoconference software, such as Zoom. This supports players with different skills and knowledge and provides opportunity

for group discussion and reflection. Available at https://www.livingsecurity.com/cyberescape-online

7. **Cybersecurity Lab:** This highly accessible free browser-based game allows players to erect defenses against notional cyberattacks with resources earned through completing mini-lessons. Available at https://www.pbs.org/wgbh/nova/labs/lab/cyber/

8. **Anti-Phishing Phil:** One of a suite of games developed at Carnegie Mellon University, this game is now available commercially from Wombat Security in volume licenses for less than $20. Available at https://www.cmu.edu/iso/aware/phil/index.html

9. **Targeted Attack:** Players take on the role of chief information officer of a fictional company and must make decisions to successfully complete an important project. The game progresses in a "choose your own adventure" style through a series of well-produced live-action video clips. Available at http://targetedattacks.trendmicro.com/

10. **Hot Spot:** In this short, free web-based hidden object game, players must quickly identify security weaknesses in an office setting. A good way to start a discussion on physical security. Available at https://hotspot.livingsecurity.com/

11. **Brute Force:** This lane-defense game was developed by the author to teach players how to choose and create strong, memorable passwords (Thornton & Francia, 2014). Hackers attempt to break through walls whose strength is determined by the password used to create them. Duplicating passwords which are broken result in the destruction of all matching passwords. Custom passwords have the potential to be the most powerful, but players must remember their created passwords to get the highest score. This game and the one following are depicted in Figure 5.

Figure 5. Brute Force (left) and Space Scams (right), author-created information awareness games

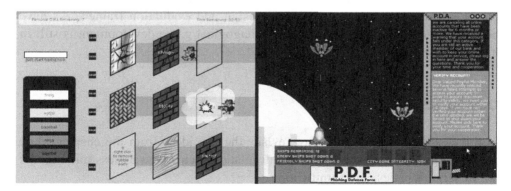

12. **Space Scams:** A phishing awareness game developed by the author in which players must determine friend from foe based on message content. Both of the above games are available for free by contacting the author at thornton@ jsu.edu.

For those information security professionals interested in gamifying their training, the tools below are recommended.

1. **ClassDojo:** This classroom management software is primarily marketed toward K-12 students but can be easily configured to appeal to older learners with minor graphical adjustments. Educators award points to students for positive behaviors and subtract them for negative ones, all of which are highly customizable. This software is free for teachers. Available at https://www.classdojo.com/
2. **Classcraft:** A gamified pedagogy framework with a fantasy setting, this software has high production values and a wide array of features. A free version is available, while premium features cost $120/year per teacher. Available at https://www.classcraft.com/
3. **Gamegogy Leaderboard and Marketplace:** Built using the Learning Tools Interoperability (LTI) standard, these author-developed apps (depicted in Figure 4) integrate easily into the Canvas LMS. The Leaderboard app displays class ranking based on total points, and the Marketplace allows instructors to create items which can be purchased with virtual currency to confer real-time in-course benefits. Both are freely available by contacting thornton@ jsu.edu.

FUTURE RESEARCH DIRECTIONS

While many information security awareness games have been developed over the last decade, many of them are focused on younger learners, and most are single-player. Moreover, while several game design and evaluation frameworks have been proposed, a unified approach to pedagogical game development is still in its formative phase.

CONCLUSION

In this closing section, the author revisits the key ideas from the chapter while providing guidance on the topics of information security awareness training, the use of serious games, and gamification.

General Training Considerations

Effective security awareness training must include not only the technical knowledge, but also the overarching concepts inherent to a safety mindset. Employees must internalize the high-level values associated with the list of prohibited and approved actions of the information security policy. As such, the best training will support trainees in developing a "mental model" of the system and how they fit into it. Scholars advise that training must reinforce self-efficacy. To do, employees must understand that non-compliant behavior is within their control and that it can affect the entire organization.

Because personality is a moderating factor between intent and behavior, security professionals must have realistic expectations of their ability to change behavior, and they should be prepared with layered defenses. Employees with high conscientiousness and agreeableness tend toward compliance once they are made aware of vulnerabilities.

As several authors have suggested, training should include social elements to be most effective. This may take the form of multiplayer discussion-based training, community mentoring, and reputation (as in gamification). To support this, consider offering additional, optional training sessions with minor incentives. These need not be monetary, but can take the form of gamified badges or certificates, in electronic or physical form. Next, offer mentoring opportunities to the high achievers who completed the advanced sessions by making them the teachers. As ever, values and ideas that come from experienced peers have more influence than those from a top-down or disembodied training format.

Serious Games Considerations

Serious games can support standardized training as an interstitial adjunctive, providing preparation or review for periodic recertifications. They can be played individually in order to prepare employees for group/discussion-based training. In either scenario, these free up precious time for the already encumbered security awareness professional.

Remember that games can be played in a variety of formats. Digital gaming has a great deal of portability and availability and easy electronic monitoring, while physical games like board and card games can be deployed in low-tech environments.

To measure the effectiveness of games in your program without overcommitting resources, consider a pilot release with a small subset of employees. Compare the assessment results of users who used games versus more traditional training before expanding.

Security professionals who wish to employ multiplayer, discussion-based games may struggle with scheduling enough training sessions to handle a large employee base. For fast throughput, Scholl (2019) recommends using a learning station format in the style of circuit training, with small groups rotating through all the stations in turn. Each station covers a particular concept, and the small groups solve problems through team discussion. A mediator at each station guides teams through the station activity, provides assessment, and facilitates reflection. Using this style allows for fast, lively, personal training.

In several of the games discussed above, such as the excellent CyberCIEGE, players' choices and progress can be reviewed by both the player and their supervisor. This provides an opportunity for analysis as well as potential for gamification. For instance, the first 50 employees to complete certain training modules could be rewarded with a virtual badge.

Gamification Considerations

If using gamification, security professionals should address the desired attitudes and behaviors, and take care in choosing extrinsic motivators. Remember that extrinsic motivators can induce intrinsic ones, especially if they incentivize new, positive habits. On the other hand, if they are used to reinforce well-established habits that are already intrinsically satisfying, the removal of the extrinsic motivators may cause a regression toward non-compliance.

With ranking mechanics like leaderboards, consider the negative effect of shaming. The use of anonymized rankings that only shows an employee their own place without identifying other coworkers may work best. Moreover, public leaderboards that are visible to all employees may actually decrease security, as the authors Blythe & Coventry (2012) rightly caution, by helping social engineers identify potential weak targets.

Even a moderate amount of gamification can lead to motivation boosts, so adoption can be done in phases. As with the pilot study suggested above, security professionals may wish to test a handful of gamification mechanics before establishing a wider framework. As an example, employees who report real-life phishing attempts could earn "security points", and security professionals could post "bounties" for the most prevalent vulnerabilities in order to promote awareness.

As with serious games, remember that gamification can be analog instead of digital, if desired. That is to say, physical manipulatives like printed cards, badges, etc. may provide a cheap and easy way to start using gamification, especially with a smaller employee base or pilot study.

REFERENCES

3rd World Farmer. (2022). *3rd World Farmer: A Thought-provoking Simulation.* Retrieved from http://www.3rdworldfarmer.com/

A World Without Oil. (2022). *A World Without Oil: Play It Before You Live It.* Retrieved from http://writerguy.com/wwo/metahome.htm

Arachchilage, N., & Love, S. (2014). Security awareness of computer users: A phishing threat avoidance perspective. *Computers in Human Behavior, 38,* 304–312.

BadgeOS. (2022). *BadgeOS.* Retrieved from https://badgeos.org/

Badgr. (2022). *Badgr: Achieve Anything, Recognize Everything.* Retrieved from https://info.badgr.com/

Baxter, R. J., Holderness, D. K. Jr, & Wood, D. A. (2016). Applying basic gamification techniques to IT compliance training: Evidence from the lab and field. *Journal of Information Systems, 30*(3), 119–133.

Bíró, G. I. (2014). Didactics 2.0: A pedagogical analysis of gamification theory from a comparative perspective with a special view to the components of learning. *Procedia: Social and Behavioral Sciences, 141,* 148–151.

Block, J. H., & Burns, R. B. (1976). Mastery learning. *Review of Research in Education, 4,* 3–49.

Blythe, J. M., & Coventry, L. (2012, September). Cyber security games: a new line of risk. In *International Conference on Entertainment Computing* (pp. 600-603). Springer.

Boss, S. R., Galletta, D. F., Lowry, P. B., Moody, G. D., & Polak, P. (2015). What do systems users have to fear? Using fear appeals to engender threats and fear that motivate protective security behaviors. *Management Information Systems Quarterly, 39*(4), 837–864.

Brecht, F., Fabian, B., Kunz, S., & Müller, S. (2012). Communication anonymizers: Personality, internet privacy literacy and their influence on technology acceptance. *Eur Conf Inf Syst, 214,* 1–13.

Brown, J. S., Heath, C., & Pea, R. (2003). *Vygotsky's educational theory in cultural context.* Cambridge University Press.

Bulgurcu, B., Cavusoglu, H., & Benbasat, I. (2010). Information security policy compliance: An empirical study of rationality-based beliefs and information security awareness. *Management Information Systems Quarterly,* 523–548.

Cialdini, R. (2021). *Influence, New and Expanded: The Psychology of Persuasion.* HarperCollins.

Credly. (2022). *Credly Digital Credentials.* Retrieved from https://info.credly.com/

Crossler, R., Johnston, A., Lowry, P., Hu, Q., Warkentin, M., & Baskerville, R. (2013). Future directions for behavioral information security research. *Computers & Security, 32*, 90-101.

Csíkszentmihályi, M. (1997). Finding flow: The psychology of engagement with everyday life. Hachette UK.

D'Arcy, J., Herath, T., & Shoss, M. K. (2014). Understanding employee responses to stressful information security requirements: A coping perspective. *Journal of Management Information Systems, 31*(2), 285–318.

Darvasi, P. (2016). *Empathy, perspective and complicity: How digital games can support peace education and conflict resolution.* Mahatmi Gandhi Institute of Education for Peace and Sustainable Development/UNESCO.

Deci, E. L., & Ryan, R. M. (2012). *Self-determination theory.* Academic Press.

El-Khuffash, A. (2013). *Gamification.* Ryerson University.

Eyre, H. L. (2007). Keller's Personalized System of Instruction: Was it a Fleeting Fancy or is there a Revival on the Horizon? *The Behavior Analyst Today, 8*(3), 317.

Fagade, T., & Tryfonas, T. (2016, July). Security by compliance? A study of insider threat implications for Nigerian banks. In *International Conference on Human Aspects of Information Security, Privacy, and Trust* (pp. 128-139). Springer.

Felicia, P. (Ed.). (2012). *Developments in current game-based learning design and deployment.* IGI Global.

Fiorella, L., & Mayer, R. (2013). The relative benefits of learning by teaching and teaching expectancy. *Contemporary Educational Psychology, 38*(4), 281–288.

Fox, J., & Bailenson, J. N. (2009). Virtual self-modeling: The effects of vicarious reinforcement and identification on exercise behaviors. *Media Psychology, 12*(1), 1–25.

Gee, J. (2007). *Good video games + good learning: Collected essays on video games, learning, and literacy.* Peter Lang.

Gibbons, P. (2002). *Scaffolding language, scaffolding learning.* Heinemann.

Glassman, M., & Kang, M. J. (2012). Intelligence in the internet age: The emergence and evolution of Open Source Intelligence (OSINT). *Computers in Human Behavior*, *28*(2), 673–682.

Habitica. (2022). *Habitica - Gamify Your Life*. Retrieved from https://habitica.com/

Hamari, J., Koivisto, J., & Sarsa, H. (2014). Does gamification work?--a literature review of empirical studies on gamification. In *2014 47th Hawaii international conference on system sciences* (pp. 3025-3034). IEEE.

Haney, J., & Lutters, W. (2020). Security Awareness Training for the Workforce: Moving Beyond "Check-the-Box" Compliance. *Computer*, *53*(10).

Haucke, A., & Pokoyski, D. (2018). Mea culpa–Schuld, Scham und Opferrolle bei Social Engineering. In KES (Vol. 1, pp. 6-8). Academic Press.

Herath, T., & Rao, H. (2009). Protection motivation and deterrence: A framework for security policy compliance in organisations. *European Journal of Information Systems*, *18*(2), 106–125.

Hirschi, T. (1969). *Causes of Delinquency*. University of California Press.

Hu, Q., Dinev, T., Hart, P., & Cooke, D. (2012). Managing employee compliance with information security policies: The critical role of top management and organizational culture. *Decision Sciences*, *43*(4), 615–660.

Huang, Y., Xu, J., Yu, B., & Shull, P. B. (2016). Validity of FitBit, Jawbone UP, Nike+ and other wearable devices for level and stair walking. *Gait & Posture*, *48*, 36–41.

IBM Security & Ponemon Institute. (2020). *Cost of Insider Threats: Global Report*. Retrieved from https://www.ibm.com/downloads/cas/61KLOPV5

Kirlappos, I., Beautement, A., & Sasse, M. A. (2013, April). "Comply or Die" Is Dead: Long live security-aware principal agents. In *International conference on financial cryptography and data security* (pp. 70-82). Springer.

Kobayashi, S., & Schultz, W. (2008). Influence of reward delays on responses of dopamine neurons. *The Journal of Neuroscience: The Official Journal of the Society for Neuroscience*, *28*(31), 7837–7846.

Life is Strange: True Colors [Video game]. (2021). Deck Nine Games.

Mayo, M. J. (2007). Games for science and engineering education. *Communications of the ACM*, *50*(7), 30–35.

McCrae, R. R., & John, O. P. (1992). An introduction to the five-factor model and its applications. *Journal of Personality*, *60*(2), 175–215.

McDougall, S. J., Curry, M. B., & De Bruijn, O. (2001). The effects of visual information on users' mental models: An evaluation of Pathfinder analysis as a measure of icon usability. *International Journal of Cognitive Ergonomics*, *5*(1), 59–84.

McGonigal, J. (2011). *Reality is broken: Why games make us better and how they can change the world*. Penguin.

Microsoft. (2022). *Ribbon Hero 2: How to play the game*. Retrieved from https://www.microsoft.com/en-us/microsoft-365/blog/2011/04/26/ribbon-hero-2-how-to-play-the-game-video/

National Institute of Justice. (2016). *Five Things About Deterrence*. Retrieved from https://nij.ojp.gov/topics/articles/five-things-about-deterrence

Naval Postgraduate School. (2022). *CyberCIEGE Downloads*. Retrieved from https://nps.edu/web/c3o/downloads

Pahnila, S., Siponen, M., & Mahmood, A. (2007, January). Employees' behavior towards IS security policy compliance. In *2007 40th Annual Hawaii International Conference on System Sciences (HICSS'07)* (pp. 156b-156b). IEEE.

Parable of the Polygons. (2022). *Parable of the Polygons: A Playable Post on the Shape of Society*. Retrieved from https://ncase.me/polygons/

Pop Sugar. (2022). *Organize Your Life: 7 Apps For Family Organization*. Retrieved from https://www.popsugar.com/family/photo-gallery/21393586/image/21393602/Chore-Hero

Proofpoint. (2021). *2021 Human Factor Report*. Retrieved from https://www.proofpoint.com/sites/default/files/threat-reports/pfpt-us-tr-human-factor-report.pdf

Reality Drop. (2022). *Reality Drop*. Retrieved from https://www.realitydrop.org/

Safa, N., & Ismail, M. (2013). A customer loyalty formation model in electronic commerce. *Economic Modelling*, *35*, 559–564.

Safa, N., Von Solms, R., & Furnell, S. (2016). Information security policy compliance model in organizations. *Computers & Security, 56*, 70-82.

SANS. (2021). *2021 Security Awareness Report: Managing Human Cyber Risk*. Retrieved from https://go.sans.org/lp-wp-2021-sans-security-awareness-report

Scholl, M. (2018). Play the Game! Analogue Gamification for Raising Information Security Awareness. *Systemics. Cybernetics and Informatics, 16*(3), 32–35.

Scholl, M. (2019). Sensitizing students to information security and privacy awareness with analogue gamification. *Wissenschaftliche Beiträge, 2019*(23), 19–26.

Shropshire, J., Warkentin, M., & Sharma, S. (2015). Personality, attitudes, and intentions: Predicting initial adoption of information security behavior. *Computers & Security, 49*, 177-191.

Silic, M., & Lowry, P. B. (2020). Using design-science based gamification to improve organizational security training and compliance. *Journal of Management Information Systems, 37*(1), 129–161.

Siponen, M., Pahnila, S., & Mahmood, M. (2010). Compliance with information security policies: An empirical investigation. *Computer, 43*(2), 64–71.

Sommestad, T., Hallberg, J., Lundholm, K., & Bengtsson, J. (2014). Variables influencing information security policy compliance: A systematic review of quantitative studies. *Information Management & Computer Security*.

Spent. (2022). *Spent: It's Just Stuff, Until You Don't Have It*. Retrieved from https://playspent.org/

Stipek, D. J. (1996). Motivation and instruction. Handbook of Educational Psychology, 1, 85-113.

Thornton, D., & Francia, G. (2014). Gamification of information systems and security training: Issues and case studies. *Information Security Education Journal, 1*(1), 16–24.

Vail, J. (2015). Gamification of an information security management course. In EdMedia+ Innovate Learning (pp. 1720-1731). Association for the Advancement of Computing in Education (AACE).

Vance, A., Siponen, M., & Pahnila, S. (2012). Motivating IS security compliance: Insights from habit and protection motivation theory. *Information & Management, 49*(3-4), 190–198.

Verizon. (2021). *2021 Verizon Data Breach Investigations Report*. Retrieved from https://www.verizon.com/business/resources/reports/2021/2021-data-breach-investigations-report.pdf

Vonnegut, K. (2010). *Cat's cradle*. Dial Press Trade Paperbacks.

Warkentin, M., McBride, M., Carter, L., & Johnston, A. (2012). The role of individual characteristics on insider abuse intentions. *Proc Am Conf Inf Syst*, *28*, 1-10.

Warkentin, M., & Willison, R. (2009). Behavioral and policy issues in information systems security: The insider threat. *European Journal of Information Systems*, *18*(2), 101–105.

Werbach, K., & Hunter, D. (2012). *For the Win: How Game Thinking Can Revolutionize Your Business*. Wharton Digital Press.

Yazdanmehr, A., Wang, J., & Yang, Z. (2020). Peers matter: The moderating role of social influence on information security policy compliance. *Information Systems Journal*, *30*(5), 791–844.

Zichermann, G., & Cunningham, C. (2011). *Gamification by design: Implementing game mechanics in web and mobile apps*. O'Reilly Media, Inc.

ADDITIONAL READING

Arachchilage, N. A. G., & Hameed, M. A. (2017). *Integrating self-efficacy into a gamified approach to thwart phishing attacks*. arXiv preprint arXiv:1706.07748.

Farber, M. (2016). Gamify your classroom. *Education Digest*, *81*(5), 37.

Goo, J., Yim, M., & Kim, D. (2014). A path to successful management of employee security compliance: An empirical study of information security climate. *IEEE Transactions on Professional Communication*, *57*(4), 286–308. doi:10.1109/TPC.2014.2374011

Hunicke, R. (2005, June). The case for dynamic difficulty adjustment in games. In *Proceedings of the 2005 ACM SIGCHI International Conference on Advances in computer entertainment technology* (pp. 429-433). 10.1145/1178477.1178573

Mitnick, K. D., & Simon, W. L. (2003). *The art of deception: Controlling the human element of security*. John Wiley & Sons.

Scholl, M., Gube, S., & Koppatz, P. (2021). *Development of Game-Based Learning Scenarios for Social Engineering and Security Risk Management for SMEs in the Manufacturing Industry*. In *12th International Multi-Conference on Complexity, Informatics and Cybernetics*. IMCIC.

Sheldon, L. (2020). *The multiplayer classroom: Designing coursework as a game*. CRC Press. doi:10.1201/9780429285035

Wu, T., Tien, K., Hsu, W., & Wen, F. (2021). Assessing the Effects of Gamification on Enhancing Information Security Awareness Knowledge. *Applied Sciences (Basel, Switzerland)*, *11*(19), 9266. doi:10.3390/app11199266

Zichermann, G. (2022). *Gamification Co - The Leading Source for Gamification News & Info*. Retrieved from https://www.gamification.co/

KEY TERMS AND DEFINITIONS

Autonomy: The perception of self-governance.

Big Five: A collection of personality traits in psychology. They include extraversion, agreeableness, openness, conscientiousness, and neuroticism.

Electroencephalography: The measurement of the brain's electrical activity applied to a visual display or graph.

Flow: An intense, ego-free, hyper-focused state of attention brought about by compelling activities at the appropriate challenge level.

Gamification: The use of game mechanics in a non-game context in order to motivate desired behavior.

Normative Belief: An individual's belief about what behavior is expected of them by other people within their group.

Self-Efficacy: An individual's belief that they are capable of attaining their desired goals.

Serious Game: A game whose primary purpose is not to entertain, but to impart knowledge or persuade.

Section 3
Cybersecurity Consulting and Assurance

Chapter 5

Using the NIST Framework and COBIT 2019 in Offering Cybersecurity Consulting and Assurance Services

Jeffrey S. Zanzig
Jacksonville State University, USA

ABSTRACT

Information processing in a cyber environment offers tremendous benefits but is also accompanied by inevitable dangers including compromised confidentiality and malware such as ransomware that can shut down major segments of a country's operations. A variety of forms of guidance and regulation have been developed to deal with these cybersecurity issues. The professions of public accounting and internal audit have long worked with organizations to protect the integrity of their information systems. Both of these professions are working diligently to guide organization management in the area of cybersecurity. An important aspect of such services is an appropriate framework to use as a basis for advisement and assurance. One such framework is the Framework for Improving Critical Infrastructure Cybersecurity issued by the National Institute of Standards and Technology.

INTRODUCTION

Organizations have achieved significant benefits from their ability to harness the power of the Internet to reach customers and process a variety of types of information. However, this power has come at a cost in that the use of company networks and

DOI: 10.4018/978-1-7998-8390-6.ch005

Copyright © 2022, IGI Global. Copying or distributing in print or electronic forms without written permission of IGI Global is prohibited.

their connections to the Internet have provided entry points for malicious persons to inappropriately access and manipulate and/or steal company information. For example, a cybersecurity breach in December 2020 at a large American software development company named Solarwinds drew the attention of the United States Congress when hackers were able to introduce malicious code into the company's Orion IT infrastructure monitoring and administration platform. This code was then transferred to over 250 companies and government agencies by means of updates and patches that Solarwinds sent out to its customers. The SUNBURST malware produced backdoors allowing hackers to enter the systems of Solarwinds customers while bypassing normal authentication procedures (Mar, 2021). In another incident, the largest fuel pipeline in the United States was brought down when hackers got into a virtual private network of the Colonial Pipeline Company in April 2021. This ransomware attack resulted in Colonial shutting down its entire gasoline pipeline for the first time in its 57-year history (Turton and Mehrotra, 2021). As a result of incidents such as these, there have been an increasing number of regulations and other forms of guidance that organizations must comply with to protect the confidentiality, integrity, and availability of information.

Certified public accountants (CPAs) and internal auditors are well known and respected for their extensive efforts in advising organizations regarding internal controls over information processing. Both professions are working conscientiously to serve organizations in advising them in how to address cybersecurity risks. In addition, the American Institute of Certified Public Accountants (AICPA) has issued guidance on how CPAs can evaluate and report on cybersecurity programs. Of course, the offering of consulting and assurance services must be accompanied by an appropriate framework. Such frameworks must address a variety of forms of guidance and government regulation, while at the same time allowing for continuous improvement to address the constantly changing threats in a cybersecurity environment.

The Cybersecurity Enhancement Act of 2014 revised the purpose of the National Institute of Standards and Technology (NIST) to encompass finding and advancing cybersecurity risk frameworks. On April 16, 2018, the NIST issued version 1.1 of their Framework for Improving Critical Infrastructure Cybersecurity (NIST Framework). The NIST Framework recognizes that organizations will continue to have unique risks in that they face different threats and have their own levels of risk tolerance. It is for this reason that organizations will tailor practices in the NIST Framework to their specific situations. The NIST Framework may be described as consisting of four basic components:

1. **The Framework Core:** An arrangement of cybersecurity actions, anticipated outcomes, and appropriate references that are customary across infrastructure sectors.
2. **Framework Implementation Tiers:** Describe an organization's procedures over a range, from Partial (Tier 1) to Adaptive (Tier 4).

3. **Framework Profile:** Can be used to ascertain opportunities for advancing cybersecurity position by contrasting a "Current" Profile (the "as is" state) with a "Target" Profile (the "to be" state).
4. **Coordination of Framework Implementation:** Describes a common flow of information and decisions.

Any framework of cybersecurity must be based on appropriate guidance from various organizations respected for their knowledge of technology and cybersecurity issues. The NIST Framework is indeed based on guidance from several informative references including those of the ISACA. The ISACA is well known for its development of international information system auditing and control standards. One of their most significant contributions is a continuing project known as the Control Objectives for Information and related Technology (COBIT). The management process of COBIT 2019 contains four management domains:

*   **Align, Plan and Organize (APO)**
*   **Build, Acquire and Implement (BAI)**
*   **Deliver, Service and Support (DSS)**
*   **Monitor, Evaluate and Assess (MEA)**

COBIT 2019 contains explanations of specific management practices than can be tailored to the development of various objectives that a company may wish to accomplish within each domain. Each organization should decide on its own combination of management practices based on the unique environment in which it operates (ISACA, 2019).

The remainder of this chapter is conceptually divided into four major topics:

1. The first is some background describing factors that have increased concerns over cybersecurity including: remote working, cloud computing, and information processing services at organizations like CPA firms.
2. The main focus of the chapter considers some guidance regarding how the professions of public accounting and internal auditing are offering consulting and assurance services for cybersecurity programs. The section concludes with a description of the NIST Framework.
3. Solutions and recommendations present illustrations regarding how key elements of a cybersecurity framework are addressed by the NIST Framework Core in a way that links them to COBIT 2019. This section closes with steps described in the NIST Framework to establish or improve a cybersecurity program.
4. Concluding sections are then presented to describe some future research directions and a conclusion.

BACKGROUND

Organizations continue to face a variety of threats from predators waiting for the chance to obtain inappropriate access into an organization's network and information being transmitted over the Internet. Security measures such as encryption, employee training, and virtual private networks have helped organizations to make significant accomplishments to protect their information technology environments. However, the last few years have seen increases in cybersecurity issues due to both remote working and cloud computing. In addition, it is interesting to note that information processing organizations like CPA firms have been recognized as having some specific issues regarding cybersecurity risks.

Remote Working

Nabe (2021) points out that government restrictions in response to the Covid-19 pandemic have encouraged or required employees to work remotely from home. However, many organizations were not adequately prepared to address the cybersecurity risks associated with this environment. For example, home Wi-Fi networks are often more susceptible to attacks and employees may not regularly run programs to scan for viruses and malware. In addition, before the pandemic organizations may have been more reluctant to allow employees to remotely access confidential data. With the pandemic, organizations were required to relax some of these restrictions due to employees working at home for extended periods.

Cloud Computing

Hodge (2021) points out concerns raised by a cybersecurity strategy consultant named Shawn Chaput, who describes some key risks that internal auditors need to keep in mind in regard to cloud computing:

- **Identity and Access Management:** Establishing the identity of the end user is an important issue because the separation of the processing from the client organization provides more of an opportunity for unauthorized access into an organization's information processing.
- **Supplier Management:** Organizations depend on third parties to perform processing tasks and handle data security. Internal audit should help company management to consider the possibility of a third-party information processer experiencing a data breach and how the organization intends to respond.
- **Data Classification:** Organizations may attempt to protect all cloud data at the highest possible level of security. Instead, data should be classified at

various security levels. Assigning all data at a high security level can result in some highly sensitive data being under protected because so much is being spent on security that corners are cut to keep security costs at a reasonable level.

- **Talent Deficiencies:** The variety of cloud computing services includes an assortment of technologies that are in a constant state of change. When processing is performed in-house, companies can hire technology staff familiar with the specific technologies they employ. However, with the use of cloud computing, organizations can never be sure whether the technical people they hire will be able to stay up to date with the ever-changing technologies of third-party providers.

Cybersecurity Risks for CPA Firms

Although CPAs are an excellent source of service in assisting their clients in their programs of cybersecurity, CPA firms must also consider that their access to client information subjects them to being an attractive candidate for a cybersecurity attack. The Private Companies Practice Section (PCPS) is an accounting firm membership section of the AICPA that looks out for the interests of small and mid-sized firms and the clients they serve. In 2018, they issued a paper entitled A CPA's introduction to Cybersecurity in which they point out several reasons why CPA firms should be well acquainted with their own cybersecurity position:

- **They Offer a Single Access Point:** Attackers have come to realize that CPA firms contain an extensive repository of sensitive data for a large number of organizations, that can all be accessed by simply getting into to the records of a single firm.
- **The Data of CPA Firm Clients Lives in Many Places:** CPA firm employees probably have client data stored in numerous places including servers on the CPA firm's network, staff laptops, email systems, and cloud-based storage. The more places that sensitive data is stored, the greater the difficulty in ensuring that each location has appropriate security measures in place to protect data. The reputation of a CPA firm can be seriously damaged when there is a data breach causing businesses to lose faith in the special trust that clients attribute to CPAs in protecting the confidentiality of their data.
- **CPA Firms Have Compliance Obligations:** Some CPA firms may be unaware that they already have cybersecurity compliance obligations regarding three common areas. One area is personally identifiable information (PII) such as social security numbers. Most states in America have laws that state that "if at any point the company or organization has reason to believe

that an unauthorized user has accessed PII, the entity must acknowledge that breach directly to the affected individuals and through public notification." In addition, when a CPA firm has a client that possesses protected health information (PHI), the firm may become subject to implementing a cybersecurity program that follows the Health Insurance Portability and Accountability Act (HIPAA), which is a federal law protecting PHI. Finally, if a CPA firm accepts credit cards, they must comply with a set of cybersecurity measures covering the proper handling of credit card information.

MAIN FOCUS OF THE CHAPTER

The large volume of regulations and ever-changing threats that exist in the cybersecurity environment of today's organizations poses significant challenges regarding compliance that many organizational leaders may be poorly equipped to handle. Organizational leadership needs the assistance of trusted professionals to guide them in the creation and continuous updating of an appropriate set of cybersecurity policies. If properly rooted in an appropriate cybersecurity framework, these policies can be used to structure recommendations and provide a set of standards against which cybersecurity assurance can be provided. The main focus section discusses cybersecurity guidance by considering literature from the areas of public accounting and internal audit, and concludes with an introduction to the NIST Cybersecurity Framework.

CPAs and Cybersecurity

CPAs are well trained regarding internal controls over financial reporting and providing assurance concerning an organization's basic financial statements. The profession of public accounting continues its efforts to improve its competence to address security over information technology and the emerging threats of a cybersecurity environment. This section discusses a risk assessment process that CPAs can follow in offering cybersecurity consulting, examples of cybersecurity guidance, and an assurance service known as a The Cybersecurity Risk Management Examination.

Cybersecurity Consulting by CPAs

Bwerinofa-Petrozzello (2021) points out that the increasing rate of cyber fraud places CPAs in a good position to assist their clients in preparing for a potential cyberattack by helping them to conduct a three-step risk assessment including:

1. Recognizing inherent fraud risks that a client is subject to.
2. Assessing the probability and magnitude of each inherent fraud risk, and
3. Responding to inherent risks that are both probable and significant in magnitude.

In particular, she mentions the following regarding an evaluation of IT security and controls:

* **Avoid Simple Passwords:** Employees should be cautioned against using passwords which are easy to remember but simple to guess. For example, the name of a favorite pet or a birthday. In addition, even a sufficiently complex password should be changed regularly due to the availability of technology to eventually break even the best password.
* **Apply the Principle of Least Privilege:** Employees should only possess the smallest amount of access needed to conduct their job responsibilities.
* **Automate IT Security Updates:** To the greatest extent possible, organizations should automate security updates and put in place employee evaluation criteria that encourages employees to appropriately consider the importance of keeping up-to-date security measures.
* **Terminate End-of-Life Software:** The organization should ensure that end-of-life software that is no longer supported by the vendor is replaced with updated software receiving proper vendor support.
* **Consider Remote Access Security:** A virtual private network (VPN) can be used to address the risks associated with remote staff accessing an organization's private network. A VPN allows users to logically extend an organization's private network through encryption technology that helps to prevent the ability of outsiders on the Internet to intercept and interpret data. In addition, multifactor authentication can be used to require a user to present two or more forms of identification before access is granted.
* **Regularly Train Employees on Cybersecurity:** It is not possible to have a technological safeguard to protect against every one of a vast number of ever-changing cybersecurity risks. One of the most important safeguards is having competent employees who have been appropriately trained to be on their guard to recognize and report such incidents. Bucher (2021) notes that organization employees need to be aware of red flags. For example, an attacker may just send out emails without any suspicious links or files for the purpose of just soliciting a response from the recipient. If the recipient responds, the attacker learns that the recipient exists along with other information like the format of the email and design of the signature. This can make it easier to steal the identity of the victim.

Lanz (2016) suggests the following strategies to assist those in a position of governance in managing cybersecurity:

- **Perform a Risk Assessment:** To properly allocate resources it is important for board members to fully comprehend the threats they face, and the accompanying costs should they occur.
- **Choosing What to Protect:** It would be too expensive to protect every part of the organization. Companies should evaluate what assets are in most need of protection. The analysis should include the probability and potential financial loss from the threat. Suggested controls should include an estimate the benefits of the control along with an approximation of the time and costs to implement and maintain it.
- **Properly Report the Results of Vulnerability Testing:** All too often there has been a patch available for a vulnerability for months or even years before the vulnerability is exploited. This could be attributable to audit committees receiving vulnerability reports in the form of an extremely long document that is filled with technical jargon. An improved approach might be one in which data and servers are classified using a data classification policy ranked by risk level (i.e., high, medium, or low), presenting results for only high-ranked resources. Similar to the idea of providing an aged analysis of accounts receivable, it would also be helpful to present the amount of time overdue for remediations to address vulnerabilities. Written explanations should be provided for delays along with compensating controls that may assist in protecting against a vulnerability until it is addressed.

The Cybersecurity Risk Management Examination

In 2017, the American Institute of Certified Public Accountants (AICPA) issued guidance to CPAs in "Reporting on an Entity's Cyber Security Risk Management Program and Controls" ("Cybersecurity Guidance"). The focus of this guidance is to allow CPAs to attest as to whether a client's cybersecurity risk management program achieves its overall business objectives. The Cybersecurity Guidance describes the following three components of the standard examination report:

1. A management description of the organization's cybersecurity risk management program covering how an organization identifies its information assets, the approach management takes in addressing the cybersecurity risks faced by those assets, and what security measures have been put in place to protect the information assets.
2. A management assertion addressing (i) whether the description is presented in agreement with the description criteria and (ii) the effectiveness of

Table 1. Other opinion possibilities

Nature of Matter Giving Rise to the Modification	Practitioner's Professional Judgment About the Pervasiveness of the Effect or Possible Effects on the Description or on the Effectiveness of Controls	
	Material but Not Pervasive	*Material and Pervasive*
Scope limitation • The practitioner is unable to obtain sufficient appropriate evidence.	Qualified opinion	Disclaimer of opinion
Material misstatements • Subject Matter 1: The description is materially misstated. Or • Subject Matter 2: The controls were not effective to achieve the entity's cybersecurity objectives.	Qualified opinion	Adverse opinion
It is possible for different opinions to be issued regarding the two subject matters.		

the organization's cybersecurity risk management controls in achieving cybersecurity objectives.

3. A report by the CPA firm as to whether the above components of management's assertion have been met.

A CPA firm would issue a standard examination report when the management description is appropriately presented, and cybersecurity risk management controls are effective in achieving cybersecurity objectives. Table 1 taken from the Cybersecurity Guidance presents some other opinion possibilities.

Zanzig and Francia (2020) point out that the Cybersecurity Guidance also allows for both design-only and partial examinations. A design-only examination would be appropriate in situations where there has not been enough time to evaluate the effectiveness of newly implemented controls. Such situations may arise when an organization is new or has significantly changed its cybersecurity program. A partial examination may be appropriate depending on the needs of the report user. For example, selling off a portion of a business may involve a partial examination to meet the needs of potential buyers.

Internal Audit and Cybersecurity

Internal auditors are normally employees of the companies they audit and are therefore ever present to assist company management and the board in establishing and maintaining a program of cybersecurity. Pundmann (2021) states that the management and boards of today's organizations require internal audit to provide forward-looking advice concerning cyber risks and controls to deal with them. However, it can be a formidable task to begin a discussion in regard to understanding theoretical cybersecurity risks as many members of management and the board may not have sufficient experience in dealing with such issues. Pundmann suggests that the conversation can be expedited by framing the talk around risks that have happened at other organizations. For example, one approach would be to take a headline, incident, or a case study and ask the following questions:

- Could an incident or risk like this happen at our organization?
- What are we doing to block or identify such situations?
- How would our organization know if this threat has materialized?
- In what way would our organization react?
- Who would be responsible for dealing with the threat and solving the problem?
- If third parties are involved, what role would they play?
- What are our organization's most vulnerable links?

Internal audit could facilitate the cybersecurity discussion by staging a simulation where participants would summarize steps and action plans for a cyberattack scenario.

Reporting Cybersecurity Issues to Those Charged with Governance

Organizations should ideally have a board of directors composed of both upper company management and competent outside representatives. This allows for a balance of persons with an intricate knowledge of company operations along with persons independent of management who can help to ensure that management does not go astray. To preserve the independence of an audit process, it is advisable for a company to have an audit committee composed entirely of independent members of the board of directors. Issues involving either significant disagreements with management regarding the implementation of appropriate controls or situations concerning management integrity may need to be referred directly to the audit committee. In summary, portions of the prior discussion provided examples of literature from both public accounting and internal audit regarding issues that should be considered in advising organizations on issues of cybersecurity. Obviously, this guidance could be equally applicable to either CPAs or internal auditors providing consulting services to those charged with organizational governance.

Components of the National Institute of Standards and Technology Framework

The National Institute of Standards and Technology (2018) Framework may be described as consisting of four basic components: (1) Framework Core, (2) Framework Implementation Tiers, (3) Framework Profiles, and (4) Coordination of Framework Implementation. The discussion in this section describes the basic components.

Framework Core

The Framework Core consists of the following elements:

- **Functions:** Serve to describe cybersecurity activities at their highest level.
- **Categories:** Subdivides Functions into sets of cybersecurity outcomes.
- **Subcategories:** Subdivides Categories to provide a set of outcomes that support the achievement of each category.
- **Informative References:** Provides guidelines, practices, and standards to illustrate approaches to achieving outcomes associated with individual Subcategories.

The NIST Framework points out that the Core Functions are not supposed to simply provide a path to a static desired state. Rather, they are to be performed on a continuous basis to provide an operational approach to manage the ever-changing nature of cybersecurity risk. The Core Functions may be defined as follows:

- **Identify:** It is imperative that the business context of the organization be well understood. The Identify function considers the critical functions of the business and the cybersecurity risks that are associated with them.
- **Protect:** Serves to develop and put into operation the right security measures to ensure the continued functioning of critical functions.
- **Detect:** Activities are developed and implemented to ensure timely discovery of cybersecurity events.
- **Respond:** Develop and put into operation actions to control the impact of probable cybersecurity occurrences.
- **Recover:** To minimize the impact from a cybersecurity event, the recover function serves to minimize the effect of a cybersecurity event.

Table 2. Function and category unique identifiers

Function Unique Identifier	Function	Category Unique Identifier	Category
ID	Identify	ID.AM	Asset Management
		ID.BE	Business Environment
		ID.GV	Governance
		ID.RA	Risk Assessment
		ID.RM	Risk Management Strategy
		ID.SC	Supply Chain Risk Management
PR	Protect	PR.AC	Identity Management and Access Control
		PR.AT	Awareness and Training
		PR.DS	Data Security
		PR.IP	Information Protection Processes and Procedures
		PR.MA	Maintenance
		PR.PT	Protective Technology
DE	Detect	DE.AE	Anomalies and Events
		DE.CM	Security Continuous Monitoring
		DE.DP	Detection Processes
RS	Respond	RS.RP	Response Planning
		RS.CO	Communications
		RS.AN	Analysis
		RS.MI	Mitigation
		RS.IM	Improvements
RC	Recover	RC.RP	Recovery Planning
		RC.IM	Improvements
		RC.CO	Communications

Table 2 from the NIST Framework shows the Core Functions and the categories that have been assigned to each of them.

Framework Implementation Tiers

Framework implementation tiers "describe an increasing degree of rigor and sophistication in cybersecurity risk management practices." An organization should choose a level that satisfies organization goals, keeps cybersecurity risk at a reasonable level, and is practical to implement. The four tiers in increasing order are:

1. **Partial:** Risk management practices are conducted using an ad hoc and occasionally reactive approach with little understanding of cybersecurity risk at an organizational level.
2. **Risk Informed:** Risk management practices are authorized by management but are not necessarily created at a level of organizational-wide policy.
3. **Repeatable:** Risk management practices are officially approved and adopted as organizational policy, allowing the organization to effectively respond to changes in risk using a consistently applied approach
4. **Adaptive:** "Organization adapts its cybersecurity practices based on previous and current cybersecurity activities, including lessons learned and predictive indicators", allowing decisions to be made with a clear understanding of the relationship between cybersecurity risks and organizational objectives.

The Framework points out that although organizations at the level of the "Partial" tier are urged to move to higher levels, progression to a higher level is only "encouraged when a cost-benefit analysis indicates a feasible and cost-effective reduction of cybersecurity risk."

Framework Profiles

"The Framework Profile is the alignment of the Functions, Categories, and Subcategories with the business requirements, risk tolerance, and resources of the organization." To address complexity, organizations may desire to develop numerous profiles that align with a variety of organization components. Profiles can be used to describe both a current and target profile. To allow for flexibility in application, the NIST Framework does not describe specific Profile templates.

Coordination of Framework Implementation

The NIST Framework states that coordination involves customary flows of information and decisions specifically defining them as follows:

- **Executive level:** "Communicates the mission priorities, available resources, and overall risk to the business/process level."
- **Business/process level:** "Uses the information as inputs into the risk management process, and then collaborates with the implementation/ operations level to communicate business needs and create a Profile."
- **Implementation/operations level:** "Communicates the Profile implementation progress to the business/process level."

SOLUTIONS AND RECOMMENDATIONS

This chapter points out that both CPAs and internal auditors have continuously improved their services to offer organizations valuable consulting services on cybersecurity. In addition, the American Institute of Certified Public Accountants has issued guidance on how CPAs can offer a Cybersecurity Risk Management Examination to provide assurance on organization cybersecurity programs. Whether such professionals are providing consulting advice or assurance services, the overall process of either type of engagement is based on an organization having a cybersecurity program that is rooted in an appropriate framework. Due to the rapidly changing cyber environment, such a framework must be continuously updated using guidance from authoritative cybersecurity literature. One such framework is the previously described NIST Framework, which is based in part on authoritative guidance from the well-respected Control Objectives for Information and related Technology (COBIT) issued by the ISACA. The current edition of the guidance is known as COBIT 2019. This section describes fundamental elements of a cybersecurity framework and how they can be tied to the NIST Framework and COBIT 2019. It closes with the steps to establish or improve a cybersecurity program.

Fundamental Elements of a Cybersecurity Framework

Blackwell (2021) describes six fundamental elements that should be contained within a cybersecurity framework. In the following discussion, sample tables are provided for each of Blackwell's fundamental elements to illustrate how they can be linked to an NIST Framework (2018) Core Function, Category, and Subcategory. For each NIST Framework Subcategory, the tables also provide an informative reference, suggested activity, and metric from COBIT 2019 to demonstrate how the Framework is linked to authoritative literature on cybersecurity (ISACA, 2019).

Fundamental Element 1 - Governance

An organization must establish an attitude of accountability around its data and IT by providing resources to support cybersecurity and establishing lines of reporting responsibility. Since not all risks can be addressed, an organization should also clearly define its risk appetite to establish a baseline to determine what is a significant risk. Table 3 illustrates how the NIST Framework can be applied regarding governance to achieve an attitude of accountability.

Table 3. Governance – attitude of accountability

Framework Function: Identify (ID)
Develop an organizational understanding to manage cybersecurity risks to systems, people, assets, data, and capabilities.

Framework Category: Governance (ID.GV) *The policies, procedures, and processes to manage and monitor the organization's regulatory, legal, risk, environmental, and operational requirements are understood and inform the management of cybersecurity risk.*	**Informative Reference from COBIT 2019 (MEA03.01 – Identify External Compliance Requirements)** *On a continuous basis, monitor changes in local and international laws, regulations and other external requirements and identify mandates for compliance from and I&T (information and technology) perspective.*
Framework Subcategory: (ID.GV-3) *Legal and regulatory requirements regarding cybersecurity, including privacy and civil liberties obligations, are understood and managed.*	**Suggested Activity from COBIT 2019** *Assign responsibility for identifying and monitoring any changes of legal, regulatory and other external contractual requirements relevant to the use of I&T resources and the processing of information within the business and I&T operations of the enterprise.* **Suggested Metric from COBIT 2019** *Frequency of compliance requirements reviews.*

Fundamental Element 2 - Risk Identification and Assessment

A risk management strategy should maintain a regularly updated inventory of its assets and business processes. For each item, a determination should be made regarding vulnerabilities and threats along with the consequences of what could happen should the item be compromised. Currently existing controls should be identified and linked to the identified vulnerabilities and threats. Table 4 illustrates how the NIST Framework can be applied to properly account for critical information and technology assets.

Fundamental Element 3 - Controls

The controls include a collection of tools and processes that protect data and IT. Some examples include intrusion detection, firewalls, password conventions, physical access controls, and software patching practices. Table 5 illustrates how the NIST Framework can be applied so that appropriate controls are put in place to prevent unauthorized access to information and technology resources.

Table 6 illustrates how the NIST Framework can be applied to put in place controls to ensure proper monitoring for cybersecurity incidents.

Table 4. Identification of resources

Framework Function: Identify (ID) Develop an organizational understanding to manage cybersecurity risks to systems, people, assets, data, and capabilities.	
Framework Category: Asset Management (ID.AM) *The data, personnel, devices, systems, and facilities that enable the organization to achieve business purposes are identified and managed consistent with their relative importance to organizational objectives and the organization's risk strategy.*	**Informative Reference from COBIT 2019** **(BAI09.02 – Manage Critical Assets)** *Identify assets that are critical in providing service capability. Maximize their reliability and availability to support business needs.*
Framework Subcategory: **(ID.AM-1)** *Physical devices and systems within the organization are inventoried.*	**Suggested Activity from COBIT 2019** *Identify assets that are critical in providing service capability by referencing requirements in service definitions, service level agreements (from vendors) and the configuration management system.* **Suggested Metric from COBIT 2019** *Number of critical assets.*

Table 5. Access to resources

Framework Function: Protect (PR) Develop and implement appropriate safeguards to ensure delivery of critical services.	
Framework Category: Identity Management, Authentication, and Access Control (PR.AC) *Access to physical and logical assets and associated facilities is limited to authorized users, processes, and devices, and is managed consistent with the assessed risk of unauthorized access to authorized activities and transactions.*	**Informative Reference from COBIT 2019** **(DSS05.04 – Manage User Identity and Logical Access)** *Ensure that all users have information access rights in accordance with business requirements. Coordinate with business units that manage their own access rights within business processes.*
Framework Subcategory: **(PR.AC-4)** *Access permissions and authorizations are managed, incorporating the principles of least privilege, and separation of duties.*	**Suggested Activity from COBIT 2019** *Maintain user access rights in accordance with business function, process requirements, and security policies. Align the management of identities and access rights to the defined roles and responsibilities, based on least-privilege, need-to-have, and need-to-know principles.* **Suggested Metric from COBIT 2019** *Number of incidents relating to unauthorized access of information.*

Fundamental Element 4 - Response Planning

It is generally understood that all organizations are likely to experience an occasional successful cyberattack. When this occurs, it is imperative to be able to recover quickly with a minimum amount of damage. Internal audit should work with organizational leaders to ensure that incident response should be a top priority and that business

Table 6. Monitoring for cybersecurity incidents

Framework Function: Detect (DE)	
Develop and implement appropriate activities to identify the occurrence of a cybersecurity event.	
Framework Category: Security Continuous Monitoring ***(DE.CM)*** *The information system and assets are monitored to identify cybersecurity events and verify the effectiveness of protective measures.*	***Informative Reference from COBIT 2019*** ***(DSS05.07 – Manage Vulnerabilities and Monitor the Infrastructure for Security-Related Events)*** *Using a portfolio of tools and technologies (e.g., intrusion detection tools), manage vulnerabilities and monitor the infrastructure for unauthorized access. Ensure the security tools, technologies, and detection are integrated with general event monitoring and incident management.*
Framework Subcategory: ***(DE.CM-3)*** *Personnel activity is monitored to detect potential cybersecurity events.*	***Suggested Activity from COBIT 2019*** *Regularly review the event logs for incidents.* ***Suggested Metric from COBIT 2019*** *Number of vulnerabilities discovered during testing.*

Table 7. Responding and minimizing loss

Framework Function: Respond (RS)	
Develop and implement appropriate activities to take action regarding a detected cybersecurity incident.	
Framework Category: Mitigation ***(RS.MI)*** *Activities are performed to prevent expansion of an event, mitigate its effects, and resolve the incident.*	***Informative Reference from COBIT 2019*** ***(APO12.06 – Respond to Risk)*** *Respond in a timely manner to materialized risk events with effective measures to limit the magnitude of loss.*
Framework Subcategory: ***(RS.MI-1)*** *Incidents are contained.*	***Suggested Activity from COBIT 2019*** *Apply the appropriate response plan to minimize the impact when risk incidents occur.* ***Suggested Metric from COBIT 2019*** *Percent of I&T (information and technology) risk action plans executed as designed.*

continuity plans remain up to date and cover every vital business function. Planning should also include how and when to inform essential internal personnel, customers, authorities, employees, and the public. Table 7 illustrates how the NIST Framework can be applied in a way to help ensure that losses from cybersecurity incidents are minimized.

Fundamental Element 5 – Communication

Employee understanding is a key defense against cyberattacks and employees should be regularly trained in cybersecurity issues regarding recognition and reporting. Table 8 shows that the NIST Framework can be used to address ensuring that employees understand their cybersecurity roles.

Table 8. Define employee roles

Framework Function: Respond (RS)
Develop and implement appropriate activities to take action regarding a detected cybersecurity incident.

Framework Category: Communication (RS.CO) *Response activities are coordinated with internal and external stakeholders.*	*Informative Reference from COBIT 2019 (APO01.05 – Establish Roles and Responsibilities)* *Define and communicate roles and responsibilities for enterprise I&T (information and technology), including authority levels, responsibilities, and accountability.*
Framework Subcategory: (RS.CO-1) *Personnel know their roles and order of operations when a response is needed.*	*Suggested Activity from COBIT 2019* *Establish, agree on, and communicate I&T-related roles and responsibilities for all personnel in the enterprise, in alignment with business needs and objectives. Clearly delineate responsibilities and accountabilities, especially for decision making and approvals.* *Suggested Metric from COBIT 2019* *Number of completed role descriptions.*

Table 9. Sharing information

Framework Function: Respond (RS)
Develop and implement appropriate activities to take action regarding a detected cybersecurity incident.

Framework Category: Communication (RS.CO) *Response activities are coordinated with internal and external stakeholders.*	*Informative Reference from COBIT 2019 (BAI08.03 – Use and Share Knowledge)* *Propagate available knowledge resources to relevant stakeholders and communicate how these resources can be used to address different needs (e.g., problem solving, learning, strategic planning, and decision making).*
Framework Subcategory: (RS.CO-5) *Voluntary information sharing occurs with external stakeholders to achieve broader cybersecurity situational awareness.*	*Suggested Activity from COBIT 2019* *Set management expectations and demonstrate appropriate attitude regarding the usefulness of knowledge and the need to share knowledge related to the governance and management of enterprise I&T (information and technology).* *Suggested Metric from COBIT 2019* *Percent of knowledge user satisfaction.*

In addition, sharing information with outside organizations encourages a cooperative effort to deal with current and future cyber risks as organizations can learn from and assist one another. Table 9 shows that the NIST Framework can be used to consider the importance of sharing information about cybersecurity events.

Table 10. Recovery and documenting lessons learned

Framework Function: Recover (RC)	
Develop and implement appropriate activities to maintain plans for resilience and to restore any capabilities or services that were impaired due to a cybersecurity incident.	
Framework Category: Recovery Planning (RC.RP) *Recovery processes and procedures are executed and maintained to ensure restoration of systems or assets affected by cybersecurity events.*	***Informative Reference from COBIT 2019 (DSS02.05 – Resolve and Recover from Incidents)*** *Document, apply, and test the identified solutions or workarounds. Perform recovery actions to restore the I&T (information and technology) related service.*
Framework Subcategory: (RC.RP-1) *Recovery Plan is executed during or after a cybersecurity event.*	***Suggested Activity from COBIT 2019*** *Document incident resolution and assess if the resolution can be used as a future knowledge source.* ***Suggested Metric from COBIT 2019*** *Percent of stakeholder satisfaction with resolution and recovery from incident.*

Fundamental Element 6 - Continuous Improvement

Studying real-life occurrences in addition to system tests and internal audit findings can provide important lessons to improve cybersecurity. It is therefore crucial that a cyber security framework include a process for incident review and self-evaluation. Table 10 illustrates how the NIST framework can be used to address both recovery and continuous improvement through documentation of incident resolutions.

Steps to Establish or Improve a Cybersecurity Program

The NIST Framework (2018) defines the following steps that should be repeated as needed to achieve a program of continuous cybersecurity improvement:

Step 1: **Prioritize and Scope:** "Organization identifies its business/mission objectives and high-level organizational priorities. With this information, the organization makes strategic decisions regarding cybersecurity implementations and determines the scope of systems and assets that support the selected business line or process."

Step 2: **Orient:** "Organization identifies related systems and assets, regulatory requirements, and overall risk approach."

Step 3: **Create a Current Profile:** "Organization develops a Current Profile by indicating which Category and Subcategory outcomes from the Framework Core are currently being achieved."

Step 4: **Conduct a Risk Assessment:** "Organization analyzes the operational environment in order to discern the likelihood of a cybersecurity event and the impact that the event could have on the organization."

Step 5: **Create a Target Profile**: "Create a Target Profile that focuses on the assessment of the Framework Categories and Subcategories describing the organization's desired cybersecurity outcomes."

Step 6: **Determine, Analyze, and Prioritize Gaps:** "Organization compares the Current Profile and the Target Profile to determine gaps. Next, it creates a prioritized action plan to address gaps – reflecting mission drivers, costs and benefits, and risks – to achieve the outcomes in the Target Profile."

Step 7: **Implement Action Plan:** "Organization determines which actions to take to address the gaps, if any, identified in the previous step and then adjusts its current cybersecurity practices in order to achieve the Target Profile."

CPAs and internal auditors can strategically assist an organization's management and board of directors in achieving the above steps. This will allow organizations to implement action plans to address gaps between current and target profiles.

FUTURE RESEARCH DIRECTIONS

Organization programs of cybersecurity are complex and can be difficult to maintain. Some of the following suggestions for future research could help:

- Organizations may have difficulty in deciding which elements of an extensive cybersecurity framework are most important for them to implement. It would be helpful if some cybersecurity elements could be identified as essential to certain types of businesses or industries.
- Accounting education focuses extensively on learning the standards applicable to internal accounting controls, financial reporting, and financial statement audits. Although continued emphasis on these areas is very important, further research should address additional technological training that should be offered to accounting students who want to pursue a specialization in cybersecurity.
- A company's board of directors and audit committee are generally regarded as the persons responsible for the governance of an organization. Future research should further evaluate what and how certain issues regarding cybersecurity should be reported to those charged with governance.

CONCLUSION

Both CPAs and internal auditors have long been instrumental in providing guidance to organization management in regard to internal accounting controls and assurance over traditional financial statement reporting. In addition, both are also known for offering operational auditing, which deals with the effectiveness and efficiency of practically any aspect of company operations. The development of the Internet and accompanying networking capabilities has also resulted in these professionals expanding their capabilities and services to include the realm of cybersecurity.

Regardless of whether services are offered in the form of consulting advice or assurance of the proper functioning an organization's cybersecurity program, such services must be embedded in a framework that is derived from authoritative guidance that is continuously updated to reflect a constantly changing environment. The ISACA is recognized for its contributions to international information system auditing and control standards. One of their most noteworthy contributions is an ongoing project known as the Control Objectives for Information and related Technology (COBIT). This chapter illustrates how the current edition of the National Institute of Standards and Technology (NIST) Framework includes key fundamental elements of a cybersecurity framework that can be linked to authoritative cybersecurity literature including specific references, activities, and metrics from COBIT 2019.

REFERENCES

American Institute of Certified Public Accountants (AICPA). (2018). *A CPA's Introduction to Cybersecurity.* Accessed September 11, 2021. Retrieved from https://www.aicpa.org/InterestAreas/PrivateCompaniesPracticeSection/QualityServicesDelivery/InformationTechnology/DownloadableDocuments/cpa-guide-to-cybersecurity.pdf

Blackwell, L. (2021). Key Aspects of a Cybersecurity Framework. *Internal Auditor*, 14-15. Accessed September 11, 2021. Retrieved from https://theiia.texterity.com/ia/august_2021_internal_auditor/MobilePagedReplica.action?pm=2&folio=14#pg16

Bucher, D. (2021). Protecting against cyberattacks. *Strategic Finance.*

Bwerinofa-Petrozzello, R. (2021). Helping clients before a cyberattack: CPAs play critical roles in building defenses against breaches, fraud and other online threats. *The Journal of Accountancy.* Accessed September 10, 2021. Retrieved from https://www.journalofaccountancy.com/issues/2021/sep/help-clients-before-a-cyberattack.html

Hodge, N. (2021). Reigning in Cyber Risk. *Internal Auditor*, 25-29. Accessed on September 15, 2021. Retrieved from: https://theiia.texterity.com/ia/august_2021_internal_auditor/MobilePagedReplica.action?pm=2&folio=24#pg26

ISACA. (2019). *COBIT 2019 Framework: Introduction and Methodology.* Author.

Lanz, J. (2016). Communication Cybersecurity Risks to the Audit Committee. *The CPA Journal*. Accessed on September 12, 2021. Retrieved from https://www.cpajournal.com/2016/05/21/communicating-cybersecurity-risks-audit-committee/

Mar, S. (2021). The Aftermath of Solarwinds. *Internal Auditor*, (June), 18–19.

Nabe, C. (2021). *Impact of COVID-19 on Cybersecurity*. Deloitte. Accessed September 25, 2021. Retrieved from: https://www2.deloitte.com/ch/en/pages/risk/articles/impact-covid-cybersecurity.html

National Institute of Standards and Technology (NIST). (2018). *Framework for Improving Critical Infrastructure Cybersecurity, version 1.1*. Accessed on September 18, 2021. Retrieved from https://nvlpubs.nist.gov/nistpubs/CSWP/NIST.CSWP.04162018.pdf

Pundmann, S. (2021). Cyber Risk and the Board. *Internal Auditor*, (August), 31–33.

Reporting on an Entity's Cybersecurity Risk Management Program and Controls. (2017). American Institute of Certified Public Accountants.

Turton, W., & Mehrotra, K. (2021). Hackers Breached Colonial Pipeline Using a Compromised Password. *Bloomberg*. Accessed on October 9, 2021. Retrieved from: https://www.bloomberg.com/news/articles/2021-06-04/hackers-breached-colonial-pipeline-using-compromised-password

Zanzig & Francia. (2020). Auditor Evaluation and Reporting on Cybersecurity Risks. In *Encyclopedia of Organizational Knowledge, Administration, and Technology*. Hershey, PA: IGI Global Publishing. www.igi-global.com

ADDITIONAL READING

Al-Moshaigeh, A., Dickins, D., & Higgs, J. (2019). Cybersecurity Risks and Controls: Is the AICPA's SOC for Cybersecurity a Solution? *The CPA Journal*. Accessed September 30, 2021. Retrieved from https://www.cpajournal.com/2019/07/08/cybersecurity-risks-and-controls/

Anders, S. (2020). Cybersecurity Resources for a Remote Workforce. *The CPA Journal*. Accessed October 7, 2021. Retrieved from: https://www.cpajournal.com/2020/09/07/cybersecurity-resources-for-a-remote-workforce/

Bozkus Kahyaoglu, S., & Caliyurt, K. (2018). Cyber security assurance process from the internal audit perspective. *Managerial Auditing Journal*, *33*(4), 360–376. doi:10.1108/MAJ-02-2018-1804

Brazina, P. R., Leauby, B. A., & Sgrillo, C. (2019). Cybersecurity Opportunities for CPA Firms. *Pennsylvania CPA Journal*. Accessed October 7, 2021. Retrieved from https://www.picpa.org/articles/picpa-news/2019/04/24/pa-cpa-journal-cybersecurity-opportunities-for-cpa-firms

Chang, Y. T., Chen, H., Cheng, R. K., & Chi, W. (2019). The impact of internal audit attributes on the effectiveness of internal control over operations and compliance. *Journal of Contemporary Accounting & Economics*, *15*(1), 1–19. doi:10.1016/j.jcae.2018.11.002

Drew, J. (2018). Paving the way to a new digital world. *Journal of Accountancy*, *225*(6), 18–22. Retrieved October 7, 2021, from https://www.journalofaccountancy.com/issues/2018/jun/accounting-technology-roundtable.html

Fine, T., & Tysiac, K. (2021). Cybersecurity requirements provide new opportunities for CPAS. *Journal of Accountancy*. Accessed on October 7, 2021. Retrieved from: https://www.journalofaccountancy.com/news/2021/mar/cybersecurity-requirements-provide-new-opportunity-for-cpas.html

Hamm, K. (2019). Cybersecurity: Where Are We, and What More Can Be Done? *The CPA Journal*. Accessed October 7, 2021. Retrieved from: https://www.cpajournal.com/2019/09/16/cybersecurity-where-are-we-and-what-more-can-be-done/

KEY TERMS AND DEFINITIONS

Assurance: An independent professional service that increases the value of information for the decision maker.

Audit Committee: A committee composed of outside members of a company's board of directors, that is responsible for oversight involving a company's internal controls and information reporting.

Cloud Computing: Data centers that offer data storage and computing power to various organizations; relieving the user organizations of the need to invest resources to establish, maintain, and manage the data centers.

Cybersecurity: A set of processes, practices, and technologies designed to protect, on the realm of cyberspace, and the three tenets of information security: confidentiality, integrity, and availability.

Framework: A grouping of rules and related concepts into a logical approach that can be used to identify complex problems and decide upon appropriate courses of action to address them.

Internal Audit: A group of professionals who work within an organization to perform an independent appraisal activity to achieve efficiency and effectiveness in regard to both operating activities and information reporting.

Internal Controls: Systematic measures instituted by an organization to ensure the integrity of its operations.

Chapter 6
Service Organization Control (SOC) Reports and Their Usefulness

Thomas Tribunella
State University of New York at Oswego, USA

Heidi Tribunella
University of Rochester, USA

ABSTRACT

Many organizations outsource their business processes to service providers. The service providers must be audited by certified public accountants (CPA) to check the design and operation of their security procedures and internal controls (IC). These reports are called service organization control (SOC) reports. Through these reports, a CPA can express an opinion on the ICs of the services provider. SOC reports come in several different formats depending on the circumstance. As outsourcing becomes more popular and computer crimes increase, SOC reports will be more important. The objective of this chapter is to explain SOC reports, how they are compiled, and how they are used. Accordingly, this chapter gives a technical description of SOC reports so that professionals in the areas of accounting, auditing, and risk management can understand the purpose, application, and value of SOC reports. The authors conclude that as managers put more information on the cloud, SOC reports will fill an important need since they inform managers about risk management issues such as internal controls.

DOI: 10.4018/978-1-7998-8390-6.ch006

Copyright © 2022, IGI Global. Copying or distributing in print or electronic forms without written permission of IGI Global is prohibited.

INTRODUCTION

With most organizations accumulating big databases, managers are aware of susceptibility to data breaches. Accordingly, organizations and auditors may require proof that a third-party cloud service company is taking reasonable precautions to protect their data and information. Even if a cloud service processor does not handle financial data but hosts various other types of transactions and processes, a Service and Organization Control (SOC) report may mitigate the risk and impact of a data breach (Shedari, 2013).

The triple interaction framework of internal controls refers to a set of interactions between a service organization, client, and CPA firm, to foster confidence in the internal controls of the service organization. As the knowledge economy expands, more organizations will outsource to cloud-based service providers. This requires an audit of the service organization's internal control to reduce the probability of material errors and fraud. In the triple interaction model of internal controls, each organization is represented by a rectangle, with arrows showing interactions between the three agents. The client in Figure 1 is receiving payroll (PR) services from the service organization. Accordingly, the client's CPA must audit the internal controls over PR at the service organization to be able to complete the client's audit.

SOC reports are relatively new, having started in 2011. They were created by the American Institute of Certified Public Accountants (AICPA). SOC reports can only be issued by a CPA (Certified Public Accounting) firm as the reports are the result of an attestation engagement. An attestation engagement is an examination performed by an independent CPA who checks the system to see if it conforms to industry standards. In addition, similar to auditing, CPA firms that provide SOC reports must commit to a peer review process (Maloney + Novotny, 2020).

Figure 1. Triple interaction framework related to SOC reports

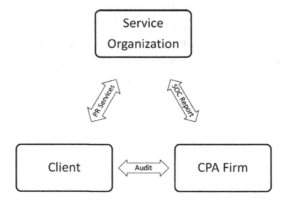

A SOC report (not to be confused with the acronym for security operations center) is a way to verify that a third-party processor, such as a cloud service, is following best or reasonable practices before outsourcing a business function to that third party. SOC reports enable managers and auditors to feel confident that service providers are operating with proper security and internal controls (ICs). Also, auditors will refer to these reports when analyzing the internal control design and operation during an audit of a company that uses a third-party processor for some of their business functions.

A third-party processor should pursue SOC reports if the services impact a client's financial or operational reporting. For example, if a cloud service hosts software and databases that process clients' accounts receivable, billing, and collections data, this affects the client's cash and accounts receivable on the balance sheet (financial reporting). Accordingly, a SOC report is appropriate. Another reason why outside processors pursue SOC reports is if their clients or auditors ask for a "right to audit." Without SOC reporting, this could be a costly and time-intensive process, especially if several clients submit similar requests related to internal controls and cybersecurity (ISACA, 2011). The objective of this chapter is to review SOC reports and the issues related to their completion such as internal controls, types of SOC reports, and audit procedures.

LITERATURE REVIEW

With the growth of cloud services, the importance of SOC reports is growing along with the demand for these reports from CPA firms. Ninety-three percent of companies are considering or already have outsourced some of their operations to a cloud service (Dautovic, 2021). Large and small organizations outsource to save costs and improve efficiency. The most common services outsourced include accounting, customer service, human resource management, financial services, and information technology. Accordingly, IT departments spend 13.6% of their budgets on outsourcing to cloud services (Dautovic, 2021). This has increased from 12.7% in 2019 (Dautovic, 2021). Even though 78% of companies are satisfied with their outsourced functions, 68% percent of these companies are concerned with cloud service dependability (Tech Explore, 2019). This is their biggest concern. They worry about issues such as cybersecurity, stability, reliability, compliance, and intellectual property loss (Laudon & Laudon, 2022).

Proofpoint researchers have found that 92% of Fortune 500 companies were targeted by hackers in 2019 and 60% of those cloud services were successfully hacked. The study showed that there were 15 million unauthorized login attempts with 400,000 successful hacks (Tech Explore, 2019).

For health care organizations, the use of service providers brings even greater risks as health care organizations can be held accountable for data breaches of private health information under the Health Insurance Portability and Accountability Act (HIPAA). Penalties for one violation can be $50,000. There is a cap of $1.5 million annually under HIPAA (McAuliffe, 2020).

SOC reports are a type of internal control report that are issued by a service organization. These reports provide information regarding the risks with an outsourced service. A review of the literature reveals that there are few scholarly articles in the area of SOC reports. Most of the literature is from practitioner-based journals, websites, and blogs. Henk (2020) provided a literature review of internal controls in 2020. This scholarly article addresses the theoretical framework of internal control and the definition of internal control. The literature review makes reference to the Sarbanes Oxley Act of 2002 but does not mention SOC reports. Schoenfeld (2021) has posted a business working paper on cyber risk and SOC audits on the Social Science Research Network (SSRN). This study analyzes the benefits and costs of SOC audits. Based on the study Schoenfeld found:

- Twenty-nine percent of firms in the S&P 500 partake in a SOC audit.
- Business-model exposure to technology predicts that a SOC audit will be undertaken.
- The SOC audits include internal controls over data integrity.
- The average SOC fee is $900,000.

After SOC reports emerged in 2011, Ahmed et al. (2015) found the following trends emerged back in 2015 for early adopters of SOC reports once they had some experience:

- Adopters found it easier to determine the SOC report type to issue.
- Continued improvement allows management assertions to be clearer, risk assessments had better documentation, and system descriptions are more effective.
- Adopters used better technology to execute multiple SOC audits if issuing both SOC 1 and SOC 2 reports.
- Service organizations have been successful at using their internal audit departments to reduce the cost of SOC audits.
- Adopters increased the implementation of user-entity controls.
- Increased interim visits by service auditors allows issues to be identified earlier in the cycle and possibly corrected before the end of the audit period.

Stewart et al. (2021), in a *Wall Street Journal* advertorial, noted the impacts of COVID-19 and the shift to remote work on SOC testing procedures. They noted the following changes:

- There has been a shift to using local auditors to perform physical observations.
- Auditors are conducting walkthrough virtual inspections with the use of video conferencing.
- When multiple locations are involved, the auditor might take a site sampling approach.
- There has been an increase in the reliance on the work of internal audit departments at the service providers.
- Auditors gather other types of evidence such as videos from cameras and physical access mechanisms such as badge reader logs.

Bourke (2016) noted an increased interest in SOC than when SOC was introduced in 2011. Bourke notes the purpose of SOC reporting and the three different types of SOC reports that will be discussed later in this chapter. The differences between SOC 1 and SOC 2 were discussed by Johnson (2021) in a StrongDM blog post and the differences between SOC 2 and SOC 3 reports were discussed in a Linford & Company LLP blog post (Jones, 2020).

METHODOLOGY AND CONTRIBUTION

The methodology of this chapter is qualitative. It is a technical and descriptive chapter. Therefore, this chapter gives a technical description of SOC reports so that professionals concerned with accounting, auditing, and risk management can understand the purpose, application, and value of SOC reports.

As managers put more information on the cloud, SOC reports fill an important need since they inform managers about risk management issues such as internal controls. A review of the literature on SOC reports reveals a conspicuous absence of detailed description and explanation of SOC reports. Accordingly, this chapter contributes to the literature by providing a technical description of SOC reports so that professionals in the areas of accounting, auditing, and risk management can understand the purpose, application, and value of SOC reports. This chapter also adds to the literature by providing a comprehensive overview of all three types of SOC reports and provides much more background information than the Bourke article, which does cover all three SOC reports.

Background of Internal Controls

Internal controls (IC) are methods and procedures for making sure the processing and storage of data are accurate and secure (Anders, 2020). Below the authors review major types of ICs. IC is a voluminous topic that could fill a book by itself. Here the authors want to give the reader a working understanding of IC so they can put SOC reports in the proper context.

Baseline and General Controls

These types of controls can be applied to all parts of the organization. They are the controls that are usually required by upper management and can be implemented by all departments such as the separation of duties. Separation of duties tries to ensure that incompatible functions are not being performed by the same person. The incompatible duties are custody, authorization, and recording (CAR). If these duties are combined within the same employee, it gives the employee the opportunity to commit fraud and cover it up. For example, if the same employee is receiving cash and doing the recordkeeping, they can pocket the cash, not record it, and the company is none the wiser (Romney et al., 2020).

Application Controls

These controls are applied to specific application areas but are not appropriate for all situations. For example, controls over cash receipts are not appropriate for property, plant, and equipment. Application controls include a range of activities as diverse as approvals, authorizations, verifications, reconciliations, operational performance reviews, and asset safety (Romney et al., 2020).

Backup Disaster Recovery (Hot, Warm or Cold Sites)

All organizations should have a backup plan for their information systems. The backup facility should be at another location in case an emergency destroys the primary location. For example, a flood could damage the primary system and the backup if they are at the same facility. Accordingly, the backup should be off-site. The backup locations also need to be configured to minimize delays in operations. Management must choose between a hot, warm, or cold site. A hot site is the most comprehensive of the options as it is a complete copy of your data, systems, and hardware. A hot site could be compared to a natural gas generator where the household members do not really notice when the power goes off and the generator kicks in as soon as it is needed. The opposite of a hot site would be a cold site. The cold site would include just the bare minimum, such as just your data. It would probably not include the hardware. So, when disaster strikes, your users are definitely going to know, and it may take some time to get back up and running. The middle of the road is the warm site. This would include more infrastructure than a cold site, but not be as elaborate as a hot site (Otava, 2016).

TYPES OF SOC REPORTS

SOC 1: Internal Controls Over Financial Reporting

The American Institute of Certified Public Accountants (AICPA) developed SOC 1 to determine the effectiveness of service organization controls on financial reporting. SOC 1 reports cover the general controls that address the risks to users related to the utilization of an online service. The SOC 1 Type 1 report is different from SOC 1 Type 2. Type 1 reports assess the design of security processes and controls at a specific point in time, whereas a Type 2 report assesses how effective those controls are over time by observing operations over a period of time. Type 1 is a snapshot, similar to a balance sheet, while Type 2 covers a period of time, like an income statement does (Johnson, 2021).

SOC 2: Data Security and the 5 Trust Principles (Restricted Use Report)

After the AICPA developed SOC 1 reports, they followed up with SOC 2 in response to growing concerns over data privacy and security. SOC 2 applies to all service providers that process and store customer data. In producing the SOC 2 attestation of compliance, auditors refer to the AICPA's Statement on Standards for Attestation Engagements number 18 (SSAE 18), which emphasizes data security (Johnson, 2021).

SOC 2 Type 1 and 2 reports address a service organization's controls that are relevant to their operations and compliance (Brown, 2022). SOC 2 Type 1 is different from Type 2 in that a Type 1 assesses the design of security processes at a specific point in time, such as documenting the design of internal controls, whereas a Type 2 report assesses how effective those controls are over time by observing operations for a period of time (Brown, 2022). Accordingly, a SOC 2 audit will test the operation of internal controls and security procedures. SOC 2 reports are based on AICPA's Trust Principles. The five Trust Principles are outlined below (Romney et al., 2020):

- **Security:** Systems and data must be protected against unauthorized access.
- **Availability:** Systems need to be available for use and operation when needed by users.
- **Processing integrity:** System processing must be timely, accurate, complete, and authorized.
- **Confidentiality:** Information designated as confidential must be protected from unauthorized access.
- **Privacy:** Personal information must be used, retained, disclosed, and disposed of appropriately.

Once a company obtains a SOC 2 Type 1 report, which attests to compliance at a single point in time, it can follow up with an annual Type 2 audit, which measures ongoing SOC 2 compliance over a period of time.

SOC 2 requires organizations to establish and follow information security policies and procedures. Having the SOC 2 report attesting to an enterprise's compliance means that user of the information can have confidence that the data processing is protected by security and internal controls (Johnson, 2021).

SOC 3: Data Security and the 5 Trust Principles (General Use Report)

Managers often need to show their auditors, bankers, investors, and other interested parties that the organization has adhered to the five Trust Services Principles—Security, Availability, Processing Integrity, Confidentiality, and Privacy—for all shared data and information. A SOC 3 report is meant to be distributed widely and publicly. Therefore, it does not contain as much detailed information as a SOC 2 report. For instance, a SOC 2 report contains details of the internal controls tested, whereas a SOC 3 report would not contain such details since it is intended for a public audience. A SOC 2 is directed toward management and can be used by management to improve the existing internal controls around data security (Kovash, 2019).

SOC Reports for Cybersecurity

SOC for Cybersecurity is a reporting framework through which organizations can communicate relevant useful information about the effectiveness of their cybersecurity risk management design and implementation program. CPAs can report on such information to meet the cybersecurity information needs of a broad range of interested parties and stakeholders. This can give boards of directors, analysts, investors, auditors, regulators, bankers, and other users an assessment and evaluation of an organization's risk management program related to information technology infrastructure and processes (AICPA, n.d.a).

SOC Reports for Supply Chains

This is an internal control report on an entity's system and security related to producing, manufacturing, and distributing products. It helps managers understand the cybersecurity risks and impact in the organization's internal value chains and external supply chains (AICPA, n.d.b).

TYPES OF TESTS AUDITORS APPLY TO SERVICE ORGANIZATIONS

Type 1 Report Tests

This type of investigation examines the design of ICs without looking at the detailed transactions. Here the ICs are analyzed like a blueprint without testing the execution. Below the authors discuss the more popular techniques that auditors use.

Documentation

Auditors can ask if the ICs are formally documented in manuals that are available to the employees. When was the last time these manuals were updated? Do the narratives related to ICs clearly communicate to the reader the details of how the ICs are applied to different business processes? Models of IC can be documented effectively with tools such as an input control matrix (ICM) or a data dictionary, which would list the controls related to database attributes. An example of an ICM related to payroll information is displayed in Table 1. Other models can explain processing, output, preventative, detective, and corrective controls as well as time-based controls and controls in layers (Romney et al., 2020).

Charts

Has the organization formally documented the flow of data and information? Has there been a documentation of the program logic that is used to process data? Accordingly, technology controls related to networks such as intrusion detection systems, routers, servers, the demilitarized zone, and firewalls lend themselves to charts that depict their organization (Arens et al., 2020).

Table 1. Example of an input control matrix

Database attributes	Employee Number	First Name	Last Name	Base Pay	Overtime	Pay Rate
Internal controls						
Auto number	X					
Field length		X	X			
Validation rule						
Maximum value				X	X	X
Minimum value				X		X
Character type	Number	Alpha	Alpha	Number	Number	Number
Required field	X	X	X	X		X

Table 2. Example of an access control matrix (ACM)

Database Attributes	Employee Last Name	Employee Number	Base Pay Rate	Overtime	Fed. Tax Withholding Rate	Payroll Calculation Program
Username						
Jones	CRUD	CRUD				
Qu			RUD	RUD	CR	
Smith						
Zhang						E

Policy

Are there policies that delineate the various authorizations that employees have that allow them to create, read, update, delete, and execute (CRUDE) items in the database? CRUDE can be documented on an access control matrix (ACM). An example of an ACM related to payroll information is displayed in Table 2. Policies can also explain who is involved in ICs. For example, is there a chief security officer, chief information officer, chief technology officer, or vice president of risk management on the upper management team? If so, does this individual report directly to the board? Is there a Computer Emergency Response Team or IT committee that is trained and ready to jump into action in the event of a crisis? Are external communications sent over the public internet encrypted (Romney et al., 2020)?

ACM Legend

- C: Create
- R: Read
- U: Update
- D: Delete
- E: Execute

Environment

Auditors ask: What type of environment is set by the board of directors and upper management? Do they set a tone at the top that emphasizes the importance of ethics and ICs? Auditors can review the board minutes to see how often ICs are discussed. Do they communicate to the rest of the organization that ICs are critical to the operation of the organization? Are these communications documented with memos and email (Arens et al., 2020)?

Type 2 Report Tests

These types of tests are testing IC and detailed transactions over a period of time (Halterman, 2011). Since there may be millions of transactions the auditors will employ statistical sampling. When testing internal controls auditors employ the following tests: Inquiry, Observation, Reperformance, and Inspection.

Inquiry

Inquiry is the first step and allows the auditor to understand the internal control structure. Inquiry involves interviewing members of the client's management team and staff to understand the internal control structure. They may ask the staff person to describe how a particular transaction is processed. After the interview the auditor typically documents the business process in a narrative or flowchart. See below for a detailed description of the internal control documentation methods. Once the process has been documented, it is a good idea to have the client review the auditor's documentation to ensure that the auditor appropriately understood the client's description of the internal control structure (Arens et al., 2020).

Observation

Once the auditor has an understanding of the internal control structure, the auditor can observe the particular business process or transaction occurring while the client is operating. This serves to ensure that the auditor's understanding of the internal control system is correct. It can also serve as a test of internal controls to see if the controls are operating as designed (Arens et al., 2020).

Reperformance

Another way to test the internal control system is to reperform a transaction. You take one transaction and walk it through the entire internal control system. This should allow the auditor to test that the controls are functioning as designed (Arens et al., 2020).

Inspection

Inspection involves reviewing various business documents that show signs of review or authorization. Usually, a sample of transactions is used for inspection. While inspecting, auditors are looking for evidence of a review such as a signature, a type of checkmark, or a stamp. Auditors have to be cautious in this area, as it is possible for client personnel to sign or indicate they reviewed when in fact they did not review the transaction at all. Here some additional inquiry might be helpful to get comfort that the supervisor is actually reviewing the transactions that auditors are testing (Arens et al., 2020).

INTERNAL CONTROL DOCUMENTATION

Documentation of internal control systems and the auditor's testing is extremely important. Auditing standards require auditors to understand the ICs and that understanding must be documented in their workpapers. Different types of documentation are discussed below.

Narratives

A narrative is a memo-type documentation that tells the story of the internal control structure. It is a written description of internal controls and processes of a particular business cycle. Structured narratives are narratives that have been organized in a matrix where the columns identify items such as data sources (e.g., customers), data storage, information processing, and data destinations (e.g., management; Arens et al., 2020).

Data Flow Diagram

A data flow diagram is another way of documenting internal controls but instead of "telling a story," it draws a picture of how data flows through the internal control system. It uses a number of different symbols to draw the picture of the internal controls. The data flow diagram depicts the logic of the system rather than the physical attributes of the system (Romney et al., 2020).

Flowcharts

Flowcharts are the most popular diagram, and they are often used to understand the internal controls. There are various versions of flowcharts. A document flowchart is a picture of how documents move through the internal control system. Document flowcharts are frequently used by auditors. System flowcharts, like data flow diagrams, show how data flows through an internal controls system and shows controls that are in place in the business process. System flowcharts focus more on the computer architecture of a system. They are used more by computer scientists. Both document and systems flowcharts document the physical attributes of the system.

A program flowchart shows how data flows and is processed within a computer program. This tool can be used by software engineers to document the program logic and the particular algorithm being employed (Romney et al., 2020).

Internal Control Questionnaires

Internal control questionnaires are a predefined list of questions that assist the auditor in understanding the internal control structure. These questionnaires can be used to help guide inquiry meetings when first gaining an understanding of the internal controls (Arens et al., 2020).

Process Diagrams

A process diagram is a flowchart that documents the relationships between major components of an internal control system and how different systems interact, such as the revenue cycle with the cash receipts cycle. Process diagrams also highlight who is responsible for which controls and processes (Romney et al., 2020).

EXAMPLE STANDARD SOC REPORT

SOC Report Opinions

CPAs will audit and investigate a service organization and check the design and function of the security and internal controls. When CPAs issue a SOC report they express an opinion on how well the security and internal controls are working based on the five trust standards. Listed below are the various types of SOC report opinions (Arens et al., 2020):

- **Standard Unqualified:** This is a clean opinion, and the auditor supports the findings with no modifications to the standard unqualified report.
- **Unqualified:** The auditor writes an unqualified report but adds an explanatory paragraph to emphasize an issue.
- **Qualified:** The auditor cannot express an unqualified opinion. However, the issues are not material enough to issue an adverse report. The auditor adds an explanatory paragraph to point out a potential problem which may be significant.
- **Adverse:** The auditor believes that there are material and pervasive issues with the security or internal controls. Report readers should not rely on the vendor's system.
- **Disclaimer:** The auditors' scope was limited, or the auditors are not independent, and they are unable to express an opinion.

Below is an example of a standard SOC report. The auditors are Smith and Company CPAs, and the service organization is XYZ Service Corporation, providing Platform as a Service (PaaS) to clients. The report is a SOC 2 type 2 report. XYZ corporation in turn uses Amazon Web Services (AWS) as an infrastructure provider. This shows the complex web of relationships that can occur between various service providers and clients (AICPA, 2014).

Independent Auditor's Report To:

XYZ Service Corporation

Assessment Scope

Smith and Company CPAs has examined XYZ Service Corporation's description of its Platform as a Service (PaaS), the suitability of the design of internal controls, and the operating effectiveness of controls during the period from January 1, 2020, to December 31, 2020, to achieve the related control objectives. The documentation indicates that certain control objectives specified in the description can be achieved only if complementary controls and operating effectiveness of XYZ Corporation's controls are designed and operating effectively, along with related controls at the service organization. We have not evaluated the suitability of the design and operating effectiveness of such complementary user entity controls. XYZ Corporation uses the Amazon Web Services (AWS) Infrastructure as a Service (IaaS) platform for clients' production and backup services. The description of the system in this report includes only the controls of XYZ Corporation and excludes the related controls of AWS. Our examination did not extend to controls of AWS.

Service Organization's Responsibilities

XYZ Corporation has provided an assertion about the fair presentation of the description and the suitability of the design of their internal controls to achieve the related control objectives. XYZ is responsible for preparing the description and for its assertion, including the completeness, accuracy, and presentation of the description. XYZ is also responsible for providing the services covered by the description, specifying the control objectives, identifying the risks related to the achievement of the control objectives, selecting the criteria and designing, implementing, and documenting controls to achieve the related control objectives.

Service Auditors' Responsibilities

Our responsibility is to express an opinion on the fairness of the presentation of the description and on the suitability of the design and operating effectiveness of the controls to achieve the related control objectives, based on our examination. We conducted our examination in accordance with attestation standards established by the American Institute of Certified Public Accountants. Those standards require that we plan and perform our examination to obtain reasonable assurance about whether, in all material respects, the description is fairly presented, and the controls were suitably designed and operating effectively to achieve the related control objectives stated in the description of assessment period. An examination of a description of a service organization's system and the suitability of the design of the service organization's controls to achieve the related control objectives involves the design suitability and operating effectiveness of those controls to achieve the related control objectives. Our procedures included assessing the risks that the description is not fairly presented and that the controls were not suitably designed and operating effectively to achieve the related control objectives stated in the description. An examination engagement of this type also includes evaluating the overall description and the suitability of the control objectives, and the appropriateness of the criteria specified by the service organization and described in Management's assertion. We believe that the evidence we obtained is sufficient and appropriate to provide a reasonable basis for our opinion.

Inherent Limitations

Because of their nature, internal controls at a service organization may not prevent, or detect and correct, all errors and omissions. Furthermore, the projection into the future of any evaluation of the fairness of the description, or conclusions about the suitability of the design of the controls to achieve the related control objectives, is subject to the risk that controls at a service organization may become inadequate or fail.

Description of the Tests of Controls

The specific controls reviewed are listed in the section titled Control Objectives and Related Controls.

Assessors' Opinion

We have examined the attached description titled "XYZ Service Corporation's Description of its Platform as a Service (PaaS) throughout the period January 1, 2020 to December 31, 2020" and the suitability of the design and operating effectiveness of controls to meet the criteria for the Security, Availability, Processing Integrity, Confidentiality, and Privacy principles set forth in TSP section 100, Trust Services Principles and Criteria, throughout the period January 1, 2020, to December 31, 2020. The description indicates that certain applicable trust services criteria specified in the description can be achieved only if complementary user entity controls contemplated in the design of XYZ Corporation's controls are suitably designed and operating effectively, along with related controls at the service organization. We have not evaluated the suitability of the design or operating effectiveness of such complementary user-entity controls. XYZ Corporation utilizes the Amazon Web Services (AWS) Infrastructure as a Service (IaaS) platform for data center hosting services. XYZ Corporation's control objectives and related controls, which are listed in Section C of this report, include only the control objectives and related controls of XYZ Corporation.

XYZ Corporation has provided the attached assertion titled "XYZ Corporation's Description of its Platform as a Service (PaaS) throughout the period January 1, 2020, to December 31, 2020," which is based on the criteria identified by management. XYZ Corporation is responsible for (1) preparing the description and assertion; (2) the completeness, accuracy, and method of presentation of both the description and assertion; (3) providing the services covered by the description; (4) specifying the controls that meet the applicable trust services criteria and stating them in the description; and (5) designing, implementing, and documenting the controls to meet the applicable trust services criteria.

Our responsibility is to express an opinion on the fairness of the presentation based on the description criteria set forth in XYZ Corporation's assertion and on the suitability of the design and operating effectiveness of the controls to meet the applicable trust services criteria, based on our examination. We conducted our examination in accordance with attestation standards established by the American Institute of Certified Public Accountants.

Those standards require that we plan and perform our examination to obtain reasonable assurance about whether, in all material respects, (1) the description is fairly presented based on the description criteria, and (2) the controls were suitably designed and operating effectively to meet the applicable trust services criteria throughout the period January 1, 2020, to December 31, 2020.

Our examination involved performing procedures to obtain evidence about the fairness of the presentation of the description based on the description criteria and the suitability of the design and operating effectiveness of those controls to meet the applicable trust services criteria. Our procedures included assessing the risks that the description is not fairly presented and that the controls were not suitably designed or operating effectively to meet the applicable trust services criteria. Our procedures also included testing the operating effectiveness of those controls that we consider necessary to provide reasonable assurance that the applicable trust services criteria were met.

Our examination also included evaluating the overall presentation of the description. We believe that the evidence we obtained is sufficient and appropriate to provide a reasonable basis for our opinion.

Because of their nature and inherent limitations, controls at a service organization may not always operate effectively to meet the applicable trust services criteria. Furthermore, the projection into the future of any evaluation of the fairness of the presentation of the description or conclusions about the suitability of the design or operating effectiveness of the controls to meet the applicable trust services criteria is subject to the risks that the system may change or that controls at a service organization may become inadequate and fail. In our opinion, in all material respects, based on the description criteria identified in XYZ Corporation's assertion and the applicable trust services criteria:

- The description fairly presents the system that was designed and implemented throughout the period January 1, 2020, to December 31, 2020.
- The controls stated in the description were suitably designed to provide reasonable assurance that the applicable trust services criteria would be met if the controls operated effectively throughout the period January 1, 2020, to December 31, 2020, and user entities applied the complementary controls in the design of XYZ Corporation controls throughout the period.
- The controls tested, which together with the complementary user-entity controls, if operating effectively, were those necessary to provide reasonable assurance that the applicable trust services criteria were met, operated effectively throughout the period January 1, 2020, to December 31, 2020.

The specific controls we tested, and the nature, timing, and results of our tests, are presented in section C our report.

This report and the description of tests of controls and results thereof are intended solely for the information and use of XYZ Corporation user entities of Platform as a Service (PaaS) during some or all of the period January 1, 2020, to December 31, 2020; and prospective user entities, independent auditors, and practitioners providing services to such user entities, and regulators who have sufficient knowledge and understanding of the following:

- The nature of the service provided by the service organization.
- How the service organization's system interacts with user entities, subservice organizations, or other parties.
- Internal control and its limitations.
- Complementary user-entity controls and how they interact with related controls at the service organization to meet the applicable trust services criteria.
- The applicable trust services criteria.
- The risks that may threaten the achievement of the applicable trust services criteria and how controls address those risks.

Restricted Use

This report and the description of the suitability of the design and operating effectiveness of controls in this report are intended solely for the information and use of XYZ's Platform as a Service (PaaS) for the assessment period and the independent auditors of such user entities, who have a sufficient understanding to consider it, along with other information including information about the controls implemented by user entities themselves, when assessing the risks and regulatory compliance of non-financial reporting controls. This report is not intended to be and should not be used by anyone other than those specified parties.

Sincerely,

Sue Smith, CPA

Smith CPAs

123 Jones Street

New York, NY

ARE SOC REPORTS REQUIRED?

These reports are required by an organization seeking an external auditor's independent opinion on the organization's financial statements. A company can outsource processing and data storage related to business functions such as human resources. However, a company cannot outsource its ownership and responsibility for the integrity of financial information and operational data. If a company is publicly traded (issues stock and bonds to the public over a U.S. exchange), it will need to pursue a SOC 1 report as part of the Sarbanes-Oxley Act (SOX). Below, the authors have highlighted more information about the various regulators and the regulations they follow.

American Institute of Certified Public Accountants (AICPA)

The AICPA is the world's largest member association representing the accounting profession. AICPA produces a number of different guidance documents on a variety of accounting and auditing issues. They have the following guidance available related to SOC reporting:

- Reporting on an Examination of Controls at a Service Organization Relevant to User Entities' Internal Control of Financial Reporting (SOC 1).
- SOC 2 Reporting on an Examination of Controls at a Service Organization Relevant to Security, Availability, Processing Integrity, Confidentiality or Privacy.
- Trust Services Criteria for Security, Availability, Processing Integrity, Confidentiality and Privacy. The five trust services criteria were developed by the AICPA and the Canadian Institute of Chartered Accountants.
- 2018 Description Criteria for a Description of a Service Organizations System in a SOC 2 Report.
- 2015 Description Criteria for a Description of a Service Organizations System in a SOC 2 Report.

Securities and Exchange Commission (SEC)

This is a division of the federal government that is responsible for overseeing the security exchanges, such as the New York Stock Exchange, securities brokers and dealers, investment advisors, and mutual funds. Their main concerns in this oversight are to promote fair dealing of security transactions and disclosure of important market information, and to prevent fraud.

Sarbanes-Oxley Act

The Sarbanes-Oxley Act of 2002 (SOX) was passed by Congress in response to a number of accounting and financial statement fraud cases that occurred in the very late 1990s and early 2000s. This act has several key areas that affected the accounting profession (Romney et al., 2020):

1. Requirement of the chief executive officer and chief financial officer to certify the financial statements.
2. Creation of management assessment of internal controls and the auditor's assessment of internal controls. This requires management to annually assess their internal control structure for material weaknesses in their system and for the auditors of the financial statements to express an opinion on management's assessment of internal controls. These requirements were included in Section 404 of SOX.
3. Creation of the Public Company Accounting Oversight Board (PCAOB). This including regulating the public accounting firms that audit public companies.

Public Company Accounting Oversight Board

This oversight board was created by SOX. This oversight board oversees the audits and auditing firms of public companies. This was a large change to the accounting profession because it greatly increased government regulations of public accounting firms.

Most publicly traded companies are now required to issue their SOC reports under the Statement on Standards for Attestation Engagements (SSAE) 18, the standard for a SOC 1 report. SSAE 18 is an auditing standard that auditors use to investigate the controls of technology vendors (such as cloud service providers) and other service providers so that clients using those vendors can be confident that the vendors' internal controls and security are designed well and functioning reasonably. SOC 1 reports include the design and testing of controls to report on the operational effectiveness of controls related to financial reporting (Johnson, 2021).

Many financial statement users will also want a SOC 2 report. A SOC 2 report is an engagement performed under the standards of AICPA (SSAE 18). Another auditing standard used by auditors is AT (attest engagements) section 101. It is based on the existing SysTrust and WebTrust principles developed by AICPA. AT section 101 was written by the Public Company Accounting Oversight Board (PCAOB) and relates to attest engagements of publicly traded company by certified public accountants (CPAs). However, not only do many companies expect SOC 2 compliance from their service providers, but having a SOC 2 report attesting to compliance confers confidence in the resulting data and information such as financial statements (PCAOB, 2016).

Internal Control Frameworks: COSO and COBIT

COSO stands for the Committee of Sponsoring Organizations of the Treadway Commission. They wrote the Enterprise Risk Management (ERM) framework. This is the most popular IC framework in the United States, and it has five components known as CRIME (Arens et al., 2020):

- **Control activities:** The policies and procedures that help ensure that IC directives are adhered to. They occur throughout the organization from strategic to operational levels.
- **Risk assessment:** Each organization faces a wide variety of risks from external and internal sources. Risk assessment is a prerequisite for determining how risks should be estimated and managed by administrators.
- **Information and communication:** Information communication plays an important role in IC systems. Effective communication with internal and external parties increases the probability of compliance.
- **Monitoring:** IC systems must be continuously monitored, which is the process of evaluating the effectiveness of system performance over time.
- **Environment:** Sets the tone of an organization since the board and management are influencing the control consciousness of its employees.

COBIT stands for Control Objectives for Information and Related Technologies. It is not as popular as the COSO framework but is still influential with internal auditors. It was developed by the Information Systems Audit and Control Association which offers various certification programs (Romney et al., 2020).

SOLUTIONS AND RECOMMENDATIONS

As more organizations outsource their business processes to service providers such as cloud providers, problems occur with security and ICs. Clients can outsource their processes to service providers, but they cannot eliminate their responsibility for security and ICs. As a result, service providers must maintain ICs and those controls must be examined for effectiveness. Accordingly, a CPA can audit the controls at service providers and express an opinion on those controls, though the issuance of a SOC report. There is a variety of SOC reports depending on the needs of the client, discussed earlier in the chapter.

LIMITATION OF THE CHAPTER AND FUTURE RESEARCH DIRECTIONS

The major limitation of this chapter is that it is not empirical. The methodology of this chapter is qualitative. This is a technical and descriptive chapter. The objective is to explain and describe the function of SOC reports from a technical point of view.

As noted in the literature review, there are few scholarly articles on SOC reports. This is a new area where research could be conducted. Researchers could do an empirical analysis in the future to determine the economic efficiency of SOC reports. There are several empirical questions that could be addressed. For example: Are SOC reports correlated with reduced fraud and errors? Do SOC reports lower costs by reducing audit fees? Furthermore, users and providers could provide their perceptions of SOC reports. A survey could be developed and distributed asking managers and other SOC report users if they believe SOC reports add value to financial information. In addition, researchers could ask: Do service providers believe that SOC reports add confidence to the services they offer? Studies could be done to see if the issuance of a particular opinion in a SOC report has any impact on the stock price of the service provider. Studies might focus on if there are differences in the SOC opinions and the opinions on the internal controls over financial reporting of certain companies. Since SOX and SOC reports are both focused on ICs, some of the academic research conducted around SOX could be updated to include SOC reports. Comparison research could also be done on what procedures were used in SOC testing before the shift to remote work because of COVID and what the procedures look like now, after the shift to remote work that seems to be here to stay. This is a new area of auditing and will provide new areas of research for academics.

The future of SOC reports is related to the way service organization will be audited. These organizations will be audited remotely and continuously in the future. Since a client can outsource through the internet, the service organization can be located anywhere in the world. This lends itself to remote work. In addition, rather than auditing a service provider once per period, auditors could continuously audit service providers to continually check their security and internal controls. As outsourcing increases, this issue will grow in importance.

SUMMARY AND CONCLUSION

The objective of this chapter is to explain SOC reports, how they are compiled, and how they are used. The usefulness of SOC reports is also explained. Accordingly, this chapter gives a technical description of SOC reports so that professionals in the areas of accounting, auditing, and risk management can understand the purpose, application, and value of SOC reports. While the SOC 1 report is mainly concerned with examining controls over financial reporting, the SOC 2 and SOC 3 reports focus more on the predefined, standardized benchmarks for controls related to security, processing integrity, confidentiality, or privacy of the data center's system and information (Otava, 2011). SOC 1 and 2 reports offer both Type 1 and Type 2 reports. A Type 1 report demonstrates that a company's internal controls are properly designed. In addition, a Type 2 report further demonstrates that the controls operate effectively over a period of time (Otava, 2011).

In conclusion, a service organization should consider investing in the audit required for a SOC report. Many companies expect SOC compliance from their service providers and IT vendors. Accordingly, a SOC report attesting to compliance with security standards confers confidence in the system.

ACKNOWLEDGMENT

This research received no specific grant from any funding agency in the public, commercial, or not-for-profit sectors.

REFERENCES

Ahmed, A., Horn, S., & Smith, R. (2015). *Lessons from the first three years of SOC reporting.* Crowe Horwath LLP. https://www.crowe.com/-/media/Crowe/LLP/folio-pdf/Lessons-From-First-Three-Years-of-SOC-Reporting_RISK15910.pdf

AICPA. (2014). *Illustrative type 2 SOC 2^{SM} report with the criteria in the cloud security (CSA) cloud controls matrix (CCM)*. https://us.aicpa.org/content/dam/aicpa/interestareas/frc/assuranceadvisoryservices/downloadabledocuments/soc2_csa_ccm_report.pdf

AICPA. (n.d.a). *SOC for cybersecurity*. https://www.aicpa.org/interestareas/frc/assuranceadvisoryservices/aicpacybersecurityinitiative.html

AICPA. (n.d.b). *SOC for supply chain*. https://us.aicpa.org/interestareas/frc/assuranceadvisoryservices/soc-for-supply-chain

Anders, S. B. (2020, February). System organization controls resources. *The CPA Journal*. https://www.cpajournal.com/2020/03/23/system-organization-controls-resources/

Arens, A., Elder, R., Beasley, M., & Hogan, C. (2020). *Auditing and assurance services* (17th ed.). Pearson.

Bourke, J. C. (2016, June 13). Explaining the 3 faces of SOC. *Journal of Accountancy*. https://www.journalofaccountancy.com/newsletters/2016/jun/3-face-of-soc.html

Brown, S. (2022, March 7). *SOC2 Type 1 Guide: Everything You need To Know*. StrongDM Blog. https://www.strongdm.com/blog/what-is-soc-2-type-1

Dautovic, G. (2021). *15 must-know outsourcing statistics for 2021*. https://fortunly.com/statistics/outsourcing-statistics/#gref

Halterman, C. (2011, June 30). Expanding service organization controls reporting. *Journal of Accountancy*. https://www.journalofaccountancy.com/issues/2011/jul/20103500.html

Henk, O. (2020). Internal control through the lens of institutional work: A systematic literature Review. *Journal of Management Control, 31*(3), 239–273. doi:10.100700187-020-00301-4

Information Systems Audit and Control Association (ISACA). (2011). Understanding the new SOC Reports. *ISACA Journal*. https://www.isaca.org/resources/isaca-journal/past-issues/2011/understanding-the-new-soc-reports

Johnson, B. (2021). The differences between SOC 1 vs SOC 2. *StrongDM*. https://www.strongdm.com/blog/soc-1-vs-soc-2

Jones, S. (2021, December 2). 6 reasons why you need SOC 2 compliance. *Reciprocity*. https://reciprocity.com/6-reasons-why-you-need-soc-2-compliance/

Kovash, M. (2019). *SOC 2 vs. SOC 3 reports: What is the difference?* Linford & Co LLP Blog. https://linfordco.com/blog/soc-2-vs-soc-3/

Laudon, K. C., & Laudon, J. P. (2022). *Management information systems: Managing the digital firm* (17th ed.). Pearson.

Maloney + Novotny LLC. (2020). *History of SOC reports*. https://socreport.com/history-of-soc-reports/

McAuliffe, S. M. (2020). System and organization controls for healthcare organizations. *Keiter CPAs blog*. https://keitercpa.com/blog/system-organization-controls-for-healthcare/

Otava. (2011, August 19). *Service Organization Control Reports: SOC1, SOC2 & SOC3*. https://www.otava.com/blog/soc-1-soc-2-soc-3-report-comparison/

Otava. (2016, January 28). *What is the difference between a cold, warm and hot disaster recovery site?* https://www.otava.com/blog/what-is-the-difference-between-a-cold-warm-and-hot-disaster-recovery-site/

Romney, M., Steinbart, P., Summers, S., & Wood, D. (2020). *Accounting information systems* (15th ed.). Prentice.

Schoenfeld, J. (2022, February 8). *Cyber risk and voluntary Service Organization Control (SOC) Audits*. Tuck School of Business Working Paper No. 3596065. doi:10.2139/ssrn.3596065

Shedari, D. (2013, March 1). Common myths of service organization controls (SOC) reports. *ISACA Journal*. https://www.isaca.org/resources/isaca-journal/past-issues/2013/common-myths-of-service-organization-controls-soc-reports

Tech Explore. (2019, September 15). *60% of major US firms have been hacked in cloud: Study*. https://techxplore.com/news/2019-09-major-firms-hacked-cloud.html

ADDITIONAL READING

Brown, C. (2018). *The state of cloud adoption*. Deloitte. https://deloitte.wsj.com/articles/the-state-of-cloud-adoption-1541988132

GoCardless. (n.d.). *What are tests of control in auditing?* https://gocardless.com/en-au/guides/posts/what-are-tests-of-control-in-auditing/

Pierce, R. (2020, December 29). *What is a SOC 1 report? Expert advice you need to know*. Linford & Co LLP Blog. https://linfordco.com/blog/what-is-soc-1-report/

Public Company Accounting Oversite Board (PCAOB). (2016). *Attestation standards (AT 101)*. https://pcaobus.org/oversight/standards/attestation-standards/details/AT101

Stewart, C., Jay, C., Rubin, S., & Kaewert, K. (2021). *SOC audits adapt to COVID-19 conditions*. Deloitte. https://deloitte.wsj.com/articles/soc-audits-adapt-to-covid-19-conditions-01616698928

KEY TERMS AND DEFINITIONS

Attestation Engagement: An examination performed by an independent CPA who checks the system to see if it conforms to industry standards.

Auditing: The process of examining compliance with regulations or other standards. Financial auditing is usually done by external CPAs, internal auditors can assist the external CPAs. All publicly traded companies in the United States must be audited once per year.

Certified Public Accountant (CPA): An individual who holds a state license which allows them to practice auditing services. They also do a wide variety of other financial services such as tax, consulting, and other financial statement services.

Cybersecurity: Security of computer-based systems. These systems employ a wide variety of methods such as encryption, firewalls, backup, and internal controls.

Information Systems: Any system that reports information to the management of an organization. These systems also receive and store data as well as process and output information.

Internal Controls: Controls that assure the privacy, accuracy, and security of data and information. These controls can be broad-based or specific to a particular application.

Sarbanes-Oxley (SOX) Act: Passed in 2002 after a series of corporate frauds, SOX requires management of publicly traded companies to take responsibility for financial statements. It also requires auditors to express an opinion on a company's ICs (section 404) as well as their financial statements. SOX created the Public Company Accounting Oversite Board (PCAOB) to regulate the auditing profession.

Securities and Exchange Commission (SEC): This is a regulatory governmental organization that sets standards for publicly traded companies and securities. They also create regulations for the CPA profession through the PCAOB. It was created in 1934 as a reaction to the stock market crash of 1929.

Service Organization Control (SOC) Reports: Reports completed by CPAs that express an opinion on the design and operation of a service organization's security and ICs. There are several types of SOC reports.

Service Organizations: Organizations that provide services for clients. In the context of this chapter, service organizations provide a variety of financial and information type services to clients such as cloud storage and data processing.

Section 4
Other Information Security Concerns

Chapter 7
Corporate Governance and Financial Risk Disclosure:
Empirical Evidence in the Portuguese Capital Market

Kátia Lemos
ⓘ https://orcid.org/0000-0002-3961-5964
Research Centre on Accounting and Taxation, Polytechnic Institute of Cávado and Ave, Portugal

Sara Serra
ⓘ https://orcid.org/0000-0003-3107-1752
Research Centre on Accounting and Taxation, Polytechnic Institute of Cávado and Ave, Portugal

Filipa Pacheco
Management School, Polytechnic Institute of Cávado and Ave, Portugal

Maria Sofia Martins
Management School, Polytechnic Institute of Cávado and Ave, Portugal

ABSTRACT

The aim of this study is to analyze the influence of certain characteristics associated with the corporate governance model on the level of disclosure of financial risks in non-financial entities listed in Euronext Lisbon. For this purpose, a content analysis of the reports and accounts of those companies was conducted for the periods 2017 to 2019 through a disclosure index based on the disclosure requirements contained in international financial reporting standards. Subsequently, in order to assess the influence of the corporate governance model on the level of risk disclosure, several simple linear regression models were estimated, which correlate the disclosure index with certain characteristics associated with the board of directors and the auditor. The results obtained show that larger boards of directors with greater

DOI: 10.4018/978-1-7998-8390-6.ch007

Copyright © 2022, IGI Global. Copying or distributing in print or electronic forms without written permission of IGI Global is prohibited.

gender diversity and auditors belonging to the Big 4 positively influence the level of disclosure of financial risks.

INTRODUCTION

The events that marked the most recent international financial crisis have highlighted the importance of transparency in financial information, especially with regard to the risks incurred by companies and the strategies adopted to mitigate and manage those risks.

For users of financial information to be able to make the right decisions, it is necessary that they have sufficient and reliable information. As such, there has been a great concern with the levels of information disclosure, both in terms of quantitative and qualitative aspects. In fact, the occurrence of numerous financial scandals has led stakeholders to demand more transparent and reliable financial information. One of the measures found to address this problem, as well as to promote the credibility of the financial statements, is the existence of corporate governance mechanisms, namely, the bodies' management and supervisory bodies.

Therefore, companies sought solutions to improve their financial reports and one of those solutions is the disclosure of information to shareholders (Salehi et al., 2017 and Alsuwaigh et al., 2020), who need reliable and complete information to make their decisions. Disclosure about risks and the strategies adopted in their management helps investors to assess companies' risks and predict their market value (Abdullah et al., 2017 and Veltri et al., 2020), reducing information asymmetries and increasing market liquidity (Elshandidy & Neri, 2015). On the other hand, corporate governance is considered fundamental in companies, especially after the financial collapse of some companies, and aims to optimize the performance of organizations through a set of rules and procedures.

The main objective of this work is to study the influence of the corporate governance model on the level of disclosure of risk information in non-financial entities listed on Euronext Lisbon. To this end, we have conducted a content analysis on the consolidated annual Reports and Accounts of the companies that compose the sample, for the periods of 2017, 2018 and 2019.

To measure the level of risk disclosure, we have used a disclosure index, based on the disclosure requirements contained in International Financial Reporting Standards, and later, using simple linear regression models, we have tested if certain characteristics associated with the corporate governance model have some influence on the levels of disclosure presented by the companies under analysis.

This work pretends to contribute to the investigation on the financial risk disclosure practices adopted by companies and on the influence of corporate governance mechanisms on the information disclosed, and may be useful for researchers, accounting standards bodies and entities responsible for defining enforcement mechanisms.

To carry out the defined objectives, after this introduction, this chapter is divided into 6 sections. In the next section, a brief literature review is carried out and the research hypotheses are defined in the following section. The subsequent section is dedicated to the research design, by defining the sample and describing the collection and treatment of data. Afterwards the results obtained are presented and discussed. Finally, the solutions and recommendations, the future research directions and the conclusion are presented.

BACKGROUND

Over the years, the concept of risk has gained more importance and, according to Solomon et al. (2000), Mohobbot and Noriyuki (2005), Linsley and Shrives (2006), Oliveira et al. (2011b), Bessis (2015), and Abdullah et al. (2017), the risk is inherent to all businesses and companies. However, according to ICAEW (2011), the risks are specific to the business model and the circumstances of each company. There is a variety of risks.

According to Amaral (2015), risks can be classified as financial risks and non-financial risks. The first risks are related to the institution's monetary assets and liabilities, and are subdivided into credit risk, market risk, and liquidity risk. In turn, non-financial risks result from external circumstances (social, political, or economic phenomena) or internal (human resources, technologies, procedures, and others) to the institution. These risks are subdivided into several sub-categories such as business risk, strategic risk, conflict of interest risk and legal risk. There are also other risks, such as specific risks, whose negative impact results in a strong imbalance for the entire financial system.

Therefore, disclosure of risks is relevant for companies and investors (Mohobbot & Noriyuki, 2005; Gonidakis, Koutupis, Tsamis & Agoraki, 2020; Jaffar, Al Sheikh, Hassan & Abdullah, 2021; Saha & Kabra, 2021). According to Combes-Thue et al. (2006), the disclosure of risks is central to the communication of companies and is considered one of the most valued information by investors (Bozzolan & Miihkinen, 2021). In fact, according to Serrasqueiro (2010), one of the main reasons for risks disclosure is to guarantee investors the information necessary to assess their investment decisions.

For Bushman and Landsman (2010), market discipline depends on transparency in financial reporting, as this will allow investors to monitor the institution's financial health and make investment decisions. Thus, one of the first objectives of risks disclosure is to keep the investor informed, allowing for a better risk assessment and definition of the company's risk profile. According to Beretta and Bozzolan (2004), investors need to understand the risks that a company takes to create value.

The disclosure of risk reduces information asymmetries between investors and companies (Serrasqueiro, 2010). Kim and Yasuda (2018) and Deumes and Knechel (2008) report that disclosure of risk reduces the cost of capital by disclosing reliable information to investors. They will be reassured and end up demanding a lower cost of capital. Solomon et al. (2000) and Saleem and Usman (2021) add that, in addition to reducing information asymmetries, the disclosure of risk information improves investor relations since they are informed about the company's prospects.

According to Ebrahimi Maimand and Namazi (2021), in addition to contributing to capital reduction, risk disclosure helps to manage changes and report the future trajectory of the entity's business model. As such, risk disclosure should be mandatory for all companies.

Despite the stated advantages, companies tend to disclose little information about risks. In fact, according to Linsley and Shrives (2006), ICAEW (2011), Oliveira et al. (2011a), and Kravet and Muslu (2013), currently, information about risks is not enough for stakeholders to be able to make their decisions. One of the reasons is related to the threat of litigation by shareholders and other stakeholders. Moreover, according to Deumes and Knechel (2008), when the managers make statements that may be wrong endangering their reputation.

Furthermore, the fact that the process of collecting, evaluating, and disseminating information involves costs (Healy & Palepu, 2001; Prencipe, 2002; Linsley & Shrives, 2006), which can be disproportionately higher for smaller companies (Deumes & Knechel, 2008). Another reason for the limited disclosure of risks is related to the competitiveness of companies. When a company discloses detailed information about risks, it may be revealing information with commercial sensitivity and may lose market competitiveness to other companies and, consequently, its market value (Verrecchia, 2001; Deumes & Knechel, 2008). Kravet and Muslu (2013) also report that risk assessments are often considered negative information, causing managers to omit them because of concerns about their careers. Furthermore, given its nature and constant change, it is difficult to measure the disclosure of risks.

RESEARCH HYPOTHESES

Board of Directors' Size

Fathi (2013) and Martins (2014) state that the board of directors' size has a positive impact on the quality of the financial information disclosed. In this context, the results of the studies by Ntim et al. (2013), Elshandidy and Neri (2015), Moumen et al. (2016), Carmona et al. (2016), Saggar and Singh (2017) Akbar et al. (2017), Alkurdi et al. (2019) revealed that larger boards of directors contribute to increased risk disclosure. In contrast, Oliveira et al. (2018), Alshirah et al. (2020), as well as Bufarwa et al. (2020) did not find a statistically significant relationship between board size and the level of risk disclosure. Contrary to all the studies mentioned, Hemrit (2018) found that the board of directors' size is negatively associated with risk disclosure.

Despite the contradictory results obtained, it is expected that the board of directors' size will influence the level of risk disclosure. Thus, the following research hypothesis was formulated:

Hypothesis One: The board of directors' size influences the level of financial risks disclosure.

Board of Directors' Diversity

The monitoring role played by the board of directors is an important corporate governance control mechanism. However, the board of directors' diversity can affect the quality of this monitoring function and, therefore, the company's financial performance (Campbell & Mínguez-Vera, 2008). The study by Ain et al. (2020) also revealed that the participation of women on the board of directors reduces agency costs. Therefore, boards with more women are associated with more transparent information disclosure policies (DeBoskey et al., 2018).

In this context, the studies by Carmona et al. (2016), Saggar and Singh (2017), Bufarwa et al. (2020), as well as Seebeck and Vetter (2021) revealed that board of directors' diversity is positively related to risk disclosure. However, Oliveira et al. (2018) and Biswas (2021) did not find a statistically significant relationship between the board of directors' diversity and the level of risk disclosure.

Despite the contradictory results obtained, it is expected that the gender diversity of the board of directors will influence the level of disclosure about risks, formulating the following research hypothesis:

Hypothesis Two: The board of directors' diversity influences the level of financial risks disclosure.

Independent Directors on the Board

According to Barros et al. (2013) and Thenmozhi and Sasidharan (2020), the independent directors on the board are essential to protect the interests of shareholders, essentially, minority shareholders. Cai et al. (2005) add that a board of directors with more independent members is more effective, as they can better verify and monitor managers and reduce agency problems. Furthermore, they better meet shareholder preferences in terms of accountability and transparency, being the principal indicator of the quality of corporate governance (Abraham & Cox, 2007).

Given the above, Abraham and Cox (2007) and Oliveira et al. (2011b) state that independent directors can influence the disclosure information level because they have incentives to require the disclosure of more information to balance the levels of risk to their reputation. Therefore, a higher level of disclosure can be expected from companies with more independent directors, since they have access to privileged information (Lopes & Rodrigues, 2007).

Following this thought, Lajili (2009), Oliveira et al. (2011b), Barakat and Hussainey (2013), Elshandidy and Neri (2015), Carmona et al. (2016), Moumen et al. (2016), Ashfaq et al. (2016), Akbar et al. (2017), Hemrit (2018), Oliveira et al. (2018), Alkurdi et al. (2019), Ibrahim et al. (2019) and Elamer et al. (2020) obtained empirical evidence of the existence of a positive association between the level of risk disclosure and the number of independent directors on the board of directors. However, the study by Ismail and Rahman (2011) and Buckby et al. (2015) revealed the lack of association between the disclosure of risks and the number of independent directors on the board of directors.

Given the inconsistency of results, the following research hypothesis was formulated:

Hypothesis Three: The number of independent members on the board of directors influences the level of financial risks disclosure.

Type of Auditor

According to Chalmers and Godfrey (2004) and Deumes and Knechel (2008), the largest auditing companies, such as the Big4, are more likely to require high levels of information disclosure, to maintain their reputation and avoid costs of reputation. Lennox (1999) also states that the Big4 require their customers to disclose more information about risk due to the greater risk of litigation.

Based on the above premises, the empirical studies by Oliveira et al. (2011b), Mokhtar and Mellett (2013), Campbell et al. (2014), Carmona et al. 2016, Zango et al. (2016), Fukukawa and Kim (2017), Habtoor et al. (2017), Dey et al. (2018), Mcchlery and Hussainey (2021), revealed a positive association between risk disclosure and the type of audit firm, that is, specifically a Big4. This association was not verified in the studies by Deumes and Knechel (2008), Buckby et al. (2015),

Ibrahim et al. (2019), Bozzolan and Miihkinen (2021), Mcchlery and Hussainey (2021). Hay's research results (2021) also revealed that there is a general effect of the Big4 risk disclosure, but it has been proved that some Big4 are associated with a superior quality of risk disclosure.

In view of these results, the following research hypothesis was developed:

Hypothesis Four: The type of auditor (Big4) influences the level of financial risks disclosure.

Auditor's Gender

The auditor's gender influences the way that information is collected, processed and evaluated (Breesch & Branson, 2009). As such, behavioral differences between male and female auditors can have important implications for the audit quality and financial reports (Ittonen et al., 2013). In fact, Montenegro and Brás (2015), Hardies et al. (2016), Garcia-Blandon et al. (2019) found in their studies that female auditors provide higher quality audit services. The study by Abdelfattah et al. (2020) revealed that female auditors tend to be more cautious about risk, providing more detailed reports and requiring more detailed reports from audited entities.

In this context, the study by Bozzolan and Miihkinen (2021) proved that the quality of risk disclosures is associated with the auditor's gender. In turn, Hay (2021) found that female auditors are associated with better risk disclosure.

Given the results, the following research hypothesis was obtained:

Hypothesis Five: The auditor's gender influences the level of financial risks disclosure.

Audit Committee

According to IBGC (2015), the Board of Directors can form multiple committees to support it in carrying out its functions. Among the committees that can be formed, the audit committee stands out, responsible for overseeing the financial statements, internal controls, financial area, internal audit, and risk management. Therefore, and as reported by Felo et al. (2003) and De Vlaminck and Sarens (2015), the existence of an audit committee is related to the quality of the financial statements.

Proving this premise, the study by Abdullah et al. (2017) and Agyei-Mensah (2019) found that the existence of an audit committee positively influences the disclosure of risks. Zhang et al. (2013) also found a statistically significant relationship between the independence of the audit committee and the level of risk disclosure. However, the existence of this relationship was not validated in the study by Oliveira et al. (2018).

In view of these results, the following research hypothesis was developed:

Hypothesis Six: The existence of an audit committee influences the level of financial risks disclosure.

RESEARCH DESIGN

Sample

In view of the main objective of this work of verifying the influence of certain characteristics associated with the corporate governance model in the disclosure of financial risks in non-financial companies, during the period 2017-2019, companies listed on Euronext Lisbon were selected as the target population.

In this sense, the list of companies listed on Euronext Lisbon, on November 16, 2018, was obtained, in a total of 47 companies.

Of these 47 companies, entities linked to the sports sector were excluded (whose reporting period does not coincide with the calendar year), financial sector entities and companies for which it was not possible to obtain information on some of the variables considered or whose reports and accounts referring to the 3 periods analyzed were not available for consultation. That said, 32 companies remain in the sample of this study.

Table 1 shows the selection and constitution of the study sample:

Table 1. Selection and constitution of the sample companies

	Number of Companies
Total entities listed on Euronext Lisbon on 11/16/2018[1]	**47**
Excluded entities:	
Sports Limited Companies	3
Financial Companies	2
Lack of information	10
Total entities included in the study	**32**

Methodology

In analyzing the information disclosed, the content analysis technique was used, coding the information collected into a risk disclosure index, whose sum of the items disclosed over the total of items considered results in the risk disclosure index for each company, per year. The source for obtaining the information was the management reports and accounts of each of the companies for the periods of 2017, 2018 and 2019.

According to Amran *et al.* (2009), the content analysis method is the most common and widely used in the evaluation of disclosure. "It is chosen because the study focuses on the extent or quantity and not on the quality of risk disclosures" (Amran *et al.*, 2009).

That said, for the preparation of this study, the management reports and accounts for each of the companies were collected through the Portuguese Securities Market Commission website, as they are considered a credible source of information.

Dependent Variable

Since the objective of this work is to study the level of disclosure about risks of non-financial companies, a disclosure index (DI) was built (which appears in Table 25 in Appendix 1). Since what we intend to analyze is the level of disclosure about risks, specifically financial risks, the information disclosure requirements contained in IFRS 7 were considered.

This index consists of 30 items of disclosure and can be divided into 6 main categories:

1. Accounting policies
2. Specific information on risk disclosure
3. Hedging
4. Credit risk
5. Liquidity risk
6. Market risk

The use of these type of indices as a tool to measure the level of disclosure is something that already exists in the literature, such as for example in the studies carried out by Madrigal *et al.* (2015), Malafronte *et al.* (2016), Ashfaq *et al.* (2016), Neifar and Jarboui (2018), Coelho *et al.* (2018) and Adam-Muller & Erkens (2020).

Subsequently, all the management reports and accounts of the companies that make up the sample were collected, and their analysis was carried out through the constructed index. When checking each of the items that make up the disclosure index, each of them was given a weight of 0 or 1, where 0 means that the item is not disclosed and 1 means that the item is disclosed. Thus, after verifying each of the items for each of the companies' reports, the value of the risk disclosure index per company and per year, is obtained through the quotient between the sum of the total items disclosed by the company in question and the total of items that constitute the disclosure index. The higher the value of the index, the higher the level of disclosure presented by the company.

Subsequently, the dependent variable, consisting of the average value of the disclosure index per company was calculated for the period analyzed, considering the following formula:

$$DI = (DI\_2017 + DI\_2018 + DI\_2019) / 3$$

Independent Variables

The independent variables used in this study are based on the research hypotheses previously formulated and represent the characteristics associated to the corporate governance model that we believe influence the level of disclosure about companies' risks, as shown in Table 2.

Table 2. Independent variables

Variable	Determination Form	Hypothesis
Board of Directors' Size (BDS)	number of members on the board of directors	H1
Board of directors' Diversity (BDD)	% of female members on the board of directors	H2
Independent Directors on the board (IDBD)	% of independent directors on the board of directors	H3
Type of auditor (BIG 4)	Dummy: 0 - not belonging to the Big 4 1 - belonging to the Big 4	H4
Auditor's Gender (AG)	Dummy: 0 – the auditor is male 1 – the auditor is female	H5
Audit Committee (AC)	Dummy: 0 - the company does not have an auditing commission 1 - the company has an auditing commission	H6

Regression Models

In order to analyze the relationship between the corporate governance model and the level of disclosure on financial risks, several simple linear regression models were developed, crossing the dependent variable, with each of the independent variables previously described, which are presented in Table 3.

Table 3. Simple linear regression models

$$DI = \alpha_{0+} \beta_1 \; BDS + \varepsilon_i$$

$$DI = \alpha_{0+} \beta_1 \; BDD + \varepsilon_i$$

$$DI = \alpha_{0+} \beta_1 \; IDBD + \varepsilon_i$$

$$DI = \alpha_{0+} \beta_1 \; Big4 + \varepsilon_i$$

$$DI = \alpha_{0+} \beta_1 \; AG + \varepsilon_i$$

$$DI = \alpha_{0+} \beta_1 \; AC + \varepsilon_i$$

DI – Value of Financial risk disclosure index
BDS – Board of Director's Size
BDD – Board of Director's Diversity
IDBG – Independent Directors on the Board of Directors
BIG4 – Type of Auditor
AG – Auditor's Gender
AC – Audit Committee

ANALYSIS AND DISCUSSION OF RESULTS

At this point, we will proceed to the analysis and discussion of the results obtained in our study.

Sample Characterization

From the total companies that compose the sample, through Table 4, we can conclude that, mainly, the companies belong to the sectors of consumption services activity and industry (28% each).

Finally, through the analysis of Table 5, about geographic location, we conclude that there are no companies located in Alentejo, Algarve, Azores, and Madeira. That said, most companies are located in the metropolitan area of Lisbon, representing about 59,4% of the total sample, with the remaining 37,5% of companies located in the north of the country.

Table 4. Characterization of the sample by sector of activity

Activity Sector	Frequency	Percentage
Gás, Petróleo e Energia	5	15,6%
Materiais básicos	1	3,1%
Indústria	9	28,1%
Bens de consumo	2	6,3%
Serviços ao consumidor	9	28,1%
Telecomunicações	4	12,5%
Tecnologia	2	6,3%
Total	32	100%

Table 5. Characterization of the sample by geographic location

Location	Frequency	Percentage
North	12	37,5%
Center	1	3,1%
Lisbon	19	59,4%
Alentejo	0	0,0%
Algarve	0	0,0%
Azores	0	0,0%
Madeira	0	0,0%
Total	**32**	**100,0%**

Descriptive Analysis

Table 6 presents the result of the descriptive statistics of the disclosure index, considering the index values for the periods 2017, 2018, and 2019, respectively, and the average index value (which is the dependent variable of the regression models presented in the next point).

As it is possible to conclude, by analyzing the values presented in Table 6, the average value of the index evolved positively over the period analyzed, but the variation verified is not significant. The average value of the index is 0.6466, indicating that Portuguese companies do not disclose all of the disclosure requirements contained in IFRS. However, in all analyzed periods, it is possible to identify a maximum disclosure value of 0.93, indicating that there is at least one entity that presents almost all the considered disclosure items. On the other hand, it is possible to verify that in the 2017 period there was at least one entity that did not present any expected

Table 6. Disclosure Index – descriptive statistics

		DI 2017	DI 2018	DI 2019	DI Mean
N	Valid	32	32	32	32
	Missing	0	0	0	0
Mean		0,6392	0,6498	0,6509	0,6466
Deviation error		0,23020	0,22282	0,21843	0,21223
Minimum		0,00	0,10	0,10	0,12
Maximum		0,93	0,93	0,93	0,93

disclosure item (since the minimum value was equal to zero), but in the following two periods there are no entities that do not present any disclosure item (since the minimum value is 0.10).

The results obtained prove that Portuguese companies are concerned about revealing some type of information about the risks incurred, but they are probably also afraid to disclose information that, as Kravet and Muslu (2013) defend, could be interpreted as negative.

Regression Models Analysis

In order to analyze the influence of the composition of the board of directors on the disclosure of financial risks, three simple linear regressions were estimated, relating the disclosure index to each of the previously defined variables, according to hypotheses 1, 2 3 formulated. The results are shown below.

Board of Directors' Size

Table 7, Table 8, and Table 9 present the results of the simple linear regression model for the independent variable size of the board of directors.

Table 7. Model summary

Model	R	R Squared	R Squared Adjusted	Standard Error of Estimate	Durbin-Watson
1	,370[a]	0,137	0,108	0,20039	2,462

a. Predictors: (Constant), BDS
b. Dependent variable: ID

Table 8. ANOVA[a]

	Model	Sum of Squares	df	Medium Square	Z	Sig.
1	Regression	0,192	1	0,192	4,772	,037[b]
	Residue	1,205	30	0,040		
	Total	1,396	31			

a. Dependent variable: ID
b. Predictors: (Constant), BDS

Table 9. Coefficients[a]

	Model	Non-standardized Coefficients		Standardized Coefficients	t	Sig.
		B	Error	Beta		
1	(Constant)	0,491	0,080		6,167	0,000
	BDS	0,017	0,008	0,370	2,184	0,037

As can be seen from the analysis of Table 9, the independent variable size of the board of directors (BDS) is significantly and positively associated with the disclosure index, so it is possible to conclude that the level of disclosure of financial risks will be higher in companies with larger boards of directors. In this way, it is possible to validate hypothesis 1.

The value of R squared (shown in Table 7) indicates that the model allows explaining about 13.7% of the disclosure index variation, and the F test (Z value in Table 8) presents a significant value indicating that the model is adequate in general terms.

The results obtained are consistent with the results obtained by Ntim et al. (2013), Elshandidy and Neri (2015), Moumen et al. (2016), Carmona et al. (2016), Saggar and Singh (2017), Akbar et al. (2017), Alkurdi et al. (2019), who also obtained evidence of the existence of a positive association between board size and risk disclosure. However, they are contrary to the results obtained by Hemrit (2018), who obtained evidence of a negative association between those two variables.

Board of Directors' Diversity

Table 10, Table 11, and Table 12 present the results of the simple linear regression model for the independent variable diversity of the board of directors (BDD).

Table 10. Model summary

Model	R	R Squared	R Squared Adjusted	Standard Error of Estimate	Durbin-Watson
1	,333[a]	0,111	0,081	0,20343	2,370

a. Predictors: (Constant), BDD
b. Dependent variable: ID

Table 11. ANOVAa

Model		Sum of Squares	df	Medium Square	Z	Sig.
1	Regression	0,155	1	0,155	3,740	,063[b]
	Residue	1,242	30	0,041		
	Total	1,396	31			

a. Dependent variable: ID
b. Predictors: (Constant), BDD

Table 12. Coefficients[a]

Model		Non-standardized Coefficients		Standardized Coefficients	t	Sig.
		B	Error	Beta		
1	(Constant)	0,549	0,062		8,820	0,000
	BDD	0,590	0,305	0,333	1,934	0,063

The results presented in Table 12 allow us to verify that, for a significance level of 5%, the variable diversity of the board of directors does not prove to be statistically significant. However, the p value = 0.063, indicating that, if we increase the significance level to 10%, it is possible to state that gender diversity influences the level of disclosure about financial risks. Thus, it is concluded that the greater the percentage of female members on the board of directors, the greater the level of disclosure on financial risks presented, allowing the validation of hypothesis 2 as well.

The value of R squared (shown in Table 10) allows us to conclude that the estimated model explains about 11% of the disclosure index variation. Regarding the F test (in Table 11), the value of p = 0.063, so that, for a significance level of 10%, the model is adequate to explain that variation.

The results obtained are consistent with the results of Carmona et al. (2016), Saggar and Singh (2017), Bufarwa et al. (2020), and Seebeck and Vetter (2021), who also proved the existence of a positive association between the board of directors' gender diversity and risk disclosure.

Board of Directors' Members Independency

The results of the simple linear regression for the independent variable Independence of the board of directors' members are presented in Table 13, Table 14, and Table 15.

Table 13. Model summary

Model	R	R Squared	R Squared Adjusted	Standard Error of Estimate	Durbin-Watson
1	,108[a]	0,012	-0,022	0,21650	2,382

a. Predictors: (Constant), IDBD
b. Dependent variable: ID

Table 14. ANOVA[a]

Model		Sum of Squares	df	Medium Square	Z	Sig.
1	Regression	0,016	1	0,016	0,344	,562[b]
	Residue	1,359	29	0,047		
	Total	1,375	30			

a. Dependent variable: ID
b. Predictors: (Constant), IDBD

Table 15. Coefficients[a]

Model		Non-standardized Coefficients		Standardized Coefficients	t	Sig.
		B	Error	Beta		
1	(Constant)	0,672	0,065		10,398	0,000
	IDBD	-0,095	0,162	-0,108	-0,586	0,562

As it is possible to analyze by the results presented in Table 15, the variable independence of the members of the board of directors is not statistically significant (p value >0,05), and therefore it is not possible to validate hypothesis 3.

These results are consistent with the results obtained by Ismail and Rahman (2011) and Buckby et al. (2015), who also did not obtain evidence of the existence of any association between the independence of the members of the board of directors and the disclosure of risks. However, they are contrary to the results obtained by Lajili (2009), Oliveira et al. (2011b), Barakat and Hussainey (2013), Elshandidy and Neri (2015), Carmona et al. (2016), Moumen et al. (2016), Ashfaq et al. (2016), Akbar et al. (2017), Hemrit (2018), Oliveira et al. (2018), Alkurdi et al. (2019), Ibrahim et al. (2019), Elamer et al. (2020), who proved the existence of a positive association between the number of independent members on the board of directors and the disclosure of risks.

Likewise, in order to verify the auditor's influence on the disclosure of financial risks, three simple linear regressions were also estimated that relate the disclosure index with the type of auditor, the auditor's gender and the existence of an audit committee, as per defined in hypotheses 4, 5 and 6.

Type of Auditor

The results of the simple linear regression model for the independent variable type of auditor (Big4) are presented in Table 16, Table 17, and Table 18.

Table 16. Model summary

Model	R	R Squared	R Squared Adjusted	Standard Error of Estimate	Durbin-Watson
1	,508[a]	0,258	0,233	0,18582	2,182

a. Predictors: (Constant), Big4
b. Dependent variable: ID

Table 17. ANOVA[a]

Model		Sum of Squares	df	Medium Square	Z	Sig.
1	Regression	0,360	1	0,360	10,441	,003[b]
	Residue	1,036	30	0,035		
	Total	1,396	31			

a. Dependent variable: ID
b. Predictors: (Constant), Big4

Table 18. Coefficients[a]

Model		Non-standardized Coefficients		Standardized Coefficients	t	Sig.
		B	Error	Beta		
1	(Constant)	0,400	0,083		4,814	0,000
	Big4	0,292	0,090	0,508	3,231	0,003

The value presented for the variable type of auditor (shown in Table 18) is significant (p value <0.05), so it is possible to conclude that the level of disclosure about financial risks will be higher in companies whose external auditor belongs to one of the 4 largest auditing companies, being possible to validate hypothesis 4.

The model explains 25,8% of the variation in the disclosure index value and the F test result (p value <0.05) allows validating the model in general terms.

These results are consistent with the results obtained by other authors, such as Oliveira et al. (2011b), Mokhtar and Mellett (2013), Campbell et al. (2014), Carmona et al. 2016, Zango et al. (2016), Fukukawa and Kim (2017), Habtoor et al. (2017), Dey et al. (2018), Mcchlery and Hussainey (2021), and Hay (2021) who also proved the existence of a positive association between the type of audit firm and the disclosure of risks.

Auditor's Gender

Regarding the auditor's gender variable, the results of the simple linear regression are presented in Table 19, Table 20, and Table 21.

Table 19. Model summary

Model	R	R Squared	R Squared Adjusted	Standard Error of Estimate	Durbin-Watson
1	,123[a]	0,015	-0,018	0,21410	2,433

a. Predictors: (Constant), AG
b. Dependent variable: ID

As it is possible to prove, by the values presented in Table 21, it is proven that the auditor's gender does not exert any influence on the level of disclosure on financial risks (p value $>0,05$), and hypothesis 5 cannot be validated.

Table 20. ANOVA[a]

	Model	Sum of Squares	df	Medium Square	Z	Sig.
1	Regression	0,021	1	0,021	0,462	,502[b]
	Residue	1,375	30	0,046		
	Total	1,396	31			

a. Dependent variable: ID
b. Predictors: (Constant), AG

Table 21. Coefficients[a]

	Model	Non-standardized Coefficients		Standardized Coefficients	t	Sig.
		B	Error	Beta		
1	(Constant)	0,567	0,124		4,584	0,000
	AG	0,088	0,130	0,123	0,680	0,502

This result contradicts the results of the studies by Bozzolan and Miihkinen (2021) and Hay (2021), which proved that the quality of risk disclosure is associated with the auditor's gender.

Audit Committee

For the variable existence of an audit committee, the results of the simple linear regression model are presented in Table 22, Table 23, and Table 24.

Table 22. Model summary

Model	R	R Squared	R Squared Adjusted	Standard Error of Estimate	Durbin-Watson
1	,256[a]	0,066	0,035	0,20853	2,583

a. Predictors: (Constant), AC
b. Dependent variable: ID

Once again, as in the previous variable, it is not possible to prove the existence of influence of the audit committee in the disclosure of financial risks (p value >0,05, in Table 24).

Table 23. ANOVA[a]

Model		Sum of Squares	df	Medium Square	Z	Sig.
1	Regression	0,092	1	0,092	2,111	,157[b]
	Residue	1,305	30	0,043		
	Total	1,396	31			

a. Dependent variable: ID
b. Predictors: (Constant), AC

Table 24. Coefficients[a]

Model		Non-standardized Coefficients		Standardized Coefficients	t	Sig.
		B	Error	Beta		
1	(Constant)	0,624	0,040		15,539	0,000
	AC	0,148	0,102	0,256	1,453	0,157

This result corroborates the result obtained by Oliveira et al. (2018), who also failed to prove the existence of an association between those two variables but contradicts the results of Abdullah et al. (2017) and Agyei-Mensah (2019), who obtained evidence of a positive association between the variable existence of an audit committee and risk disclosure.

In conclusion, from the analysis of the linear regressions models, it is possible to conclude that, for a significance level of 5%, the variables size of the board of directors and type of auditor significantly and positively influence the level of disclosure about financial risks, being possible to validate hypothesis 1 and 4. Thus, the greater the number of members on the board of directors, the greater the level of disclosure about financial risks, indicating that the composition of the board of directors may influence the definition of disclosure practices.

On the other hand, the level of disclosure about financial risks will also be higher if the auditor belongs to one of the 4 largest international auditing companies, indicating that these companies are concerned with maintaining their reputation and influence their clients to disclose information about risks incurred

If we increase the significance level to 10%, the diversity of the board of directors also positively influences the level of disclosure about financial risks, also validating hypothesis 2. Thus, it is concluded that the greater the number of female members on the board, the greater the level of disclosure, indicating that female members are more concerned with disclosing the risks to which the entity is exposed.

The remaining variables associated with the corporate governance model were not significant, indicating that the percentage of independent members on the board of directors, the gender of the auditor and the existence of an audit committee do not influence the level of disclosure on financial risks, not being possible to validate hypothesis 3, 5 and 6.

SOLUTIONS AND RECOMMENDATIONS

This study allowed us to conclude that Portuguese companies listed on Euronext Lisbon do not present high levels of disclosure on financial risks, indicating that these companies may not be duly complying with the disclosure requirements contained in the applicable standards. Thus, the results obtained may be of special interest to the bodies responsible for defining enforcement mechanisms.

On the other hand, this study also allowed us to conclude that the greater the number of members on the board of directors and the greater the number of female members, the greater the disclosure of risks. Regarding the auditor, it was proven that the fact that the auditor belongs to one of the Big4 also positively influences the disclosure of risks. In this sense, these results may be useful for companies, in defining the composition of their boards of directors and choosing the auditor.

FUTURE RESEARCH DIRECTIONS

This study has some limitations that must also be addressed. The first is related to the fact that the sample used is small in size, and the results obtained cannot be extrapolated to all non-financial companies in Portugal, since it is limited to a pre-defined list of listed companies.

Since the standards regarding the disclosure of risk information are constantly reviewed and evolving, it is suggested for future research, the analysis of disclosure and verification of the degree of compliance with future mandatory requirements.

Taking into account the current context, it will also be interesting to see how companies have introduced information in their reports and accounts related to the risks associated with Covid 19 and its impacts. Finally, it is also suggested to extend this study to unlisted companies, also covering small and medium-sized companies that are the most representative of the business fabric in Portugal.

CONCLUSION

The objectives of this study were to measure the level of disclosure about financial risks and analyze the influence of the corporate governance model on the level of disclosure. To this end, in a first stage, a content analysis was carried out on the management reports and accounts of the companies, through a disclosure index, created based on the disclosure requirements contained in the International Financial Reporting Standard No. 7 - Financial Instruments: Disclosures. In a second phase of the study, through simple linear regressions, this disclosure index was related to a set of independent variables related to certain characteristics of the board of directors (size of the board, diversity of the board and independence of the board) and the auditor (type of auditor, gender of the auditor and existence of an audit committee).

The financial risk disclosure index presents an average value of 0,6466 which represents little more than half of the information that is required to companies, also revealing a level of disclosure insufficient in relation to what would be desirable. Only two companies managed to reach the maximum disclosure value of 0,93.

With regard to the relationship between the variables associated with the board of directors and the level of disclosure about financial risks, it was possible to prove that the size of the board of directors and the gender of the board members (for a significance level of 10%) positively influence the level of disclosure. Thus, it was possible to conclude that larger boards of directors and with a greater number of female members exert greater pressure for the disclosure of risks to increase. However, it was not possible to prove the influence of the number of independent board members on the disclosure of financial risks.

Regarding the auditor, it was possible to prove the existence of influence of the type of auditor, concluding that, if the auditor belongs to one of the four largest auditing companies, the higher the level of disclosure about financial risks will be. However, it was not possible to prove the influence of the auditor's gender and the existence of an audit committee at the level of disclosure.

REFERENCES

Abdullah, M., Shukor, Z., & Rahmat, M. (2017). The influences of risk management committee and audit committee towards voluntary risk management disclosure. *Jurnal Pengurusan*, *50*, 83–95. doi:10.17576/pengurusan-2017-50-08

Abraham, S., & Cox, P. (2007). Analysing the determinants of narrative risk information in UK FTSE 100 annual reports. *The British Accounting Review*, *39*(3), 227–248. doi:10.1016/j.bar.2007.06.002

Adam-Muller, A., & Erkens, M. (2020). Risk disclosure noncompliance. *Journal of Accounting and Public Policy, 39*(3), 106739. doi:10.1016/j.jaccpubpol.2020.106739

Agyei-Mensah, B. (2019). The effect of audit committee effectiveness and audit quality on corporate voluntary disclosure quality. *African Journal of Economic and Management Studies, 10*(1), 17–31. doi:10.1108/AJEMS-04-2018-0102

Ain, Q., Yuan, X., Javaid, H., Usman, M., & Haris, M. (2020). (forthcoming). Female directors and agency costs: Evidence from Chinese listed firms. *International Journal of Emerging Markets.*

Akbar, S., Kharabsheh, B., Poletti-Hughes, J., & Shah, S. (2017). Board structure and corporate risk taking in the UK financial sector. *International Review of Financial Analysis, 50*, 101–110. doi:10.1016/j.irfa.2017.02.001

Alkurdi, A., Hussainey, K., Tahat, Y., & Aladwan, M. (2019). The impact of corporate governance on risk disclosure: Jordanian evidence. *Academy of Accounting and Financial Studies Journal, 23*(1), 1–16.

Alshirah, M., Rahman, A., & Mustapa, I. (2020). Board of directors' characteristics and corporate risk disclosure: The moderating role of family ownership. *EuroMed Journal of Business, 15*(2), 219–252. doi:10.1108/EMJB-09-2019-0115

Amaral, M. (2015). Tipos de riscos na actividade bancária. *Revisores e Auditores, 69*, 37–42.

Amran, A., Bin, A. M. R., & Hassan, B. C. H. M. (2009). Risk reporting: An exploratory study on risk management disclosure in Malaysian annual reports. *Managerial Auditing Journal, 24*(1), 39–57. doi:10.1108/02686900910919893

Ashfaq, K., Zhang, R., Munaim, A., & Razzaq, N. (2016). An investigation into the determinants of risk disclosure in banks: Evidence from financial sector of Pakistan. *International Journal of Economics and Financial Issues, 6*(3), 1049–1058.

Barakat, A., & Hussainey, K. (2013). Bank governance, regulation, supervision, and risk reporting: Evidence from operational risk disclosures in European banks. *International Review of Financial Analysis, 30*, 254–273. doi:10.1016/j. irfa.2013.07.002Barros, C., Boubakar, S., & Hamrouni, A. (2013). Corporate governance and voluntary disclosure in France. *Journal of Applied Business Research, 29*(2), 561–578. doi:10.19030/jabr.v29i2.7657

Beretta, S., & Bozzolan, S. (2004). A framework for the analysis of firm risk communication. *The International Journal of Accounting, 39*(3), 265–288. doi:10.1016/j.intacc.2004.06.006

Biswas, S. (2021). Female directors and risk-taking behavior of Indian firms. *Managerial Finance, 47*(7), 1016–1037. doi:10.1108/MF-05-2020-0274

Bozzolan, S., & Miihkinen, A. (2021). The quality of mandatory non-financial (risk) disclosures: The moderating role of audit firm and partner characteristics. *The International Journal of Accounting, 56*(02), 2150008. doi:10.1142/S1094406021500086

Breesch, D., & Branson, J. (2009). The effects of auditor gender on audit quality. *The IUP Journal of Accounting Research & Audit Practices, 8*(3-4), 78–107.

Buckby, S., Gallery, G., & Ma, J. (2015). An analysis of risk management disclosures: Australian evidence. *Managerial Auditing Journal, 30*(8/9), 812–869. doi:10.1108/MAJ-09-2013-0934

Bufarwa, I., Elamer, A., Ntim, C., & AlHares, A. (2020). Gender diversity, corporate governance and financial risk disclosure in the UK. *International Journal of Law and Management, 62*(6), 521–538. doi:10.1108/IJLMA-10-2018-0245

Bushman, R., & Landsman, W. (2010). The pros and cons of regulating corporate reporting: A critical review of the arguments. *Accounting and Business Research, 40*(3), 259–273. doi:10.1080/00014788.2010.9663400

Cai, C., Keasey, K., & Short, H. (2005). Corporate governance and information efficiency in security markets. *European Financial Management, 12*(5), 763–787. doi:10.1111/j.1468-036X.2006.00276.x

Campbell, K., & Mínguez-Vera, A. (2008). Gender diversity in the boardroom and firm financial performance. *Journal of Business Ethics, 83*(3), 435–451. doi:10.100710551-007-9630-y

Carmona, P., Fuebtes, C., & Ruiz, C. (2016). Risk disclosure analysis in the corporate governance annual report using fuzzy-set qualitative comparative analysis. *Revista de Administração de Empresas, 56*(3), 342–352. doi:10.1590/S0034-759020160307

Chalmers, K., & Godfrey, J. (2004). Reputation costs: The impetus for voluntary derivative financial instruments reporting. *Accounting, Organizations and Society, 29*(2), 95–125. doi:10.1016/S0361-3682(02)00034-X

Coelho, S., Amaral, M., & Lemos, K. (2018). Divulgação de informação sobre riscos financeiros nas entidades bancárias : Evidência empírica em Portugal. *European Journal of Applied Business Management. Special Issue of ICABM, 2018*, 205–225.

Combes-ThuÚlin, E., Henneron, S., & Touron, P. (2006). Risk regulations and financial disclosure: An investigation based on corporate communication in French traded companies. *Corporate Communications, 11*(3), 303–326. doi:10.1108/13563280610680876

De Vlaminck, N., & Sarens, G. (2015). The relationship between audit committee characteristics and financial statement quality: Evidence from Belgium. *The Journal of Management and Governance, 19*(1), 145–166. doi:10.100710997-013-9282-5

DeBoskey, D., Luo, Y., & Wang, J. (2018). Does board gender diversity affect the transparency of corporate political disclosure? *Asian Review of Accounting, 26*(4), 444–463. doi:10.1108/ARA-09-2017-0141

Deumes, R., & Knechel, W. (2008). Economic incentives for voluntary reporting on internal risk management and control systems. *Auditing, 27*(1), 35–66. doi:10.2308/aud.2008.27.1.35

Dey, R., Hossain, S., & Rezae, Z. (2018). Financial risk disclosure and financial attributes among publicly traded manufacturing companies: Evidence from Bangladesh. *Journal of Risk and Financial Management, 11*(50), 1–16. doi:10.3390/jrfm11030050

Ebrahimi Maimand, M., & Namazi, M. (2021). (in press). Firms' risk disclosure and reporting: A comprehensive framework. *Journal of Knowledge Accounting.*

Elamer, A. A., Ntim, C. G., Abdou, H. A., & Pyke, C. (2020). Sharia supervisory boards, governance structures and operational risk disclosures: Evidence from Islamic banks in MENA countries. *Global Finance Journal, 46*, 1–44. doi:10.1016/j.gfj.2019.100488

Elshandidy, T., & Neri, L. (2015). Corporate governance, risk disclosure practices, and market liquidity: Comparative evidence from the UK and Italy. *Corporate Governance, 23*(4), 331–356. doi:10.1111/corg.12095

Fathi, J. (2013). The determinants of the quality of financial information disclosed by French listed companies. *Mediterranean Journal of Social Sciences, 4*(2), 319–319. doi:10.5901/mjss.2013.v4n2p319

FeloA.KrishnamurthyS.SolieriS. (2003). Audit committee characteristics and the perceived quality of financial reporting: an empirical analysis. *Available at* SSRN 401240. doi:10.2139/ssrn.401240

Field, L., Lowry, M., & Mkrtchyan, A. (2013). Are busy boards detrimental? *Journal of Financial Economics, 109*(1), 63–82. doi:10.1016/j.jfineco.2013.02.004

Fukukawa, H., & Kim, H. (2017). Effects of audit partners on clients' business risk disclosure. *Accounting and Business Research, 47*(7), 780–809. doi:10.1080/0001 4788.2017.1299619

Gonidakis, F., Koutoupis, A., Tsamis, A., & Agoraki, M. (2020). Risk disclosure in listed Greek companies: The effects of the financial crisis. *Accounting Research Journal, 33*(4/5), 615–633. doi:10.1108/ARJ-03-2020-0050

Habtoor, O., Ahmad, N., Mohamad, N., & Haat, M. (2017). Linking corporate risk disclosure practices with firm-specific characteristics in Saudi Arabia. *Gadjah Mada International Journal of Business, 19*(3), 247–267. doi:10.22146/gamaijb.26769

Hardies, K., Breesch, D., & Branson, J. (2016). Do (Fe)Male Auditors Impair Audit Quality? Evidence from Going-Concern Opinions. *European Accounting Review, 25*(1), 7–34. doi:10.1080/09638180.2014.921445

Hay, D. C. (2021). Discussion of "The Quality of Mandatory Nonfinancial Risk Disclosures and the Moderating Effect of Audit Firm and Partner Characteristics". *The International Journal of Accounting, 56*(02), 2180004. doi:10.1142/ S1094406021800044

Healy, P., & Palepu, K. (2001). Information asymmetry, corporate disclosure, and the capital markets: A review of the empirical disclosure literature. *Journal of Accounting Research, 31*(1-3), 405–440.

Hemrit, W. (2018). Risk reporting appraisal in post-revolutionary Tunisia. *Journal of Financial Reporting and Accounting, 16*(4), 522–542. doi:10.1108/JFRA-05-2016-0040

IBGC. (2015). *Código das melhores práticas de governança corporativa. 5ª Edição.* Instituto Brasileiro de Governança Corporativa.

Ibrahim, A., Habbash, M., & Hussainey, K. (2019). Corporate governance and risk disclosure: Evidence from Saudi Arabia. *International Journal of Accounting. Auditing and Performance Evaluation, 15*(1), 89–111. doi:10.1504/IJAAPE.2019.096748

ICAEW. (2011). *Reporting business risks: Meeting expectations - Information for better markets initiative.* Institute of Chartered Accountants in England and Wales.

Ismail, R., & Rahman, A. (2011). Institutional investors and board of directors' monitoring role on risk management disclosure level in Malaysia. *The IUP Journal of Corporate Governance, 10*(2), 37–61.

Ittonen, K., Vähämaa, E., & Vähämaa, S. (2013). Female auditors and accruals quality. *Accounting Horizons, 27*(2), 205–228. doi:10.2308/acch-50400

Jaffar, R., Al Sheikh, W., Hassan, M. S., & Abdullah, M. (2021). Voluntary Risk Disclosures of Islamic Financial Institutions: The Role of AAOIFI Standards Implementation. *Asian Journal of Accounting and Governance*, *15*, 1–14. doi:10.17576/AJAG-2021-15-04

Kim, H., & Yasuda, Y. (2018). Business risk disclosure and firm risk: Evidence from Japan. *Research in International Business and Finance*, *45*, 413–426. doi:10.1016/j.ribaf.2017.07.172

Kravet, T., & Muslu, V. (2013). Textual risk disclosures and investors' risk perceptions. *Review of Accounting Studies*, *18*(4), 1088–1122. doi:10.100711142-013-9228-9

Lennox, C. S. (1999). Audit quality and auditor size: An evaluation of reputation and deep pockets hypotheses. *Journal of Business Finance & Accounting*, *26*(7-8), 779–805. doi:10.1111/1468-5957.00275

Linsley, P., & Shrives, P. (2006). Risk reporting: A study of risk disclosures in the annual reports of UK companies. *The British Accounting Review*, *38*(4), 387–404. doi:10.1016/j.bar.2006.05.002

Lopes, P., & Rodrigues, L. (2007). Accounting for financial instruments : An analysis of the determinants of disclosure in the Portuguese. *The International Journal of Accounting*, *42*(1), 25–56. doi:10.1016/j.intacc.2006.12.002

Madrigal, M., Guzmán, B., & Guzmán, C. (2015). Determinants of corporate risk disclosure in large Spanish companies: A snapshot. *Contaduría y Administración*, *60*(4), 757–775. doi:10.1016/j.cya.2015.05.014

Malafronte, I., Porzio, C., & Starita, M. (2016). The nature and determinants of disclosure practices in the insurance industry: Evidence from European insurers. *International Review of Financial Analysis*, *45*, 367–382. doi:10.1016/j.irfa.2015.02.003

Mcchlery, S., & Hussainey, K. (2021). Risk disclosure behaviour: Evidence from the UK extractive industry. *Journal of Applied Accounting Research*, *22*(3), 484–506. doi:10.1108/JAAR-09-2019-0134

Mohobbot, A., & Noriyuki, K. (2005). The UK guidelines for company risk reporting - An evaluation. *Okayama Economic Review*, *37*(1), 1–18.

Mokhtar, E., & Mellett, H. (2013). Competition, corporate governance, ownership structure and risk reporting. *Managerial Auditing Journal*, *28*(9), 838–865. doi:10.1108/MAJ-11-2012-0776

Montenegro, T., & Bras, F. (2015). Audit quality: Does gender composition of audit firms matter? *Spanish Journal of Finance and Accounting. Revista Española de Financiación y Contabilidad, 44*(3), 264–297. doi:10.1080/02102412.2015.1035578

Moumen, N., Othman, H., & Hussainey, K. (2016). Board structure and the informativeness of risk disclosure: Evidence from MENA emerging markets. *Advances in International Accounting, 35*, 82–97. doi:10.1016/j.adiac.2016.09.001

Neifar, S., & Jarboui, A. (2018). Corporate governance and operational risk voluntary disclosure: Evidence from Islamic banks. *Research in International Business and Finance, 46*, 43–54. doi:10.1016/j.ribaf.2017.09.006

Oliveira, J., Rodrigues, L., & Craig, R. (2011a). Risk-related disclosure practices in the annual reports of Portuguese credit institutions: An exploratory study. *Journal of Banking Regulation, 12*(2), 100–118. doi:10.1057/jbr.2010.20

Oliveira, J., Rodrigues, L., & Craig, R. (2011b). Risk-related disclosures by non-finance companies: Portuguese practices and disclosure characteristics. *Managerial Auditing Journal, 26*(9), 817–839. doi:10.1108/02686901111171466

Oliveira, J., Serrasqueiro, R., & Mota, S. (2018). Determinants of risk reporting by portuguese and spanish non-finance companies. *European Business Review, 3*(1), 311–339. doi:10.1108/EBR-04-2017-0076

Prencipe, A. (2002). Proprietary costs and voluntary segment disclosure: evidence from Italian listed companies. SSRN *Electronic Journal.* doi:10.2139/ssrn.319502

Saggar, R., & Singh, B. (2017). Corporate governance and risk reporting: Indian evidence. *Managerial Auditing Journal, 32*(4/5), 378–405. doi:10.1108/MAJ-03-2016-1341

Saha, R., & Kabra, K. (2021). *Is Voluntary Disclosure Value Relevant? Evidence from Top Listed Firms in India.* Vision - The Journal of Business Perspective., doi:10.1177/0972262920986293

Saleem, S., & Usman, M. (2021). Information risk and cost of equity: The role of stock price crash risk. *The Journal of Asian Finance, Economics, and Business, 8*(1), 623–635.

Seebeck, A., & Vetter, J. (2021). Not Just a Gender Numbers Game: How Board Gender Diversity Affects Corporate Risk Disclosure. *Journal of Business Ethics,* 1–26. doi:10.100710551-020-04690-3

Serrasqueiro, R. M. (2009). *A divulgação da informação sobre riscos empresariais* [Paper presentation]. XIV Encuentro AECA, Instituto Superior de Contabilidade e Administração de Coimbra.

Solomon, J., Solomon, A., Norton, S., & Joseph, N. (2000). A conceptual framework for corporate risk disclosure emerging from the agenda for corporate governance reform. *The British Accounting Review, 32*(4), 447–478. doi:10.1006/bare.2000.0145

Thenmozhi, M., & Sasidharan, A. (2020). Does board independence enhance firm value of state-owned enterprises? Evidence from India and China. *European Business Review, 32*(5), 785–800. doi:10.1108/EBR-09-2019-0224

Verrecchia, R. E. (2001). Essays on disclosure. *Journal of Accounting and Economics, 32*(1-3), 97–180. doi:10.1016/S0165-4101(01)00025-8

Watts, R., & Zimmerman, J. (1990). Positive accounting theory: A ten year perspective. *The Accounting Review, 65*(1), 131–156.

Zhang, X., Taylor, D., Qu, W., & Oliver, J. (2013). Corporate risk disclosures: influence of institutional shareholders and audit committee. *Corporate Ownership and Control, 10*(4), 341-353.

ADDITIONAL READING

Al-Hadi, A., Hasan, M., & Habib, A. (2016). Risk committee, firm life cycle, and market risk disclosures. *Corporate Governance, 24*(2), 145–170. doi:10.1111/corg.12115

Al-Yahyaee, K. H., Al-Hadi, A. K., & Hussain, S. M. (2017). Market risk disclosures and board gender diversity in Gulf Cooperation Council (GCC) firms. *International Review of Finance, 17*(4), 645–658. doi:10.1111/irfi.12123

Allini, A., Rossi, F., & Hussainey, K. (2016). The board's role in risk disclosure: An exploratory study of Italian listed state-owned enterprises. *Public Money & Management, 36*(2), 113–120. doi:10.1080/09540962.2016.1118935

Amran, A., Bin, A., & Hassan, B. (2009). Risk reporting: An exploratory study on risk management disclosure in Malaysian annual reports. *Managerial Auditing Journal, 24*(1), 39–57. doi:10.1108/02686900910919893

Barako, D., Hancock, P., & Izan, H. (2006). Corporate disclosure by kenyan companies. *Corporate Governance, 14*(2), 107–125. doi:10.1111/j.1467-8683.2006.00491.x

Carter, D. A., D'Souza, F., Simkins, B. J., & Simpson, W. G. (2010). The gender and ethnic diversity of US boards and board committees and firm financial performance. *Corporate Governance, 18*(5), 396–414. doi:10.1111/j.1467-8683.2010.00809.x

Chantachaimongkol, N., & Chen, S. (2018). The Effects of Board Compositions and Audit Committee Characteristics on Information Disclosure Practices: A Case of Singapore. *Asian Journal of Finance & Accounting, 10*(1), 407–427. doi:10.5296/ajfa.v10i1.13261

Dobler, M., Lajili, K., & Zéghal, D. (2011). Attributes of corporate risk disclosure: An international investigation in the manufacturing sector. *Journal of International Accounting Research, 10*(2), 1–22. doi:10.2308/jiar-10081

Höring, D., & Gründl, H. (2011). Investigating risk disclosure practices in the european insurance industry. *The Geneva Papers, 36*(2002), 380–413.

Kongpraiya, C. (2010). *The study of corporate risk disclosure in the case of Thai listed companies* [Unpublished doctoral dissertation]. University of Nottingham.

Lemos, K. (2011). *Contabilidade de instrumentos derivados. Estudo da informação divulgada pelas empresas portuguesas* [Unpublished doctoral dissertation]. Universidad de Santiago de Compostela - Facultade de Ciencias Económicas y Empresariales, Spain.

Lenard, M. J., Yu, B., York, E. A., & Wu, S. (2014). Impact of board gender diversity on firm risk. *Managerial Finance, 40*(8), 787–803. doi:10.1108/MF-06-2013-0164

Martins, R. (2014). *O governo das sociedades e o relato voluntário das entidades do PSI-20* [Unpublished master dissertation]. Universidade do Minho, Portugal.

Miranda, C. (2014). *A influência do governo das sociedades na qualidade dos resultados* [Unpublished master dissertation]. Universidade do Porto, Portugal.

Oliveira, G. (2016). *Estudo da relação entre o governo das sociedades e a divulgação voluntária pelas empresas do PSI-20* [Unpublished doctoral dissertation]. Universidade do Minho, Portugal.

Peters, G., & Abbott, L. (2001). *Voluntary disclosures and auditor specialization: the case of commodity derivative disclosures.* Western Regional Association Meeting, San Jose, CA.

Salehi, M., Moradi, M., & Paiydarmanesh, N. (2017). The effect of corporate governance and audit quality on disclosure quality: Evidence from Tehran stock exchange. *Periodica Polytechnica Social and Management Sciences, 25*(1), 32–48. doi:10.3311/PPso.8354

KEY TERMS AND DEFINITIONS

Audit Committee: A control body created to oversee internal processes and controls for the production of financial reports, to protect the interests of stakeholders.

Auditor: An audit professional whose main function is to issue an opinion on the company's accounts.

Corporate Governance Model: Corporate governance structure, comprising the bodies responsible for managing and controlling companies.

Credit Risk: Risk of loss caused by non-payment by the counterparty or deterioration of the credit position.

Disclosure Index: Indicator of the extent of the disclosure presented by a certain company, relative to certain information, measured by the sum of the items disclosed on the total items considered.

Liquidity Risk: Inability of a company to meet its obligations due to lack of financial resources, thus incurring losses.

Market Risk: Risk of loss arising from adverse changes in market rates and prices, such as interest rates and exchange rates.

ENDNOTE

[1]   Date of collection of the list of companies listed on Euronext Lisbon.

APPENDIX 1

Table 25 presents the items that compose the Financial risk disclosure index.

Table 25. Financial risk disclosure index

	Accounting Policies
1	Entity risk management policy
2	Accounting policies adopted for the recognition and measurement of financial instruments
3	Use of additional estimates and judgments
4	Purpose of holding derivative instruments
5	Description of hedging operations
6	Fair value of held financial instruments
7	Methods used to determine fair value
	Specific Information on Risk
8	The entity's risk exposure
9	Origin of risks
10	The entity's risk management objectives, policies and procedures
11	Methods used to measure this risk
12	Changes related to the previous period in relation to: exposure to risk, source of risks, political objectives and risk management procedures and risk measurement
13	Summary of the entity's exposure to that risk at the reporting date
	Hedging
14	Description of each type of hedge operation
15	Description of the financial instruments chosen as hedging instruments
16	Fair values of hedging instruments at the reporting date
17	Gains and losses on the hedging instrument
18	Gains and losses on the hedged instrument
19	Hedging ineffectiveness
	Credit Risk
20	Amount that best represents the entity's maximum exposure to credit risk at the reporting date, without taking into account any guarantees held or other improvements in credit quality (for example, clearing agreements not eligible for compensation under IAS 32)
21	Regarding the amount that best represents the entity's maximum exposure to risk, a description of collateral held as caution and other improvements in credit quality
22	Information about the credit quality of financial assets that are neither past due nor impaired
23	The carrying amount of financial assets whose terms have been renegotiated and which, otherwise, would be past due or impaired

continued on following page

Table 25. Continued

	Liquidity Risk
24	An analysis of the maturity of the financial liabilities that indicates the remaining contractual maturities
25	A description of how the entity manages the liquidity risk inherent in the previous paragraph
	Market Risk
26	A sensitivity analysis for each type of market risk to which the entity is exposed at the reporting date, showing how the results and equity would have been affected by changes in the risk variable in question reasonably possible at that date
27	The methods and assumptions used in preparing the sensitivity analysis
28	The changes introduced in the methods and assumptions used compared to the previous period, as well as the reasons for these changes
29	A description of the method used in preparing this sensitivity analysis, as well as the main criteria and assumptions underlying the data provided
30	An explanation of the purpose of the method used and the limitations that may result from the fact that the information does not fully reflect the fair value of the asset and liability involved

Chapter 8

Implications of Artificial Intelligence–Driven Deepfakes for Cybersecurity and Regulation in Nigeria:
Theorising for Cyberfakes and Cyberviolence

Adamkolo Mohammed Ibrahim
iD https://orcid.org/0000-0003-1662-7054
University of Maiduguri, Nigeria

Bukar Jamri
Yobe State University, Damaturu, Nigeria

Abubakar Zakari
Federal Polytechnic, Damaturu, Nigeria

ABSTRACT

The first quarter of the 21st century has barely passed, but a barrage of 'disrupting' surprises emerged – from the proliferation of information and communication technologies (ICT) to the weaponisation of ICT itself. Hence, cyberfakes or cyber deceptions (e.g., deepfakes, fake news, and even hate speech) have the potential to cause monumental problems related to cybersecurity and other online information management for organisations, nations, and individuals. Because literature and theories related the novel cyber deceptions may be scanty, this chapter attempted to close this research and theoretical gaps by deriving concepts leading to the development of a 'modelled framework' for the study of deepfakes and other related

DOI: 10.4018/978-1-7998-8390-6.ch008

Copyright © 2022, IGI Global. Copying or distributing in print or electronic forms without written permission of IGI Global is prohibited.

cyber deceptions and violence in social, organisational, or national contexts. Performing brainstorming reviews of extant literature, several theoretical concepts were derived leading to the development of the unified model of digital deception and online hate pronouncement. Policy recommendations were offered at the end.

INTRODUCTION

Barely has the world lived the first quarter of the 21st century than a swarm of disruptive surprises emerged. These surprises range from the so-called 'millennium bug', to the proliferation of information and communication technologies, and to the emergence, growth, and development of social media. Additional surprises include the revolutionary development of artificial intelligence (AI) technologies, to the weaponisation of the internet. The weaponisaion of the internet is a phenomenon that can cause harm not only to organisations and nations' cyber resources and cyber assets but also to online users' safety and wellbeing which often escalates into real-life mayhems with devastating consequences (Ahmad, Zhang, Huang, Zhang, Dai, Song, & Chen, 2021). Last but not the least of the surprises of the 21st century is the outbreak of the COVID-19 pandemic, which has caused global public health problems with devastating socio-economic consequences and implications for disruptive cybersecurity and online information management. Hence, cyberfakes or cyber deceptions (e.g., deepfakes, cheap fakes, fake news, and even hate speech) have the potential to cause monumental problems related to cyber security and other online information management for organisations, nations, and individuals (Paris & Donovan, 2019). In 2017, Nigeria was scored fifth in terms of cybersecurity (readiness, legislation, etc.) in Africa. In the same period, it was scored between 50th and 89th globally. Nigeria scored a very high rating in terms of cybersecurity legislation in Africa in 2017 (Garba & Bade, 2021; Ogundokun, Awotunde, Sadiku, Adeniyi, Abiodun, & Dauda, 2021). While in 2020, according to Global Cybersecurity Index (GCI), it was ranked 4th out of 43 countries in Africa, and 47th out of 182 countries (GCI, 2020).

The early years of the new millennium were dominated by the predominant model of internet connectivity which was rooted in population disparities worldwide. Consequently, national well as international security brings people into contact with "vast informational circuits that increasingly organise life on a global scale" (Ahmad et al., 2021; Reid, 2009, p. 608). As described in that utopian vision, this idea was undermined by an additional assumption. The assumption is that internet users will automatically be drawn to learn and grow by searching for new sources of knowledge in the current crisis of digital deceits online including misinformation, deepfakes, and cheap fakes. The utopian assumption further envisages the rise of authoritarian populism in Western liberal democracies (Bradshaw & Howard,

2019; Paris & Donovan, 2019; Taylor, 2021). Various studies and analyses have all agreed that these transformations have contributed to the emergence of a new and confounding state of both national and international insecurity (Sayler, 2019, 2019 Oct. 14; Horowitz, Allen, Saravelle, Cho, Frederick, & Scharre, 2018; Tolosana, Vera-Rodriguez, Fierrez, Morales, & Ortega-Garcia, 2020).

To find a suitable theoretical background for this chapter, we decided to focus on one of the most significant consequences of the condition: reflexive securitisation of digital media. This term refers to two important aspects of digital media (Karpf, 2017; Taylor, 2020). The primary source of this information is the fact that such media are known to allow for the delivery of messages, the collection and analysis of data about that delivery, and possibly a third function, all in one go. These capabilities, on the other hand, have been progressively growing more attractive to corporations, governments, and non-governmental organisations and groups who are now intervening to maximise beneficial outcomes and to reduce adverse risks for valued interests (Meinrath & Vitka, 2014; Mirghani, 2011; Taylor, 2020). As Perl, Howlett, and Ramesh (2018) noted, although this approach may, in some cases, lead to the designation of digital media as a cybersecurity threat, it has an alternative effect. It is clear to see that these assertions are inevitable. However, the presumption points out that such outcomes can appear obvious or automatic, but they are not.

In this chapter, we reviewed extant literature on the current cybersecuritisation of digital technology (e.g., internet, and social media) in the contexts of "deepfakes", and even cheap fakes, fake news and hate speech. While fake news and hate speech have become popular with research on the internet or social media use, 'deepfakes' is a novel online phenomenon (Paris & Donovan, 2019). Concisely, deepfakes is a term that is used to describe "recent advancements in computer configuration, artificial intelligence, multi-media editing tools, and digital data preservation" (Hao, 2019; Nwafor, 2021; Taylor, 2020). Hao further explains that users of deepfake employ "generative adversarial networks" (GANs) to create, test, and revise audio-visual texts, which are created by applying to compete for machine-learning algorithms (De Vries, 2020; Hao, 2019). Paris and Donovan (2019) coined the term "cheapfakes" to demonstrate that successfully deceptive media creation has never needed advanced processing technologies, such as today's machine learning tools. According to them, "a 'deepfake' is a video that has been altered through some form of machine learning to 'hybridise or generate human bodies and faces,' whereas a 'cheap fake' is an AV [audio-visual] manipulation created with cheaper, more accessible software (or none at all). Cheapfakes can be rendered through Photoshop, lookalikes, re-contextualizing footage, speeding, or slowing. a deepfake is a video that has been altered in some way" (p. 2).

This chapter focuses on providing an understanding of the impacts, influences, effects, correlation, and dynamics of digital deception (deepfakes and/or cheapfakes, and fake news) and online hate speech in the context of Nigerian national cybersecurity. Also looked at in this chapter are the relationships between these online deceptions and offensive speech and Nigerian national cybersecurity can be understood using some theoretical underpinnings. Although there are theoretical/conceptual frameworks for studying fake news and even hate speech in the African (or Nigerian) context, not quite deep advances have been made in research in that scholarly domain. This chapter aimed to close that theoretical/conceptual gap by the development of the UMDDOHP through the modification of the Theory of reasoned action (Fishbein & Ajzen, 1975). Furthermore, although deepfakes technology has yet to be implemented in Nigeria at the time of writing, arguably it is only a matter of time. Since the proliferation of publicly available mobile applications and software tools, anyone with a knack for genuine creativity or mischief has been able to create and use deepfakes. This has sparked social and ethical debates and raised several legal quandaries. Those wronged by deepfakes (individuals or corporations) may have legal recourse. When it comes to deepfakes, how important is intellectual property? What is the best way to deal with deepfakes should they proliferate in Nigeria, regulatory-wise? The purpose of this piece is to provide answers to the queries earlier mentioned.

To give a general overview, the introductory discourse of this chapter is followed by the 'Background' section, which presents the problem statement. Next, is the Literature Review section, which critically examines the issues, problems, and concept of deepfakes, the underlying technology, reasons for growth, and challenges inherent in the underlying technology in more detail. Also discussed in this section are the various applications of deepfakes, the drawbacks when exploited for criminal or illegal purposes, and how deepfakes can be used in commercially innovative ventures. Furthermore, in this section issues related to the regulation of cyber technology based on how Nigerian laws and regulations (both civil and criminal) can be used to combat the new technology are critically discussed, along with suggestions for other ways to combat the rise of deepfakes. The conclusion remarks which is preceded by the section on future research direction wraps up the chapter with some final thoughts on the subject.

BACKGROUND

Nigeria and Access to Public Information

Nigeria is a federal republic with 36 states and a Federal Capital Territory (FCT) in Abuja, and the 1999 Constitution serves as its primary source of law (as amended). Nigeria's legal system, as a former British colony, conforms to the common law history, but it also allows for the application of traditional or indigenous customary laws, as well as Islamic law, or Shari'ah. Previously, customary and Shari'ah law were limited to civil conflicts involving all parties, but after 1999, several northern Nigerian states extended Shari'ah law to criminal and social contacts. With a population of about 209 million and 105 million active internet users, Nigeria is home to the highest population of internet users in Arica. Over 33 million Nigerians use social media (DataReportal, 2021 February). In the last few years, the Nigerian government has introduced social media regulation as well as hate speech and fake news (prohibition) laws at the federal level. However, only a few state governments have so far domesticated them, with Ebonyi State (in the southern part of the country) being one of the pioneer states to adopt the laws and Kano State (in the northern part) moderating the fake news prohibition law to focus on matters related to COVID-19.

The Freedom of Information Act (FOIA) of Nigeria was enacted in 2011 to promote public access to public records and information held by government entities. FOIA makes it illegal for government entities to share personal data with the public unless consent is obtained or the information is publicly available. It does, however, make an exception for personal data and information, as well as personal privacy issues (Nwoke, 2019). Section 14 of the Freedom of Information Act prohibits government entities from sharing personal information on citizens unless they have consent, or the information is publicly available (Adibe, Ike, & Udeogu, 2017; Obi, 2020 September). The Freedom of Information Act (FOIA) of Nigeria. The act was passed in 2011 to improve public access to government records and information.

The Privacy Right

Privacy is defended as a fundamental human right in several international human rights accords. It is essential for the preservation of human dignity and serves as the bedrock of any democratic society. Other rights, including freedom of expression, information, and association, are preserved, and strengthened. The right to privacy implies that individuals should have a space for independent development, interaction, and liberty. Surveillance and censorship, for example, are only acceptable when authorised by law, necessary to achieve a legal goal, and proportionate to the goal pursued (Humble, 2021; Paradigm Initiative & Privacy International, 2018 March). As advances in information technology have enabled previously unimagined methods of gathering, storing, and transferring personal data, the right to privacy has developed to encompass state obligations relating to personal data protection (Seubert, S& Becker, 2021; Zharova & Elin, 2017). Concepts of data protection are established in several international treaties, and they have been adopted by several domestic legislatures (Kusamotu, 2007; Paradigm Initiative & Privacy International, 2018 March).

Nigerian Domestic Law of Privacy

The Federal Republic of Nigeria's 1999 Constitution recognises privacy as a basic right. "[t]he privacy of citizens, their homes, correspondence, telephone conversations, and telegraphic communications is hereby guaranteed and protected," Section IV, Article 37 of the Nigerian Constitution states. Observers have labelled Article 37 "probably one of the most under-researched, under-litigated, and under-developed rights in the Nigerian Constitution" (Akintola & Akinpelu, 2021; Paradigm Initiative & Privacy International, 2018 March).

Despite the Constitution's explicit protection of privacy, Nigeria lacks comprehensive law to protect personal information, with the National Assembly actively discussing two bills on the subject as of March 2018. Individual portions of agency-specific law (such as the National Identity Management Commission Act 2007, which controls the country's identity management system) and industry-specific regulations comprise most data privacy rules. The National Information Technology Development Agency (NITDA) produced Draft Guidelines on Data Protection in 2013, which comprised a precise set of provisions governing government agencies' acquisition, processing, storage, and transfer of personal data. The guidelines, however, are not yet legally binding (Akintola & Akinpelu, 2021; Paradigm Initiative & Privacy International, 2018 March; Suraj, 2020).

Countries are increasingly relying on information and communication technology (ICT) to create more inclusive governance, better commercial opportunities, and economic growth. The internet and its accompanying cyberspace are at the centre of ICT, enabling applications that are not constrained by physical or geographical borders (Ulnicane, Knight, Leach, Stahl, & Wanjiku, 2021). Cyberspace has become a crucial communication medium for the 21st century and beyond because it facilitates globalisation and drives operations in both critical and non-critical fields. The use of the internet for illegal purposes can have major consequences for the economy, national security, and the safety and privacy of the people (Eboibi, 2017; Froehlich, Ringas, & Wilson, 2021) especially Nigerians. According to the office of the National Security Adviser (ONSA), this reality necessitates the development of a policy that directs government efforts toward the creation of a safe online for Nigerians (Bello & Griffiths, 2021; ONSA, 2017 November).

The Federal Government of Nigeria announced the National Cybersecurity Policy (ONSA, 2015) in February 2015 to provide cohesive measures and strategic efforts to ensure the country's presence in cyberspace is secure and protected. The two texts work together to implement Nigerian Cybersecurity Programs through a multi-stakeholder partnership that includes government Ministries, Departments, and Agencies (MDA) and civil society organisations. Nigeria's National Cybersecurity

Strategy aims to defend the country from cybercrime, espionage, terrorism, and child internet abuse, among other things. Section 41 of the Cybercrime (Prohibition, Prevention, and Other Measures) Act, 2015 (CPPA, 2015; Osho & Onoja, 2015) requires the ONSA to "ensure the formulation and effective implementation" of Nigeria's comprehensive national cybersecurity strategy and policy. The National Cybersecurity Policy and National Cybersecurity Strategy emphasise the significance of analysing, appraising, and prioritising cyber risks to develop effective responses and a framework for a cybersecurity action plan as shown in Figure 1 (Akinyetun, 2021; ONSA, November 2017).

Figure 1. A sketch of the graphical representation of the Nigerian national cybersecurity policy 2015 architecture.

National Strategy for Engaging Cyber Threats Inimical to National Interest

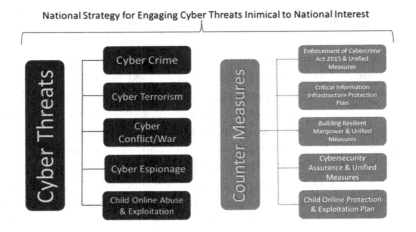

Nigeria's National Cybersecurity Strategy aims to safeguard key information infrastructure while also fostering a trustworthy cybercommunity. The strategy lays forth national priorities, principles, and procedures for identifying and reducing cybersecurity risks. It is a detailed document that outlines a series of procedures and strategic actions targeted at ensuring cyberspace security (ONSA, 2017 November; Osho & Onoja, 2015). These topics are a national priority, with 31 actions to be carried out by relevant governmental and private sector partners. Further, the National Cybersecurity Strategy is based on three important approaches: multi-stakeholder participation, public-private partnerships, and international collaboration. These approaches are utilised to implement the seven theme areas of legal and regulatory frameworks, critical information infrastructure protection and resilience, cybersecurity awareness and child online safety, capacity building and personnel development, and cybersecurity governance (Orji, 2018; Osho & Onoja, 2015). ONSA designed this Action Plan framework for implementing the National Cybersecurity Strategy to realise the Government's goal of securing Nigerian cyberspace per the National Cybersecurity Policy. The Action Plan framework contains all the government's priorities, plans, and strategies for putting the Strategy into action. It divides the strategy's seven theme sections into concrete programmes with measurable objectives (ONSA, 2017 November). As a result, Key Performance Indicators (KPI) with dates for each effort and delivery have been supplied to aid in progress assessment assiduously by the government.

REVIEW OF RELATED LITERATURE ON THE ISSUES AND PROBLEMS

Overview of Emerging Cybersecurity Issues in Nigeria

For many people and companies, the year 2020 has been a rollercoaster of "transformations" and various adaptations, as it is called the year of transformations. It is safe to say that the pandemic has played a major role in many world events, including those that took place online. To sum up, cybersecurity attacks and data breaches against businesses, health institutions, government agencies, and non-profit organisations will have increased significantly in scale in 2020 and 2021, compared to what they were in 2019 (Gafni & Pavel, 2021; Williams, Chaturvedi, & Chakravarthy, 2020). The attacks targeted many personal computers and cloud-based software applications. During this time, the remote work infrastructure was utilised. Despite a very positive outlook due to vaccine development in various countries, the economic and social situation remains largely the same as we entered 2021. Cybersecurity in Nigeria may be affected by global trends in social, economic, and political events (Aladenusi, 2021; Sule, Zennaro, & Thomas, 2021).

Related to issues on cybersecurity is the sudden and dramatic increase in sophisticated fakes in cyberspace. Misinformation and 'fake news' have become common terms in political discourse in recent years. What is more, this phenomenon poses a growing threat not only in Nigeria's social media space but also around the world. We live in a time when information is readily available, as is the ability to create and consume commercially viable merchandise content. Realising this, a variety of people produce content aimed at shaping narratives and social discourse. Some people are intentionally spreading misinformation and fake news to change people's perceptions and social attitudes. They do this by creating content that is either incorrect or altered, including videos and images (Mare, Mabweazara, & Moyo, 2019; Wasserman & Madrid-Morales, 2019). While attempting to do so, misinformation is on the rise, and a new, more sophisticated digital threat may emerge – deepfakes, on the other hand, are much more difficult to detect (Ibrahim, 2019). Deepfakes are artificially intelligent and machine learning-created hyper-realistic digital contents, such as sounds, videos, and images. To put it in another way, deepfakes are digital representations that are meant to look and sound as real as possible (Nwafor, 2021). According to Tope Aladenusi, who is the Leader, Cyber Risk Services, Deloitte West Africa, by 2021, a spike in Nigerian cyberspace-based deepfakes is expected. This is a crucial time to check the legality of various forms of media on the Internet (Aladenusi, 2021).

Discourse on social, political, and economic issues indicate that it is critical for the public to be on guard when it comes to online content and to check the usage of various tools before discarding them. Nigerian cyberspace may see an increase in deepfakes by 2021, according to expert predictions (Apuke & Omar, 2020). Cyber-attacks on major technology and cybersecurity firms, including FireEye and SolarWinds, were significant and unprecedented in 2020's fourth quarter. Some nation-state actors and advanced persistent threat (APT) groups have been identified as the primary perpetrators of these attacks. As a result of these attacks, private, internal, and unpublished security tools have been stolen, and SolarWinds' security monitoring system has been breached by taking advantage of a security flaw in the programme's code (Khweiled, Jazzar, & Eleyan, 2021). Yet to see the full impact of these attacks, we are still close to seeing tools and exploits like these in more tools, skills, and forums on the dark web and eventually out in the "wild". There is a lot to learn from these attacks, and as the probes continue, we will probably see more data breaches associated with them. These cyberattacks show that no matter how innovative a company is, it will have to deal with cybersecurity threats. There is an increase in the number of daring attacks on ISPs, cyber security solutions, and technical institutions as attackers become more creative and daring (Aladenusi, 2021; Paris & Donovan, 2019).

Obviously, Nigerian cyberspace is prone to cyberattacks and other nefarious activities such as cyber fraud, or 'Yahoo-Yahoo' as it is popularly known. Regulations governing cyber security and data privacy/protection will be tighter than they are now. Plentiful organisations in Nigeria have implemented the Nigerian Data Privacy Regulation (NDPR) over the past two years. More attacks, data leaks and breaches mean stricter cybersecurity regulations and enforcement of security safeguards in place by businesses, particularly those in data-sensitive sectors, are likely (Richards & Eboibi, 2021). The social media bill will continue to be a hot topic in 2020 and beyond (Aladenusi, 2021). To combat misinformation, the government has investigated ways to regulate social media, especially during the #EndSARS protests. Because of a series of intense anti-police brutality and anti-government demonstrations, the hashtag #EndSARS was created in Nigeria in October 2020. So many hacking groups have been linked to anti-government protests that the spotlight may now shift to Nigerian companies where cyber attackers may feel they are easier targets because they are perceived as being more vulnerable. Data leaks, breaches of sensitive information and deceptive contents such as deepfakes, cheap fakes and misinformation are likely to occur in government and public institutions and go viral online due to both domestic and foreign motivations (Paris & Donovan, 2019). On the other hand, an increase in financial support for cybersecurity awareness can be expected. Also, more discussion about social media regulations and possible government regulations to address a variety of concerns, despite the strong opposition can be expected (Eigbedion, 2021; Ojedokun, Ogunleye, & Aderinto, 2021; Richards & Eboibi, 2021).

The Concept of Deepfakes

Many manipulated videos have surfaced recently showing people doing or saying things they never did or being in places they never were as if they really happened. This technology, dubbed "Deepfakes," has been put to use for a variety of purposes (Fallis, 2020; Giansiracusa, 2021). Even if it is a video of Barack Obama calling President Donald Trump a "complete dipshit," or Mark Zuckerberg boasting about having "total control over billions" of people's data, the deepfakes phenomenon is still on the rise (Cole, 2019; Greengard, 2019). Since social media is such an important part of the digital space, it is safe to say that despite deepfakes' enormous potential, most of its demonstrations to date have shown how this technology has spread misinformation, triggered fraud, and privacy concerns, and more importantly the threat it poses to our already vulnerable information ecosystem by creating uncertainty about our shared reality (Cole, 2019; Eigbedion, 2021; Yadlin-Segal & Oppenheim, 2021).

A deepfake is a digitally manipulated image, video, or audio that presents people saying or doing things that have never occurred in real life. Videos of celebrities in unflattering sexual situations, which were later discovered to be faked, went viral on Reddit in 2017. Deepfakes is a mashup of the terms "deep learning" and "fake" used to describe the technology. Deepfakes rely on neural networks to learn how to mimic a person's facial expressions, mannerisms, voice, and inflexions by analysing large amounts of data (Chesney & Citron, 2019; Kerner & Risse, 2021; Westerlund, 2019). Though decontextualisation ("photoshopping") of still images and content fabrication is at the heart of digital society, a quick look at history shows that photography has long lost its innocence, as the art of 'photo tampering has been used by respected leaders like Abraham Lincoln or even dictators like Joseph Stalin who used photo retouchers to remove his political opponents from official photographs (Giansiracusa, 2021). That is why people who know about the technology and anyone who relies on audio-visual evidence are worried about deepfake technology's steady rise in the manipulated videos of people now increasingly making their way online (Blakemore, 2020 April 28; Eigbedion, 2021; Westerlund, 2019).

An artificial intelligence (AI) technology called "generative adversarial networks" (GANs) is the primary source of deepfaking technology; it combines two artificial neural networks to produce remarkably realistic images, videos, and sounds. GANs work by using a dataset of images, videos, or sounds to train a 'generator' and a 'discriminator', where the generator tries to create images that fool the discriminator into thinking they are real. Feeding a deep learning algorithm footage of two people trains it to swap faces, in other words (Eigbedion, 2021; Fallis, 2020; Nwafor, 2021; Yadlin-Segal & Oppenheim, 2021). Many images are required for deepfakes to create an authentic forgery, but current research shows that GANs can be trained on less information because researchers and even tech companies are already developing techniques to generate a fake video by feeding it only one photo, such as a selfie (Mesky, Liaudanskas, Kalpokiene, & Jurcys, 2020; Solsman, 2019 May 24; Westerlund, 2019).

Deepfakes have grown rapidly due to several factors, including the development of large image databases, particularly with the active participation of hundreds of millions on various social media or social networking platforms; the improvement in the computing power of graphics processing units (GPUs) and neural networks (an AI variant); and the growing commodification of tools and services that lower the barrier for non-experts to create deepfakes (Eigbedion, 2021; Green, 2019 October 30). However, no matter how far deepfakes have come in the last few years, there are still several issues that need to be addressed. Cyber or digital anonymity is a problem because most deepfake creators hide their identities, making it impossible for their victims or regulatory bodies to track them down. This problem is exacerbated if the creator is based in a different country. Second, the internet has no boundaries when it comes to the speed at which news, and particularly misinformation, spread across the globe. Individuals' wrongdoing about deepfakes and related cyberattacks can have long-term repercussions on others, leaving impressions that can be difficult to correct in the future. Using deepfakes to evade accountability for the truth poses another problem. Occasionally, someone is accused of wrong use of adapted videos or audio evidence to cast doubt on the charge or contradict it outright by labelling the real video or content as a deepfake. These situations do happen occasionally. Also known as the "liar's dividend," this is a common term (Eigbedion, 2021; Fallis, 2020; Yadlin-Segal & Oppenheim, 2021). There is also concern that as technology advances, it will become increasingly difficult to distinguish between a deepfake and a genuine product. As a result, people will be sceptical of all images and videos they see moving forward (Chesney & Citron, 2019; Hall, 2018; Krefetz, 2020 February 26).

The Various Uses of Deepfakes

It is often said that "a tool is only as good as the hands of the one who wields it" (see Eigbedion, 2021, p. 4); the same thing can be said of deepfakes. Whilst deepfakes could be highly innovative with an inherently creative and commercial value, there have been numerous attempts to create socially harmful deepfakes (Eigbedion, 2021; Dobber, Metoui, Trilling, Helberger, & de Vreese, 2021). Mesky and colleagues have highlighted the various uses of the deepfake technology, which, according to them, can be traced to the following creators:

1. deepfake hobbyists;
2. political and various activists;
3. other malevolent actors such as fraudsters; and
4. legitimate creators, such as e-commerce companies, movie production companies, educational and health institutes etc.

In discussing the forms of deepfakes, this chapter classifies the use of deepfake technology into two broad categories – criminal uses and commercial uses.

The Use of Deepfakes in Crime

Deepfakes Creation and Use Concerning Cybersecurity: Cybersecurity issues constitute one of the major threats imposed by deepfakes. The corporate world is gradually witnessing deepfakes being deployed by fraudsters to commit financial fraud. Criminals can make use of deepfake technology for market and stock manipulation; create real-time visual and audio impersonations of executives announcing a fake product launch, or fake acquisition/merger, making false statements of financial losses, bankruptcy or even the capabilities of a product, or portraying them as if committing a crime, or even giving instructions to an employee to perform an urgent cash transfer or provide confidential information; the list is endless (de Ruiter, 2021; Kirchengast, 2020). As such, with the quality of these videos improving rapidly, businesses need to be aware of how to spot fake videos, if not they stand the risk of brand sabotage, blackmail, falsification of evidence against a business in court, embarrass management, subvert procurement process, disrupt business relationships, and ultimately result in loss of business (Eigbedion, 2021; O'Sullivan, 2019 June 13).

Deepfakes Creation and Use in Politics: Deepfakes may also be used as a catalyst by various political players, including political agitators, hacktivists, terrorists, and foreign state intelligence agencies in disinformation campaigns to manipulate public opinion and to erode trust in public institutions (Ahmed, 2021). The negative impacts of deepfake videos/news reports to democratic societies could extend to targeting the reputation of certain individuals (e.g., a deepfake video of a politician offering/ receiving a bribe), portraying false or fabricated events (a fake terrorist attack or kidnap), or impact such democratic processes as electoral campaigns (a deepfake of a presidential candidate giving a racist speech or a presidential candidate confessing complicity in a crime), or and to deepen polarisation among social groups (Gosse & Burkell, 2020; Siekierski, 2019; Vaccari & Chadwick, 2020). Also, if used by hostile governments, deepfakes could even pose threats to national security or impair international relations (Eigbedion, 2021; Mesky et al., 2020). While the foregoing examples of deepfakes possess the likelihood of causing domestic unrest, riots, and disruptions in elections, other nation-states could even choose to act out their foreign policies based on unreality, leading to international conflicts. The result is that such deepfakes are likely to hamper citizens' trust toward authority-provided information and therefore come to regard everything as untrue (Ahmed, 2021; Eigbedion, 2021; Evans, 2018 April 17).

Sex-Related Deepfakes: The very first use case of generative adversarial networks (GANs) was to create deepfake sex videos; in particular, face-swapped celebrity porn and revenge porn. In the former category, celebrities' images are superimposed on the bodies of porn stars in adult movies. This kind of non-consensual celebrity pornography still accounts for about the majority of all the deepfakes (Gosse & Burkell, 2020; Maddocks, 2020). On the other hand, revenge porn has been subsequently expanded to deepfake sex videos, where non-consensual pornographic deepfakes are distributed by hackers or anyone seeking financial gain or notoriety rather than merely as revenge for the loss of a romantic relationship (Haris, 2018; Mesky et al., 2020). Although, the earliest deepfake pornography featured such famous actresses as Scarlett Johannsson and Gal Gadot, however, the reality is that anyone could have his or her face superimposed onto the bodies of porn stars engaged in sexual acts. Hence deepfake sex videos raise issues of breach of privacy, violation of image rights (where applicable), and consent, often resulting in victims suffering sexual humiliation and exploitation; physical, mental, or financial abuse, damage to reputation, to mention but a few (Eigbedion, 2021; Maddocks, 2020; Mesky et al., 2020).

The Use of Deepfakes as Commodities: Deepfake technology also has positive uses in many industries, including entertainment, social media and healthcare, educational media and digital communications, and various business fields, such as e-commerce and fashion. Businesses in the e-commerce and advertising sector interested in brand distinction can adopt deepfake technology in transforming their products or services in significant ways thereby making the same easily distinguishable by customers. For example, an e-fashion store may allow customers to create digital clones/avatars of themselves and try on attires before final purchase (Baron, 2019 July 19; Holliday, 2021).

The movie industry can benefit from deepfake technology in several ways. Initially, movie studios faced diverse challenges in bringing the imaginations of creators (writers/directors) into reality owing to the limitations of technology, and where said technology was available, visual storytelling remained prohibitively expensive for most creators. However, deepfake tech incorporates the ability to merge imagery, thereby giving smaller-scale and upcoming producers a similar capacity for bringing imaginative creativity to life at a reduced cost. Examples of the use and potentials of deepfake in the movie industry include - updating film footage instead of reshooting it, a recreation of classic scenes in movies, creating new movies starring long-dead actors, making use of special effects and advanced face editing in post-production, rendition of digital voices for actors who lost theirs due to disease etc. (Ayers, 2021; Brandon, 2018 February 16; Dhillon, 2019 July 4).

Similarly, deepfake technology can break the language barrier on video conference calls by translating speech and simultaneously altering facial and mouth movements to improve eye contact and make everyone appear to be speaking the same language (Ahmed, 2021; Ballantine, 2019 July 3). This can be extended to creating a realistic voice-over or dubbing for movies in any language, thus allowing diverse audiences to better enjoy films and educational media. A good example is the 2019 global malaria awareness campaign featuring David Beckham wherein visual and voice-altering technology was used to make him appear multilingual. In the same vein, deep fakes could be generated as a form of parody or satire (e.g., videos, memes, etc.). GANs certainly empower creators to create new content and develop innovative forms of creative expression. Accordingly, deep fakes could be seen as a medium that facilitates creative interactions and political debates. Creative deep fakes could be considered a constitutive part of free speech. The possibilities of deepfakes are endless and the true potentials are yet to be fully exploited (Dhillon, 2019; Eigbedion, 2021; Vaccari & Chadwick, 2020). Nevertheless, this discourse on deepfakes and other technologies with the potential to cause serious cybersecurity problems highlights the need for regulatory mechanisms.

The Regulation of Deepfakes

The Regulation of Data Protection and Privacy

The importance of regulation and even legislation cannot be overstated considering the potential uses and abuses of deepfakes as discussed earlier in this chapter. It is necessary to have a comprehensive legislative policy that lays out an efficient framework for the creation, ownership, distribution, and responsible exploitation of deepfakes as commercial commodities. Additionally, new criminal laws and/or regulations, as well as revisions to existing ones, should be enacted to reflect these previously unanticipated realities in cases of criminal use. Deepfakes are currently not specifically mentioned in Nigerian civil or criminal laws (Perot & Mostert, 2020; Yadlin-Segal & Oppenheim, 2021). The current laws and regulations, however, show that they can be adapted to address issues like privacy and data protection, intellectual property, defamation, identity fraud, or impersonation resulting from the use of deepfakes, and further help to allow the creators or users of deepfakes to know what types of deepfakes are permissible and not permissible (Ballantine, 2019 July 3; Eigbedion, 2021).

In the 1999 Constitution of the Federal Republic of Nigeria (as amended), Section 37 establishes Nigeria's regulatory framework for data protection and privacy (as Amended). There are several ways in which an individual's privacy has been violated, including an "invasion of personal life" (depending on how the information was obtained), public disclosure, publicity cast in a false light, and unauthorised appropriation (Spivak, 2019). If someone is the victim of deepfake, he or she may be able to sue for violation of his constitutional right to privacy by convincing the court that the constitutional right to privacy covers invasions of one's private life, particularly concerning how photos or videos are obtained and then 'deepfaked' (Fallis, 2020; Yadlin-Segal & Oppenheim, 2021). Contrary to popular belief, Nigerian law does not protect the right to privacy as other countries have done. Other nations, for example, have passed laws protecting personal identity and image rights, just to name a few (Eigbedion, 2021).

The Nigeria Data Protection Regulation 2019 (TNDPR) is the only data protection regulation in place in Nigeria now (NITDA, 2019). TNDPR's primary goal is to protect the personal data of all Nigerians and non-Nigerian residents in Nigeria as an advancement in privacy rights. Aside from that, TNDPR applies to all transactions involving the processing of an individual's private and confidential information. Personal data refers to "any" information about a specific identified or identifiable natural person. Other terms for personal information (sensitive or not) include names, photographs, and any other information about a natural person's physical, physiological, genetic, economic, cultural, or social identity (Fallis, 2020; Yadlin-Segal & Oppenheim, 2021). TNDPR goes on to define the term "processing" as "any" operation or set of operations performed on personal data, whether by automated means, such as collection, recording, organisation, structuring, storage, adaptation or alteration, retrieval, consultation, use, disclosure by transmission, dissemination or otherwise making available, alignment or combination, restriction, erasure, or destruction (Eigbedion, 2021; NITDA, 2019).

TNDPR mandates that data controllers obtain consent from individuals before processing their personal data or disclosing it to third parties. That is why inserting provisions in terms and conditions that give developers the global right to "permanently" use any image created on a face-swapping app for free or the right to transfer images to any third party without the user's further permission would be a clear data breach under the TNDPR's terms and conditions. To the extent that deepfakes use personal information about individuals, those activities fall under the scope of TNDPR (NITDA, 2019). When an organisation intends to use data for purposes not readily apparent to the individual, it is critical to obtain the appropriate consent before using the data for any unlawful purpose. Although obtaining consent before processing any personal information is critical, TNDPR also allows for other situations in which data may be processed without obtaining consent first, such as when the data subject is a contractual party, or the controller is bound by legal obligations that require the processing of the data. Legitimate creators, like e-commerce companies or movie production companies, may not be required to obtain 'consent before processing personal data if they rely on the aforementioned grounds (Fallis, 2020; NITDA, 2019; Yadlin-Segal & Oppenheim, 2021).

Defamation as a Form of Tort

Defamation is a tort that gives victims of false or defamatory statements or representations compensation for their suffering. Libel and slander are the twin torts that constitute defamation in Nigerian law. Defamation published in permanent forms, such as writing, sign, picture, cartoon, or electronic broadcasts, falls under the first category, while defamation spoken or uttered falls under the second. People who have been victimised by deepfakes may be entitled to damages under a libel action for defamation, since deepfakes are often expressed permanently (Araromi, 2018 November 28; Eigbedion, 2021). It has become a problem in the age of the computer to defame someone online and spread false information through web content to harm their reputation. When it comes to the scope of a defamation claim, this type can go much further than the usual one. The effect and description of generic defamation closely match those of online defamation because deepfakes are widely disseminated via the internet and other electronic means. There must be serious harm caused to the victim by the statement before a case of online defamation can be brought to court. Additionally, there must be evidence of the publication for a case to proceed. All these conditions must be met before an online defamation case can be brought to court (Eigbedion, 2021; Gerstner, 2020). Someone who has spent their entire life working hard to build a solid reputation only to have it shattered by an adult video depicting sexual acts in which they appear to engage when those actions run counter to their reputation is likely to have a case that meets the criteria for a defamation suit (Atake, Gbahabo, & Ushiadi, 2019 April 3; Holliday, 2021).

In the case of online defamation, a claimant must show that the alleged defamatory material was accessed and downloaded by identifiable persons within the jurisdiction of the court and that reputational harm resulted from the publication of the alleged defamatory material, in the context of a deepfake claim. The readership of the defamatory material must be considered when calculating the reputational damage suffered by the defamation victim because of an online defamation claim (Gerstner, 2020). The more people who read the offending post, the more likely it is that the post's reputation will be tarnished. Also, in the opposite case where the number of readers is low, a defamation claim may very well be unsuccessful unless evidence can be established that the posting has caused or will cause serious reputational harm. It is important to remember that not all online "defamation" is defamation (Fallis, 2020; Yadlin-Segal & Oppenheim, 2021). Unless there is clear and convincing evidence of actual malice by the creator of deepfake, a defendant facing a defamation claim based on deepfake creations may rely on the defence of – fair comment, statements of opinion reached based on facts; statements about public officials; and where it is proven that the communication was true (Spivak, 2019).

Furthermore, The Federal Competition and Consumer Protection Act 2018 (TFCCPA) governs Nigeria's current competition regime. Protecting consumer interests and welfare, as well as prohibiting unfair business practices, are just a few of the many goals of the FCCPA. TFCCPA also establishes the Federal Competition and Consumer Protection Commission (FCCPC), which acts as the competition regulator empowered to prevent and punish anti-competitive practices in every sector in Nigeria. Consumer protection and competition protection are two important responsibilities of The Federal Competition and Consumer Protection Act 2018 (FCCPC), making it a viable option for regulating Nigeria's deepfakes. FCCPC may have limited powers because not all deepfake creations include a 'commercial' component. Because of this, the FCCPC's regulatory jurisdiction in dealing with deepfake pornography or videos would most likely be limited when they are made for sexual gratification, the humiliation of a victim, or for other non-commercial purposes as a parody for entertainment (Eigbedion, 2021; Fallis, 2020; Holliday, 2021).

Trademarks and Patents

Content modification like that seen with deepfakes usually raises concerns about copyright and other forms of intellectual property protection. When it comes to deep fakes, there are a variety of issues to consider, including whether the person who created the fake can claim authorship of the new deep fake or whether using the original material (one or more copyright works) without permission constitutes a violation of third-party copyright and/or image rights. Two elements must be proven to establish infringement under Nigeria's primary copyright legislation: ownership of a valid copyright and copying of the work's original constituent elements (Gerstner, 2020). While a claimant can establish ownership by showing that she is the work's original author, she usually has no copyright claim because she does not own the source material's underlying copyright. As a result, the only person with the authority to sue for copyright infringement is the original author of the copyrighted source material from which the deepfake was derived. As an illustration, since the copyrights to a photograph are owned by the person who took it (the photographer), only that photographer has the standing to sue a deepfake creator for infringement (LFN, 2010; Nema, 2021). For example, if the deepfake uses a victim's own photo, the author of the deepfake may be able to make a copyright claim against the person who made the fake. Nevertheless, the chances for a victory in such legal actions are uncertain as deepfake creators may avoid liability by invoking statutory exceptions showing that the deepfake is intended for educational, artistic, or other expressive purposes as a parody or satire or that only a small part of the original work was used to create the deepfake are uncertain (e.g., if only a short snippet of a film was used in creating a parody). When it comes to liability, whether the person who created the deepfake can get away with it or not depends on the facts of each case. More importantly, whether the alleged infringer can convince a court that fair use analysis tilts the scales in his or her favour by showing that the deepfake is transformative in nature and that it is intended to be used for non-commercial purposes will also be a factor (Gerstner, 2020; Yadlin-Segal & Oppenheim, 2021).

Based on the Nigerian Communications Commission (NCC) guidelines, to ensure that infringing content is removed, a victim can file a complaint with an internet service provider (ISP) and request that it remove the identified content (a takedown notice). Image rights/publicity rights can be asserted as an additional option for redress. This intellectual property right has been defined as every human being's inherent right to control the commercial use of aspects of his personality such as appearance, pictures, likeness or caricatures and computer-generated images as well as signature and personal logos and slogans (Ahmed, 2021; Eigbedion, 2021). Image rights are also known as the right of publicity in some jurisdictions like the United States. To put it another way, "the image right" according to Eigbedion (2021, p. 9), refers to the economic right to make use of one's own fame and notoriety for economic gain. Images rights were once only granted to celebrities, professional athletes, artists, and entertainers. However, as time has gone on, "they are now granted to anyone" (Iwu, 2017; Spivak, 2019, p. 383).

A claim for infringement of image rights may also be an option for dealing with the problems caused by deepfakes. As a result, the person whose likeness appears in a deepfake may be able to bring an image right claim if a creator makes money from using that person's image without their consent (Nema, 2021). In an image rights suit, a claimant need only show that he has goodwill or considerable influence that entitles him to a financial interest in his identity and that this identity has been commercially exploited by a defendant without his consent to prevail in court (Ahmed, 2021; Iwu, 2017). For victims suing for infringement of their image rights, unlike copyright actions, the right to sue is not conditional on legal ownership of the image (Ahmed, 2021; Caldera, 2019). A defendant, on the other hand, may raise the defence that the work was produced solely for expression through parody or satire, or that no commercial benefit was derived from the creation of the work in question. Nigeria does not yet have a comprehensive image rights law. As an extension of artistic works and cinematographic films, image rights may be protected under Nigerian copyright laws as an extension of the country's copyright laws. For image rights claims stemming from deepfakes in Nigeria, it is suggested that tort actions under the torts of "passing-off" and "defamation" are a more viable option (Ahmed, 2021; Eigbedion, 2021, p. 10; Oturu, 2019 October 29).

Solutions and Recommendations

Countering Techniques of Deepfakes

Additionally, regulation can be used to address deepfake-related concerns, but other "combative approaches" approaches can be used to combat the harm that deepfakes cause, which includes, first, education and training. The public is still unaware of the dangers of deepfakes. Public awareness must be raised about the dangers of technology misuse. In addition to training employees, businesses and organisations must maintain a state of alertness and develop plans for cyber resilience. For example, implementing a comprehensive verification strategy or system, or using slogans and codes that are only known to certain individuals within the organisation or team (Ahmed, 2021; Nwafor, 2021). The second approach involves research and development of technology to detect and prevent deepfake attacks. This opens up a slew of new business opportunities for cybersecurity and artificial intelligence (AI) start-ups (Eigbedion, 2021, p. 14; Hawell, 2019 June 13; Nwafor, 2021). The third approach involves corporate policies and voluntary actions. These involve policies by social media makers to report, block, or remove deepfake content; suspension of violators' user accounts; investment in detection technologies; training of staff to identify deepfakes, etc. (Schwartz, 2019 June 24; Westerlund, 2019).

The Penalty for Criminal/Offensive Use of Deepfakes

To address issues arising from deepfakes, several Nigerian criminal statutes are relevant. These include laws against cyberstalking, blackmail, extortion, impersonation, and criminal defamation. To this day, the Cybercrime Act of 2015 has been the most effective tool in the fight against criminal activities that take place in cyberspace (Nwafor, 2021). Messages or other materials intentionally disseminated over computer systems or networks that are grossly offensive, pornographic, or otherwise indecent or obscene, or menacing to another, knowing that the message is false, are prohibited under Section 24 of the Cybercrimes Act. This includes messages that cause someone else to be irritated or inconvenienced or to cause them harm or unnecessary anxiety by insulting, injuring, or criminally intimidating them (Cunliffe-Jones, Diagne, Finlay, & Schiffrin, 2021). In this way, "the posting of deepfakes in connection with the targeting of individuals, for example, where non-consensual pornographic deepfakes are shared would be in violation of the provisions of the said Sections 24" (Ahmed, 2021; Eigbedion, 2021, p. 12).

The Cybercrimes Act's Sections 13, 14 and 22 criminalise activities related to impersonation crimes (computer-related forgery, fraud and identity theft), particularly when someone knowingly accesses a computer or network and inputs, alters, deletes, or suppresses any data that results in inauthentic data with the intention that such inauthentic data will be considered or acted upon as authentic, or where such actions (alteration, deletion, or suppression) "causes any loss of property to another, whether or not to confer any economic benefits on himself or another person" (Eigbedion, 2021, p. 13). Sending electronic messages that materially misrepresent any fact with the intent to defraud another is also included in the offence. Therefore, the Nigerian Cybercrime Act may apply to penalise actions such as making a deepfake video and disseminating it to cause another "annoyance, inconvenience danger, obstruction, insult, injury, criminal intimidation, hatred, ill will, or needless anxiety," or to perpetrate fraud. Section 26 of the Cybercrimes Act "criminalizes activities involving the creation or distribution of racist or xenophobic materials to the public through a computer system or network" (Eigbedion, 2021, p. 14) to address broader societal harms. It follows then that any deep fake that spreads racist or hate speech with the intent of inciting violence would fall under the purview of this section of the Cybercrimes Act (Ahmed, 2021; Cunliffe-Jones et al., 2021).

In addition to criminal defamation charges, creators of deep fakes could be held liable for posting videos they knew were fakes or were reckless about their truth or falsity. Instead of preventing a situation where defamation takes on the tendency to arouse angry passion, provoke revenge, and ignite society, criminal defamation seeks to prevent a situation where public peace is endangered by defamation (Ahmed, 2021; Babalola, 2019 October 23). To be defamed means to expose someone to hatred, contempt, or ridicule, or to harm someone in their profession or trade by damaging their reputation. This is defined in Section 373 of the Criminal Code as "a matter likely to injure the reputation of any person by exposing him to hatred, contempt or ridicule, or likely to damage any person in his profession or trade by injury to his reputation" (Eigbedion, 2021, p. 13). Slander can be used to describe defamatory statements made or published in a short time, much like the tort of defamation. An indefinite publication of false and harmful materials about another person, whether in a painting or a picture or the form of an effigy, caricature or an advertisement will be considered libel (Cunliffe-Jones et al., 2021; Nwafor, 2021).

Conceptualising the Unified Model of Digital Deception and Online Hate Pronouncement

From the foregoing review of the literature, it is obvious that cyber deception which comes in various ways including deepfakes, cheap fakes, fake news, and even hate speech has the potential to pose cyber security and other online information management problems. Being an emerging area of study, specific theoretical underpinnings to explain and predict behaviours related to those novel cyber deceptions may be scanty or unavailable. This chapter attempts to close this research and theoretical gaps by deriving concepts leading to the development of a 'conceptualised theoretical' model which can be used to study deepfakes and other related cyber or digital deceptions and/or violence capable of causing a lot of harm not only to organisations and nations' cyber-assets but also to individual online users, which often escalates real-life situations with devastating consequences. Hence, this chapter proposes the Unified Model of Digital Deception and Online Hate Pronouncement (UMDDOHP) for adoption (see Figure 2).

Figure 2. A graphical representation of the Unified Model of Digital Deception and Online Hate Pronouncement (UMDDHOP)

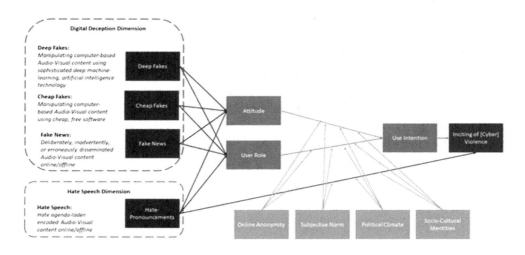

UMDDOHP is conceptualised to comprise four key dimensions, namely (i) the predicting variable dimension (PVD), (ii) the mediating variable dimension MeVD), (iii) the moderating variable dimension (MoVD), and (iv) the dependent variable dimension (DVD) (see Figure 2). The PVD, which is the dimension having the four independent variables of the model is divided into two sub-dimensions, namely the digital deception dimension (DDD) and hate pronouncement dimension (HPD); the DDD cluster consists of three predictors, namely 'deepfakes', 'cheap fakes, and 'fake news; the HPD cluster consists of only 'hate pronouncement' (HP) as its loner variable; the MeVD cluster consists of a total of three mediating variables, two of which are corresponding (direct) mediating variables – 'attitude' (AT) and 'user role' (UR) – with the third variable – 'use intention' (UI) – being a loner; while the MoD cluster consists of four moderating variables, namely 'online anonymity' (OA), 'subjective norm' (SN), 'political climate' (PC), and 'socio-cultural identities' (SCI).

To predict the behaviour – 'Inciting of Cyberviolence' (ICV), which is, the dependent variable – the predicting paths of all four predictors are conceptualised to be directly mediated by Attitude and User Role except for the Hate Pronouncement (HP) variable, which is also conceptualised to directly predict the dependent variable, Incitement of Cyberviolence (e.g., Ibrahim, 2019; Gohdes, 2018). The variables Attitude (AT) and User Role (UR) is conceptualised to be mediated by Use Intention (UI) (e.g., Wu et al., 2017), a phenomenon that bars it (the Use Intention variable) from being directly predicted by all three variables in the Digital Deception dimension cluster. Moreover, in information systems (IS) research, 'use intention' is often theorised to directly predict 'use behaviour' (e.g., Bandura, 1986; Venkatesh, Morris, Davis, & Davis, 2003); hence, this chapter conceptualises 'use intention'(UI) to directly predict the behaviour-driven action of the 'inciting of cyberviolence'. All four moderators – Online Anonymity (e.g., Arthur, 2013; Yankoski, Theisen, Verdeja, & Scheira, 2021); Subjective Norm (e.g., Arthur, 2013; Reicher & Stott, 2011); Political Climate (e.g., Adum, Ojiakor, & Nnatu, 2019; Ciboh, 2017; Ibrahim, 2019); Socio-Cultural Identities (e.g., Castells, 2007; McQuail, 2010; Tajfel & Turner, 1979) are conceptualised to moderate all three influential paths emanating from the two direct (corresponding) mediating variables 'Attitude' (e.g., Fishbein & Ajzen, 1975; Wu et al., 2017) and 'User Role' (e.g., Chen et al., 2018; Yankoski et al., 2021), as well as the only influential path emanating directly (without any mediation) from the Hate Pronouncement (HP) variable to the Inciting of Cyberviolence (ICV) variable (e.g., Wu et al., 2017; Yankoski et al., 2021).

Conceptualising Incitement of Violence as a Threat to National Security

Leveraging on the Theory of Conflict, this chapter conceptualises inciting of violence (the dependent variable) as a threat to national security. According to Mohammed and colleagues, first written by Fredrick Engel, the conflict theory was developed by Karl Marx. This was necessitated by the "failure of the functionalist theory to provide a vivid explanation of conflicts and social change in the society" (Mohammed, Danladi, & Adamu, 2020, p. 135). The conflict theory was developed in response to the failure of functionalist theory to account for conflicts and social change. Since the struggle for economic resources results in a conflict of interest between the two disparate classes, conflict theory presupposes that the economy exerts control over all other social activities (the superstructure). It was concluded that in a capitalist society, the 'haves' exercise complete control over all social activities at the expense of the 'have-nots,' who were primarily the masses (Mohammed et al., 2020; Ogunlana, 2019).

This chapter argues that the mainstream media's excessive control and regulation in presenting the public with the true picture of political events have increased street journalism's popularity, which consequently popularised cyber conflict with violent real-life repercussions such as the #EndSARS protests that went viral on social media platforms in October 2020 in Nigeria but ended up with inestimable real-life consequences – loss of lives and destruction of property worth billions of Naira. The wealthy political class in Nigeria own and control the media to spread propaganda and divide the populace, particularly educated citizens (the masses). However, rapid developments in social media technology have redefined the media landscape giving the citizens great opportunities to have their say; thus, breaking the decades-long media monopoly enjoyed by the ruling class and bourgeoisie (Ojo, 2020; Abbas, 2012).

To understand the implications of violence/conflict to national security, it is pertinent for us to understand a little about human security, which, due to the absence of a widely accepted standard for determining an individual's level of safety, is seen as ambiguous. Human security is simply defined as the "absence of fear" (United Nations, 1994). Human security is also defined as an individual's high standard of living. Because the term "security" is used by so many different actors, including governments, international organisations, researchers, and non-governmental organisations, it is difficult to address and criticise (Fukuda-Parr & Messineo, 2012; Ojo, 2020).

It has been shown that online hate speech, misinformation, and other forms of cyber deception such as deepfakes can incite online violence with real-life consequences (Hatzipanagos, 2018; Müller & Schwarz, 2018 May). A lot of advances have been made in research on hate speech and misinformation (fake news) in the Nigerian context; however, evidence on the emergence and/or impacts of deepfakes in Nigeria is still scanty. However, evidence on the use of cheap online-based technologies, or cheapfakes to manipulate content is available. For example, an action research study on the EndSARS protests conducted by Dubawa, the leading Nigerian fact-checking site concludes that with a frequency of over 50%, the content analysis of fact-check of claims on #EndSARS protests showed images were the most manipulated content (Jamiu, 2020). increased criminality, particularly in cyberspace and transnational organised crime, pose a threat to national security (KPMG, 2014; Kuol & Amegbo, 2021; Ojo, 2020).

FUTURE RESEARCH DIRECTIONS

The year 2021 has been full of surprises in the fields of economics, health, business, and cybersecurity as was the year 2020. As we have seen over the last couple of years, security will always be a top priority, even when times are tough because attackers are constantly looking for vulnerabilities to exploit. By looking back on the experiences and lessons we have learned in the past, we can gain perspective and be better prepared for the years ahead. Future research should focus on providing a specific understanding of the likely effects of deepfakes on organisations and governments' cybersecurity so that they enhance their cybersecurity programmes, implement initiatives to continuously monitor internal people and system activities, proactively manage vulnerabilities and risks, test incident response and business continuity plans, and take a stance that has already been breached to improve their cybersecurity. Future research should also focus on the criminal and business implications of deepfakes; because attackers only need one successful entry to gain access, businesses cannot afford to become complacent when it comes to security. Finally, future research should focus on testing the UMDDHOP because the scope of the present research is merely a critical review of extant literature hence, the model was not tested. It is recommended that future research should adopt a mixed-method approach to test the model to provide comprehensive exploratory reports from both qualitative and quantitative perspectives.

CONCLUSION

Without any comprehensive report on the use of deepfakes in Nigeria or any explicit mention of the term "deepfakes" in our legal or legislative tools, this chapter demonstrates that some of Nigeria's pre-existing legal tools covering intellectual property, data protection and private data protection and the legal tools regarding the competition can be used as initial approaches in addressing deepfakes-related concerns. To be sure, the need to repeal or amend Nigeria's current legislation to address any potential latent ambiguities that may arise regarding the applicability of those legal tools to deepfakes and other emerging technologies cannot be overstated. In fact, "the speed at which the law is clarified or amended to address these issues may be considered to be its rate of 'adaptation' (Eigbedion, 2021, p. 13) As a result of this process, it will be necessary to adopt measures that are based on processes that are flexible and inclusive and include innovators as well as established companies, as well as regulators, experts, and the public. There must be a well-defined strategy in place in addition to updating the existing legal tools and regulations for the deepfake technology because no one will be safe once the rubber hits the road once the legal/regulatory and sociotechnical approaches are combined.

Deepfakes are here to stay as a new technological process that opens up new possibilities. Deepfakes will inevitably be used for criminal purposes. However, this should not override the need to recognise the enormous commercial potentials of the technology, nor should it preclude efforts to limit or mitigate any harm the technology may cause. Many times, the chasm between new emerging technologies like deepfakes and the systems put in place to regulate them has only widened. In the face of rapidly changing societal and economic circumstances, systems are frequently non-responsive or slow to respond/adapt. In addition, the existing complex national systems in place for enacting new laws or amending old ones in response to recent and/or emerging developments exacerbate these regulatory challenges. Regulation in Nigeria is no exception, as there is no mechanism for informing legislators quickly and anticipatorily of advantageous new technologies.

REFERENCES

Abbass, I. M. (2012). No retreat no surrender conflict for survival between Fulani pastoralists and farmers in Northern Nigeria. *European Scientific Journal*, *8*(1), 331–346.

Adibe, R., Ike, C. C., & Udeogu, C. U. (2017). Press Freedom and Nigeria's Cybercrime Act of 2015: An Assessment. *Africa Spectrum*, *52*(2), 117–127. doi:10.1177/000203971705200206

Ahmad, T., Zhang, D., Huang, C., Zhang, H., Dai, N., Song, Y., & Chen, H. (2021). Artificial intelligence in sustainable energy industry: Status quo, challenges and opportunities. *Journal of Cleaner Production*, *125834*. Advance online publication. doi:10.1016/j.jclepro.2021.125834

Ahmed, S. (2021). Who inadvertently shares deepfakes? Analysing the role of political interest, cognitive ability, and social network size. *Telematics and Informatics, 57,* 101508. doi:10.1016/j.tele.2020.101508

Akintola, S. O., & Akinpelu, D. A. (2021). The Nigerian Data Protection Regulation 2019 and data protection in biobank research. *International Data Privacy Law, 11*(3), 307–318. doi:10.1093/idpl/ipab011

Akinyetun, T. S. (2021). Poverty, Cybercrime and National Security in Nigeria. *Journal of Contemporary Sociological Issues, 1*(2), 1–23. doi:10.19184/csi.v1i2.24188

Aladenusi, T. (2021 January). *A fresh perspective: Nigeria cyber security outlook 2021.* Cyber Risk Services Deloitte West Africa. https://www.delotte.com.ng/

Apuke, O. D., & Omar, B. (2020). Fake news proliferation in Nigeria: Consequences, motivations, and prevention through awareness strategies. *Humanities and Social Sciences Reviews, 8*(2), 318–327. doi:10.18510/hssr.2020.8236

AraromiA. (2018 November 28). Determining legal responsibilities in defamation: Crossing the dividing line between real world and internet jurisdiction. SSRN. https://www.researchgate.net/scientificcontributions/2075535661_Marcus_Araromi

Atake, A., Gbahabo, E., & Ushiadi, A. (2019 April 3). Online defamation: Just before you post it! *Templars-Thought Leadership.* https://www.templars-law.com/copyrights-and-the-music-business/

Ayers, D. (2021). The limits of transactional identity: Whiteness and embodiment in digital facial replacement. *Convergence, 27*(4), 1018–1037. doi:10.1177/13548565211027810

Babalola, A. (2019 October 23). When False Publication May Amount to Criminal Libel. *Vanguard.* https://www.vanguardngr.com/2019/10/when-false-publications-may-amount-to-criminal-libel/#:~:text=Whereas%20in%20tort%20the%20false%20publication%20must%20be,tendency%20to%20provoke%20a%20breach%20of%20the%20peace

Ballantine, M. (2019 July 3). Are deepfakes invading the office? *Forbes.* https://www.forbes.com/sites/mattballantine/2019/07/03/are-deepfakes-invading-the-office/#19bf48923ea1

Baron, K. (2019 July 19). Digital double: The deepfake tech nourishing new wave retail. *Forbes.* https://www.forbes.com/sites/katiebaron/2019/07/29/digital-do-ubles-the-deepfake-tech-nourishing-new-waveretail/#33489a044cc7

BBC News. (2021). Muhammadu Buhari: Twitter deletes Nigerian leader's "civil war" post. *BBC News*. Retrieved 25 July 2021 from https://www.bbc.com/news/world-africa-57336571.amp

Bello, M., & Griffiths, M. (2021). Routine activity theory and cybercrime investigation in Nigeria: how capable are law enforcement agencies? In T. Owen & J. Marshall (Eds.), *Rethinking Cybercrime* (pp. 213–235). Palgrave Macmillan. doi:10.1007/978-3-030-55841-3_11

Blakemore, E. (2020 April 28). How Photos Became a Weapon in Stalin's Great Purge. *History*. https://www.history.com/news/josef-stalin-great-purge-photo-retouching

Bradshaw, S., & Howard, P. (2019). *The global disinformation order*. https://comprop.oii.ox.ac.uk/research/cybertroops2019/

Brandon, J. (2018 February 16). Terrifying high-tech porn: Creepy 'deepfake' videos are on the rise. *Fox News*. https://www.foxnews.com/tech/2018/02/16/terrifying-high-tech-porn-creepy-deepfake-videos-are-on-rise.html

Caldera, E. (2019). Reject the evidence of your eyes and ears: Deepfakes and the law of virtual replicants. *Seton Hall Law Review*, *50*, 177.

Chesney, B., & Citron, D. (2019). Deep fakes: A looming challenge for privacy, democracy, and national security. *California Law Review*, *107*, 1753–1820. doi:10.2139srn.3213954

Cole, S. (2019). This deepfake of Mark Zuckerberg tests Facebook's fake video policies. *Vice*. https://www.vice.com/en/article/ywyxex/deepfake-of-mark-zuckerberg-facebook-fake-video-policy

Cunliffe-Jones, P., Diagne, A., Finlay, A., & Schiffrinet, A. (2021). Bad law – legal and regulatory responses to misinformation in Sub-Saharan Africa 2016–2020. In *Misinformation policy in Sub-Saharan Africa: From laws and regulations to media literacy* (pp. 99–218). University of Westminster Press. doi:10.16997/book53.b

Cybercrimes (Prohibition, Prevention), etc.) Act (CPPA), 2015.

DataReportal. (2021, February). *Digital 2021: Nigeria*. https://datareportal.com/reports/digital-2021-nigeria

de Ruiter, A. (2021). The distinct wrong of deepfakes. *Philosophy & Technology*, *34*, 1311–1332. doi:10.100713347-021-00459-2

De Vries, K. (2020). You never fake alone. Creative AI in action. *Information Communication and Society*, *23*(14), 2110–2127. doi:10.1080/136911 8X.2020.1754877

Dhillon, S. (2019 July 4). The optimistic view of deepfakes: Always look on the bright side of simulated life. *Tech Crunch*. https://techcrunch.com/2019/07/04/an-optimistic-view-of-deepfakes/

Dobber, T., Metoui, N., Trilling, D., Helberger, N., & de Vreese, C. (2021). Do (microtargeted) deepfakes have real effects on political attitudes? *The International Journal of Press/Politics*, *26*(1), 69–91. doi:10.1177/1940161220944364

Eboibi, F. E. (2017). A review of the legal and regulatory frameworks of Nigerian Cybercrimes Act 2015. *Computer Law & Security Review*, *33*(5), 700–717. doi:10.1016/j.clsr.2017.03.020

EigbedionA. (2020 August 1). Deepfakes: Legal & regulatory considerations in Nigeria. Available at SSRN: doi:10.2139/ssrn.3670644

Evans, C. (2018 April 17). Spotting fakes news in a world with manipulated video. *CBS News*. https://www.cbsnews.com/news/spotting-fake-news-in-a-world-with-manipulated-video/

Fallis, D. (2020). The epistemic threat of deepfakes. *Philosophy & Technology*, *34*, 623–643. doi:10.100713347-020-00419-2 PMID:32837868

Fishbein, M., & Ajzen, I. (1975). *Intention and behaviour: An introduction to theory and research*. Addison-Wesley. doi:10.4236/tel.2018.813176

Froehlich, A., Ringas, N., & Wilson, J. (2021). How space can support African civil societies: Security, peace, and development through Efficient Governance Supported by space applications. *Acta Astronautica*. Advance online publication. doi:10.1016/j.actaastro.2021.06.006

Fukuda-Parr, S., & Messineo, C. (2012). *Human security: A critical review of the literature*. Working Paper. Leuven: Centre for Research on Peace and Development.

Gafni, R., & Pavel, T. (2021). Cyberattacks against the health-care sectors during the COVID-19 pandemic. *Information & Computer Security*. 1 doi:0.1108/ICS-05-2021-0059

Garba, A. A., & Bade, A. M. (2021). The current state of cybersecurity readiness in Nigerian organizations. *International Journal of Multidisciplinary and Current Educational Research*, *3*(1), 154–162.

GCI. (2020). *Global cybersecurity index 2020.* International Telecommunication Union (ITU). https://www.itu.int/dms_pub/itu-d/opb/str/D-STR-GCI.01-2021-PDF-E.pdf

Gerstner, E. (2020). Face/off: "Deepfake" face swaps and privacy laws. *Defense Counsel Journal, 87,* 1–14.

Giansiracusa, N. (2021). Deepfake Deception. In N. Giansiracusa (Ed.), *How Algorithms create and prevent fake news* (pp. 41–66). Apress.

Gosse, C., & Burkell, J. (2020). Politics and porn: How news media characterizes problems presented by deepfakes. *Critical Studies in Media Communication, 37*(5), 497–511. doi:10.1080/15295036.2020.1832697

Green, A. (2019, October 30). Lawmakers and tech groups fight back against deepfakes. *Financial Times.* https://www.ft.com/content/b7c78624-ca57-11e9-af46-b09e8bfe60c0

Greengard, S. (2019). Will deepfakes do deep damage? *Communications of the ACM, 63*(1), 17–19. doi:10.1145/3371409

Hall, H. K. (2018). Deepfake videos: When seeing isn't believing. *Cath. U. J. L. & Tech, 27*(1), 51–76.

Hao, L. (2019). The emergence of deepfake technology: A review. *Technology Innovation Management Review, 9*(11), 39–52.

Harris, D. (2018). Deepfakes: False pornography is here and the law cannot protect you. *Duke L. & Tech. Rev., 17,* 99.

Hatzipanagos, R. (2018). How online hate turns into real-life violence. *Washington Post.* Retrieved 25 July 2021 from https://www.washingtonpost.com/nation/2018/11/30/how-online-hate-speech-is-fueling-real-life-violence/

Hawell, D. (2019 June 13). Top AI researchers race to detect 'deepfake' videos: 'We are outgunned'. *Mercury News.* https://www.washingtonpost.com/technology/2019/06/12/top-ai-researchers-race-detectdeepfake-videos-we-are-outgunned/

Holliday, C. (2021). Rewriting the stars: Surface tensions and gender troubles in the online media production of digital deepfakes. *Convergence, 27*(4), 899–918. doi:10.1177/13548565211029412

Horowitz, M., Allen, G., Saravelle, E., Cho, A., Frederick, K., & Scharre, P. (2018). *Artificial intelligence and international security*. Center for a New American Security. https://www.cnas.org/publications/reports/artificial-intelligence-and-internationalsecurity

Humble, K. P. (2021). International law, surveillance and the protection of privacy. *International Journal of Human Rights*, *25*(1), 1–25. doi:10.1080/13642987.202 0.1763315

Ibrahim, A. M. (2019). Theorizing the journalism model of disinformation and hate speech propagation in a Nigerian context. *International Journal of E-Politics*, *10*(2), 60–73. doi:10.4018/IJEP.2019070105

Iwu, P.-A. (2017). Photo privacy and media/image rights in Nigeria. *The BarCode*, *2*(2). http://barcode.stillwaterslaw.com/1.1/2017/04/01/photo-privacy-and-mediaimage-rights-in-nigeria/

Jamiu, F. (2021). Analysis of claims on #EndSARS protest in Nigeria: Images most manipulated content, Twitter as a major platform. *Dubawa*. Retrieved 25 July 2021 from https://www.dubawa.org/analysis-of-claims-on-end-sars-protest-in-nigeria-images-most-manipulated-content-twitter-as-major-platform

Karpf, D. (2017). Digital politics after Trump. *Annals of the International Communication Association*, *41*(2), 198–207.

Kerner, C., & Risse, M. (2021). Beyond Porn and Discreditation: Epistemic Promises and Perils of Deepfake Technology in Digital Lifeworlds. *Moral Philosophy and Politics*, *8*(1), 81–108. doi:10.1515/mopp-2020-0024

Khweiled, R., Jazzar, M., & Eleyan, D. (2021). Cybercrimes during COVID-19 Pandemic. *International Journal of Information Engineering & Electronic Business*, *13*(2). doi:10.5815/ijieeb.2021.02.01

Kirchengast, T. (2020). Deepfakes and image manipulation: Criminalisation and control. *Information & Communications Technology Law*, *29*(3), 308–323. doi:10 .1080/13600834.2020.1794615

KPMG. (2014). *Future state 2030: The global megatrends shaping governments*. Retrieved 25 July 2021 from https://assets.kpmg/content/dam/kpmg/pdf/2014/02/future-state-2030-v3.pdf

Krefetz, N. (2020 February 26). Deepfakes and the war on reality. *Streaming Media*. https://www.streamingmedia.com/Articles/ReadArticle.aspx?ArticleID=139414

Kuol, L., & Amegbo, J. (2021). Rethinking national security strategies in Africa. *International Relations and Diplomacy*, *9*(01), 1–17. doi:10.17265/2328-2134/2021.01.001

Kusamotu, A. (2007). Privacy law and technology in Nigeria: The legal framework will not meet the test of adequacy as mandated by article 25 of European union directive 95/46. *Information & Communications Technology Law*, *16*(2), 149–159. doi:10.1080/13600830701597616

Leetaru, K. (2019 May 16). Deepfakes: The media talks politics while the public is interested in pornography. *Forbes*. https://www.forbes.com/sites/kalevleetaru/2019/03/16/deepfakes-the-media-talks-politics-while-the-public-isinterested-in-pornography/#71ea2e528461

LFN (2010). Sections 6, 10, 15 & 16 of the Copyright Act, CAP C28, LFN, 2010.

Maddocks, S. (2020). 'A deepfake porn plot intended to silence me': Exploring continuities between pornographic and 'political' deep fakes. *Porn Studies*, *7*(4), 415–423. doi:10.1080/23268743.2020.1757499

Mare, A., Mabweazara, H. M., & Moyo, D. (2019). "Fake news" and cyber-propaganda in sub-saharan africa: Recentering the research agenda. *African Journalism Studies*, *40*(4), 1–12. doi:10.1080/23743670.2020.1788295

Meinrath, S. D., & Vitka, S. (2014). Crypto war II. *Critical Studies in Media Communication*, *31*(2), 123–128.

Mesky, E., Liaudanskas, A., Kalpokiene, J., & Jurcys, P. (2020). Regulating deepfakes: Legal & ethical considerations. *Journal of Intellectual Property Law & Practice*, *15*(1), 24–31. doi:10.1093/jiplp/jpz167

Mirghani, S. (2011). The war on piracy. *Critical Studies in Media Communication*, *28*(2), 113–134.

Mohammed, A. O., Danladi, O. H., & Adamu, R. C. (2020). Hate-speech, street journalism and national security in Nigeria. *Journal of Management Sciences*, *3*(1), 131–140.

Müller, K., & Schwarz, C. (2021 May). *Fanning the flames of hate: Social media and hate crime*. Working Paper Series, No. 373, Centre for Competitive Advantage in the Global Economy (CAGE), Department of Economics, the University of Warwick, UK.

Nema, P. (2021). Understanding copyright issues entailing deepfakes in India. *International Journal of Law and Information Technology*, *29*(3), 241–254. doi:10.1093/ijlit/eaab007

Nigerian Copyright Act. Section 51 of the Copyright Act.

NITDA (2019). The National Information Technology Development Agency (NITDA) on 25th January 2019. The said Regulation was made pursuant to the National Information Technology Development Agency Act (NITDA Act 2007).

Nwafor, I. E. (2021). AI ethical bias: A case for AI vigilantism (AIIantism) in shaping the regulation of AI. *International Journal of Law and Information Technology*, *29*(3), 225–240. doi:10.1093/ijlit/eaab008

Nwoke, U. (2019). Access to Information under the Nigerian Freedom of Information Act, 2011: Challenges to Implementation and the Rhetoric of Radical Change. *Journal of African Law*, *63*(3), 435–461. doi:10.1017/S0021855319000299

O'Sullivan, D. (2019 June 13). House Intel chair sounds alarm in Congress' first hearing on deepfake videos. *CNN*. https://edition.cnn.com/2019/06/13/tech/deepfake-congress-hearing/index.html

Obi, U. V. (2020 September). *An extensive article on data privacy and data protection law in Nigeria*. International Network of Privacy Law Professionals (INPLP). https://inplp.com/

Ogundokun, R. O., Awotunde, J. B., Sadiku, P., Adeniyi, E. A., Abiodun, M., & Dauda, O. I. (2021). An Enhanced Intrusion Detection System using Particle Swarm Optimization Feature Extraction Technique. *Procedia Computer Science*, *193*, 504–512. doi:10.1016/j.procs.2021.10.052

Ogunlana, S. O. (2019). Halting Boko Haram/Islamic State's West Africa Province propaganda in cyberspace with cybersecurity technologies. *Journal of Strategic Security*, *12*(1), 72–106. https://www.jstor.org/stable/26623078

Ojedokun, U. A., Ogunleye, Y. O., & Aderinto, A. A. (2021). Mass mobilization for police accountability: The case of Nigeria's# EndSARS protest. *Policing. Journal of Policy Practice*, *15*(3), 1894–1903. doi:10.1093/police/paab001

Ojo, J. S. (2020). Governing "ungoverned spaces" in the foliage of conspiracy: Toward (re) ordering terrorism, from Boko Haram Insurgency, Fulani militancy to banditry in Northern Nigeria. *African Security*, *13*(1), 77–110. doi:10.1080/1939 2206.2020.1731109

ONSA. (2015a). National Cybersecurity Policy 2015. Office of the National Security Adviser, Abuja, Federal Government of Nigeria.

ONSA. (2015b). National Cybersecurity Strategy 2015. Office of the National Security Adviser, Abuja, Federal Government of Nigeria.

ONSA. (2015c). *National Security Strategy 2015. Office of the National Security Adviser*. Federal Government of Nigeria.

ONSA (2017 November). *Action plan for implementation of the national cybersecurity strategy*. Office of the National Security Adviser, Abuja, Federal Government of Nigeria.

Orji, U. J. (2018). The African Union Convention on Cybersecurity: A regional response towards cyber stability? *Masaryk University Journal of Law and Technology, 12*(2), 91-129. 10.5817/MUJLT2018-2-1

Osho, O., & Onoja, A. D. (2015). National Cyber Security Policy and Strategy of Nigeria: A Qualitative Analysis. *International Journal of Cyber Criminology, 9*(1), 120–143. doi:10.5281/zenodo.22390

Oturu, D. (2019 October 29). Nigeria: Protection of Image Rights (Part 1). *AELEX*. https://www.mondaq.com/Nigeria/Intellectual-Property/858520/Protection-Of-Image-Rights-Part-1

Paradigm Initiative & Privacy International. (2018 March). *The right to privacy in Nigeria: Stakeholder report universal periodic review 31st session – Nigeria*. https://www.privacyinternational.org

Paris, B., & Donovan, J. (2019). *Deepfakes and cheap fakes: The manipulation of video and audio evidence*. Data & Society. https://datasociety.net/output/deepfakes-and-cheap-fakes/

Perl, A., Howlett, M., & Ramesh, M. (2018). Policy-making and truthiness: Can existing policy models cope with politicized evidence and wilful ignorance in a "post-fact" world? *Policy Sciences, 51*(4), 581–600. doi:10.100711077-018-9334-4

Perot, E., & Mostert, F. (2020). Fake it till you make it: An examination of the US and English approaches to persona protection as applied to deepfakes on social media. *Journal of Intellectual Property Law & Practice, 15*(1), 32–39. doi:10.1093/jiplp/jpz164

Reid, J. (2009). Politicising connectivity. *Cambridge Review of International Affairs, 22*(4), 607–623.

Richards, N. U., & Eboibi, F. E. (2021). African governments and the influence of corruption on the proliferation of cybercrime in Africa: Wherein lies the rule of law? *International Review of Law Computers & Technology, 35*(2), 131–161. doi: 10.1080/13600869.2021.1885105

Sayler, K. (2019a, Nov 21). Artificial intelligence and national security. *Congressional Research Service*. https://fas.org/sgp/crs/natsec/R45178.pdf

Sayler, K., & Harris, L. (2019b, Oct. 14). Deep fakes and national security. *Congressional Research Service*. https://crsreports.congress.gov/product/pdf/IF/IF11333

Schwartz, S. (2019 June 24). Deepfakes aren't a tech problem, they are a power problem. *The Guardian*. https://www.theguardian.com/commentisfree/2019/jun/24/deepfakes-facebook-silicon-valley-responsibility

Seubert, S., & Becker, C. (2021). The Democratic Impact of Strengthening European Fundamental Rights in the Digital Age: The Example of Privacy Protection. *German Law Journal, 22*(1), 31–44. doi:10.1017/glj.2020.101

Siekierski, B. J. (2019 April 8). *Deep fakes: What can be done about synthetic audio and video?* In Brief, Library of Parliament (LOP) papers. https://lop.parl.ca/sites/PublicWebsite/default/en_CA/ResearchPublications/201911E

Solsman, J. E. (2019 May 24). *Samsung deepfake AI could fabricate a video of you from a single profile pic: Even the Mona Lisa can be faked.* CNet Tech. https://www.cnet.com/news/samsung-aideepfake-can-fabricate-a-video-of-you-from-a-single-photo-mona-lisa-cheapfake-dumbfake/

Spivak, R. (2019). Deepfakes: The newest way to commit one of the oldest crimes. *Geo. L. Tech. Rev., 3*(2), 339-400.

Sule, M. J., Zennaro, M., & Thomas, G. (2021). Cybersecurity through the lens of digital identity and data protection: Issues and trends. *Technology in Society, 67*, 101734. doi:10.1016/j.techsoc.2021.101734

Suraj, O. A. (2020). Online surveillance and the repressive Press Council Bill 2018: A two-pronged approach to media self-censorship in Nigeria. In Journalist Safety and Self-Censorship (1st ed., pp. 80-99). Routledge. 1 doi:0.4324/9780367810139

Taylor, B. C. (2020). Defending the state from digital deceit: The reflexive securitisation of deepfake. *Critical Studies in Media Communication, 38*(1), 1–17. doi:10.1080/15295036.2020.1833058

Tolosana, R., Vera-Rodriguez, R., Fierrez, J., Morales, A., & Ortega-Garcia, J. (2020). Deepfakes and beyond: A survey of face manipulation and fake detection. *Information Fusion*, *64*, 131–148. doi:10.1016/j.inffus.2020.06.014

Ulnicane, I., Knight, W., Leach, T., Stahl, B. C., & Wanjiku, W. G. (2021). Framing governance for a contested emerging technology: Insights from AI policy. *Policy and Society*, *40*(2), 158–177. doi:10.1080/14494035.2020.1855800

United Nations. (1994). *Human development report*. Oxford University Press.

Vaccari, C., & Chadwick, A. (2020). Deepfakes and disinformation: Exploring the impact of synthetic political video on deception, uncertainty, and trust in news. *Social Media + Society*, *6*(1), 1–13. doi:10.1177/2056305120903408

Wasserman, H., & Madrid-Morales, D. (2019). An exploratory study of "fake news" and media trust in Kenya, Nigeria and South Africa. *African Journalism Studies*, *40*(1), 107–123. doi:10.1080/23743670.2019.1627230

Westerlund, M. (2019). The emergence of deepfake technology: A review. *Technology Innovation Management Review*, *9*(11), 39–52.

Williams, C. M., Chaturvedi, R., & Chakravarthy, K. (2020). Cybersecurity risks in a pandemic. *Journal of Medical Internet Research*, *22*(9), e23692. doi:10.2196/23692 PMID:32897869

Yadlin-Segal, A., & Oppenheim, Y. (2021). Whose dystopia is it anyway? Deepfakes and social media regulation. *Convergence*, *27*(1), 36–51. doi:10.1177/1354856520923963

Zharova, A. K., & Elin, V. M. (2017). The use of Big Data: A Russian perspective of personal data security. *Computer Law & Security Review*, *33*(4), 482–501. doi:10.1016/j.clsr.2017.03.025

ADDITIONAL READING

Abiodun, A. (2021). A comparative analysis of the legal framework for the criminalisation of cyberterrorism in Nigeria, England and the United States. *Nnamdi Azikiwe University Journal of International Law and Jurisprudence*, *12*(1), 99–112.

Chigozie-Okwum, C. C., Michael, D. O., & Ugboaja, S. G. (2017). Computer forensics investigation: Implications for improved cyber security in Nigeria. *AFRREV STECH: An International Journal of Science and Technology*, *6*(1), 59–73. doi:10.4314tech. v6i1.5

Garba, A. A. (2021). Cybersecurity awareness of university students in Nigeria: Analysis approach. *Turkish Journal of Computer and Mathematics Education*, *12*(12), 3739–3752.

Garba, A. A., & Bade, A. M. (2021). The current state of cybersecurity readiness in Nigerian organizations. *Educational Research*, *3*(1), 154–162.

Garba, A. A., Siraj, M. M., Othman, S. H., & Musa, M. A. (2020). A Study on Cybersecurity awareness among students in Yobe State University, Nigeria: A quantitative approach. *International Journal on Emerging Technologies*, *11*(5), 41–49.

Olayemi, O. J. (2014). A socio-technological analysis of cybercrime and cyber security in Nigeria. *International Journal of Sociology and Anthropology*, *6*(3), 116–125. doi:10.5897/IJSA2013.0510

Osho, O., & Onoja, A. D. (2015). National cyber security policy and strategy of Nigeria: A qualitative analysis. *International Journal of Cyber Criminology*, *9*(1), 120–143. doi:10.5281/zenodo.22390

Udoh, V., & Olajide, D. A. (2021). Data protection in Nigeria: A review of the Nigerian Data Protection Regulation 2019 and the need for Nigeria to sign the African Convention on Data Protection. *Available at SSRN 3766819*.

KEY TERMS AND DEFINITIONS

Artificial Intelligence: Sophisticated technology based on machine learning algorithms that can imitate human thinking capacity and movements/behaviours.

Cyber Assets: All physical property related to cyber technology and other information and communication technology possessed by a government, organisation, or individuals.

Cyber Deception: Deceptive, unreal, faked content shared online to deceive others.

Cyber Resources: This refers to all non-physical wealth, assets, properties, and other possessions that exist in cyberspace (online) such as the various form of data and other valuable information.

Cyberfakes: This term is the synonym of cyber deception. It further means any fake, or faked content in whatever form that is circulated online to confuse, deceive, threaten, or even harm or destroy others' property whether online, offline or both.

Cybersecurity: This term refers to the online peacefulness, safety, and harmony of state (nation), organisation and even individual. It also refers to the absolute absence, or a substantial degree of the guarantee of the absence of cyberviolence, 'cyberaggression', cyberconflict and other forms of online threat to a nation's, organisation's or individual entity's overall sense of being secure from any phenomenon that may cause a great deal of panic, and fear, or the absence of peace, or the prevalence of war-like situation, or all of these in the cyberspace.

Cyberviolence/Conflict: Violence or conflict that occurs between and among entities with online consequences and may have real-life consequences as well.

Chapter 9

The Effect of Protection of Personal Information Act No. 4 of 2013 on Research Data Ethics in South Africa

Nkholedzeni Sidney Netshakhuma

https://orcid.org/0000-0003-0673-7137

University of Mpumalanga, South Africa

ABSTRACT

This study aims to assess the effect of the Protection of Personal Information Act No. 4 of 2013 on research data ethics in South Africa. The Protection of Personal information Act No 4 of 2013 includes a clause on protection of confidentiality and privacy during the collection of data. This research recommends universities to develop privacy data policy and records management policy to improve compliance with the legislation. Furthermore, training and awareness of staff on data ethics is necessary in universities. The research ethics committees are to be established to provide advice on conducting of research in South African universities.

INTRODUCTION

This book chapter assesses the impact of the Protection of Personal Information Act No 4 of 2013 (POPIA) on the research data ethics of South African universities. The assessment was conducted through research, scholarship, and innovation by creating an enabling framework that guides the conduct of staff, students, and other stakeholders in undertaking research activities in compliance with POPIA. The

DOI: 10.4018/978-1-7998-8390-6.ch009

Copyright © 2022, IGI Global. Copying or distributing in print or electronic forms without written permission of IGI Global is prohibited.

author recognizes that ethical practice goes hand in hand with scientifically valid research and effective teaching. POPIA was signed into law in November 2013. The implementation of the Act was effective from 01 July 2021. The enactment of POPIA by the South Africa government is to promote a collection of data in transparency as a step towards accountability. POPIA was enacted because privacy is the basic right of individuals and organizations. Section 14 of the Constitution of the Republic of South Africa protects the right to privacy.

BACKGROUND

POPIA is based on the OECD privacy principles (OECD) and the General Data Protection Regulation (GDPR) mapping (OECD 2013). The principles are accountability, processing or use limitation, collection limitation, purpose specification, information quality, openness, security safeguards, and data subject contribution or access. The POPIA was enacted to ensure data is protected against unauthorized users. The POPIA is aligned with the Constitution of the Republic of South Africa Act of 1996 to promote privacy rights. The Constitution mentions privacy in its Bill of Human Rights as the basic human rights and dignity of all South African. The bill of Rights is the cornerstone of democracy in South Africa. This shows that part of the Constitution requires the protection of privacy rights. South African universities are required to comply with the POPIA. The Bill of Rights (Chapter 2 of the Constitution) enshrines the rights of all people and affirms the democratic values of human dignity, equality, and freedom. Section 12 (2) (c) specifies the right of the individuals "not to be subjected to medical or scientific experiments without their informed consent". Section 16 (1) (d) states that individuals have the right to freedom of expression which includes academic freedom and freedom of scientific research. Section 24 refers to the rights of individuals to an environment that is not harmful to their health or well-being, and to have the environment protected for the benefit of present and future generations.

The book chapter highlights areas of universities that need to improve compliance with POPIA. Most research on privacy has not addressed broader compliance on POPIA as the legislation is relatively new in South Africa. Prior research found that research on privacy issues was reactive based on organization functions in South Africa. There is concern about universities' potential ethical violations inherent during the collection and harvesting of student data especially during a digital era where online teaching is a norm (Parsons 2021). Questions related to privacy and ethics in connections to learning analytics have been an ongoing concern since the early days of learning analytics in education (Gasevic, Dawson, & Jovanovic 2016). Issues on privacy and autonomy are at the forefront of ethical concerns. Ethical questions related to ownership of data, access, and sharing of personal information need to be clear from various stakeholders.

Ethical behavior and compliance with POPIA are necessary for South African universities' protection of personal information and privacy. However, it appears that the implementation of POPIA is a challenge in the education sector such as universities. This is so because some universities are not yet developed systems and processes to comply with the POPIA. Hence, It is a world trend for countries to develop a private information to ensure the protection of personal information. Botha, Glober, & Eloff (2017) alluded that enactment of the act was done towards the worldwide tendency to modernize personal information protection.

Universities are recognized as knowledge-based organizations involves in all types of research themes (Adham, Kasimin, Isa, Othman, & Ahmad 2015). Universities as public institutions collect, store, and analyze data as part of research processes. Researchers are to protect the privacy of participants during research processes. This statement is alluded to by Fang and Chen (2013) who state that students and employees are components of society and are entitled to the rights in privacy protections. During the process of collection of data, it is necessary to ensure that privacy and confidentiality are maintained and protected by institutions. (Johnson & Grandison 2007). Hence, failure to safeguard private information may lead to risks to privacy and confidentiality.

It is the responsibility of universities to ensure an accredited structure for the ethical review of research following relevant legislation. To coordinate the management of personal information, universities are to assign departments, divisions, or units responsible for privacy, information, and knowledge management. Most South African universities established or assigned departments, divisions, and the unit responsible for data and information management. This statement is alluded to by Tan (2016) who states that the university has its own set of faculty members working on projects with knowledge and working experience in research work.

LITERATURE REVIEW

The international and national data privacy, personal information, universities records, and archives records were reviewed. The literature review not only provided background to this study, but it gave information as well as actively facilitated discussion throughout the research process. Data ethics is an essential information management issue that challenges organizations (Culnan and Williams 2009).

One of the factors that universities need to address their data ethics is the development of information communication technology, which has led to information explosion and increased demands for privacy and confidentiality. Adherence to data ethics is necessary especially when researchers engage in all forms of research. Universities register research projects as key issues and align with research themes identified in their research strategy. Universities embedded scientists to play a role to facilitate and leverage external research to meet the university's needs. Acknowledging ongoing and longer-term commitment required universities to publish peer-reviewed papers and book chapters. Therefore, universities are obliged in terms of POPIA to develop processes and systems to manage personal information. This implies that electronic records management system is to be enhanced to manage records effectively. Research conducted ethically considers a fuller and extensive investigation into privacy issues. Recognition of individual rights should be considered. All research conducted in South Africa is encouraged by the ethical framework to engage stakeholders meaningfully in their research., advocacy of privacy should be considered by individuals.

Universities' compliance with POPIA regulation or code of conduct may lead to legitimacy. The South African universities established the Protection of Personal Information Act Code of Conduct to ensure that their divisions, departments, and units adhere to research ethics. With the ever-increasing research in universities, there is a need to develop research ethic procedures to adhere to records management policies and procedures. The development of a code of conduct is necessary to provide guidelines and a framework to research ethically. Framework and code of practices are tools to implement privacy laws (Ferguson, Hoel, Schefel, & Drachslaer 2016). The observation and promotion of ethics are done through the development of a framework (Kaisara & Pather 2010). This shows the significance of developing the code of ethics of an organization.

Besides compliance with POPIA, organizations and individuals have moral obligations to adhere to ethical issues. Data ethics compliance is necessary beyond the private governance framework. Gry (2019) states that values such as human dignity and privacy are recognized as fundamental rights and data protection laws in Europe. Therefore, research must be guided by the research ethics committee established by the university. This statement is alluded to by Wilkinson, Slack, Crews, Singh, & Salzwedel (2021) who states that the research ethics committee plays a role to guide a collection of data. The researcher ethics committee plays a role in issues research with permission from universities to collect data. Securing research permission from the institution is important to respect universities authorities. The Research Ethics Committee assumes duties to review ethical considerations related to research for degree and non-degree purposes involving human subjects which investigate target disadvantaged communities. The research committee assumes duties for ethics clearance for institutional and external research involving staff and students of the University. The research committee is responsible to monitor the treatment of animals used in research and teaching at universities, reviewing all protocols involving animal use to ensure that they are following acceptable ethical and scientific standards, and ensuring aspects of care and use of animals in research and teaching comply with POPIA. A research Committee is instrumental to enhance university internal control as mandated by POPIA. The privacy impact assessment should be conducted by this committee as part of the organization's risk management. Risk assessment ensures that information created and maintained by an organization is maintained on regular basis.

Records managers and librarians are to respect personal privacy and the protection of personal data necessarily. Therefore, there is a need for universities to establish a records management forum to develop and implement the protection of personal information. The records Management forum makes it explicit that the role of records managers, in modern society, includes the protection of personal information.

Besides South Africa, countries all over the world enacted privacy laws to safeguard the privacy of personal information. Countries respond to issues of researching with the view to protect personal information by enacting privacy laws (Johnson and Grandison 2007). Examples of legislation by country include Canada's Personal Information Protection and Electronic Document Act of 2000, Japan's Personal Information Protection Law of 2003, Australia's Privacy Act of 1988 (Solove 2008). The European Union's Directives on Data Protection specified fundamental principles for Privacy protection in Europe, The Data Protection Act 1998 in the United Kingdom implemented the European Directive on the protection of individuals on the processing of personal data and the free movement of such data (Griffith 2017). The Data Protection Act of 1998 provides a framework to process personal data, from which a living individual can be identified, that is stored on computers or organized papers. Western concepts of privacy are alien to the cultural, historical, religious, and philosophical traditions (Ess, 2005). The European Union's attitudes towards privacy are stipulated in comprehensive statutes such as the General Data Protection Regulations (Parsons, 2021). This statute is applied to preserve personal information. Furthermore, any transfer of personal data to the non-European Union must provide an adequate level of data protection (Makulilo 2012). South Africa is subjected to these rules Ethics Advisory Committee was established in 2015 to deal with compliance on digital issues about the GDPR (Floridi 2018). The GDPR replaces the Data Protection Directive 95/ 46/EC. This legislation harmonizes the data privacy of the European Union. The ethics advisory contributed to the European Union members to compliance with the regulations. In Canada, Institutional research ethics board boards (IREBS) approve and monitor safety, privacy, and confidentiality for research participants (Kotecha, et al., 2011). They further state that lack of clarity in guidelines impedes advances in Canadian public health surveillance and research seeking to improve understanding of health determinants and chronic disease management.

EXECUTIVE MANAGEMENT SUPPORT

A component of privacy management requires support from executive management. The executive management support may be demonstrated by the organization developing a data and privacy policy to ensure organizational compliance with POPIA. Universities are to develop policies to prevent any litigation because of bridging privacy information. Procedures are to be developed to prevent the unauthorized dissemination of records in compliance with POPIA. The preliminary research shows limited support for privacy legislation by the Universities management. A study conducted by Silverman, et, al., 2015) states that developing an ethical culture facilitates and improves ethical conduct of research of universities requires support and commitment from executive management. The university management is to ensure that policies and procedures are developed to promote transparency. Accountability and transparency are necessary. This can be achieved by ensuring that monitoring and review are regularly conducted by institutions.

Executive management must ensure that staff appointed to research ethics possess high integrity, able to execute their duties and responsibilities. They must also be aligned to the policy and procedure of university research ethics. Furthermore, it is the responsibility of the executive management to allocate a budget for training and raising awareness on research ethics. Furthermore, there should be continuous monitoring and evaluation of research ethics. The review of the literature shows the level of endorsement of records management projects, funding of specialized training, and implementation of records management programs especially at the University of Witwatersrand as alluded to by (Phiri & Tough 2018)

DATA COMMERCIALIZATION

There is a data commercialization perspective to manage revenue. Commercialization must be supported by academics and administrators (Adham, Kasimin, Ma Isa, Othman, & Ahmad 2015). Academics and administrators are trained in the administration of research. Business ethics are standards used to judge the rightness or wrongness of a business 'relations to others. Ethics is defined as the methods, principles, and business a business or organization brings to comply with legislation, compliance to regulatory and professional standards, and compliance to university standards, keeping promises and commitments and abiding by general principles of values (Fatoki, 2012). In the digital economy, technology is a dominant factor influencing the production of goods and services (Kaisara & Pather, 2010). The free flow of information puts customers' needs at the core of business strategies and priorities. All business interactions are to be in line with business ethics. A framework that is relevant to the business practice of ethics includes Social Accountability 8000, Association for Computing Machinery Code of Ethics, and the Institute of Electrical and Electronics Engineers Code of Ethics is some of the tools used by e-commerce practitioners to promote business ethics. Private organizations are to develop policies and procedures in line with POPIA to ensure that their organization complies with legislation.

TRUST

It seems that there is a lack of trust by universities to provide a researcher with personal information. Lack of trust compromise autonomous informed decisions to participate in decision making. It appears that some university community members stop trusting the research team in the authorization of researching ethically. This research recommends universities build trust and mitigate privacy fears by developing and implementing their privacy policies and procedures.

DATA POLICIES

Research productivity is influenced by the attributes of individual researchers, institutions, and policy. Universities are expected to develop data policies to improve compliance with POPIA. The formalization of data management translates into the development of records management policies, processes, standards, and functional requirements (Khumalo & Baloyi, 2017). Many South African universities have not yet fully implemented data ethics management programs and are finding it hard for staff to comply with privacy management policies. This statement is alluded to by a study conducted by Johnson and Grandison (2007) who state that privacy breaches increased because of weak or ineffective enforcement of data protection laws as well as discrepancies and conflict in legal protection. As a result, most universities are at risk for privacy close violation, non-compliance, and litigation. Hence, there is a need for oversight of information management policy within an organization. It appears that most universities view records management as part of privacy management.

Asogwa (2013) states that steps to manage records are to ensure the existence and implementation of a legislative and regulatory framework for record management. The existence of a data management policy is essential for universities to improve compliance with a regulatory framework. This shows the significance to comply with data policies. Data policies to outline the provision of consent. Data ethics policy is recognized as a component of a general infrastructure development's rhythm rather than caved in ethical solutions and isolated events (Gry, 2019). Therefore, there is a need to advocate for policies on data sharing and information management systems. The enactment of the POPIA requires universities to review their research policies and procedure.

GOVERNANCE

Data stewardship by universities requires a data governance infrastructure to protect research participants and promotes equity. Personal information records are fundamental elements on the management of the knowledge capital of universities (Garaba 2018). Management of personal information facilitates good governance, accountability, transparency, and access to information. It appears that most South African universities faced a challenge to document personal information to provide access to appropriate stakeholders. This is implemented within universities, with formalized data sharing guidelines that delineate data sharing options according to dataset characteristics. These include whether data requests are from within South African universities.

PRIVACY AND CONFIDENTIALITY

Standards of privacy and confidentiality protect access, control, and dissemination of personal information and assist to protect mental or psychological integrity is necessary during the collection of data. Therefore, the privacy and confidentiality of individuals are to be maintained during data collection of research data as alluded to by (Kotecha, et al., 2011). An individual should not be identified during the collection of personal information for research. Adherence to privacy and confidentiality should be key. This is so to limit damage to the image of individuals and the profile of researchers. Efforts should be done to ensure that information contains privacy and confidentiality information to be disseminated to various stakeholders. The collection of private information must be fair and confidential within an organization.

A review of the literature shows that privacy and confidentiality of information were not viewed as significant. For example, privacy remains a largely foreign concept from many Chinese people. This statement is alluded to by Fang and Chen (2013) who raised a lack of privacy awareness. Because of confidentiality and privacy, there is a need for organizations to embark on awareness to protect privacy and confidentiality of information. Provision of access to information should be done in compliance with research ethics.

Protection of privacy is important to promote trade relations. China intends to extend trade with other countries. Globalization enforces China to adhere to the principle of privacy because they want to dominate the world. The fact that China is a member of the World Trade Organization (WTO) implies that it may influence the handling of private information by another country. Globalization led to a complex set of interactive relationships between individual organizations and states and to an unprecedented correlation of massive global systems causing system risk to increase exponentially. It is very complex to research in a global context (Beerbaum, Piechocki, & Puaschunder, 2019). Cross-Cultural Exchange Programmes are necessary for global dialogues based on mutual respect and understanding (Ess, 2005). International Convention on the personal treaty was adhered to by China to influence world politics. This may be influenced by the Chinese long tradition of collectiveness of the society, tight control by the government that practices scrutiny (Yao-Huai, 2005). This statement is alluded to by Fang and Chen (2013) who state that China highly values collectivism. Privacy and confidentiality are not considered issues to conduct business in China. Despite China's collectivism, the university's function is to ensure the protection of students' information privacy. It seems that most publications in China did not consider issues of privacy and confidentiality. Hence several efforts have been made to ensure that legislation protecting personal information to consider the following aspects:

- Personal rights such as the right to know, the right to correct, the right to open, and the right to claim for compensation.
- Collections and retention of personal data
- Usage of personal information
- Dissemination of personal information
- Compensation for privacy infringements.

The author views that the principles of respect, principles of equilibrium, and the principle of social rectification should be respected when researching within an institution.

INFORMATION COMMUNICATION TECHNOLOGY

Data protection and information communication technology are not separated (Abdulrauf and Fombad, 2017). Information communication technology is an enabler for individuals and organizations to store personal information. Information Communication technology transformed the way records are created, authenticated, and preserved (Majore, Yoo, & Shon, 2014, Recker & Muller, 2015). Records created and maintained in an electronic environment need continuous maintenance because of their dependence on hardware and software. This makes it a challenge to preserve personal information preserved on an electronic platform. Therefore, it is the role of institutions to ensure the integrity and authenticity of personal data in an electronic environment. This statement is alluded to by Dong, Ilieva, & Medeiros (2018) who state that information communication technologies and techniques are anticipated to make personal information with sensitive or legally restricted information readily discoverable and accessible. It is also the responsibility of institutions to ensure that records are preserved for long-term preservation. Records management system to be developed to ensure collection, preservation, validation, identification, analysis, interpret and document digital evidence derived from digital sources. Therefore, efforts should be done by universities to ensure that records should not be affected by media.

While it is true that ICT may play a role to limit the access and disclosure of sensitive personal information preserved in automated systems (Johnson & Grandison, 2007) may protect sensitive information of an organization. Privacy solutions should be put in the university system to manage personal records. Electronic records management systems adopted by universities must enable the long-term preservation of electronic records management systems.

TRANSPARENCY

Transparency is the requirement of researchers and participants to adhere to research ethics in South Africa public universities. This implied that research is processed effectively and efficiently, and confidentiality of participants and researchers needs to be protected. The legal and policy framework during the creation, processing, storing, and preserving of records is essential to promote accountability and transparency (Okello-Obura, 2011). Researchers must be able to access collected, processed data carried out. It is essential to know what types of data were collected by various stakeholders.

DATA ACCESS, CONTROL AND STORAGE

Privacy is a matter to restrict access to persons or information about persons. Universities' privacy policies should specifically information that is classified and categorized. Various stakeholders from whom data is collected are to be assured of the protection of their data. Organizations are to develop and establish storage for the preservation and storage of personal data or research data. There is a need for an ethical review process for the collection, management, access, control, and storage of data. Data management, control, and storage would be made transparent during the collection of data. Users must be provided with opportunities to access data collected about them. Data must be secured at different levels of institutions without compromising the integrity of information.

Universities are required to comply with security requirements if they maintain reasonable procedures. Universities are to develop a security management policy to ensure the privacy of information is protected and adhered to. Furthermore, Universities are to utilize ICT for rules to access personal information. This statement alludes to Cochran, Tatikonda, and Magid (2007) who state that individuals use rules to manage access to their personal information. These rules allow differing access to personal information.

Access and use of information is a fundamental human right as alluded to by (Garaba, 2016). Hence countries are required by the United Nations to develop privacy policies. Accessibility and understandability of data depend on storage media, file formats, hard and software environments, and the availability of context information and user know-how (Recker and Muller 2015). However, in many universities' archives repositories, access and use of personal information are low because the importance of records and their use is unknown. This is because little research on personal information for research is less used in South Africa.

Information control is essential to protect privacy. Loss of control entails the loss of private information. This means that restriction on another part of private information clarifies legal intuitions about privacy. In the case of database information, private or individuals need to access private information. The restricted access view is compatible with a portion of the intrusion account. Information Communication Technologies should be a system in such a way that privacy of information is protected by individuals who intend to access personal information.

Sharing of research data is necessary for organizations to decide future decision-making. This statement is alluded to by Parsons et al (2011) who state that data stored in information communication technology must be discoverable in the database system. Research should be conducted to ensure that records are accessible to various stakeholders. This is particularly practiced in research dealing with health issues. The information delivery mechanism is expected to act as a moderator that influences both privacy benefits and risk perceptions through its effect on the inferences consumers make regarding distributive and procedural justice (Xu, Teo, Tan, & Agarwal, 2009).

Privacy and information sharing guidelines should be culturally dependent. Data is associated with the publication of research articles. Funding of research is dependent on the availability of data from various stakeholders. The sharing of data contributed to the impact of research. Sharing of public health data depends on the trust and confidence of those from whom such data are derived and related (Denny, Silaigwana, Wassenaar, Bull & Parker 2015).

Preservation of data for the long term is important to organizations (Parsons et al 2011). This requires Information Officer to ensure that records are kept on an electronic database to retain authenticity. Electronic records increase exponentially, and information communication technology changes the way organizations, and individuals manage information using electronic platforms. Management of electronic records management requires access control, authentication of individuals. Therefore, electronic records posed a challenge to the management of personal information in university records management systems. Universities are to strengthen electronic records management systems to ensure that information generated retains its authenticity. Some information communication technology preserving information failed to preserve records for long-term preservation because of technical obsolescence. The assessment on university electronic records management systems shows that most of South Africa adopted the hybrid system, which means that they use paper-based systems and electronic records management systems. Therefore, information officers are to develop policies to promote the long-term preservation of information.

Universities and individuals can benefit to share data and the application of sophisticated analytics to larger and interconnected databases (Acguisti, Brandimarte, & Loewenstein 2015).

Sharing of privacy may also occur at the international level. For example, information about privacy boundary conditions can be obtained from a transatlantic dialog between the United States and Europe on privacy protection (Puaschunder, 2019). In countries such as Canada, there is interest to ensure the information available to various stakeholders.

There are various reasons to share data with various stakeholders by researchers. The decision to share data applies to all types of research and regardless of the organization. Disclosure of personal information is needed to build a relationship or functions within group dynamics. Organizations are to ensure that there is a rule to guide the dissemination of information.

In South Africa, the exchange of human biological materials and associated data between institutions with various countries and international organizations is a common practice in biomedical research, requiring that exchange s become formalized (Mahomed & Labuschaigne 2019). Exchange of materials becomes possible through Material Transfer Agreements (MTA) in the exchange of specimens and their associated data. The exchange program is guided by national legislation such as National Health Act No. 6 of 2003 to ethics guidelines associated with consumer protection, health research, protection of research participants, and fundamental human rights.

Research that involves the exchange or cross–border transfer of data requires specialized legal and ethical knowledge relating to the governance framework. Universities are to ensure that monitoring and evaluation processes are in place. Adherence to national legislation and national ethical guidelines and standards of selected jurisdiction is important.

STAKEHOLDER ENGAGEMENT

Stakeholder relations remain key to disseminating information to relevant stakeholders. This means that processes and procedures must be put in place to ensure information privacy information policy is in place. Engagement is necessary to understand the type of people to be involved. Data ethics is a concern to multiple stakeholders such as business leaders, private activities, scholars, government regulators, and individual consumers (Smith, Dinev, & Xu, 2011, Abdulrauf & Fombad, 2017). These stakeholders require organizations and individuals' partners to preserve personal information for third parties.

POPIA has the potential to promote an interdisciplinary and collaborative approach to records management. The author proposes university set a steering committee to facilitate the distribution and sharing of data on the management of information. Such committees should have representatives from different divisions to coordinate personal information. Such a steering committee should include the records and archives management division. Inclusion of the records management division in such a committee may alleviate the records management division in the organization. This shows that there are possibilities that universities may allocate resources to strengthen records management sections.

Ethics guidance is important to guide universities on issues of engagement (Wilkinson, Slack, Crews, Singh, Salzwedel, & Wassenaar, 2021). Data management policy and guidelines guide the management of data. This means that the community should be involved to provide guidelines on the management of personal information.

Researchers are encouraged to engage the national and international stakeholders in research management. Collaborative partnerships allow the community to become active members of the management of information. This means that suitable platforms are to be in place to promote sharing of information. Collaborative initiatives to reduce the exploitation of poor people from developing countries.

Data collection should start with the community. Research is a collaborative activity with a strong view to providing access to information. Sharing data at a community level requires organizations to develop a policy (Denny, Silaigwana, Wassenaar, Bull, & Parker, 2015. Such policy should state the re-use and use of policies. This shows the significance of policies management.

The policy should also indicate a limitation of providing access to information to international communities.

Stakeholder engagement is important in university research and research ethics discourse. Engagement may offset some of the vulnerabilities of participating communities. Stakeholders' engagement has emerged as a central component of university research. Stakeholders' engagement influence how records are to be processed and organized.

Preliminary data analysis shows that most of the researchers do not adhere to research ethics and processes. Furthermore, there is little awareness of the significance of the protection of personal information.

This research shows the significance of sharing data with various stakeholders. This is because communities consent to their researcher to provide information to various stakeholders. The author is of the view that data sharing should be in line with data management.

Compliance with POPIA requires data to be shared internationally. Universities are positioned internationally to research with various institutions (Adham, Kasimin, Mat Isa, Othman, & Ahmad, 2015). This is because POPIA complies or is aligned with GDPR. There is increased recognition of the significance of collaborative research internationally. More needs to be done to ensure that collaboration is fair and equal. However, the literature review shows that South African universities lack data policies and procedures to promote sharing and distribution of information to various stakeholders. Organizations are adopting Information communication technologies to ensure that information is disseminated to various stakeholders timeously. Embracement of data sharing is an expression of reciprocity and a sign of goodwill to collaborate at solving pressing health issues and related challenges experienced by the organization. Open access and sharing of information are showing respect for an individual and organization. International Organizations should play an essential to ensure that information and data are exchanged and properly share at the international level.

SOLUTIONS AND RECOMMENDATIONS

University records managers and information officers are capacitated to provide advice on research ethics and development. There should be continuous training and development on records management programs within an organization (Asogwa, 2013). Ethics review capacity and training are necessary for staff development. Researchers are to be trained on personal integrity and professional skills regarding collection access and service, Staff need to acquire balance on the collection, maintain an unbiased stance regarding service, and adhere to the highest standards of professional excellence (Ejedafiru, 2020).

Structures and resources are needed to research universities (Adham, Mat Isa, Othman, & Ahmad, 2015). Limited resources, not enabling culture are a challenge to research universities. The most pragmatic shortcoming identified was insufficient budget and or institutional recognition for formal research ethics education and training, as alluded to by (Davies, 2020)

Lack of awareness of POPIA is a challenge experienced by universities. Therefore, staff needs to be well trained in the management of information to ensure the dissemination of information. Regular awareness about privacy protections to improve their legal consciousness are trained on management of records are done (Fang & Chen, 2013).

The establishment of records management programs and systems in universities is a solution to implement preservation of protection of personal information. Research data access depends on the university's establishment of effective records management program. Access to the data set will fail if the university lack a records management system (Khumalo & Baloyi, 2017). Unfortunately, most African institutions lack a records management system to implement privacy information management programs (Khumalo & Baloyi 2017). A university that seeks to provide access to information must improve the management of personal information. Access to information can be hindered by a lack to retrieve and manage information. Without effective records and archives, management system records can be accessed and retrieved effectively.

FUTURE RESEARCH DIRECTIONS

Examining the existing Protection of Personal Information Act No 4 of 2013 in South Africa highlights the hierarchical nature of current regulatory efforts and exposes gaps in the management of personal information. Therefore, future research may be undertaken to assess the role of records management programs on the protection of personal information within an organization.

CONCLUSION

Ethics of research are developed and refined within an ever-evolving societal context, elements of which include the need for research and the research community, moral imperatives and ethical principles, and the POPIA. The Policy on Research Ethics is thus embedded in the values enshrined in the Constitution of the Republic of South Africa and POPIA and upholds the basic principles and values that pertain to all forms of research. This chapter presents, for the first time, the full process for handling data during the research in compliance with the POPIA. Implementation of POPIA is essential especially during this period of information communication technology development. This is because limited ethics of privacy was not the fully unexplored topic in South Africa. The topic is not fully explored in South Africa. Therefore, universities must comply with POPIA to conduct research. The current book chapter concludes that POPIA promotes universities to establish a records management system and the creation of records management professionals in universities. Organizations all over the world should develop data protection to manage personal information. Regulation and management of privacy of information are necessary within an organization. Research needs to include privacy in its discussion. Evaluating the effectiveness of a POPIA remains challenging, particularly as there are no standards to measure the ethical quality of the provision of access to information to various stakeholders.

REFERENCES

Abdulrauf, A. L., & Fombad, M. C. (2017). Personal Data Protection in Nigeria: Reflections on Opportunities, Options and Challenges to legal Reforms. *The Liverpool Law Review*, *38*(2), 105–134. doi:10.100710991-016-9189-8

Acquisit, A., Brandimarte, L., & Loewenstein, G. (2015). Privacy and Human Behavior in the age of information Review. *Science*, *347*(6221), 509.

Adham, A. K., Kasimin, H., Ma Isa, R., Othman, F., & Ahmad, F. (2015). Developing a Framework for a Viable Research University. *System Practice Res*, *28*, 503–525.

Asogwa, E. B. (2013). The readiness of universities in managing electronic records. A study of three federal universities in Nigeria. *The Electronic Library*, *31*(6), 792–807. doi:10.1108/EL-04-2012-0037

Beerbaum, D., Piechocki, M., & Puaschunder, J. M. (2019). Measuring Accounting Reporting Complexity with customized extensions XBRL – A Behavioral Economics approach. *Journal of Applied Research in the Digital Economy*, *1*(10), 3–41.

Botha, J., Globler, M. M., Hahn, J., & Eloff, M. M. (2017). A High-Level Comparison between the South African Protection of Personal Information Act and International Data Protection Laws. *Conference: The 12th International Conference on Cyber Warfare and Security (ICCWS)*, 12.

Cochran, L. P., Tatikonda, V. M., & Magid, M. J. (2007). Radio Frequency Identification and Ethics of Privacy. *Organizational Dynamics*, *36*(2), 217–229. doi:10.1016/j.orgdyn.2007.03.008

Culnan, M. J., & Williams, C. K. (2009). How ethics can enhance Organizational Privacy: Lessons from the ChoicePoint and TJX Data Breaches. *Management Information Systems Quarterly, 33*(4), 673–689. doi:10.2307/20650322

Davies, E.H.S. (2020). The Introduction of research ethics reviews procedures at a university in South Africa: Review outcomes of a social science research ethics committee. *Research Ethics, 16*(1 – 2), 1 – 26.

Denny, G. S., Silaigwana, B., Wassenaar, D., Bull, S., & Parker, M. (2015). Developing Ethical Practices for Public Health Research Data Sharing in South Africa: The Views and Experiences from a Diverse Sample of Research Stakeholders. *Journal of Empirical Research on Human Research Ethics; JERHRE, 10*(3), 290–301. doi:10.1177/1556264615592386 PMID:26297750

Dong, L., Illieva, P. & Medeiros, A. (2018). Data dreams: Planning for the Future of historical medical documents. *History Matters. Journal of the Medical Library Association, 106*(4). Doi.org/10.5195/jmla.2018.444.

Ejedafiru, E. F. (2020). Librarians' Professional Ethics and Reference Service Delivery in College of Education in South-South, Nigeria. *Library Philosophy and Practice.*

Ess, C. (2005). "Lost in translation?" Intercultural dialogues on privacy and information ethics (Introduction to a special issue on Privacy and Data Privacy Protection in Asia). *Ethics and Information Technology, 7*(1), 1–6. doi:10.100710676-005-0454-0

Fang, H., & Chen, Z. (2013). Study on Chinese University Students' Privacy Protection from Intercultural Perspective. *International Conference on Education Technology and Management Sciences (ICETMS 2013).*

Fatoki, O. (2012). The Impact of Ethics on the Availability of Trade Credit to New Small and Medium-Sized Enterprises (SMEs) in South Africa. *Journal of Social Sciences, 30*(1), 21 – 29.

Ferguson, R., Hoel, T., Scheffel, M., & Drachsler, H. (2016). Guest Editorial: Ethics and Privacy in Learning Analytics. *Journal of Learning Analytics, 3*(1), 5–15. doi:10.18608/jla.2016.31.2

Floridi, L. (2018). Soft ethics, the governance of the digital, and the General Data Protection Regulation. *Phil. Trans. R. Soc. A, 370*(2133), 20180081. doi:10.1098/rsta.2018.0081 PMID:30322997

Garaba, F. (2016). User Perceptions about Archives at the Lutheran Theological Institute Library, Pietermaritzburg, South Africa. *African Journal of Library Archives and Information Science, 26*(1), 73–83.

Garaba, F. (2018). The neglected fond in university archives: The case of sport club records at the University of Kwazulu-Natal (UKZN), Pietermaritzburg Campus, South Africa. *Records Management Journal, 28*(2), 143–158. doi:10.1108/RMJ-11-2016-0043

Gasevic, D., Dawson, S., & Jovanovic, J. (2016). Ethics and Privacy as Enablers of Learning Analytics. *Journal of Learning Analytics, 3*(1), 1–4. doi:10.18608/jla.2016.31.1

Griffith, R. (2017). Managing data subject access requests. *British Journal of Community Nursing, 22*(3), 149–151. doi:10.12968/bjcn.2017.22.3.149 PMID:28252324

Gry, H. (2019). Making Sentences of data ethics: The powers behind the data ethics debate in European policymaking, Internet Policy Review. *Alexander Von Humboldt Institute for Internet and Society, Berlin., 8*(2), 1–19.

Johnson, C. M., & Grandison, A. W. T. (2007). Compliance with data protection laws using Hippocratic Database active enforcement and auditing. *IBM Systems Journal, 46*(2), 255–264. doi:10.1147j.462.0255

Kaisara, G., & Pather, S. (2010) Relevance of Ethics in e-Governance: An Analysis of Development in the WWW era. *Conference: 6th International Conference on e-Government.*

Khumalo, B.N., & Baloyi, C. (2017). The possible benefits of freedom of information laws to the records management landscape in the ESARBICA region. *Information Development*, 1 – 15. . doi:10.1177/0266666917735879

Kotecha, J. A. (2011). Ethics and privacy issues of a practice-based surveillance system. Need for a national-level institutional research ethics board and consent standards. *Canadian Family Physician Medecin de Famille Canadien, 57*, 1165–1173. PMID:21998237

Mahomed, S., & Labuschaigne, M. (2019). The role of research ethics committees in South Africa when human biological materials are transferred between institutions. *South African Journal of Bioethics and Law, 12*(2), 79–83. doi:10.7196/SAJBL.2019.v12i2.685

Majore, S. A., Yoo, H., & Shon, T. (2014). Secure and reliable electronic records management system using digital forensic technologies. *The Journal of Supercomputing, 70*(1), 149–165. doi:10.100711227-014-1137-6

Makulilo, B. A. (2012). Privacy and data protection in Africa; a state of the art. *International Data Privacy Law.*, *2*(3), 163–178. doi:10.1093/idpl/ips014

Okello-Obura, C. (2011). Records and Archives Legal and Policy Framework in Uganda. *Library Philosophy and Practice.* https://digitalcommons.unl.edu/libphilprac/608

Organization for Economic Co-Operation and Development (OECD). (2013). *The OECD privacy framework.* Available at. www. pwc.com/gx/en/consultingservices/information-security -survey/assets/pwcgsiss-2016-financia-services.pdf

Parsons, M. A., Godøy, Ø., LeDrew, E., de Bruin, T. F., Danis, B., Tomlinson, S., & Carlson, D. (2011). A conceptual framework for managing very diverse data for complex, interdisciplinary science. *Journal of Information Science*, *37*(6), 555–569. doi:10.1177/0165551511412705

Parsons, T. D. (2021). Ethics and Educational Technologies. *Educational Technology Research and Development*, *69*(1), 335–338. doi:10.100711423-020-09846-6

Phiri, J. M., & Tough, G. A. (2018). Managing university records in the world of governance. *Records Management Journal*, *28*(1), 47–61. doi:10.1108/RMJ-11-2016-0042

Puaschunder, M. J. (2019). Artificial Diplomacy: A guide for public officials to conduct Artificial Intelligence. *Journal of Applied Research in the Digital Economy*, *1*(10). Advance online publication. doi:10.2139srn.3376302

Recker, A., & Muller, S. (2015). Preserving the Essence; Identifying the significant properties of Social Science Research data. *New Review of Information Networking*, *20*(1-2), 229–235. doi:10.1080/13614576.2015.1110404

Silverman, H., Sleem, H., Moodley, K., Kumar, N., Naidoo, S., Subramanian, T., Jaafar, R., & Moni, M. (2015). Results of a self-assessment tool to assess the operational characteristics of research ethics committees in low – and middle-income countries. *Journal of Medical Ethics*, *41*(4), 332–337. doi:10.1136/medethics-2013-101587 PMID:24748650

Smith, J. H., Dinev, T., & Xu, H. (2011). Information Privacy Research: An Interdisciplinary Review. *Management Information Systems Quarterly*, *35*(4), 989. doi:10.2307/41409970

Solove, J. D. (2008). *Understanding Privacy.* Harvard University Press.

Tan, N. C. (2016). Enhancing Knowledge sharing and research collaboration among academics: The role of knowledge management. *Higher Education*, *71*(4), 525–556. doi:10.100710734-015-9922-6

Wilkinson, A., Slack, C., Crews, C., Singh, N., Salzwedel, J., & Wassenaar, S. (2021). How can research ethics committees help to strengthen stakeholder engagement in health research in South Africa? an evaluation of REC documents. *SAJBL*, *14*, 1.

Xu, H., Teo, H.-H., Tan, C. Y. B., & Agarwal, R. (2009). The role of Push-Pull Technology in Privacy Calculus: The Case of Location-Based Services. *Journal of Management Information Systems*, *26*(3), 135–174. doi:10.2753/MIS0742-1222260305

Yao-Huai, L. (2005). Privacy and data privacy in contemporary China. *Ethics and Information Technology*, *7*(1), 7–15. doi:10.100710676-005-0456-y

ADDITIONAL READING

De Bruyn, M. (2014). The Protection of Personal Information (POPI) Act- Impact on South Africa. *International Business & Economics Research Journal*, *13*(6), 1315–1340. doi:10.19030/iber.v13i6.8922

Majatjie, M., Marnewick, L. A., & Von Solms, S. (2020). Cyber security policy and the legislative Context of the Wastewater Sector in South Africa. *Sustainability*, *13*(1), 291. doi:10.3390u13010291

McKnight, H. D., Choudhury, V., & Kacmar, C. (2002). Developing and Validating trust measures for e-commerce: An integrative typology. *Information Systems Research*, *13*(3), 334–359. doi:10.1287/isre.13.3.334.81

Netshakhuma, N. S. (2019). The Future of Archivists and Records Managers in Mpumalanga, South Africa. *Mousaion*, *37*(4), 1–17.

Netshakhuma, N. S. (2020). Assessment of a South Africa national consultative workshop on the Protection of Personal Information Act (POPIA). Global Knowledge. *Memory and Communication*, *69*(1/2), 58–74.

Seto, Y. (2015). Applications of Privacy Impact Assessment in the Smart City. *Electronics and Communications in Japan*, *98*(2), 52–61. doi:10.1002/ecj.11661

Staunto, C., Adams, R., Botes, M., Dove, E. S., Horn, L., Labuschaigne, M., Loots, G., Mahomed, S., Makuba, J., Olckers, A., Pepper, S. M., Pope, A., Ramsay, M., Loideain, N., & De Vries, J. (2019). Safeguarding the future of genomic research in South Africa: Broad consent and the Protection of Personal Information Act No. 4 of 2013. *SAMJ: South African Medical Journal, 109*(7), 468–470. doi:10.7196/SAMJ.2019.v109i7.14148 PMID:31266570

Tsai, Y. J., Egelman, S., Cranor, L., & Acquisti, A. (2011). The Effect of Online Privacy Information on Purchasing Behaviour: An Experimental Study. *Information Systems Research, 22*(2), 254–268. doi:10.1287/isre.1090.0260

KEY TERMS AND DEFINITIONS

Collectivism: The practice of principles of giving a group priority over everyone in it.

Ethics: Ethics is a field of study that addresses the principles of morality based on what is right and a decision that occurs within society.

Globalization: The Process by which countries or multinational companies influence or start operating on an international scale.

Governance: Systems such as policies, processes, and procedure framework for the operation of an organization.

Personal Information: Identifiable information such as identity number, age, color, qualifications, race, and gender.

Privacy: Barriers and manage boundaries to protect personal information.

Transparency: The accuracy of information to enable organizations to make informed decision making and take the right decision.

Trust: Authenticity and reliability of the information.

Compilation of References

3rd World Farmer. (2022). *3rd World Farmer: A Thought-provoking Simulation*. Retrieved from http://www.3rdworldfarmer.com/

A World Without Oil. (2022). *A World Without Oil: Play It Before You Live It*. Retrieved from http://writerguy.com/wwo/metahome.htm

Abbass, I. M. (2012). No retreat no surrender conflict for survival between Fulani pastoralists and farmers in Northern Nigeria. *European Scientific Journal*, *8*(1), 331–346.

Abdullah, M., Shukor, Z., & Rahmat, M. (2017). The influences of risk management committee and audit committee towards voluntary risk management disclosure. *Jurnal Pengurusan*, *50*, 83–95. doi:10.17576/pengurusan-2017-50-08

Abdulrauf, A. L., & Fombad, M. C. (2017). Personal Data Protection in Nigeria: Reflections on Opportunities, Options and Challenges to legal Reforms. *The Liverpool Law Review*, *38*(2), 105–134. doi:10.100710991-016-9189-8

Abraham, S., & Cox, P. (2007). Analysing the determinants of narrative risk information in UK FTSE 100 annual reports. *The British Accounting Review*, *39*(3), 227–248. doi:10.1016/j.bar.2007.06.002

Ackerman, E. (2017, August 4). *Slight Street Sign Modifications Can Completely Fool Machine Learning Algorithms*. Retrieved February 19, 2022, from IEEE Spectrum: https://spectrum.ieee.org/slight-street-sign-modifications-can-fool-machine-learning-algorithms

Acquisit, A., Brandimarte, L., & Loewenstein, G. (2015). Privacy and Human Behavior in the age of information Review. *Science*, *347*(6221), 509.

Adam-Muller, A., & Erkens, M. (2020). Risk disclosure noncompliance. *Journal of Accounting and Public Policy*, *39*(3), 106739. doi:10.1016/j.jaccpubpol.2020.106739

Adham, A. K., Kasimin, H., Ma Isa, R., Othman, F., & Ahmad, F. (2015). Developing a Framework for a Viable Research University. *System Practice Res*, *28*, 503–525.

Adibe, R., Ike, C. C., & Udeogu, C. U. (2017). Press Freedom and Nigeria's Cybercrime Act of 2015: An Assessment. *Africa Spectrum*, *52*(2), 117–127. doi:10.1177/000203971705200206

Agyei-Mensah, B. (2019). The effect of audit committee effectiveness and audit quality on corporate voluntary disclosure quality. *African Journal of Economic and Management Studies*, *10*(1), 17–31. doi:10.1108/AJEMS-04-2018-0102

Ahmad, T., Zhang, D., Huang, C., Zhang, H., Dai, N., Song, Y., & Chen, H. (2021). Artificial intelligence in sustainable energy industry: Status quo, challenges and opportunities. *Journal of Cleaner Production*, *125834*. Advance online publication. doi:10.1016/j.jclepro.2021.125834

Ahmed, A., Horn, S., & Smith, R. (2015). *Lessons from the first three years of SOC reporting*. Crowe Horwath LLP. https://www.crowe.com/-/media/Crowe/LLP/folio-pdf/Lessons-From-First-Three-Years-of-SOC-Reporting_RISK15910.pdf

Ahmed, S. (2021). Who inadvertently shares deepfakes? Analysing the role of political interest, cognitive ability, and social network size. *Telematics and Informatics*, *57*, 101508. doi:10.1016/j.tele.2020.101508

AICPA. (2014). *Illustrative type 2 SOC 2^{SM} report with the criteria in the cloud security (CSA) cloud controls matrix (CCM)*. https://us.aicpa.org/content/dam/aicpa/interestareas/frc/assuranceadvisoryservices/downloadabledocuments/soc2_csa_ccm_report.pdf

AICPA. (n.d.a). *SOC for cybersecurity*. https://www.aicpa.org/interestareas/frc/assuranceadvisoryservices/aicpacybersecurityinitiative.html

AICPA. (n.d.b). *SOC for supply chain*. https://us.aicpa.org/interestareas/frc/assuranceadvisoryservices/soc-for-supply-chain

Ain, Q., Yuan, X., Javaid, H., Usman, M., & Haris, M. (2020). (forthcoming). Female directors and agency costs: Evidence from Chinese listed firms. *International Journal of Emerging Markets*.

Akbar, S., Kharabsheh, B., Poletti-Hughes, J., & Shah, S. (2017). Board structure and corporate risk taking in the UK financial sector. *International Review of Financial Analysis*, *50*, 101–110. doi:10.1016/j.irfa.2017.02.001

Akintola, S. O., & Akinpelu, D. A. (2021). The Nigerian Data Protection Regulation 2019 and data protection in biobank research. *International Data Privacy Law*, *11*(3), 307–318. doi:10.1093/idpl/ipab011

Akinyetun, T. S. (2021). Poverty, Cybercrime and National Security in Nigeria. *Journal of Contemporary Sociological Issues*, *1*(2), 1–23. doi:10.19184/csi.v1i2.24188

Aladenusi, T. (2021 January). *A fresh perspective: Nigeria cyber security outlook 2021*. Cyber Risk Services Deloitte West Africa. https://www.delotte.com.ng/

Aliyev, A. I., Ibrahimova, A. N., & Rzayeva, G. A. (2020). Information security: Legal regulations in Azerbaijan and abroad. *Journal of Information Science*, 1–14. doi:10.1177/0165551520981813

Alkurdi, A., Hussainey, K., Tahat, Y., & Aladwan, M. (2019). The impact of corporate governance on risk disclosure: Jordanian evidence. *Academy of Accounting and Financial Studies Journal*, *23*(1), 1–16.

Alshirah, M., Rahman, A., & Mustapa, I. (2020). Board of directors' characteristics and corporate risk disclosure: The moderating role of family ownership. *EuroMed Journal of Business, 15*(2), 219–252. doi:10.1108/EMJB-09-2019-0115

Amaral, M. (2015). Tipos de riscos na actividade bancária. *Revisores e Auditores, 69*, 37–42.

American Institute of Certified Public Accountants (AICPA). (2018). *A CPA's Introduction to Cybersecurity.* Accessed September 11, 2021. Retrieved from https://www.aicpa.org/InterestAreas/ PrivateCompaniesPracticeSection/QualityServicesDelivery/InformationTechnology/ DownloadableDocuments/cpa-guide-to-cybersecurity.pdf

Amran, A., Bin, A. M. R., & Hassan, B. C. H. M. (2009). Risk reporting: An exploratory study on risk management disclosure in Malaysian annual reports. *Managerial Auditing Journal, 24*(1), 39–57. doi:10.1108/02686900910919893

Anders, S. B. (2020, February). System organization controls resources. *The CPA Journal.* https:// www.cpajournal.com/2020/03/23/system-organization-controls-resources/

Ani, U. D., He, H., & Tiwari, A. (2020). Vulnerability-Based Impact Criticality Estimation for Industrial Control Systems. In *2020 International Conference on Cyber Security and Protection of Digital Services (Cyber Security)* (pp. 1-8). IEEE. 10.1109/CyberSecurity49315.2020.9138886

Apuke, O. D., & Omar, B. (2020). Fake news proliferation in Nigeria: Consequences, motivations, and prevention through awareness strategies. *Humanities and Social Sciences Reviews, 8*(2), 318–327. doi:10.18510/hssr.2020.8236

Arachchilage, N., & Love, S. (2014). Security awareness of computer users: A phishing threat avoidance perspective. *Computers in Human Behavior, 38*, 304–312.

AraromiA. (2018 November 28). Determining legal responsibilities in defamation: Crossing the dividing line between real world and internet jurisdiction. SSRN. https://www.researchgate.net/ scientificcontributions/2075535661_Marcus_Araromi

Arens, A., Elder, R., Beasley, M., & Hogan, C. (2020). *Auditing and assurance services* (17th ed.). Pearson.

Argus Cyber Security. (2016, January). *SAE J3061 Cyber Security Guidebook for Cyber-Physical Vehicle Systems.* Retrieved February 2022, from Argus Cyber Security: https://argus-sec.com/ sae-j3061-cyber-security-guidebook-for-cyber-physical-vehicle-systems/

Ashfaq, K., Zhang, R., Munaim, A., & Razzaq, N. (2016). An investigation into the determinants of risk disclosure in banks: Evidence from financial sector of Pakistan. *International Journal of Economics and Financial Issues, 6*(3), 1049–1058.

Asogwa, E. B. (2013). The readiness of universities in managing electronic records. A study of three federal universities in Nigeria. *The Electronic Library, 31*(6), 792–807. doi:10.1108/ EL-04-2012-0037

Atake, A., Gbahabo, E., & Ushiadi, A. (2019 April 3). Online defamation: Just before you post it! *Templars-Thought Leadership.* https://www.templars-law.com/copyrights-and-the-music-business/

Ayers, D. (2021). The limits of transactional identity: Whiteness and embodiment in digital facial replacement. *Convergence, 27*(4), 1018–1037. doi:10.1177/13548565211027810

Babalola, A. (2019 October 23). When False Publication May Amount to Criminal Libel. *Vanguard.* https://www.vanguardngr.com/2019/10/when-false-publications-may-amount-to-criminal-libel/#:~:text=Whereas%20in%20tort%20the%20false%20publication%20must%20be,tendency%20to%20provoke%20a%20breach%20of%20the%20peace

BadgeOS. (2022). *BadgeOS.* Retrieved from https://badgeos.org/

Badgr. (2022). *Badgr: Achieve Anything, Recognize Everything.* Retrieved from https://info.badgr.com/

Ballantine, M. (2019 July 3). Are deepfakes invading the office? *Forbes.* https://www.forbes.com/sites/mattballantine/2019/07/03/are-deepfakes-invading-the-office/#19bf48923ea1

Barakat, A., & Hussainey, K. (2013). Bank governance, regulation, supervision, and risk reporting: Evidence from operational risk disclosures in European banks. *International Review of Financial Analysis, 30*, 254–273. doi:10.1016/j.irfa.2013.07.002Barros, C., Boubakar, S., & Hamrouni, A. (2013). Corporate governance and voluntary disclosure in France. *Journal of Applied Business Research, 29*(2), 561–578. doi:10.19030/jabr.v29i2.7657

Baron, K. (2019 July 19). Digital double: The deepfake tech nourishing new wave retail. *Forbes.* https://www.forbes.com/sites/katiebaron/2019/07/29/digital-do-ubles-the-deepfake-tech-nourishing-new-waveretail/#33489a044cc7

Baxter, R. J., Holderness, D. K. Jr, & Wood, D. A. (2016). Applying basic gamification techniques to IT compliance training: Evidence from the lab and field. *Journal of Information Systems, 30*(3), 119–133.

BBC News. (2021). Muhammadu Buhari: Twitter deletes Nigerian leader's "civil war" post. *BBC News.* Retrieved 25 July 2021 from https://www.bbc.com/news/world-africa-57336571.amp

Beccaria, C., Newman, G. R., & Marongiu, P. (2017). *On crimes and punishments.* Routledge. doi:10.4324/9781315125527

Beerbaum, D., Piechocki, M., & Puaschunder, J. M. (2019). Measuring Accounting Reporting Complexity with customized extensions XBRL – A Behavioral Economics approach. *Journal of Applied Research in the Digital Economy, 1*(10), 3–41.

Bello, M., & Griffiths, M. (2021). Routine activity theory and cybercrime investigation in Nigeria: how capable are law enforcement agencies? In T. Owen & J. Marshall (Eds.), *Rethinking Cybercrime* (pp. 213–235). Palgrave Macmillan. doi:10.1007/978-3-030-55841-3_11

Beretta, S., & Bozzolan, S. (2004). A framework for the analysis of firm risk communication. *The International Journal of Accounting*, *39*(3), 265–288. doi:10.1016/j.intacc.2004.06.006

Bíró, G. I. (2014). Didactics 2.0: A pedagogical analysis of gamification theory from a comparative perspective with a special view to the components of learning. *Procedia: Social and Behavioral Sciences*, *141*, 148–151.

Biswas, S. (2021). Female directors and risk-taking behavior of Indian firms. *Managerial Finance*, *47*(7), 1016–1037. doi:10.1108/MF-05-2020-0274

Blackwell, L. (2021). Key Aspects of a Cybersecurity Framework. *Internal Auditor*, 14-15. Accessed September 11, 2021. Retrieved from https://theiia.texterity.com/ia/august_2021_internal_auditor/MobilePagedReplica.action?pm=2&folio=14#pg16

Blakemore, E. (2020 April 28). How Photos Became a Weapon in Stalin's Great Purge. *History*. https://www.history.com/news/josef-stalin-great-purge-photo-retouching

Block, J. H., & Burns, R. B. (1976). Mastery learning. *Review of Research in Education*, *4*, 3–49.

Blythe, J. M., & Coventry, L. (2012, September). Cyber security games: a new line of risk. In *International Conference on Entertainment Computing* (pp. 600-603). Springer.

Boss, S. R., Galletta, D. F., Lowry, P. B., Moody, G. D., & Polak, P. (2015). What do systems users have to fear? Using fear appeals to engender threats and fear that motivate protective security behaviors. *Management Information Systems Quarterly*, *39*(4), 837–864.

Botha, J., Globler, M. M., Hahn, J., & Eloff, M. M. (2017). A High-Level Comparison between the South African Protection of Personal Information Act and International Data Protection Laws. *Conference: The 12th International Conference on Cyber Warfare and Security (ICCWS), 12.*

Bourke, J. C. (2016, June 13). Explaining the 3 faces of SOC. *Journal of Accountancy*. https://www.journalofaccountancy.com/newsletters/2016/jun/3-face-of-soc.html

Bozzolan, S., & Miihkinen, A. (2021). The quality of mandatory non-financial (risk) disclosures: The moderating role of audit firm and partner characteristics. *The International Journal of Accounting*, *56*(02), 2150008. doi:10.1142/S1094406021500086

Bradshaw, S., & Howard, P. (2019). *The global disinformation order*. https://comprop.oii.ox.ac.uk/research/cybertroops2019/

Brandon, J. (2018 February 16). Terrifying high-tech porn: Creepy 'deepfake' videos are on the rise. *Fox News*. https://www.foxnews.com/tech/2018/02/16/terrifying-high-tech-porn-creepy-deepfake-videos-are-on-rise.html

Brecht, F., Fabian, B., Kunz, S., & Müller, S. (2012). Communication anonymizers: Personality, internet privacy literacy and their influence on technology acceptance. *Eur Conf Inf Syst*, *214*, 1–13.

Breesch, D., & Branson, J. (2009). The effects of auditor gender on audit quality. *The IUP Journal of Accounting Research & Audit Practices*, *8*(3-4), 78–107.

Brown, S. (2022, March 7). *SOC2 Type 1 Guide: Everything You need To Know*. StrongDM Blog. https://www.strongdm.com/blog/what-is-soc-2-type-1

Brown, J. S., Heath, C., & Pea, R. (2003). *Vygotsky's educational theory in cultural context*. Cambridge University Press.

Bucher, D. (2021). Protecting against cyberattacks. *Strategic Finance*.

Buckby, S., Gallery, G., & Ma, J. (2015). An analysis of risk management disclosures: Australian evidence. *Managerial Auditing Journal*, *30*(8/9), 812–869. doi:10.1108/MAJ-09-2013-0934

Bufarwa, I., Elamer, A., Ntim, C., & AlHares, A. (2020). Gender diversity, corporate governance and financial risk disclosure in the UK. *International Journal of Law and Management*, *62*(6), 521–538. doi:10.1108/IJLMA-10-2018-0245

Bulgurcu, B., Cavusoglu, H., & Benbasat, I. (2010). Information security policy compliance: An empirical study of rationality-based beliefs and information security awareness. *Management Information Systems Quarterly*, 523–548.

Burkacky, O., Deichmann, J., Klein, B., Pototzky, K., & Scherf, G. (2020, March). *Cybersecurity in Automotive*. Retrieved February 2022, from McKinsensy.com: https://www.mckinsey.com/~/media/mckinsey/industries/automotive%20and%20assembly/our%20insights/cybersecurity%20in%20automotive%20mastering%20the%20challenge/cybersecurity-in-automotive-mastering-the-challenge.pdf

Bushman, R., & Landsman, W. (2010). The pros and cons of regulating corporate reporting: A critical review of the arguments. *Accounting and Business Research*, *40*(3), 259–273. doi:10.1080/00014788.2010.9663400

Bwerinofa-Petrozzello, R. (2021). Helping clients before a cyberattack: CPAs play critical roles in building defenses against breaches, fraud and other online threats. *The Journal of Accountancy*. Accessed September 10, 2021. Retrieved from https://www.journalofaccountancy.com/issues/2021/sep/help-clients-before-a-cyberattack.html

Cai, C., Keasey, K., & Short, H. (2005). Corporate governance and information efficiency in security markets. *European Financial Management*, *12*(5), 763–787. doi:10.1111/j.1468-036X.2006.00276.x

Caldera, E. (2019). Reject the evidence of your eyes and ears: Deepfakes and the law of virtual replicants. *Seton Hall Law Review*, *50*, 177.

Campbell, K., & Mínguez-Vera, A. (2008). Gender diversity in the boardroom and firm financial performance. *Journal of Business Ethics*, *83*(3), 435–451. doi:10.100710551-007-9630-y

Carmona, P., Fuebtes, C., & Ruiz, C. (2016). Risk disclosure analysis in the corporate governance annual report using fuzzy-set qualitative comparative analysis. *Revista de Administração de Empresas*, *56*(3), 342–352. doi:10.1590/S0034-759020160307

Chalmers, K., & Godfrey, J. (2004). Reputation costs: The impetus for voluntary derivative financial instruments reporting. *Accounting, Organizations and Society*, *29*(2), 95–125. doi:10.1016/S0361-3682(02)00034-X

Chesney, B., & Citron, D. (2019). Deep fakes: A looming challenge for privacy, democracy, and national security. *California Law Review*, *107*, 1753–1820. doi:10.2139srn.3213954

Cialdini, R. (2021). *Influence, New and Expanded: The Psychology of Persuasion*. HarperCollins.

Cimpanu, C. (2018). *Trump signs bill that creates the Cybersecurity and Infrastructure Security Agency*. Retrieved from https://www.zdnet.com/article/trump-signs-bill-that-creates-the-cybersecurity-and-infrastructure-security-agency/

Cochran, L. P., Tatikonda, V. M., & Magid, M. J. (2007). Radio Frequency Identification and Ethics of Privacy. *Organizational Dynamics*, *36*(2), 217–229. doi:10.1016/j.orgdyn.2007.03.008

Coelho, S., Amaral, M., & Lemos, K. (2018). Divulgação de informação sobre riscos financeiros nas entidades bancárias : Evidência empírica em Portugal. *European Journal of Applied Business Management. Special Issue of ICABM*, *2018*, 205–225.

Cohen, L. E., & Felson, M. (2003). Routine activity theory. In F. Cullen & R. Agnew (Eds.), Criminological theory: Past to present (essential readings) (pp. 70–79). Academic Press.

Cole, S. (2019). This deepfake of Mark Zuckerberg tests Facebook's fake video policies. *Vice*. https://www.vice.com/en/article/ywyxex/deepfake-of-mark-zuckerberg-facebook-fake-video-policy

Cole, J. M. (2016). *Challenges of Implementing Substation Hardware Upgrades for NERC CIP version 5 Compliance to Enhance Cybersecurity. In 2016 IEEE/PES Transmission and Distribution Conference and Exposition (T&D)*. IEEE.

Combes-ThuÚlin, E., Henneron, S., & Touron, P. (2006). Risk regulations and financial disclosure: An investigation based on corporate communication in French traded companies. *Corporate Communications*, *11*(3), 303–326. doi:10.1108/13563280610680876

Cornish, D., & Clarke, R. (1986). *The reasoning criminal*. Springer-Verlag. doi:10.1007/978-1-4613-8625-4

Credly. (2022). *Credly Digital Credentials*. Retrieved from https://info.credly.com/

Crossler, R., Johnston, A., Lowry, P., Hu, Q., Warkentin, M., & Baskerville, R. (2013). Future directions for behavioral information security research. *Computers & Security, 32*, 90-101.

Csíkszentmihályi, M. (1997). Finding flow: The psychology of engagement with everyday life. Hachette UK.

Culnan, M. J., & Williams, C. K. (2009). How ethics can enhance Organizational Privacy: Lessons from the ChoicePoint and TJX Data Breaches. *Management Information Systems Quarterly*, *33*(4), 673–689. doi:10.2307/20650322

Cunliffe-Jones, P., Diagne, A., Finlay, A., & Schiffrinet, A. (2021). Bad law – legal and regulatory responses to misinformation in Sub-Saharan Africa 2016–2020. In *Misinformation policy in Sub-Saharan Africa: From laws and regulations to media literacy* (pp. 99–218). University of Westminster Press. doi:10.16997/book53.b

Cyber, C. (2021, February 15). *The Principle of Least Functionality, Simplicity is the Ultimate Sophistication*. Retrieved February 19, 2022, from Cub Cyber: https://www.cubcyber.com/the-principle-of-least-functionality-simplicity-is-the-ultimate-sophistication

Cybercrimes (Prohibition, Prevention), etc.) Act (CPPA), 2015.

D'Arcy, J., Herath, T., & Shoss, M. K. (2014). Understanding employee responses to stressful information security requirements: A coping perspective. *Journal of Management Information Systems*, *31*(2), 285–318.

Darvasi, P. (2016). *Empathy, perspective and complicity: How digital games can support peace education and conflict resolution*. Mahatmi Gandhi Institute of Education for Peace and Sustainable Development/UNESCO.

DataReportal. (2021, February). *Digital 2021: Nigeria*. https://datareportal.com/reports/digital-2021-nigeria

Dautovic, G. (2021). *15 must-know outsourcing statistics for 2021*. https://fortunly.com/statistics/outsourcing-statistics/#gref

Davies, E.H.S. (2020). The Introduction of research ethics reviews procedures at a university in South Africa: Review outcomes of a social science research ethics committee. *Research Ethics*, *16*(1 – 2), 1 – 26.

de Ruiter, A. (2021). The distinct wrong of deepfakes. *Philosophy & Technology*, *34*, 1311–1332. doi:10.100713347-021-00459-2

De Vlaminck, N., & Sarens, G. (2015). The relationship between audit committee characteristics and financial statement quality: Evidence from Belgium. *The Journal of Management and Governance*, *19*(1), 145–166. doi:10.100710997-013-9282-5

De Vries, K. (2020). You never fake alone. Creative AI in action. *Information Communication and Society*, *23*(14), 2110–2127. doi:10.1080/1369118X.2020.1754877

DeBoskey, D., Luo, Y., & Wang, J. (2018). Does board gender diversity affect the transparency of corporate political disclosure? *Asian Review of Accounting*, *26*(4), 444–463. doi:10.1108/ARA-09-2017-0141

Dechand, S. (2020, October 8). *Automotive Software: 6 Tips to Comply With ISO 21434 Cheat Sheet)*. Retrieved February 2022, from Code Intelligence: https://www.code-intelligence.com/blog/iso-21434-compliance?utm_term=automotive%20software&utm_campaign=&utm_source=adwords&utm_medium=ppc&hsa_acc=1156374742&hsa_cam=14540066791&hsa_grp=121993923530&hsa_ad=544093176460&hsa_src=g&hsa_tgt=kwd-10652700&hsa_k

Deci, E. L., & Ryan, R. M. (2012). *Self-determination theory*. Academic Press.

Deflem, M., & McDonough, S. (2015). The fear of counterterrorism: Surveillance and civil liberties since 9/11. *Society, 52*(1), 70–79. doi:10.100712115-014-9855-1

Denny, G. S., Silaigwana, B., Wassenaar, D., Bull, S., & Parker, M. (2015). Developing Ethical Practices for Public Health Research Data Sharing in South Africa: The Views and Experiences from a Diverse Sample of Research Stakeholders. *Journal of Empirical Research on Human Research Ethics; JERHRE, 10*(3), 290–301. doi:10.1177/1556264615592386 PMID:26297750

Deumes, R., & Knechel, W. (2008). Economic incentives for voluntary reporting on internal risk management and control systems. *Auditing, 27*(1), 35–66. doi:10.2308/aud.2008.27.1.35

Dey, R., Hossain, S., & Rezae, Z. (2018). Financial risk disclosure and financial attributes among publicly traded manufacturing companies: Evidence from Bangladesh. *Journal of Risk and Financial Management, 11*(50), 1–16. doi:10.3390/jrfm11030050

Dhillon, S. (2019 July 4). The optimistic view of deepfakes: Always look on the bright side of simulated life. *Tech Crunch*. https://techcrunch.com/2019/07/04/an-optimistic-view-of-deepfakes/

Dobber, T., Metoui, N., Trilling, D., Helberger, N., & de Vreese, C. (2021). Do (microtargeted) deepfakes have real effects on political attitudes? *The International Journal of Press/Politics, 26*(1), 69–91. doi:10.1177/1940161220944364

Dong, L., Illieva, P. & Medeiros, A. (2018). Data dreams: Planning for the Future of historical medical documents. *History Matters. Journal of the Medical Library Association, 106*(4). Doi. org/10.5195/jmla.2018.444.

Eboibi, F. E. (2017). A review of the legal and regulatory frameworks of Nigerian Cybercrimes Act 2015. *Computer Law & Security Review, 33*(5), 700–717. doi:10.1016/j.clsr.2017.03.020

Ebrahimi Maimand, M., & Namazi, M. (2021). (in press). Firms' risk disclosure and reporting: A comprehensive framework. *Journal of Knowledge Accounting*.

EigbedionA. (2020 August 1). Deepfakes: Legal & regulatory considerations in Nigeria. Available at SSRN: doi:10.2139/ssrn.3670644

Ejedafiru, E. F. (2020). Librarians' Professional Ethics and Reference Service Delivery in College of Education in South-South, Nigeria. *Library Philosophy and Practice*.

Elamer, A. A., Ntim, C. G., Abdou, H. A., & Pyke, C. (2020). Sharia supervisory boards, governance structures and operational risk disclosures: Evidence from Islamic banks in MENA countries. *Global Finance Journal, 46*, 1–44. doi:10.1016/j.gfj.2019.100488

Electronics, C. S. S. (2019). *A Simple Intro to LIN bus*. Retrieved October 2019, from CSS Electrnoics: https://www.csselectronics.com/screen/page/lin-bus-protocol-intro-basics/language/en

El-Khuffash, A. (2013). *Gamification*. Ryerson University.

Elshandidy, T., & Neri, L. (2015). Corporate governance, risk disclosure practices, and market liquidity: Comparative evidence from the UK and Italy. *Corporate Governance, 23*(4), 331–356. doi:10.1111/corg.12095

Ess, C. (2005). "Lost in translation?" Intercultural dialogues on privacy and information ethics (Introduction to a special issue on Privacy and Data Privacy Protection in Asia). *Ethics and Information Technology, 7*(1), 1–6. doi:10.100710676-005-0454-0

Etigowni, S., Tian, D., Hernandez, G., Zonouz, S., & Butler, K. (2016). CPAC: Securing Critical Infrastructure with Cyber-Physical Access Control. In *32nd Annual Conference on Computer Security Applications*. Los Angeles, CA: ACM. 10.1145/2991079.2991126

Evans, C. (2018 April 17). Spotting fakes news in a world with manipulated video. *CBS News.* https://www.cbsnews.com/news/spotting-fake-news-in-a-world-with-manipulated-video/

Eyre, H. L. (2007). Keller's Personalized System of Instruction: Was it a Fleeting Fancy or is there a Revival on the Horizon? *The Behavior Analyst Today, 8*(3), 317.

Fagade, T., & Tryfonas, T. (2016, July). Security by compliance? A study of insider threat implications for Nigerian banks. In *International Conference on Human Aspects of Information Security, Privacy, and Trust* (pp. 128-139). Springer.

Fallis, D. (2020). The epistemic threat of deepfakes. *Philosophy & Technology, 34*, 623–643. doi:10.100713347-020-00419-2 PMID:32837868

Fang, H., & Chen, Z. (2013). Study on Chinese University Students' Privacy Protection from Intercultural Perspective. *International Conference on Education Technology and Management Sciences (ICETMS 2013).*

Fathi, J. (2013). The determinants of the quality of financial information disclosed by French listed companies. *Mediterranean Journal of Social Sciences, 4*(2), 319–319. doi:10.5901/mjss.2013.v4n2p319

Fatoki, O. (2012). The Impact of Ethics on the Availability of Trade Credit to New Small and Medium-Sized Enterprises (SMEs) in South Africa. *Journal of Social Sciences, 30*(1), 21 – 29.

Felicia, P. (Ed.). (2012). *Developments in current game-based learning design and deployment.* IGI Global.

FeloA.KrishnamurthyS.SolieriS. (2003). Audit committee characteristics and the perceived quality of financial reporting: an empirical analysis. *Available at* SSRN 401240. doi:10.2139/ssrn.401240

Ferguson, R., Hoel, T., Scheffel, M., & Drachsler, H. (2016). Guest Editorial: Ethics and Privacy in Learning Analytics. *Journal of Learning Analytics, 3*(1), 5–15. doi:10.18608/jla.2016.31.2

Field, L., Lowry, M., & Mkrtchyan, A. (2013). Are busy boards detrimental? *Journal of Financial Economics, 109*(1), 63–82. doi:10.1016/j.jfineco.2013.02.004

Fiorella, L., & Mayer, R. (2013). The relative benefits of learning by teaching and teaching expectancy. *Contemporary Educational Psychology, 38*(4), 281–288.

Fishbein, M., & Ajzen, I. (1975). *Intention and behaviour: An introduction to theory and research.* Addison-Wesley. doi:10.4236/tel.2018.813176

Floridi, L. (2018). Soft ethics, the governance of the digital, and the General Data Protection Regulation. *Phil. Trans. R. Soc. A, 370*(2133), 20180081. doi:10.1098/rsta.2018.0081 PMID:30322997

Forsyth, B. (2015). Banning bulk: Passage of the USA FREEDOM Act and ending bulk collection. *Washington and Lee Law Review, 72*, 1307.

Fox, J., & Bailenson, J. N. (2009). Virtual self-modeling: The effects of vicarious reinforcement and identification on exercise behaviors. *Media Psychology, 12*(1), 1–25.

Francia, G. A. (2020). Connected Vehicle Security. *15th International Conference on Cyber Warfare and Security (ICCWS 2020)*, 173-181.

Francia, G. A. III. (2021). Vehicle Network Security Metrics. In K. Daimi & C. Peoples (Eds.), *Advances in Cybersecurity Management* (pp. 55–73). Springer Nature. doi:10.1007/978-3-030-71381-2_4

Francia, G. A. III, & El-Sheikh, E. (2021). Applied Machine Learning to Vehicle Security. In Y. Maleh, M. Shojafar, M. Alazab, & Y. Baddi (Eds.), *Machine Intelligence and Big Data Analytics for Cybersecurity Applications* (pp. 423–442). Springer Nature Switzerland AG. doi:10.1007/978-3-030-57024-8_19

Froehlich, A., Ringas, N., & Wilson, J. (2021). How space can support African civil societies: Security, peace, and development through Efficient Governance Supported by space applications. *Acta Astronautica.* Advance online publication. doi:10.1016/j.actaastro.2021.06.006

Fukuda-Parr, S., & Messineo, C. (2012). *Human security: A critical review of the literature.* Working Paper. Leuven: Centre for Research on Peace and Development.

Fukukawa, H., & Kim, H. (2017). Effects of audit partners on clients' business risk disclosure. *Accounting and Business Research, 47*(7), 780–809. doi:10.1080/00014788.2017.1299619

Gafni, R., & Pavel, T. (2021). Cyberattacks against the health-care sectors during the COVID-19 pandemic. *Information & Computer Security.* 1 doi:0.1108/ICS-05-2021-0059

Garaba, F. (2016). User Perceptions about Archives at the Lutheran Theological Institute Library, Pietermaritzburg, South Africa. *African Journal of Library Archives and Information Science, 26*(1), 73–83.

Garaba, F. (2018). The neglected fond in university archives: The case of sport club records at the University of Kwazulu-Natal (UKZN), Pietermaritzburg Campus, South Africa. *Records Management Journal, 28*(2), 143–158. doi:10.1108/RMJ-11-2016-0043

Garba, A. A., & Bade, A. M. (2021). The current state of cybersecurity readiness in Nigerian organizations. *International Journal of Multidisciplinary and Current Educational Research*, *3*(1), 154–162.

Gasevic, D., Dawson, S., & Jovanovic, J. (2016). Ethics and Privacy as Enablers of Learning Analytics. *Journal of Learning Analytics*, *3*(1), 1–4. doi:10.18608/jla.2016.31.1

GCI. (2020). *Global cybersecurity index 2020*. International Telecommunication Union (ITU). https://www.itu.int/dms_pub/itu-d/opb/str/D-STR-GCI.01-2021-PDF-E.pdf

Gee, J. (2007). *Good video games + good learning: Collected essays on video games, learning, and literacy*. Peter Lang.

Gerstner, E. (2020). Face/off: "Deepfake" face swaps and privacy laws. *Defense Counsel Journal*, *87*, 1–14.

Giansiracusa, N. (2021). Deepfake Deception. In N. Giansiracusa (Ed.), *How Algorithms create and prevent fake news* (pp. 41–66). Apress.

Gibbons, P. (2002). *Scaffolding language, scaffolding learning*. Heinemann.

Glahe, F. R. (Ed.). (1993). *Adam Smith's an inquiry into the nature and causes of the wealth of nations: A concordance*. Rowman & Littlefield Pub Incorporated.

Glassman, M., & Kang, M. J. (2012). Intelligence in the internet age: The emergence and evolution of Open Source Intelligence (OSINT). *Computers in Human Behavior*, *28*(2), 673–682.

Goldman, Z. K., & McCoy, D. (2016). Deterring Financially Motivated Cybercrime. *Journal of National Security Law & Policy*, *8*(3), 1.

Goldstein, F. (2020). *Understanding the UNECE WP.29*. Retrieved February 2022, from Upstream: https://upstream.auto/blog/understanding-the-unece-wp-29-cybersecurity-regulation

Gonidakis, F., Koutoupis, A., Tsamis, A., & Agoraki, M. (2020). Risk disclosure in listed Greek companies: The effects of the financial crisis. *Accounting Research Journal*, *33*(4/5), 615–633. doi:10.1108/ARJ-03-2020-0050

Gosse, C., & Burkell, J. (2020). Politics and porn: How news media characterizes problems presented by deepfakes. *Critical Studies in Media Communication*, *37*(5), 497–511. doi:10.1080/15295036.2020.1832697

Granger, D. (2017). *Karmen Ransomware Variant Introduced by Russian Hacker*. Retrieved from https://www.recordedfuture.com/karmen-ransomware-variant/

Green, A. (2019, October 30). Lawmakers and tech groups fight back against deepfakes. *Financial Times*. https://www.ft.com/content/b7c78624-ca57-11e9-af46-b09e8bfe60c0

Greengard, S. (2019). Will deepfakes do deep damage? *Communications of the ACM*, *63*(1), 17–19. doi:10.1145/3371409

Griffith, R. (2017). Managing data subject access requests. *British Journal of Community Nursing*, *22*(3), 149–151. doi:10.12968/bjcn.2017.22.3.149 PMID:28252324

Gry, H. (2019). Making Sentences of data ethics: The powers behind the data ethics debate in European policymaking, Internet Policy Review. *Alexander Von Humboldt Institute for Internet and Society, Berlin.*, *8*(2), 1–19.

Gupta, S. (2020). Assuring compliance with government certification and accreditation regulations. In *Cloud computing security* (2nd ed., pp. 387–394). CRC Press. doi:10.1201/9780429055126-32

Habitica. (2022). *Habitica - Gamify Your Life*. Retrieved from https://habitica.com/

Habtoor, O., Ahmad, N., Mohamad, N., & Haat, M. (2017). Linking corporate risk disclosure practices with firm-specific characteristics in Saudi Arabia. *Gadjah Mada International Journal of Business*, *19*(3), 247–267. doi:10.22146/gamaijb.26769

Hall, H. K. (2018). Deepfake videos: When seeing isn't believing. *Cath. U. J. L. & Tech*, *27*(1), 51–76.

Halterman, C. (2011, June 30). Expanding service organization controls reporting. *Journal of Accountancy*. https://www.journalofaccountancy.com/issues/2011/jul/20103500.html

Hamari, J., Koivisto, J., & Sarsa, H. (2014). Does gamification work?--a literature review of empirical studies on gamification. In *2014 47th Hawaii international conference on system sciences* (pp. 3025-3034). IEEE.

Hamm, M. S. (2016). The USA patriot act and the politics of fear. In *Cultural criminology unleashed* (pp. 301–314). Routledge-Cavendish.

Haney, J., & Lutters, W. (2020). Security Awareness Training for the Workforce: Moving Beyond "Check-the-Box" Compliance. *Computer*, *53*(10).

Hao, L. (2019). The emergence of deepfake technology: A review. *Technology Innovation Management Review*, *9*(11), 39–52.

Hardies, K., Breesch, D., & Branson, J. (2016). Do (Fe)Male Auditors Impair Audit Quality? Evidence from Going-Concern Opinions. *European Accounting Review*, *25*(1), 7–34. doi:10.1 080/09638180.2014.921445

Harris, D. (2018). Deepfakes: False pornography is here and the law cannot protect you. *Duke L. & Tech. Rev.*, *17*, 99.

Hatzipanagos, R. (2018). How online hate turns into real-life violence. *Washington Post*. Retrieved 25 July 2021 from https://www.washingtonpost.com/nation/2018/11/30/how-online-hate-speech-is-fueling-real-life-violence/

Haucke, A., & Pokoyski, D. (2018). Mea culpa–Schuld, Scham und Opferrolle bei Social Engineering. In KES (Vol. 1, pp. 6-8). Academic Press.

Hawell, D. (2019 June 13). Top AI researchers race to detect 'deepfake' videos: 'We are outgunned'. *Mercury News*. https://www.washingtonpost.com/technology/2019/06/12/top-ai-researchers-race-detectdeepfake-videos-we-are-outgunned/

Hay, D. C. (2021). Discussion of "The Quality of Mandatory Nonfinancial Risk Disclosures and the Moderating Effect of Audit Firm and Partner Characteristics". *The International Journal of Accounting*, *56*(02), 2180004. doi:10.1142/S1094406021800044

Healy, P., & Palepu, K. (2001). Information asymmetry, corporate disclosure, and the capital markets: A review of the empirical disclosure literature. *Journal of Accounting Research*, *31*(1-3), 405–440.

Hemrit, W. (2018). Risk reporting appraisal in post-revolutionary Tunisia. *Journal of Financial Reporting and Accounting*, *16*(4), 522–542. doi:10.1108/JFRA-05-2016-0040

Henk, O. (2020). Internal control through the lens of institutional work: A systematic literature Review. *Journal of Management Control*, *31*(3), 239–273. doi:10.100700187-020-00301-4

Herath, T., & Rao, H. (2009). Protection motivation and deterrence: A framework for security policy compliance in organisations. *European Journal of Information Systems*, *18*(2), 106–125.

Hirschi, T. (1969). *Causes of Delinquency*. University of California Press.

Hodge, N. (2021). Reigning in Cyber Risk. *Internal Auditor*, 25-29. Accessed on September 15, 2021. Retrieved from: https://theiia.texterity.com/ia/august_2021_internal_auditor/MobilePagedReplica.action?pm=2&folio=24#pg26

Holliday, C. (2021). Rewriting the stars: Surface tensions and gender troubles in the online media production of digital deepfakes. *Convergence*, *27*(4), 899–918. doi:10.1177/13548565211029412

Hooper, C., Martini, B., & Choo, K.-K. R. (2013). Cloud computing and its implications for cybercrime investigations in Australia. *Computer Law & Security Review*, *29*(2), 152–163. doi:10.1016/j.clsr.2013.01.006

Horowitz, M., Allen, G., Saravelle, E., Cho, A., Frederick, K., & Scharre, P. (2018). *Artificial intelligence and international security*. Center for a New American Security. https://www.cnas.org/publications/reports/artificial-intelligence-and-internationalsecurity

Huang, Y., Xu, J., Yu, B., & Shull, P. B. (2016). Validity of FitBit, Jawbone UP, Nike+ and other wearable devices for level and stair walking. *Gait & Posture*, *48*, 36–41.

Hui, K. L., Kim, S. H., & Wang, Q. H. (2017). Cybercrime deterrence and international legislation: Evidence from distributed denial of service attacks. *Management Information Systems Quarterly*, *41*(2), 497–523. doi:10.25300/MISQ/2017/41.2.08

Humble, K. P. (2021). International law, surveillance and the protection of privacy. *International Journal of Human Rights*, *25*(1), 1–25. doi:10.1080/13642987.2020.1763315

Hu, Q., Dinev, T., Hart, P., & Cooke, D. (2012). Managing employee compliance with information security policies: The critical role of top management and organizational culture. *Decision Sciences*, *43*(4), 615–660.

Hyder, B., & Govindarasu, M. (2020). *Optimization of Cybersecurity Investment Strategies in the Smart Grid Using Game-Theory. In 2020 IEEE Power & Energy Society Innovative Smart Grid Technologies Conference (ISGT)*. IEEE.

IBGC. (2015). *Código das melhores práticas de governança corporativa. 5ª Edição*. Instituto Brasileiro de Governança Corporativa.

IBM Security & Ponemon Institute. (2020). *Cost of Insider Threats: Global Report*. Retrieved from https://www.ibm.com/downloads/cas/61KLOPV5

Ibrahim, A. M. (2019). Theorizing the journalism model of disinformation and hate speech propagation in a Nigerian context. *International Journal of E-Politics*, *10*(2), 60–73. doi:10.4018/IJEP.2019070105

Ibrahim, A., Habbash, M., & Hussainey, K. (2019). Corporate governance and risk disclosure: Evidence from Saudi Arabia. *International Journal of Accounting. Auditing and Performance Evaluation*, *15*(1), 89–111. doi:10.1504/IJAAPE.2019.096748

ICAEW. (2011). *Reporting business risks: Meeting expectations - Information for better markets initiative*. Institute of Chartered Accountants in England and Wales.

Information Systems Audit and Control Association (ISACA). (2011). Understanding the new SOC Reports. *ISACA Journal*. https://www.isaca.org/resources/isaca-journal/past-issues/2011/understanding-the-new-soc-reports

Information Technology-Information Sharing and Analysis Center. (2022). Retrieved February 22, 2022, from About Us: https://www.it-isac.org/about

International Telecommunications Union (ITU). (2008). *ITU-TX.1205: Sries X: Data networks, open system communications and security: Telecommunication security: Overview of cybersecurity 2008*. Retrieved from https://www.itu.int/rec/dologin_pub.asp?lang=s&id=T-REC-X.1205-200804-I!!PDF-E&type=items

International, S. A. E. (1998, August 1). *CAN Specification 2.0: Protocol and Implementations*. Retrieved October 13, 2019, from SAE Mobilus: https://www.sae.org/publications/technical-papers/content/921603/

International, S. A. E. (2020, July 23). *V2X Communications Message Set Dictionary*. Retrieved February 2022, from SAE Mobilus: https://www.sae.org/standards/content/j2735_202007/

ISA/IEC. (2020, June). *Your Guide to Cybersecurity Standards*. Retrieved from Global Cybersecurity Alliance: https://gca.isa.org/isagca-quick-start-guide-62443-standards?__hstc=16245038. c309ffdf29b0a2e310f4400349939d99.1634749414522.1634749414522.1634749414522.1&__hssc=16245038.1.1634749414522&__hsfp=970585634

ISACA. (2019). *COBIT 2019 Framework: Governance and Management Objectives*. ISACA.

ISACA. (2019). *COBIT 2019 Framework: Introduction and Methodology*. Author.

Ismail, R., & Rahman, A. (2011). Institutional investors and board of directors' monitoring role on risk management disclosure level in Malaysia. *The IUP Journal of Corporate Governance, 10*(2), 37–61.

Ittonen, K., Vähämaa, E., & Vähämaa, S. (2013). Female auditors and accruals quality. *Accounting Horizons, 27*(2), 205–228. doi:10.2308/acch-50400

Iwu, P.-A. (2017). Photo privacy and media/image rights in Nigeria. *The BarCode, 2*(2). http://barcode.stillwaterslaw.com/1.1/2017/04/01/photo-privacy-and-mediaimage-rights-in-nigeria/

Jaffar, R., Al Sheikh, W., Hassan, M. S., & Abdullah, M. (2021). Voluntary Risk Disclosures of Islamic Financial Institutions: The Role of AAOIFI Standards Implementation. *Asian Journal of Accounting and Governance, 15*, 1–14. doi:10.17576/AJAG-2021-15-04

Jamiu, F. (2021). Analysis of claims on #EndSARS protest in Nigeria: Images most manipulated content, Twitter as a major platform. *Dubawa*. Retrieved 25 July 2021 from https://www.dubawa.org/analysis-of-claims-on-end-sars-protest-in-nigeria-images-most-manipulated-content-twitter-as-major-platform

Jeffery, L., & Ramachandran, V. (2021). *Why ransomware attacks are on the rise — and what can be done to stop them*. https://www.pbs.org/newshour/nation/why-ransomware-attacks-are-on-the-rise-and-what-can-be-done-to-stop-them

Johnson, B. (2021). The differences between SOC 1 vs SOC 2. *StrongDM*. https://www.strongdm.com/blog/soc-1-vs-soc-2

Johnson, C. M., & Grandison, A. W. T. (2007). Compliance with data protection laws using Hippocratic Database active enforcement and auditing. *IBM Systems Journal, 46*(2), 255–264. doi:10.1147j.462.0255

Jones, S. (2021, December 2). 6 reasons why you need SOC 2 compliance. *Reciprocity*. https://reciprocity.com/6-reasons-why-you-need-soc-2-compliance/

Juniper Research. (2020, September). *Cars With Embedded Connectivity To Reach 200 Million by 2025, With 5G Adoption Set to Soar*. Retrieved February 2022, from Juniper Research: https://www.juniperresearch.com/press/cars-with-embedded-connectivity-to-reach-200

Kaisara, G., & Pather, S. (2010) Relevance of Ethics in e-Governance: An Analysis of Development in the WWW era. *Conference: 6th International Conference on e-Government*.

Karpf, D. (2017). Digital politics after Trump. *Annals of the International Communication Association, 41*(2), 198–207.

Kerner, C., & Risse, M. (2021). Beyond Porn and Discreditation: Epistemic Promises and Perils of Deepfake Technology in Digital Lifeworlds. *Moral Philosophy and Politics*, *8*(1), 81–108. doi:10.1515/mopp-2020-0024

Keysight. (2019, February 28). *From Standard Ethernet to Automotive Ethernet.* Retrieved November 6, 2020, from Keysight: https://www.keysight.com/us/en/assets/7018-06530/flyers/5992-3742.pdf

Khumalo, B.N., & Baloyi, C. (2017). The possible benefits of freedom of information laws to the records management landscape in the ESARBICA region. *Information Development*, 1 – 15. . doi:10.1177/0266666917735879

Khweiled, R., Jazzar, M., & Eleyan, D. (2021). Cybercrimes during COVID-19 Pandemic. *International Journal of Information Engineering & Electronic Business, 13*(2). doi:10.5815/ijieeb.2021.02.01

Kim, H., & Yasuda, Y. (2018). Business risk disclosure and firm risk: Evidence from Japan. *Research in International Business and Finance*, *45*, 413–426. doi:10.1016/j.ribaf.2017.07.172

Kirchengast, T. (2020). Deepfakes and image manipulation: Criminalisation and control. *Information & Communications Technology Law*, *29*(3), 308–323. doi:10.1080/13600834.2020.1794615

Kirlappos, I., Beautement, A., & Sasse, M. A. (2013, April). "Comply or Die" Is Dead: Long live security-aware principal agents. In *International conference on financial cryptography and data security* (pp. 70-82). Springer.

Klimburg, A. (2012). *National cyber security framework manual.* NATO Cooperative Cyber Defense Center of Excellence.

Kobayashi, S., & Schultz, W. (2008). Influence of reward delays on responses of dopamine neurons. *The Journal of Neuroscience: The Official Journal of the Society for Neuroscience*, *28*(31), 7837–7846.

Koepke, P. (2017). *Cybersecurity information sharing incentives and barriers.* Sloan School of Management at MIT University. Working Paper CISL# 2017-13.

Kotecha, J. A. (2011). Ethics and privacy issues of a practice-based surveillance system. Need for a national-level institutional research ethics board and consent standards. *Canadian Family Physician Medecin de Famille Canadien*, *57*, 1165–1173. PMID:21998237

Kovash, M. (2019). *SOC 2 vs. SOC 3 reports: What is the difference?* Linford & Co LLP Blog. https://linfordco.com/blog/soc-2-vs-soc-3/

KPMG. (2014). *Future state 2030: The global megatrends shaping governments.* Retrieved 25 July 2021 from https://assets.kpmg/content/dam/kpmg/pdf/2014/02/future-state-2030-v3.pdf

Kravet, T., & Muslu, V. (2013). Textual risk disclosures and investors' risk perceptions. *Review of Accounting Studies*, *18*(4), 1088–1122. doi:10.100711142-013-9228-9

Krefetz, N. (2020 February 26). Deepfakes and the war on reality. *Streaming Media*. https://www. streamingmedia.com/Articles/ReadArticle.aspx?ArticleID=139414

Kuol, L., & Amegbo, J. (2021). Rethinking national security strategies in Africa. *International Relations and Diplomacy*, *9*(01), 1–17. doi:10.17265/2328-2134/2021.01.001

Kusamotu, A. (2007). Privacy law and technology in Nigeria: The legal framework will not meet the test of adequacy as mandated by article 25 of European union directive 95/46. *Information & Communications Technology Law*, *16*(2), 149–159. doi:10.1080/13600830701597616

Kushner, D. (2013, February 26). *The Real Story of Stuxnet*. Retrieved from IEEE Spectrum: https://spectrum.ieee.org/the-real-story-of-stuxnet#toggle-gdpr

Lanz, J. (2016). Communication Cybersecurity Risks to the Audit Committee. *The CPA Journal*. Accessed on September 12, 2021. Retrieved from https://www.cpajournal.com/2016/05/21/communicating-cybersecurity-risks-audit-committee/

Laudon, K. C., & Laudon, J. P. (2022). *Management information systems: Managing the digital firm* (17th ed.). Pearson.

Leeper Piquero, N., Lyn Exum, M., & Simpson, S. S. (2005). Integrating the desire–for–control and rational choice in a corporate crime context. *Justice Quarterly*, *22*(2), 252–280. doi:10.1080/07418820500089034

Leetaru, K. (2019 May 16). Deepfakes: The media talks politics while the public is interested in pornography. *Forbes*. https://www.forbes.com/sites/kalevleetaru/2019/03/16/deepfakes-the-media-talks-politics-while-the-public-isinterested-in-pornography/#71ea2e528461

Lennox, C. S. (1999). Audit quality and auditor size: An evaluation of reputation and deep pockets hypotheses. *Journal of Business Finance & Accounting*, *26*(7-8), 779–805. doi:10.1111/1468-5957.00275

Lévesque, F. L., Fernandez, J. M., & Batchelder, D. (2017). Age and gender as independent risk factors for malware victimisation. *Proceedings of the 31st British Computer Society Human Computer Interaction Conference*. 10.14236/ewic/HCI2017.48

Lewis, J. (2018). *Economic impact of cybercrime-No slowing down*. Santa Clara: McAfee & CSI (Center for Strategic and International Studies). Retrieved from https://www.csis.org/analysis/economic-impact-cybercrime

LFN (2010). Sections 6, 10, 15 & 16 of the Copyright Act, CAP C28, LFN, 2010.

Life is Strange: True Colors [Video game]. (2021). Deck Nine Games.

Linsley, P., & Shrives, P. (2006). Risk reporting: A study of risk disclosures in the annual reports of UK companies. *The British Accounting Review*, *38*(4), 387–404. doi:10.1016/j.bar.2006.05.002

Llinares, F. M. (2015). *That Cyber Routine, That Cyber Victimization: Profiling Victims of Cybercrime. In Cybercrime Risks and Responses*. Springer. doi:10.1057/9781137474162.0011

Lopes, P., & Rodrigues, L. (2007). Accounting for financial instruments : An analysis of the determinants of disclosure in the Portuguese. *The International Journal of Accounting, 42*(1), 25–56. doi:10.1016/j.intacc.2006.12.002

Macher, G., Schmittner, C., Veledar, O., & Brenner, E. (2020). ISO/SAE DIS 21434 Automotive Cybersecurity Standard - In a Nutshell. In A. Casimiro, F. Ortmeier, E. Schoitsch, F. Bitsch, & P. Ferreira (Eds.), Lecture Notes in Computer Science: Vol. 12235. *Computer Safety, Reliability, and Security. SAFECOMP 2020 Workshops. SAFECOMP 2020.* Springer. doi:10.1007/978-3-030-55583-2_9

Mack, D. (2017). Implementing a Modern, Secure Relay Integration Solution with Existing IEDs. In *2017 70th Annual Conference for Protective Relay Engineers (CPRE)* (pp. 1-3). IEEE.

Maddocks, S. (2020). 'A deepfake porn plot intended to silence me': Exploring continuities between pornographic and 'political' deep fakes. *Porn Studies, 7*(4), 415–423. doi:10.1080/23 268743.2020.1757499

Madrigal, M., Guzmán, B., & Guzmán, C. (2015). Determinants of corporate risk disclosure in large Spanish companies: A snapshot. *Contaduría y Administración, 60*(4), 757–775. doi:10.1016/j. cya.2015.05.014

Mahomed, S., & Labuschaigne, M. (2019). The role of research ethics committees in South Africa when human biological materials are transferred between institutions. *South African Journal of Bioethics and Law, 12*(2), 79–83. doi:10.7196/SAJBL.2019.v12i2.685

Majore, S. A., Yoo, H., & Shon, T. (2014). Secure and reliable electronic records management system using digital forensic technologies. *The Journal of Supercomputing, 70*(1), 149–165. doi:10.100711227-014-1137-6

Makulilo, B. A. (2012). Privacy and data protection in Africa; a state of the art. *International Data Privacy Law., 2*(3), 163–178. doi:10.1093/idpl/ips014

Malafronte, I., Porzio, C., & Starita, M. (2016). The nature and determinants of disclosure practices in the insurance industry: Evidence from European insurers. *International Review of Financial Analysis, 45*, 367–382. doi:10.1016/j.irfa.2015.02.003

Maloney + Novotny LLC. (2020). *History of SOC reports.* https://socreport.com/history-of-soc-reports/

Mandelcorn, S., Modarres, M., & Mosleh, A. (2013). An explanatory model of cyberattacks drawn from rational choice theory. *Transactions of the American Nuclear Society, 109.*

Mare, A., Mabweazara, H. M., & Moyo, D. (2019). "Fake news" and cyber-propaganda in sub-saharan africa: Recentering the research agenda. *African Journalism Studies, 40*(4), 1–12. doi: 10.1080/23743670.2020.1788295

Marron, J., Gopstein, A., & Bogle, D. (2021, September 29). *Benefits of an Updated Mapping between the NIST Cybersecurity Framework and the NERC Critical Infrastructure Protection Standards*. Retrieved October 2021, from National Institute of Standards and Technology: https://nvlpubs.nist.gov/nistpubs/CSWP/NIST.CSWP.09292021.pdf

Mar, S. (2021). The Aftermath of Solarwinds. *Internal Auditor*, (June), 18–19.

Mayo, M. J. (2007). Games for science and engineering education. *Communications of the ACM*, *50*(7), 30–35.

McAfee. (2020, August 25). *What is GPS Spoofing?* Retrieved February 19, 2022, from McAfee: https://www.mcafee.com/blogs/internet-security/what-is-gps-spoofing/

McAuliffe, S. M. (2020). System and organization controls for healthcare organizations. *Keiter CPAs blog*. https://keitercpa.com/blog/system-organization-controls-for-healthcare/

Mcchlery, S., & Hussainey, K. (2021). Risk disclosure behaviour: Evidence from the UK extractive industry. *Journal of Applied Accounting Research*, *22*(3), 484–506. doi:10.1108/JAAR-09-2019-0134

McCrae, R. R., & John, O. P. (1992). An introduction to the five-factor model and its applications. *Journal of Personality*, *60*(2), 175–215.

McDougall, S. J., Curry, M. B., & De Bruijn, O. (2001). The effects of visual information on users' mental models: An evaluation of Pathfinder analysis as a measure of icon usability. *International Journal of Cognitive Ergonomics*, *5*(1), 59–84.

McGonigal, J. (2011). *Reality is broken: Why games make us better and how they can change the world*. Penguin.

McKinsey & Company. (2020, March). *Cybersecurity in automotive*. Retrieved February 22, 2022, from https://www.mckinsey.com/~/media/mckinsey/industries/automotive%20and%20assembly/our%20insights/cybersecurity%20in%20automotive%20mastering%20the%20challenge/cybersecurity-in-automotive-mastering-the-challenge.pdf

Meinrath, S. D., & Vitka, S. (2014). Crypto war II. *Critical Studies in Media Communication*, *31*(2), 123–128.

Mesky, E., Liaudanskas, A., Kalpokiene, J., & Jurcys, P. (2020). Regulating deepfakes: Legal & ethical considerations. *Journal of Intellectual Property Law & Practice*, *15*(1), 24–31. doi:10.1093/jiplp/jpz167

Microsoft. (2022). *Ribbon Hero 2: How to play the game*. Retrieved from https://www.microsoft.com/en-us/microsoft-365/blog/2011/04/26/ribbon-hero-2-how-to-play-the-game-video/

Mirghani, S. (2011). The war on piracy. *Critical Studies in Media Communication*, *28*(2), 113–134.

Mohammed, A. O., Danladi, O. H., & Adamu, R. C. (2020). Hate-speech, street journalism and national security in Nigeria. *Journal of Management Sciences*, *3*(1), 131–140.

Mohobbot, A., & Noriyuki, K. (2005). The UK guidelines for company risk reporting - An evaluation. *Okayama Economic Review, 37*(1), 1–18.

Mokhtar, E., & Mellett, H. (2013). Competition, corporate governance, ownership structure and risk reporting. *Managerial Auditing Journal, 28*(9), 838–865. doi:10.1108/MAJ-11-2012-0776

Montenegro, T., & Bras, F. (2015). Audit quality: Does gender composition of audit firms matter? *Spanish Journal of Finance and Accounting. Revista Española de Financiación y Contabilidad, 44*(3), 264–297. doi:10.1080/02102412.2015.1035578

Moumen, N., Othman, H., & Hussainey, K. (2016). Board structure and the informativeness of risk disclosure: Evidence from MENA emerging markets. *Advances in International Accounting, 35*, 82–97. doi:10.1016/j.adiac.2016.09.001

Mukherjee, S. (2015). *Applying the Distribution System in Grid Restoration/NERC CIP-014 Risk Assessment. In 2015 IEEE Rural Electric Power Conference.* IEEE.

Müller, K., & Schwarz, C. (2021 May). *Fanning the flames of hate: Social media and hate crime.* Working Paper Series, No. 373, Centre for Competitive Advantage in the Global Economy (CAGE), Department of Economics, the University of Warwick, UK.

Muncaster, P. (2021). *One Ransomware Victim Every 10 Seconds in 2020.* Retrieved from https://www.infosecurity-magazine.com/news/one-ransomware-victim-every-10/

Mylrea, M., Bishop, R., Johnson, M., & Gupta Gourisetti, S. N. (2018). *Keyless Signature Blockchain Infrastructure: Facilitating NERC CIP Compliance and Responding to Evolving Cyber Threats and Vulnerabilities to Energy Infrastructure. In 2018 IEEE/PES Transmission and Distribution Conference and Exposition (T&D).* IEEE.

Nabe, C. (2021). *Impact of COVID-19 on Cybersecurity.* Deloitte. Accessed September 25, 2021. Retrieved from: https://www2.deloitte.com/ch/en/pages/risk/articles/impact-covid-cybersecurity.html

Nakao, M., Loo, S., & Melville, L. (2015). Integrating Modern Substation Automation Systems with Enterprise-level Management. In *2015 68th Annual Conference for Protective Relay Engineers* (pp. 557-562). IEEE.

National Highway Traffic Safety Administration (NHTSA). (2020). *Cybersecurity Best Practices for the Safety of Modern Vehicles.* Retrieved February 13, 2022, from UD Department of Transportation National Highway Traffic Safety Administration: https://www.nhtsa.gov/sites/nhtsa.gov/files/documents/vehicle_cybersecurity_best_practices_01072021.pdf

National Highway Traffic Safety Administration (NHTSA). (n.d.). *Vehicle Cybersecurity.* Retrieved February 22, 2022, from U.S. Department of Transportation NHTSA: https://www.nhtsa.gov/technology-innovation/vehicle-cybersecurity

National Institute of Justice. (2016). *Five Things About Deterrence.* Retrieved from https://nij.ojp.gov/topics/articles/five-things-about-deterrence

National Institute of Standards and Technology (NIST). (2018). *Framework for Improving Critical Infrastructure Cybersecurity, version 1.1.* Accessed on September 18, 2021. Retrieved from https://nvlpubs.nist.gov/nistpubs/CSWP/NIST.CSWP.04162018.pdf

National Institute of Standards and Technology. (2018, April 16). *Framework for Improving Critical Infrastructure Security.* Retrieved February 17, 2022, from https://nvlpubs.nist.gov/nistpubs/cswp/nist.cswp.04162018.pdf

National Instruments. (2019, May 28). *FlexRay Automotive Communication Bus Overview.* Retrieved October 13, 2019, from National Instruments: https://www.ni.com/en-us/innovations/white-papers/06/flexray-automotive-communication-bus-overview.html

Naval Postgraduate School. (2022). *CyberCIEGE Downloads.* Retrieved from https://nps.edu/web/c3o/downloads

Neifar, S., & Jarboui, A. (2018). Corporate governance and operational risk voluntary disclosure: Evidence from Islamic banks. *Research in International Business and Finance, 46,* 43–54. doi:10.1016/j.ribaf.2017.09.006

Nema, P. (2021). Understanding copyright issues entailing deepfakes in India. *International Journal of Law and Information Technology, 29*(3), 241–254. doi:10.1093/ijlit/eaab007

NERC CIP 003-8. (2021, October 23). *CIP-003-8.* Retrieved from North American Electric Reliability Corporation: https://www.nerc.com/_layouts/15/PrintStandard.aspx?standardnumber=CIP-003-8&title=Cyber%20Security%20—%20Security%20Management%20Controls&Jurisdiction=United%20States

NERC CIP 004-6. (2021, October 23). *CIP-004-6.* Retrieved from North American Electric Reliability Corporation: https://www.nerc.com/_layouts/15/PrintStandard.aspx?standardnumber=CIP-004-6&title=Cyber%20Security%20-%20Personnel%20&%20Training&Jurisdiction=United%20States

NERC CIP 005-6. (2021, October 23). *CIP-005-6.* Retrieved from North American Electric Reliability Corporation: https://www.nerc.com/pa/Stand/Reliability%20Standards/CIP-005-6.pdf

NERC CIP 006-6. (2021, October 23). *CIP-006-6.* Retrieved from North American Electric Reliability Corporation: https://www.nerc.com/pa/Stand/Reliability%20Standards/CIP-006-6.pdf

NERC CIP. (2021, October 23). *CIP Standards.* Retrieved from North American Electric Reliability Corporation (NERC): https://www.nerc.com/pa/Stand/Pages/CIPStandards.aspx

NERC CIP002-5.1a. (2021, October 23). *CIP-002-5.1a.* Retrieved from North American Electric Reliability Corporation (NERC): https://www.nerc.com/_layouts/15/PrintStandard.aspx?standardnumber=CIP-002-5.1a&title=Cyber%20Security%20—%20BES%20Cyber%20System%20Categorization&Jurisdiction=United%20States

NERC CIP-007-6. (2021, October 23). *CIP 007-6.* Retrieved from North American Electric Reliability Corporation: https://www.nerc.com/pa/Stand/Reliability%20Standards/CIP-007-6.pdf

NERC CIP-008-6. (2021, October 23). *CIP-008-6*. Retrieved from North American Electric Reliability Corporation: https://www.nerc.com/pa/Stand/Reliability%20Standards/CIP-008-6.pdf

NERC CIP-009-6. (2021, October 23). *CIP 009-6*. Retrieved from North American Electric Reliability Corporation: https://www.nerc.com/pa/Stand/Reliability%20Standards/CIP-009-6.pdf

NERC CIP-010-3. (2021, October 23). *CIP-010-3*. Retrieved from North American Electric Reliability Corporation: https://www.nerc.com/pa/Stand/Reliability%20Standards/CIP-010-3.pdf

NERC CIP-011-2. (2021, October 23). *CIP-011-2*. Retrieved from North American Electric Reliability Corporation: https://www.nerc.com/pa/Stand/Reliability%20Standards/CIP-011-2.pdf

NERC CIP-013-1. (2021, October 23). *CIP-013-1*. Retrieved from North American Electric Reliability Corporation: https://www.nerc.com/pa/Stand/Reliability%20Standards/CIP-013-1.pdf

NERC CIP-014-2. (2021, October 23). *CIP-014-2*. Retrieved from North American Electric Reliability Corporation: https://www.nerc.com/pa/Stand/Reliability%20Standards/CIP-014-2.pdf

Nigerian Copyright Act. Section 51 of the Copyright Act.

NIST CSF Mapping. (2020, June 8). *Mapping of NIST Cybersecurity Framework v1.1 to NERC CIP Reliability Standards*. Retrieved from National Institute of Standards and Technology: https://data.nist.gov/od/id/mds2-2348

NIST CSF. (2018, April 16). *Cybersecurity Framework versions 1.1*. Retrieved from National Institute of Standards and Technology: https://nvlpubs.nist.gov/nistpubs/CSWP/NIST.CSWP.04162018.pdf

NITDA (2019). The National Information Technology Development Agency (NITDA) on 25th January 2019. The said Regulation was made pursuant to the National Information Technology Development Agency Act (NITDA Act 2007).

Nwafor, I. E. (2021). AI ethical bias: A case for AI vigilantism (AIlantism) in shaping the regulation of AI. *International Journal of Law and Information Technology*, 29(3), 225–240. doi:10.1093/ijlit/eaab008

Nwoke, U. (2019). Access to Information under the Nigerian Freedom of Information Act, 2011: Challenges to Implementation and the Rhetoric of Radical Change. *Journal of African Law*, 63(3), 435–461. doi:10.1017/S0021855319000299

O'Sullivan, D. (2019 June 13). House Intel chair sounds alarm in Congress' first hearing on deepfake videos. *CNN*. https://edition.cnn.com/2019/06/13/tech/deepfake-congress-hearing/index.html

Obi, U. V. (2020 September). *An extensive article on data privacy and data protection law in Nigeria*. International Network of Privacy Law Professionals (INPLP). https://inplp.com/

Ogundokun, R. O., Awotunde, J. B., Sadiku, P., Adeniyi, E. A., Abiodun, M., & Dauda, O. I. (2021). An Enhanced Intrusion Detection System using Particle Swarm Optimization Feature Extraction Technique. *Procedia Computer Science*, *193*, 504–512. doi:10.1016/j.procs.2021.10.052

Ogunlana, S. O. (2019). Halting Boko Haram/Islamic State's West Africa Province propaganda in cyberspace with cybersecurity technologies. *Journal of Strategic Security*, *12*(1), 72–106. https://www.jstor.org/stable/26623078

Ojedokun, U. A., Ogunleye, Y. O., & Aderinto, A. A. (2021). Mass mobilization for police accountability: The case of Nigeria's# EndSARS protest. *Policing. Journal of Policy Practice*, *15*(3), 1894–1903. doi:10.1093/police/paab001

Ojo, J. S. (2020). Governing "ungoverned spaces" in the foliage of conspiracy: Toward (re) ordering terrorism, from Boko Haram Insurgency, Fulani militancy to banditry in Northern Nigeria. *African Security*, *13*(1), 77–110. doi:10.1080/19392206.2020.1731109

Okello-Obura, C. (2011). Records and Archives Legal and Policy Framework in Uganda. *Library Philosophy and Practice*. https://digitalcommons.unl.edu/libphilprac/608

Oliveira, J., Rodrigues, L., & Craig, R. (2011a). Risk-related disclosure practices in the annual reports of Portuguese credit institutions: An exploratory study. *Journal of Banking Regulation*, *12*(2), 100–118. doi:10.1057/jbr.2010.20

Oliveira, J., Rodrigues, L., & Craig, R. (2011b). Risk-related disclosures by non-finance companies: Portuguese practices and disclosure characteristics. *Managerial Auditing Journal*, *26*(9), 817–839. doi:10.1108/02686901111171466

Oliveira, J., Serrasqueiro, R., & Mota, S. (2018). Determinants of risk reporting by portuguese and spanish non-finance companies. *European Business Review*, *3*(1), 311–339. doi:10.1108/EBR-04-2017-0076

ONSA (2017 November). *Action plan for implementation of the national cybersecurity strategy.* Office of the National Security Adviser, Abuja, Federal Government of Nigeria.

ONSA. (2015a). National Cybersecurity Policy 2015. Office of the National Security Adviser, Abuja, Federal Government of Nigeria.

ONSA. (2015b). National Cybersecurity Strategy 2015. Office of the National Security Adviser, Abuja, Federal Government of Nigeria.

ONSA. (2015c). *National Security Strategy 2015. Office of the National Security Adviser.* Federal Government of Nigeria.

Organization for Economic Co-Operation and Development (OECD). (2013). *The OECD privacy framework*. Available at. www.pwc.com/gx/en/consultingservices/information-security-survey/assets/pwcgsiss-2016-financia-services.pdf

Orji, U. J. (2018). The African Union Convention on Cybersecurity: A regional response towards cyber stability? *Masaryk University Journal of Law and Technology, 12*(2), 91-129. 10.5817/MUJLT2018-2-1

Osho, O., & Onoja, A. D. (2015). National Cyber Security Policy and Strategy of Nigeria: A Qualitative Analysis. *International Journal of Cyber Criminology, 9*(1), 120–143. doi:10.5281/zenodo.22390

Otava. (2011, August 19). *Service Organization Control Reports: SOC1, SOC2 & SOC3.* https://www.otava.com/blog/soc-1-soc-2-soc-3-report-comparison/

Otava. (2016, January 28). *What is the difference between a cold, warm and hot disaster recovery site?* https://www.otava.com/blog/what-is-the-difference-between-a-cold-warm-and-hot-disaster-recovery-site/

Oturu, D. (2019 October 29). Nigeria: Protection of Image Rights (Part 1). *AELEX.* https://www.mondaq.com/Nigeria/Intellectual-Property/858520/Protection-Of-Image-Rights-Part-1

Pahnila, S., Siponen, M., & Mahmood, A. (2007, January). Employees' behavior towards IS security policy compliance. In *2007 40th Annual Hawaii International Conference on System Sciences (HICSS'07)* (pp. 156b-156b). IEEE.

Parable of the Polygons. (2022). *Parable of the Polygons: A Playable Post on the Shape of Society.* Retrieved from https://ncase.me/polygons/

Paradigm Initiative & Privacy International. (2018 March). *The right to privacy in Nigeria: Stakeholder report universal periodic review 31st session – Nigeria.* https://www.privacyinternational.org

Paris, B., & Donovan, J. (2019). *Deepfakes and cheap fakes: The manipulation of video and audio evidence.* Data & Society. https://datasociety.net/output/deepfakes-and-cheap-fakes/

Parsons, M. A., Godøy, Ø., LeDrew, E., de Bruin, T. F., Danis, B., Tomlinson, S., & Carlson, D. (2011). A conceptual framework for managing very diverse data for complex, interdisciplinary science. *Journal of Information Science, 37*(6), 555–569. doi:10.1177/0165551511412705

Parsons, T. D. (2021). Ethics and Educational Technologies. *Educational Technology Research and Development, 69*(1), 335–338. doi:10.100711423-020-09846-6

Paternoster, R., & Simpson, S. (1993). Rational Choice Theory of Corporate Crime. In Routine Activity and Rational Choice: Advances in Criminological Theory (vol. 5, pp. 37-58). Academic Press.

Paternoster, R., Jaynes, C. M., & Wilson, T. (2017). Rational choice theory and interest in the "fortune of others". *Journal of Research in Crime and Delinquency, 54*(6), 847–868. doi:10.1177/0022427817707240

Perl, A., Howlett, M., & Ramesh, M. (2018). Policy-making and truthiness: Can existing policy models cope with politicized evidence and wilful ignorance in a "post-fact" world? *Policy Sciences*, *51*(4), 581–600. doi:10.100711077-018-9334-4

Perot, E., & Mostert, F. (2020). Fake it till you make it: An examination of the US and English approaches to persona protection as applied to deepfakes on social media. *Journal of Intellectual Property Law & Practice*, *15*(1), 32–39. doi:10.1093/jiplp/jpz164

Phiri, J. M., & Tough, G. A. (2018). Managing university records in the world of governance. *Records Management Journal*, *28*(1), 47–61. doi:10.1108/RMJ-11-2016-0042

Polityuk, P. (2016, February 12). *Ukraine sees Russian hand in cyber attacks on power grid*. Retrieved from REUTERS: https://www.reuters.com/article/idUSKCN0VL18E

Pop Sugar. (2022). *Organize Your Life: 7 Apps For Family Organization*. Retrieved from https://www.popsugar.com/family/photo-gallery/21393586/image/21393602/Chore-Hero

Prencipe, A. (2002). Proprietary costs and voluntary segment disclosure: evidence from Italian listed companies. SSRN *Electronic Journal*. doi:10.2139/ssrn.319502

Proctor, M., & Smith, T. (2017). Lessons Learned from NERC CIP Applied to the Industrial World. In *2017 70th Annual Conference for Protective Relay Engineers (CPRE)* (pp. 1-6). IEEE.

Proofpoint. (2021). *2021 Human Factor Report*. Retrieved from https://www.proofpoint.com/sites/default/files/threat-reports/pfpt-us-tr-human-factor-report.pdf

Puaschunder, M. J. (2019). Artificial Diplomacy: A guide for public officials to conduct Artificial Intelligence. *Journal of Applied Research in the Digital Economy*, *1*(10). Advance online publication. doi:10.2139srn.3376302

Pundmann, S. (2021). Cyber Risk and the Board. *Internal Auditor*, (August), 31–33.

Qais, S. Q., Jamil, N., Daud, M., Patel, A., & Norhamadi, J. (2019). A Review of Security Assessment Metodologies in Industrial Control Systems. *Information and Computer Security*, *27*(1), 47–61. doi:10.1108/ICS-04-2018-0048

Ramanathan, R., Popat, A., Papic, M., & Ciniglio, O. (2017). *Idaho Power Experience of Implementaing Cascade Analysis Study Using the Node/Breaker Model. In 2017 IEEE Power & Energy Society General Meeting*. IEEE.

Ransbotham, S., & Mitra, S. (2009). Choice and chance: A conceptual model of paths to information security compromise. *Information Systems Research*, *20*(1), 121–139. doi:10.1287/isre.1080.0174

Reality Drop. (2022). *Reality Drop*. Retrieved from https://www.realitydrop.org/

Recker, A., & Muller, S. (2015). Preserving the Essence; Identifying the significant properties of Social Science Research data. *New Review of Information Networking*, *20*(1-2), 229–235. doi:10.1080/13614576.2015.1110404

Reid, J. (2009). Politicising connectivity. *Cambridge Review of International Affairs*, *22*(4), 607–623.

Reporting on an Entity's Cybersecurity Risk Management Program and Controls. (2017). American Institute of Certified Public Accountants.

Richards, N. U., & Eboibi, F. E. (2021). African governments and the influence of corruption on the proliferation of cybercrime in Africa: Wherein lies the rule of law? *International Review of Law Computers & Technology*, *35*(2), 131–161. doi:10.1080/13600869.2021.1885105

Robinson, M. (2014). Why do people commit crime? An integrated systems perspective. Applying Complexity Theory: Whole Systems Approaches to Criminal Justice and Social Work, *59*.

Romney, M., Steinbart, P., Summers, S., & Wood, D. (2020). *Accounting information systems* (15th ed.). Prentice.

Safa, N., Von Solms, R., & Furnell, S. (2016). Information security policy compliance model in organizations. *Computers & Security, 56*, 70-82.

Safa, N., & Ismail, M. (2013). A customer loyalty formation model in electronic commerce. *Economic Modelling*, *35*, 559–564.

Saggar, R., & Singh, B. (2017). Corporate governance and risk reporting: Indian evidence. *Managerial Auditing Journal*, *32*(4/5), 378–405. doi:10.1108/MAJ-03-2016-1341

Saha, R., & Kabra, K. (2021). *Is Voluntary Disclosure Value Relevant? Evidence from Top Listed Firms in India*. Vision - The Journal of Business Perspective., doi:10.1177/0972262920986293

Saleem, S., & Usman, M. (2021). Information risk and cost of equity: The role of stock price crash risk. *The Journal of Asian Finance, Economics, and Business*, *8*(1), 623–635.

Salehi, M., & Bayat-Sarmadi, S. (2021, May 1). PLCDefender: Improving Remote Attestation Techniques for PLCs Using Physical Model. *IEEE Internet of Things Journal*, *8*(9), 7372–7379. doi:10.1109/JIOT.2020.3040237

Sales, N. A. (2012). Regulating cyber-security. *Northwestern University Law Review*, *107*, 1503.

Salvador, A., Mack, D., & Carnegie, C. (2016). Secure IED Management Case Studies. In *2016 IEEE International Conference on Power System Technologies (POWERCON)* (pp. 1-4). IEEE.

SANS. (2021). *2021 Security Awareness Report: Managing Human Cyber Risk*. Retrieved from https://go.sans.org/lp-wp-2021-sans-security-awareness-report

Sayler, K. (2019a, Nov 21). Artificial intelligence and national security. *Congressional Research Service*. https://fas.org/sgp/crs/natsec/R45178.pdf

Sayler, K., & Harris, L. (2019b, Oct. 14). Deep fakes and national security. *Congressional Research Service*. https://crsreports.congress.gov/product/pdf/IF/IF11333

Schmittner, C., Griessnig, G., & Ma, Z. (2018). Status of the Development of ISO/SAE 21434. *Proc of the 25th European Conference, EuroSPI 2018*. 10.1007/978-3-319-97925-0_43

Schoenfeld, J. (2022, February 8). *Cyber risk and voluntary Service Organization Control (SOC) Audits*. Tuck School of Business Working Paper No. 3596065. doi:10.2139/ssrn.3596065

Scholl, M. (2018). Play the Game! Analogue Gamification for Raising Information Security Awareness. *Systemics. Cybernetics and Informatics*, *16*(3), 32–35.

Scholl, M. (2019). Sensitizing students to information security and privacy awareness with analogue gamification. *Wissenschaftliche Beiträge*, *2019*(23), 19–26.

Schwartz, S. (2019 June 24). Deepfakes aren't a tech problem, they are a power problem. *The Guardian*. https://www.theguardian.com/commentisfree/2019/jun/24/deepfakes-facebook-silicon-valley-responsibility

Security, B. (2020, August 4). *To Fuzz or Not to Fuzz: 8 Reasons to Include Fuzz Testing in Your SDLC*. Retrieved February 19, 2022, from Beyond Security: https://blog.beyondsecurity.com/fuzz-testing-sdlc/

Security, C. (n.d.). *Contrast Security*. Retrieved February 20, 2022, from Fuzz Testing: https://www.contrastsecurity.com/knowledge-hub/glossary/fuzz-testing

SecurityScorecard. (2020, August 17). *Best Practices for Cybersecurity Auditing [A Step-by-step Checklist]*. Retrieved February 13, 2022, from SecurityScorecard: https://securityscorecard.com/blog/best-practices-for-a-cybersecurity-audit

Seebeck, A., & Vetter, J. (2021). Not Just a Gender Numbers Game: How Board Gender Diversity Affects Corporate Risk Disclosure. *Journal of Business Ethics*, 1–26. doi:10.100710551-020-04690-3

Serrasqueiro, R. M. (2009). *A divulgação da informação sobre riscos empresariais* [Paper presentation]. XIV Encuentro AECA, Instituto Superior de Contabilidade e Administração de Coimbra.

Seubert, S., & Becker, C. (2021). The Democratic Impact of Strengthening European Fundamental Rights in the Digital Age: The Example of Privacy Protection. *German Law Journal*, *22*(1), 31–44. doi:10.1017/glj.2020.101

Shedari, D. (2013, March 1). Common myths of service organization controls (SOC) reports. *ISACA Journal*. https://www.isaca.org/resources/isaca-journal/past-issues/2013/common-myths-of-service-organization-controls-soc-reports

Shropshire, J., Warkentin, M., & Sharma, S. (2015). Personality, attitudes, and intentions: Predicting initial adoption of information security behavior. *Computers & Security, 49*, 177-191.

Siekierski, B. J. (2019 April 8). *Deep fakes: What can be done about synthetic audio and video?* In Brief, Library of Parliament (LOP) papers. https://lop.parl.ca/sites/PublicWebsite/default/en_CA/ResearchPublications/201911E

Silic, M., & Lowry, P. B. (2020). Using design-science based gamification to improve organizational security training and compliance. *Journal of Management Information Systems, 37*(1), 129–161.

Silverman, H., Sleem, H., Moodley, K., Kumar, N., Naidoo, S., Subramanian, T., Jaafar, R., & Moni, M. (2015). Results of a self-assessment tool to assess the operational characteristics of research ethics committees in low – and middle-income countries. *Journal of Medical Ethics, 41*(4), 332–337. doi:10.1136/medethics-2013-101587 PMID:24748650

Siponen, M., Pahnila, S., & Mahmood, M. (2010). Compliance with information security policies: An empirical investigation. *Computer, 43*(2), 64–71.

Sivan-Sevilla, I. (2017). Trading privacy for security in cyberspace: A study across the dynamics of US federal laws and regulations between 1967 and 2016. *9th International Conference on Cyber Conflict (CyCon).*

Smith, R., & Barry, R. (2019, November 24). *Utilities Targeted in Cyberattacks Identified.* Retrieved from The Wall Street Journal: https://www.wsj.com/articles/utilities-targeted-in-cyberattacks-identified-11574611200

Smith, J. H., Dinev, T., & Xu, H. (2011). Information Privacy Research: An Interdisciplinary Review. *Management Information Systems Quarterly, 35*(4), 989. doi:10.2307/41409970

Solomon, J., Solomon, A., Norton, S., & Joseph, N. (2000). A conceptual framework for corporate risk disclosure emerging from the agenda for corporate governance reform. *The British Accounting Review, 32*(4), 447–478. doi:10.1006/bare.2000.0145

Solove, J. D. (2008). *Understanding Privacy.* Harvard University Press.

Solsman, J. E. (2019 May 24). *Samsung deepfake AI could fabricate a video of you from a single profile pic: Even the Mona Lisa can be faked.* CNet Tech. https://www.cnet.com/news/samsung-aideepfake-can-fabricate-a-video-of-you-from-a-single-photo-mona-lisa-cheapfake-dumbfake/

Sommestad, T., Hallberg, J., Lundholm, K., & Bengtsson, J. (2014). Variables influencing information security policy compliance: A systematic review of quantitative studies. *Information Management & Computer Security.*

Spent. (2022). *Spent: It's Just Stuff, Until You Don't Have It.* Retrieved from https://playspent.org/

Spivak, R. (2019). Deepfakes: The newest way to commit one of the oldest crimes. *Geo. L. Tech. Rev., 3*(2), 339-400.

Srinivas, J., Das, A. K., & Kumar, N. (2019). Government regulations in cyber security: Framework, standards and recommendations. *Future Generation Computer Systems, 92*, 178–188. doi:10.1016/j.future.2018.09.063

Stanculescu, M., Badea, C. A., Marinescu, I., Andrei, P., Drosu, O., & Andrei, H. (2019). Vulnerability of SCADA and Security Solutions for a Waste Water Treatment Plant. In *11th International Symposium on Advanced Topics in Electrical Engineering.* Bucharest, Romania: IEEE. 10.1109/ATEE.2019.8724889

Stipek, D. J. (1996). Motivation and instruction. Handbook of Educational Psychology, 1, 85-113.

Sule, M. J., Zennaro, M., & Thomas, G. (2021). Cybersecurity through the lens of digital identity and data protection: Issues and trends. *Technology in Society, 67*, 101734. doi:10.1016/j. techsoc.2021.101734

Suraj, O. A. (2020). Online surveillance and the repressive Press Council Bill 2018: A two-pronged approach to media self-censorship in Nigeria. In Journalist Safety and Self-Censorship (1st ed., pp. 80-99). Routledge. 1 doi:0.4324/9780367810139

Tan, N. C. (2016). Enhancing Knowledge sharing and research collaboration among academics: The role of knowledge management. *Higher Education, 71*(4), 525–556. doi:10.100710734-015-9922-6

Taub, E. (2021, March 18). *Carmakers Strive to Stay Ahead of Hackers.* Retrieved February 24, 2022, from New York Times: https://www.nytimes.com/2021/03/18/business/hacking-cars-cybersecurity.html#:~:text=The%20effects%20of%20a%20breach,and%20a%20lot%20of%20firewalls.&text=In%20your%20garage%20or%20driveway,than%20a%20modern%20passenger%20jet

Taylor, B. C. (2020). Defending the state from digital deceit: The reflexive securitisation of deepfake. *Critical Studies in Media Communication, 38*(1), 1–17. doi:10.1080/15295036.2020.1833058

Tech Explore. (2019, September 15). *60% of major US firms have been hacked in cloud: Study.* https://techxplore.com/news/2019-09-major-firms-hacked-cloud.html

Thenmozhi, M., & Sasidharan, A. (2020). Does board independence enhance firm value of state-owned enterprises? Evidence from India and China. *European Business Review, 32*(5), 785–800. doi:10.1108/EBR-09-2019-0224

Thornton, D., & Francia, G. (2014). Gamification of information systems and security training: Issues and case studies. *Information Security Education Journal, 1*(1), 16–24.

Tolosana, R., Vera-Rodriguez, R., Fierrez, J., Morales, A., & Ortega-Garcia, J. (2020). Deepfakes and beyond: A survey of face manipulation and fake detection. *Information Fusion, 64*, 131–148. doi:10.1016/j.inffus.2020.06.014

Turton, W., & Mehrotra, K. (2021). Hackers Breached Colonial Pipeline Using a Compromised Password. *Bloomberg.* Accessed on October 9, 2021. Retrieved from: https://www.bloomberg.com/news/articles/2021-06-04/hackers-breached-colonial-pipeline-using-compromised-password

UL. (2022). *Automotive Cybersecurity Auditing and Testing.* Retrieved February 13, 2022, from https://www.ul.com/services/automotive-cybersecurity-auditing-and-testing

Ulnicane, I., Knight, W., Leach, T., Stahl, B. C., & Wanjiku, W. G. (2021). Framing governance for a contested emerging technology: Insights from AI policy. *Policy and Society, 40*(2), 158–177. doi:10.1080/14494035.2020.1855800

Compilation of References

United Nations Economic Commission for Europe (UNECE). (2021, April 3). *UN Regulation No. 156*. Retrieved February 2022, from Uniform Provisions Concerning the Approval of Vehicles with Regards to Software Update and Software Updates Management System: https://unece.org/sites/default/files/2021-03/R156e.pdf

United Nations Economic Commission for Europe (UNECE). (2021, May 27). *World Forum for Harmonization of Vehicle Regulations (WP.29) Terms of Reference and Rules of Procedure--Revision 2*. Retrieved February 2022, from UNECE: https://unece.org/transport/documents/2021/05/standards/world-forum-harmonization-vehicle-regulations-wp29-terms-0

United Nations. (1994). *Human development report*. Oxford University Press.

Upstream Security Ltd. (2020). *ISO/SAE 21434: Setting the Standard for Automotive Cybersecurity*. Retrieved November 5, 2020, from Upstream: https://info.upstream.auto/hubfs/White_papers/Upstream_Security_Setting_the_Standard_for_Automotive_Cybersecurity_WP.pdf?_hsmi=87208721&_hsenc=p2ANqtz-8ke_6RWU7hkISDBzRoHFeUhfbaRRQ7E9-Z2bvc4YMlP3JNvc42_oh1ZxJ5jtWQOUlTehUaSmp7MfNDcwzbzUWoZjrGHw

Vaccari, C., & Chadwick, A. (2020). Deepfakes and disinformation: Exploring the impact of synthetic political video on deception, uncertainty, and trust in news. *Social Media + Society*, *6*(1), 1–13. doi:10.1177/2056305120903408

Vail, J. (2015). Gamification of an information security management course. In EdMedia+ Innovate Learning (pp. 1720-1731). Association for the Advancement of Computing in Education (AACE).

Vailshery, L. S. (2021). *Number of internet of things (IoT) connected devices worldwide in 2018, 2025 and 2030*. Retrieved from https://www.statista.com/statistics/802690/worldwide-connected-devices-by-access-technology/

Vance, A., Siponen, M., & Pahnila, S. (2012). Motivating IS security compliance: Insights from habit and protection motivation theory. *Information & Management*, *49*(3-4), 190–198.

Vasistha, D. K. (2017, August). *Detecting Anomalies in Controller Area Network (CAN) for Automobiles*. Retrieved April 13, 2020, from http://cesg.tamu.edu/wp-content/uploads/2012/01/VASISTHA-THESIS-2017.pdf

Vector Informatik Gmb, H. (2020). *Media Oriented Systems Transport (MOST)*. Retrieved November 5, 2020, from Vector: https://www.vector.com/int/en/know-how/technologies/networks/most/#c21313

Verizon. (2021). *2021 Verizon Data Breach Investigations Report*. Retrieved from https://www.verizon.com/business/resources/reports/2021/2021-data-breach-investigations-report.pdf

Verrecchia, R. E. (2001). Essays on disclosure. *Journal of Accounting and Economics*, *32*(1-3), 97–180. doi:10.1016/S0165-4101(01)00025-8

Von Solms, R., & Van Niekerk, J. (2013). From information security to cyber security. *Computers & Security*, *38*, 97–102. doi:10.1016/j.cose.2013.04.004

Vonnegut, K. (2010). *Cat's cradle*. Dial Press Trade Paperbacks.

Wang, W., Chen, L., Han, L., Zhou, Z., Xia, Z., & Chen, X. (2020). Vulnerability Assessment for ICS System Based on Zero-day Attack Graph. In *2020 International Conference on Intelligent Computing, Automation, and Systems (ICICAS)*. IEEE. 10.1109/ICICAS51530.2020.00009

Warkentin, M., McBride, M., Carter, L., & Johnston, A. (2012). The role of individual characteristics on insider abuse intentions. *Proc Am Conf Inf Syst, 28*, 1-10.

Warkentin, M., & Willison, R. (2009). Behavioral and policy issues in information systems security: The insider threat. *European Journal of Information Systems, 18*(2), 101–105.

Wasserman, H., & Madrid-Morales, D. (2019). An exploratory study of "fake news" and media trust in Kenya, Nigeria and South Africa. *African Journalism Studies, 40*(1), 107–123. doi:10.1080/23743670.2019.1627230

Watts, R., & Zimmerman, J. (1990). Positive accounting theory: A ten year perspective. *The Accounting Review, 65*(1), 131–156.

Weaver, G. A., Cheh, C., Rogers, E. J., Sanders, W. H., & Gammel, D. (2013). Toward a Cyber-Physical Topolgy Language: Applications to NERC CIP Audit. *First ACM Workshop on Smart Energy Grid Security* (pp. 93-104). Berlin, Germany: ACM. 10.1145/2516930.2516934

Weerathunga, P. E., & Cioraca, A. (2016). The Importance of Testing Smart Grid IEDs Against Security Vulnerabilities. In *2016 59th Annual Conference for Protective Relay Engineers (CPRE)* (pp. 1-21). IEEE.

Welsh, W. N., & Harris, P. W. (2016). *Criminal justice policy and planning: Planned change*. Routledge. doi:10.4324/9781315638614

Werbach, K., & Hunter, D. (2012). *For the Win: How Game Thinking Can Revolutionize Your Business*. Wharton Digital Press.

Whitehouse. (2011). *International strategy for cyberspace: prosperity, security, and openness in a networked world*. Retrieved from https://obamawhitehouse.archives.gov/sites/default/files/rss_viewer/international_strategy_for_cyberspace.pdf

Wikipedia. (2022, February). Retrieved February 21, 2022, from Zero-day (computing): https://en.wikipedia.org/wiki/Zero-day_(computing)

Wilkinson, A., Slack, C., Crews, C., Singh, N., Salzwedel, J., & Wassenaar, S. (2021). How can research ethics committees help to strengthen stakeholder engagement in health research in South Africa? an evaluation of REC documents. *SAJBL, 14*, 1.

Williams, C. M., Chaturvedi, R., & Chakravarthy, K. (2020). Cybersecurity risks in a pandemic. *Journal of Medical Internet Research, 22*(9), e23692. doi:10.2196/23692 PMID:32897869

Willison, R., & Siponen, M. (2009). Overcoming the insider: Reducing employee computer crime through Situational Crime Prevention. *Communications of the ACM, 52*(9), 133–137. doi:10.1145/1562164.1562198

Woo, P.-S., & Kim, B. H. (2020). Contingency Analysis to Evaluate the Robustness in Large-Scale Smart Grids: Based on Information Security Objectives and Frequency Stability. *Energies*, *13*(6267), 6267. doi:10.3390/en13236267

Wright, V. (2010). *Deterrence in criminal justice: Evaluating certainty vs. severity of punishment.* Sentencing Project.

Xu, H., Teo, H.-H., Tan, C. Y. B., & Agarwal, R. (2009). The role of Push-Pull Technology in Privacy Calculus: The Case of Location-Based Services. *Journal of Management Information Systems*, *26*(3), 135–174. doi:10.2753/MIS0742-1222260305

Yadlin-Segal, A., & Oppenheim, Y. (2021). Whose dystopia is it anyway? Deepfakes and social media regulation. *Convergence*, *27*(1), 36–51. doi:10.1177/1354856520923963

Yao-Huai, L. (2005). Privacy and data privacy in contemporary China. *Ethics and Information Technology*, *7*(1), 7–15. doi:10.100710676-005-0456-y

Yazdanmehr, A., Wang, J., & Yang, Z. (2020). Peers matter: The moderating role of social influence on information security policy compliance. *Information Systems Journal*, *30*(5), 791–844.

Zanzig & Francia. (2020). Auditor Evaluation and Reporting on Cybersecurity Risks. In *Encyclopedia of Organizational Knowledge, Administration, and Technology*. Hershey, PA: IGI Global Publishing. www.igi-global.com

Zetter, K. (2016, January 28). *Everything We Know About Ukraine's Power Plant Hack.* Retrieved from WIRED: https://www.wired.com/2016/01/everything-we-know-about-ukraines-power-plant-hack/

Zhang, X., Taylor, D., Qu, W., & Oliver, J. (2013). Corporate risk disclosures: influence of institutional shareholders and audit committee. *Corporate Ownership and Control, 10*(4), 341-353.

Zhang, F., & Li, Q. (2018). Security Vulnerability and Patch Management in Electric Utilities: A Data-driven Analysis. In *First Workshop on Radical and Experiential Security* (pp. 65-68). ACM. 10.1145/3203422.3203432

Zhang, Z. (2011). Environmental Review & Case Study: NERC's Cybersecurity Standards for the Electtric Grid: Fulfilling its Reliability Day Job and Moonlighting as a Cybersecurity Model. *Environmental Practice*, *13*(3), 250–264. doi:10.1017/S1466046611000275

Zharova, A. K., & Elin, V. M. (2017). The use of Big Data: A Russian perspective of personal data security. *Computer Law & Security Review*, *33*(4), 482–501. doi:10.1016/j.clsr.2017.03.025

Zhou, A., Li, Z., & Shen, Y. (2019). Anomaly Detection of CAN Bus Messages Using A Deep Neural Network for Autonomous Vehicles. *Applied Sciences (Basel, Switzerland)*, *9*(3174), 3174. doi:10.3390/app9153174

Zichermann, G., & Cunningham, C. (2011). *Gamification by design: Implementing game mechanics in web and mobile apps.* O'Reilly Media, Inc.

Related References

To continue our tradition of advancing media and communications research, we have compiled a list of recommended IGI Global readings. These references will provide additional information and guidance to further enrich your knowledge and assist you with your own research and future publications.

Abashian, N., & Fisher, S. (2018). Intercultural Effectiveness in Libraries: Supporting Success Through Collaboration With Co-Curricular Programs. In B. Blummer, J. Kenton, & M. Wiatrowski (Eds.), *Promoting Ethnic Diversity and Multiculturalism in Higher Education* (pp. 219–236). Hershey, PA: IGI Global. doi:10.4018/978-1-5225-4097-7.ch012

Adebayo, O., Fagbohun, M. O., Esse, U. C., & Nwokeoma, N. M. (2018). Change Management in the Academic Library: Transition From Print to Digital Collections. In R. Bhardwaj (Ed.), *Digitizing the Modern Library and the Transition From Print to Electronic* (pp. 1–28). Hershey, PA: IGI Global. doi:10.4018/978-1-5225-2119-8.ch001

Adegbore, A. M., Quadri, M. O., & Oyewo, O. R. (2018). A Theoretical Approach to the Adoption of Electronic Resource Management Systems (ERMS) in Nigerian University Libraries. In A. Tella & T. Kwanya (Eds.), *Handbook of Research on Managing Intellectual Property in Digital Libraries* (pp. 292–311). Hershey, PA: IGI Global. doi:10.4018/978-1-5225-3093-0.ch015

Adesola, A. P., & Olla, G. O. (2018). Unlocking the Unlimited Potentials of Koha OSS/ILS for Library House-Keeping Functions: A Global View. In M. Khosrow-Pour (Ed.), *Optimizing Contemporary Application and Processes in Open Source Software* (pp. 124–163). Hershey, PA: IGI Global. doi:10.4018/978-1-5225-5314-4.ch006

Related References

Adesola, A. P., & Olla, G. O. (2019). Bridging the Digital Divide in Nigerian Information Landscape: The Role of the Library. *International Journal of Digital Literacy and Digital Competence*, *10*(3), 10–31. doi:10.4018/IJDLDC.2019070102

Adetayo, A. J. (2021). Fake News and Social Media Censorship: Examining the Librarian Role. In R. Blankenship (Ed.), *Deep Fakes, Fake News, and Misinformation in Online Teaching and Learning Technologies* (pp. 69–92). IGI Global. https://doi.org/10.4018/978-1-7998-6474-5.ch004

Adetayo, A. J. (2022). Building Civic Engagement in Smart Cities: Role of Smart Libraries. In M. Taher (Ed.), *Handbook of Research on the Role of Libraries, Archives, and Museums in Achieving Civic Engagement and Social Justice in Smart Cities* (pp. 314–333). IGI Global. https://doi.org/10.4018/978-1-7998-8363-0.ch017

Adigun, G. O., Sobalaje, A. J., & Salau, S. A. (2018). Social Media and Copyright in Digital Libraries. In A. Tella & T. Kwanya (Eds.), *Handbook of Research on Managing Intellectual Property in Digital Libraries* (pp. 19–36). Hershey, PA: IGI Global. doi:10.4018/978-1-5225-3093-0.ch002

Adriyana, L., & Fitrina Cahyaningtyas, D. (2022). The Importance of Rural Library Services Based on Social Inclusion in Indonesia. In M. Taher (Ed.), *Handbook of Research on the Role of Libraries, Archives, and Museums in Achieving Civic Engagement and Social Justice in Smart Cities* (pp. 201–218). IGI Global. https://doi.org/10.4018/978-1-7998-8363-0.ch010

Afolabi, O. A. (2018). Myths and Challenges of Building an Effective Digital Library in Developing Nations: An African Perspective. In A. Tella & T. Kwanya (Eds.), *Handbook of Research on Managing Intellectual Property in Digital Libraries* (pp. 51–79). Hershey, PA: IGI Global. doi:10.4018/978-1-5225-3093-0.ch004

Ahuja, Y., & Kumar, P. (2017). Web 2.0 Tools and Application: Knowledge Management and Sharing in Libraries. In B. Gunjal (Ed.), *Managing Knowledge and Scholarly Assets in Academic Libraries* (pp. 218–234). Hershey, PA: IGI Global. doi:10.4018/978-1-5225-1741-2.ch010

Ajmi, A. (2018). Developing In-House Digital Tools: Case Studies From the UMKC School of Law Library. In L. Costello & M. Powers (Eds.), *Developing In-House Digital Tools in Library Spaces* (pp. 117–139). Hershey, PA: IGI Global. doi:10.4018/978-1-5225-2676-6.ch006

Al-Kharousi, R., Al-Harrasi, N. H., Jabur, N. H., & Bouazza, A. (2018). Soft Systems Methodology (SSM) as an Interdisciplinary Approach: Reflection on the Use of SSM in Adoption of Web 2.0 Applications in Omani Academic Libraries. In M. Al-Suqri, A. Al-Kindi, S. AlKindi, & N. Saleem (Eds.), *Promoting Interdisciplinarity in Knowledge Generation and Problem Solving* (pp. 243–257). Hershey, PA: IGI Global. doi:10.4018/978-1-5225-3878-3.ch016

Alenzuela, R. (2017). Research, Leadership, and Resource-Sharing Initiatives: The Role of Local Library Consortia in Access to Medical Information. In S. Ram (Ed.), *Library and Information Services for Bioinformatics Education and Research* (pp. 199–211). Hershey, PA: IGI Global. doi:10.4018/978-1-5225-1871-6.ch012

Alenzuela, R., & Terry, M. A. (2020). Diversity, Indigenous Knowledge, and LIS Pedagogy: Conceptualizing Formal Education in Library and Information Studies in Vanuatu. In R. Alenzuela, H. Kim, & D. Baylen (Eds.), *Internationalization of Library and Information Science Education in the Asia-Pacific Region* (pp. 50–77). IGI Global. doi:10.4018/978-1-7998-2273-8.ch003

Allison, D. (2017). When Sales Talk Meets Reality: Implementing a Self-Checkout Kiosk. In E. Iglesias (Ed.), *Library Technology Funding, Planning, and Deployment* (pp. 36–54). Hershey, PA: IGI Global. doi:10.4018/978-1-5225-1735-1.ch003

Anglim, C. T., & Rusk, F. (2018). Empowering DC's Future Through Information Access. In A. Burtin, J. Fleming, & P. Hampton-Garland (Eds.), *Changing Urban Landscapes Through Public Higher Education* (pp. 57–77). Hershey, PA: IGI Global. doi:10.4018/978-1-5225-3454-9.ch003

Asmi, N. A. (2017). Social Media and Library Services. *International Journal of Library and Information Services*, 6(2), 23–36. doi:10.4018/IJLIS.2017070103

Attademo, G., & Maccaro, A. (2022). Research Ethics in the Social Sciences. In G. Punziano & A. Delli Paoli (Eds.), *Handbook of Research on Advanced Research Methodologies for a Digital Society* (pp. 54–64). IGI Global. https://doi.org/10.4018/978-1-7998-8473-6.ch005

Awoyemi, R. A. (2018). Adoption and Use of Innovative Mobile Technologies in Nigerian Academic Libraries. In J. Keengwe (Ed.), *Handbook of Research on Digital Content, Mobile Learning, and Technology Integration Models in Teacher Education* (pp. 354–389). Hershey, PA: IGI Global. doi:10.4018/978-1-5225-2953-8.ch019

Awoyemi, R. A. (2018). Adoption and Use of Innovative Mobile Technologies in Nigerian Academic Libraries. In J. Keengwe (Ed.), *Handbook of Research on Digital Content, Mobile Learning, and Technology Integration Models in Teacher Education* (pp. 354–389). Hershey, PA: IGI Global. doi:10.4018/978-1-5225-2953-8.ch019

Related References

Awoyemi, R. A., & Awoyemi, R. O. (2021). Beyond the Physical Library Space: Creating a 21st Century Digitally-Oriented Library Environment. In C. Chisita, R. Enakrire, O. Durodolu, V. Tsabedze, & J. Ngoaketsi (Eds.), *Handbook of Research on Records and Information Management Strategies for Enhanced Knowledge Coordination* (pp. 189–203). IGI Global. https://doi.org/10.4018/978-1-7998-6618-3.ch012

Babatope, I. S. (2018). Social Media Applications as Effective Service Delivery Tools for Librarians. In M. Khosrow-Pour, D.B.A. (Ed.), Encyclopedia of Information Science and Technology, Fourth Edition (pp. 5252-5261). Hershey, PA: IGI Global. doi:10.4018/978-1-5225-2255-3.ch456

Bakare, A. A. (2018). Digital Libraries and Copyright of Intellectual Property: An Ethical Practice Management. In A. Tella & T. Kwanya (Eds.), *Handbook of Research on Managing Intellectual Property in Digital Libraries* (pp. 377–395). Hershey, PA: IGI Global. doi:10.4018/978-1-5225-3093-0.ch019

Baker, A. A. (2020). To Whose Benefit? At What Cost?: Consideration for Ethical Issues in Social Science Research. In M. Baran & J. Jones (Eds.), *Applied Social Science Approaches to Mixed Methods Research* (pp. 251–260). IGI Global. https://doi.org/10.4018/978-1-7998-1025-4.ch011

Baker-Gardner, R., & Smart, C. (2017). Ignorance or Intent?: A Case Study of Plagiarism in Higher Education among LIS Students in the Caribbean. In D. Velliaris (Ed.), *Handbook of Research on Academic Misconduct in Higher Education* (pp. 182–205). Hershey, PA: IGI Global. doi:10.4018/978-1-5225-1610-1.ch008

Baker-Gardner, R., & Stewart, P. (2018). Educating Caribbean Librarians to Provide Library Education in a Dynamic Information Environment. In S. Bhattacharyya & K. Patnaik (Eds.), *Changing the Scope of Library Instruction in the Digital Age* (pp. 187–226). Hershey, PA: IGI Global. doi:10.4018/978-1-5225-2802-9.ch008

Baran, M. L., & Jones, J. E. (2020). Developing the Research Study: A Step-by-Step Approach. In M. Baran & J. Jones (Eds.), *Applied Social Science Approaches to Mixed Methods Research* (pp. 262–274). IGI Global. https://doi.org/10.4018/978-1-7998-1025-4.ch012

Baskaran, C. (2020). Altmetircs Research: An Impact and Tools. In C. Baskaran (Ed.), *Measuring and Implementing Altmetrics in Library and Information Science Research* (pp. 1–10). IGI Global. https://doi.org/10.4018/978-1-7998-1309-5.ch001

Bengtson, J. (2017). Funding a Gamification Machine. In E. Iglesias (Ed.), *Library Technology Funding, Planning, and Deployment* (pp. 99–112). Hershey, PA: IGI Global. doi:10.4018/978-1-5225-1735-1.ch006

Bhuda, M., & Koitsiwe, M. (2022). The Importance of Underpinning Indigenous Research Using African Indigenous Philosophies: Perspectives From Indigenous Scholars. In R. Tshifhumulo & T. Makhanikhe (Eds.), *Handbook of Research on Protecting and Managing Global Indigenous Knowledge Systems* (pp. 223–248). IGI Global. https://doi.org/10.4018/978-1-7998-7492-8.ch013

Blummer, B., & Kenton, J. M. (2017). Access and Accessibility of Academic Libraries' Electronic Resources and Services: Identifying Themes in the Literature From 2000 to the Present. In H. Alphin Jr, J. Lavine, & R. Chan (Eds.), *Disability and Equity in Higher Education Accessibility* (pp. 242–267). Hershey, PA: IGI Global. doi:10.4018/978-1-5225-2665-0.ch011

Blummer, B., & Kenton, J. M. (2018). Academic and Research Libraries' Portals: A Literature Review From 2003 to the Present. In R. Bhardwaj (Ed.), *Digitizing the Modern Library and the Transition From Print to Electronic* (pp. 29–63). Hershey, PA: IGI Global. doi:10.4018/978-1-5225-2119-8.ch002

Blummer, B., & Kenton, J. M. (2018). International Students and Academic Libraries: Identifying Themes in the Literature From 2001 to the Present. In B. Blummer, J. Kenton, & M. Wiatrowski (Eds.), *Promoting Ethnic Diversity and Multiculturalism in Higher Education* (pp. 237–263). Hershey, PA: IGI Global. doi:10.4018/978-1-5225-4097-7.ch013

Bohuski, L. (2020). What If Your Library Can't Go Green?: Promoting Wellness in Libraries. In A. Kaushik, A. Kumar, & P. Biswas (Eds.), *Handbook of Research on Emerging Trends and Technologies in Library and Information Science* (pp. 13–26). IGI Global. doi:10.4018/978-1-5225-9825-1.ch002

Boom, D. (2017). The Embedded Librarian: Do More With less. In B. Gunjal (Ed.), *Managing Knowledge and Scholarly Assets in Academic Libraries* (pp. 76–97). Hershey, PA: IGI Global. doi:10.4018/978-1-5225-1741-2.ch004

Bosire-Ogechi, E. (2018). Social Media, Social Networking, Copyright, and Digital Libraries. In A. Tella & T. Kwanya (Eds.), *Handbook of Research on Managing Intellectual Property in Digital Libraries* (pp. 37–50). Hershey, PA: IGI Global. doi:10.4018/978-1-5225-3093-0.ch003

Bradley-Sanders, C., & Rudshteyn, A. (2018). MyLibrary at Brooklyn College: Developing a Suite of Digital Tools. In L. Costello & M. Powers (Eds.), *Developing In-House Digital Tools in Library Spaces* (pp. 140–167). Hershey, PA: IGI Global. doi:10.4018/978-1-5225-2676-6.ch007

Brown, V. (2018). Technology Access Gap for Postsecondary Education: A Statewide Case Study. In M. Yildiz, S. Funk, & B. De Abreu (Eds.), *Promoting Global Competencies Through Media Literacy* (pp. 20–40). Hershey, PA: IGI Global. doi:10.4018/978-1-5225-3082-4.ch002

Browne, N. (2021). The IHS Library and Its Response to the COVID-19 Pandemic. In B. Holland (Eds.), *Handbook of Research on Library Response to the COVID-19 Pandemic* (pp. 298-320). IGI Global. https://doi.org/10.4018/978-1-7998-6449-3.ch016

Chaiyasoonthorn, W., & Suksa-ngiam, W. (2018). Users' Acceptance of Online Literature Databases in a Thai University: A Test of UTAUT2. *International Journal of Information Systems in the Service Sector*, *10*(1), 54–70. doi:10.4018/IJISSS.2018010104

Chaudron, G. (2018). Burst Pipes and Leaky Roofs: Small Emergencies Are a Challenge for Libraries. In K. Strang, M. Korstanje, & N. Vajjhala (Eds.), *Research, Practices, and Innovations in Global Risk and Contingency Management* (pp. 211–231). Hershey, PA: IGI Global. doi:10.4018/978-1-5225-4754-9.ch012

Chemulwo, M. J. (2018). Managing Intellectual Property in Digital Libraries and Copyright Challenges. In A. Tella & T. Kwanya (Eds.), *Handbook of Research on Managing Intellectual Property in Digital Libraries* (pp. 165–183). Hershey, PA: IGI Global. doi:10.4018/978-1-5225-3093-0.ch009

Chen, J., Lan, X., Huang, Q., Dong, J., & Chen, C. (2017). Scholarly Learning Commons. In L. Ruan, Q. Zhu, & Y. Ye (Eds.), *Academic Library Development and Administration in China* (pp. 90–109). Hershey, PA: IGI Global. doi:10.4018/978-1-5225-0550-1.ch006

Chigwada, J. P. (2018). Adoption of Open Source Software in Libraries in Developing Countries. *International Journal of Library and Information Services*, *7*(1), 15–29. doi:10.4018/IJLIS.2018010102

Chigwada, J. P. (2020). Librarian Skillsets in the 21st Century: The Changing Role of Librarians in the Digital Era. In N. Osuigwe (Ed.), *Managing and Adapting Library Information Services for Future Users* (pp. 41–58). IGI Global. https://doi.org/10.4018/978-1-7998-1116-9.ch003

Chigwada, J. P. (2020). The Role of the Librarian in the Research Life Cycle: Research Collaboration Among the Library and Faculty. In C. Chisita (Ed.), *Cooperation and Collaboration Initiatives for Libraries and Related Institutions* (pp. 335–346). IGI Global. https://doi.org/10.4018/978-1-7998-0043-9.ch017

Chigwada, J. P. (2021). Research Data Management Services in Tertiary Institutions in Zimbabwe. In B. Holland (Eds.), *Handbook of Research on Knowledge and Organization Systems in Library and Information Science* (pp. 419-437). IGI Global. https://doi.org/10.4018/978-1-7998-7258-0.ch022

Chigwada, J. P., & Maturure, R. (2019). Advocating for Library and Information Services by National Library Associations of Africa in the Context of Sustainable Development Goals. In P. Ngulube (Ed.), *Handbook of Research on Advocacy, Promotion, and Public Programming for Memory Institutions* (pp. 219–237). IGI Global. doi:10.4018/978-1-5225-7429-3.ch012

Chiparausha, B., & Chigwada, J. P. (2019). Promoting Library Services in a Digital Environment in Zimbabwe. In P. Ngulube (Ed.), *Handbook of Research on Advocacy, Promotion, and Public Programming for Memory Institutions* (pp. 284–296). IGI Global. https://doi.org/10.4018/978-1-5225-7429-3.ch015

Chisita, C. T., & Chinyemba, F. (2017). Utilising ICTs for Resource Sharing Initiatives in Academic Institutions in Zimbabwe: Towards a New Trajectory. In B. Gunjal (Ed.), *Managing Knowledge and Scholarly Assets in Academic Libraries* (pp. 174–187). Hershey, PA: IGI Global. doi:10.4018/978-1-5225-1741-2.ch008

Chu, S., Tu, S., Wang, N., & Zhang, W. (2020). Information Equity and Cultural Sharing: The Service for Migrant Workers in Hangzhou Public Library. *International Journal of Library and Information Services*, 9(1), 10–24. https://doi.org/10.4018/IJLIS.2020010102

Clarance, M. M., & Angeline, X. M. (2019). User Opinion on Library Collections and Services: A Case Study of Branch Library in Karaikudi. In S. Thanuskodi (Ed.), *Literacy Skill Development for Library Science Professionals* (pp. 343–375). IGI Global. https://doi.org/10.4018/978-1-5225-7125-4.ch015

Costello, L., & Fazal, S. (2018). Developing Unique Study Room Reservation Systems: Examples From Teachers College and Stony Brook University. In L. Costello & M. Powers (Eds.), *Developing In-House Digital Tools in Library Spaces* (pp. 168–176). Hershey, PA: IGI Global. doi:10.4018/978-1-5225-2676-6.ch008

Cui, Y. (2017). Research Data Management: Models, Challenges, and Actions. In L. Ruan, Q. Zhu, & Y. Ye (Eds.), *Academic Library Development and Administration in China* (pp. 184–195). Hershey, PA: IGI Global. doi:10.4018/978-1-5225-0550-1.ch011

Dhamdhere, S. N., De Smet, E., & Lihitkar, R. (2017). Web-Based Bibliographic Services Offered by Top World and Indian University Libraries: A Comparative Study. *International Journal of Library and Information Services*, 6(1), 53–72. doi:10.4018/IJLIS.2017010104

Related References

Eiriemiokhale, K. A. (2018). Copyright Issues in a Digital Library Environment. In A. Tella & T. Kwanya (Eds.), *Handbook of Research on Managing Intellectual Property in Digital Libraries* (pp. 142–164). Hershey, PA: IGI Global. doi:10.4018/978-1-5225-3093-0.ch008

El Mimouni, H., Anderson, J., Tempelman-Kluit, N. F., & Dolan-Mescal, A. (2018). UX Work in Libraries: How (and Why) to Do It. In L. Costello & M. Powers (Eds.), *Developing In-House Digital Tools in Library Spaces* (pp. 1–36). Hershey, PA: IGI Global. doi:10.4018/978-1-5225-2676-6.ch001

Emiri, O. T. (2017). Digital Literacy Skills Among Librarians in University Libraries In the 21st Century in Edo And Delta States, Nigeria. *International Journal of Library and Information Services*, *6*(1), 37–52. doi:10.4018/IJLIS.2017010103

Emmelhainz, C. (2020). Educating the Central Asian Librarian: Considering the International MLIS in Kazakhstan. In R. Alenzuela, H. Kim, & D. Baylen (Eds.), *Internationalization of Library and Information Science Education in the Asia-Pacific Region* (pp. 1–32). IGI Global. https://doi.org/10.4018/978-1-7998-2273-8.ch001

Esguerra, A. C. (2020). Library Education and Librarianship in Japan and the Philippines. In R. Alenzuela, H. Kim, & D. Baylen (Eds.), *Internationalization of Library and Information Science Education in the Asia-Pacific Region* (pp. 131–157). IGI Global. https://doi.org/10.4018/978-1-7998-2273-8.ch006

Esposito, T. (2018). Exploring Opportunities in Health Science Information Instructional Outreach: A Case Study Highlighting One Academic Library's Experience. In S. Bhattacharyya & K. Patnaik (Eds.), *Changing the Scope of Library Instruction in the Digital Age* (pp. 118–135). Hershey, PA: IGI Global. doi:10.4018/978-1-5225-2802-9.ch005

Fagbola, O. O., Smart, A. E., & Oluwaseun, B. O. (2020). Application of Cloud Computing Technologies in Academic Library Management: The National Open University of Nigeria Library in Perspective. In A. Tella (Ed.), *Handbook of Research on Digital Devices for Inclusivity and Engagement in Libraries* (pp. 135–159). IGI Global. https://doi.org/10.4018/978-1-5225-9034-7.ch007

Fan, Y., Zhang, X., & Li, G. (2017). Research Initiatives and Projects in Academic Libraries. In L. Ruan, Q. Zhu, & Y. Ye (Eds.), *Academic Library Development and Administration in China* (pp. 230–252). Hershey, PA: IGI Global. doi:10.4018/978-1-5225-0550-1.ch014

Farmer, L. S. (2017). ICT Literacy Integration: Issues and Sample Efforts. In J. Keengwe & P. Bull (Eds.), *Handbook of Research on Transformative Digital Content and Learning Technologies* (pp. 59–80). Hershey, PA: IGI Global. doi:10.4018/978-1-5225-2000-9.ch004

Farmer, L. S. (2017). Data Analytics for Strategic Management: Getting the Right Data. In V. Wang (Ed.), *Encyclopedia of Strategic Leadership and Management* (pp. 810–822). Hershey, PA: IGI Global. doi:10.4018/978-1-5225-1049-9.ch056

Farmer, L. S. (2017). Managing Portable Technologies for Special Education. In V. Wang (Ed.), *Encyclopedia of Strategic Leadership and Management* (pp. 977–987). Hershey, PA: IGI Global. doi:10.4018/978-1-5225-1049-9.ch068

Fujishima, D., & Kamada, T. (2017). Collective Relocation for Associative Distributed Collections of Objects. *International Journal of Software Innovation*, *5*(2), 55–69. doi:10.4018/IJSI.2017040104

Ghani, S. R. (2017). Ontology: Advancing Flawless Library Services. In T. Ashraf & N. Kumar (Eds.), *Interdisciplinary Digital Preservation Tools and Technologies* (pp. 79–102). Hershey, PA: IGI Global. doi:10.4018/978-1-5225-1653-8.ch005

Gu, J. (2017). Library Buildings on New Campuses. In L. Ruan, Q. Zhu, & Y. Ye (Eds.), *Academic Library Development and Administration in China* (pp. 110–124). Hershey, PA: IGI Global. doi:10.4018/978-1-5225-0550-1.ch007

Guan, Z., & Wang, J. (2017). The China Academic Social Sciences and Humanities Library (CASHL). In L. Ruan, Q. Zhu, & Y. Ye (Eds.), *Academic Library Development and Administration in China* (pp. 31–54). Hershey, PA: IGI Global. doi:10.4018/978-1-5225-0550-1.ch003

Gul, S., & Shueb, S. (2018). Confronting/Managing the Crisis of Indian Libraries: E-Consortia Initiatives in India - A Way Forward. In R. Bhardwaj (Ed.), *Digitizing the Modern Library and the Transition From Print to Electronic* (pp. 129–163). Hershey, PA: IGI Global. doi:10.4018/978-1-5225-2119-8.ch006

Gunjal, B. (2017). Managing Knowledge and Scholarly Assets in Academic Libraries: Issues and Challenges. In B. Gunjal (Ed.), *Managing Knowledge and Scholarly Assets in Academic Libraries* (pp. 270–279). Hershey, PA: IGI Global. doi:10.4018/978-1-5225-1741-2.ch013

Guo, J., Zhang, H., & Zong, Y. (2017). Leadership Development and Career Planning. In L. Ruan, Q. Zhu, & Y. Ye (Eds.), *Academic Library Development and Administration in China* (pp. 264–279). Hershey, PA: IGI Global. doi:10.4018/978-1-5225-0550-1.ch016

Hahn, J. (2020). Student Engagement and Smart Spaces: Library Browsing and Internet of Things Technology. In B. Holland (Eds.), *Emerging Trends and Impacts of the Internet of Things in Libraries* (pp. 52-70). IGI Global. https://doi.org/10.4018/978-1-7998-4742-7.ch003

Halder, D. (2020). A Transitional Shift From Traditional Library to Digital Library. In A. Kaushik, A. Kumar, & P. Biswas (Eds.), *Handbook of Research on Emerging Trends and Technologies in Library and Information Science* (pp. 147–155). IGI Global. https://doi.org/10.4018/978-1-5225-9825-1.ch011

Hallis, R. (2018). Leveraging Library Instruction in a Digital Age. In S. Bhattacharyya & K. Patnaik (Eds.), *Changing the Scope of Library Instruction in the Digital Age* (pp. 1–23). Hershey, PA: IGI Global. doi:10.4018/978-1-5225-2802-9.ch001

Halupa, C. (2022). An Introduction to Survey Research. In A. Zimmerman (Ed.), *Methodological Innovations in Research and Academic Writing* (pp. 41–62). IGI Global. https://doi.org/10.4018/978-1-7998-8283-1.ch003

Hartsock, R., & Alemneh, D. G. (2018). Electronic Theses and Dissertations (ETDs). In M. Khosrow-Pour, D.B.A. (Ed.), Encyclopedia of Information Science and Technology, Fourth Edition (pp. 6748-6755). Hershey, PA: IGI Global. https://doi.org/ doi:10.4018/978-1-5225-2255-3.ch584

Haugh, D. (2018). Mobile Applications for Libraries. In L. Costello & M. Powers (Eds.), *Developing In-House Digital Tools in Library Spaces* (pp. 76–90). Hershey, PA: IGI Global. doi:10.4018/978-1-5225-2676-6.ch004

Hayes, C. (2022). Methodology and Method in Case Study Research: Framing Research Design in Practice. In S. Watson, S. Austin, & J. Bell (Eds.), *Conceptual Analyses of Curriculum Inquiry Methodologies* (pp. 138-154). IGI Global. https://doi.org/10.4018/978-1-7998-8848-2.ch007

Hayes, C., & Graham, Y. N. (2022). Phenomenology: Conceptually Framing Phenomenological Research Design and Methodology. In S. Watson, S. Austin, & J. Bell (Eds.), *Conceptual Analyses of Curriculum Inquiry Methodologies* (pp. 28-50). IGI Global. https://doi.org/10.4018/978-1-7998-8848-2.ch002

Hill, V. (2017). Digital Citizens as Writers: New Literacies and New Responsibilities. In E. Monske & K. Blair (Eds.), *Handbook of Research on Writing and Composing in the Age of MOOCs* (pp. 56–74). Hershey, PA: IGI Global. doi:10.4018/978-1-5225-1718-4.ch004

Hoh, A. (2019). Expanding the Awareness and Use of Library Collections Through Social Media: A Case Study of the Library of Congress International Collections Social Media Program. In J. Joe & E. Knight (Eds.), *Social Media for Communication and Instruction in Academic Libraries* (pp. 212–236). IGI Global. doi:10.4018/978-1-5225-8097-3.ch013

Holland, B. (2020). Emerging Technology and Today's Libraries. In B. Holland (Eds.), *Emerging Trends and Impacts of the Internet of Things in Libraries* (pp. 1-33). IGI Global. https://doi.org/10.4018/978-1-7998-4742-7.ch001

Homza, A., & Fontno, T. J. (2021). Supporting Teacher Candidates as Social Justice Change-Makers: A Faculty-Librarian Collaboration for Building and Using Diverse Youth Collections. In D. Hartsfield (Ed.), *Handbook of Research on Teaching Diverse Youth Literature to Pre-Service Professionals* (pp. 398–421). IGI Global. https://doi.org/10.4018/978-1-7998-7375-4.ch020

Horne-Popp, L. M., Tessone, E. B., & Welker, J. (2018). If You Build It, They Will Come: Creating a Library Statistics Dashboard for Decision-Making. In L. Costello & M. Powers (Eds.), *Developing In-House Digital Tools in Library Spaces* (pp. 177–203). Hershey, PA: IGI Global. doi:10.4018/978-1-5225-2676-6.ch009

Huang, C., & Xue, H. F. (2017). The China Academic Digital Associative Library (CADAL). In L. Ruan, Q. Zhu, & Y. Ye (Eds.), *Academic Library Development and Administration in China* (pp. 20–30). Hershey, PA: IGI Global. doi:10.4018/978-1-5225-0550-1.ch002

Huang, J., & Vedantham, A. (2019). Cabot Science Library: Creating Transformative Learning Environments in Library Spaces. In A. Darshan Singh, S. Raghunathan, E. Robeck, & B. Sharma (Eds.), *Cases on Smart Learning Environments* (pp. 284–298). IGI Global. doi:10.4018/978-1-5225-6136-1.ch016

Hunsaker, A. J., Majewski, N., & Rocke, L. E. (2018). Pulling Content out the Back Door: Creating an Interactive Digital Collections Experience. In L. Costello & M. Powers (Eds.), *Developing In-House Digital Tools in Library Spaces* (pp. 205–226). Hershey, PA: IGI Global. doi:10.4018/978-1-5225-2676-6.ch010

Hussain, A. (2020). Cutting Edge: Technology's Impact on Library Services. In J. Jesubright & P. Saravanan (Eds.), *Innovations in the Designing and Marketing of Information Services* (pp. 16–27). IGI Global. https://doi.org/10.4018/978-1-7998-1482-5.ch002

Idiegbeyan-ose, J., Owolabi, S. E., Ayooluwa, A., Foluke, O., Toluwani, E., & Sunday, O. (2019). Digital Library and Distance Learning in Developing Countries: Benefits and Challenges. In R. Bhardwaj & P. Banks (Eds.), *Research Data Access and Management in Modern Libraries* (pp. 220–245). IGI Global. https://doi.org/10.4018/978-1-5225-8437-7.ch011

Ifijeh, G., Adebayo, O., Izuagbe, R., & Olawoyin, O. (2018). Institutional Repositories and Libraries in Nigeria: Interrogating the Nexus. *Journal of Cases on Information Technology*, 20(2), 16–29. doi:10.4018/JCIT.2018040102

Igbinovia, M. O., Solanke, E. O., & Obinyan, O. O. (2020). Building Influence: Strategising for Library Advocacy. In N. Osuigwe (Ed.), *Managing and Adapting Library Information Services for Future Users* (pp. 221–241). IGI Global. https://doi.org/10.4018/978-1-7998-1116-9.ch013

Iglesias, E. (2017). Insourcing and Outsourcing of Library Technology. In E. Iglesias (Ed.), *Library Technology Funding, Planning, and Deployment* (pp. 113–123). Hershey, PA: IGI Global. doi:10.4018/978-1-5225-1735-1.ch007

Ikolo, V. E. (2018). Transformational Leadership for Academic Libraries in Nigeria. In M. Khosrow-Pour, D.B.A. (Ed.), Encyclopedia of Information Science and Technology, Fourth Edition (pp. 5726-5735). Hershey, PA: IGI Global. doi:10.4018/978-1-5225-2255-3.ch497

Ikolo, V. E. (2020). Doctor's Awareness and Perception of Medical Library Resources and Services: A Case Study of Delta State University Teaching Hospital (Delsuth), Nigeria. *International Journal of Library and Information Services*, 9(2), 58–71. https://doi.org/10.4018/IJLIS.2020070104

Joe, J. A. (2018). Changing Expectations of Academic Libraries. In M. Khosrow-Pour, D.B.A. (Ed.), Encyclopedia of Information Science and Technology, Fourth Edition (pp. 5204-5212). Hershey, PA: IGI Global. doi:10.4018/978-1-5225-2255-3.ch452

Juliana, I., Izuagbe, R., Itsekor, V., Fagbohun, M. O., Asaolu, A., & Nwokeoma, M. N. (2018). The Role of the School Library in Empowering Visually Impaired Children With Lifelong Information Literacy Skills. In P. Epler (Ed.), *Instructional Strategies in General Education and Putting the Individuals With Disabilities Act (IDEA) Into Practice* (pp. 245–271). Hershey, PA: IGI Global. doi:10.4018/978-1-5225-3111-1.ch009

Kalu, C. O., Chidi-Kalu, E. I., & Mafe, T. A. (2021). Research Data Management in an Academic Library. In J. Chigwada & G. Tsvuura (Eds.), *Handbook of Research on Information and Records Management in the Fourth Industrial Revolution* (pp. 38–55). IGI Global. https://doi.org/10.4018/978-1-7998-7740-0.ch003

Kalusopa, T. (2018). Preservation and Access to Digital Materials: Strategic Policy Options for Africa. In P. Ngulube (Ed.), *Handbook of Research on Heritage Management and Preservation* (pp. 150–174). Hershey, PA: IGI Global. doi:10.4018/978-1-5225-3137-1.ch008

Kamau, G. W. (2018). Copyright Challenges in Digital Libraries in Kenya From the Lens of a Librarian. In A. Tella & T. Kwanya (Eds.), *Handbook of Research on Managing Intellectual Property in Digital Libraries* (pp. 312–336). Hershey, PA: IGI Global. doi:10.4018/978-1-5225-3093-0.ch016

Karagöz, E., Güney, L. Ö., & Baran, B. (2022). The Collaborative Digital Content Library Fostering Faculty Members' Collaboratively Building Learning Sources. In G. Durak & S. Çankaya (Eds.), *Handbook of Research on Managing and Designing Online Courses in Synchronous and Asynchronous Environments* (pp. 196–213). IGI Global. doi:10.4018/978-1-7998-8701-0.ch010

Karmakar, R. (2018). Development and Management of Digital Libraries in the Regime of IPR Paradigm. *International Journal of Library and Information Services*, 7(1), 44–57. doi:10.4018/IJLIS.2018010104

Kasemsap, K. (2017). Mastering Knowledge Management in Academic Libraries. In B. Gunjal (Ed.), *Managing Knowledge and Scholarly Assets in Academic Libraries* (pp. 27–55). Hershey, PA: IGI Global. doi:10.4018/978-1-5225-1741-2.ch002

Kehinde, A. (2018). Digital Libraries and the Role of Digital Librarians. In A. Tella & T. Kwanya (Eds.), *Handbook of Research on Managing Intellectual Property in Digital Libraries* (pp. 98–119). Hershey, PA: IGI Global. doi:10.4018/978-1-5225-3093-0.ch006

Kenausis, V., & Herman, D. (2017). Don't Make Us Use the "Get Along Shirt": Communication and Consensus Building in an RFP Process. In E. Iglesias (Ed.), *Library Technology Funding, Planning, and Deployment* (pp. 1–22). Hershey, PA: IGI Global. doi:10.4018/978-1-5225-1735-1.ch001

Kohl, L. E., Lombardi, P., & Moroney, M. (2017). Moving from Local to Global via the Integrated Library System: Cost-Savings, ILS Management, Teams, and End-Users. In E. Iglesias (Ed.), *Library Technology Funding, Planning, and Deployment* (pp. 23–35). Hershey, PA: IGI Global. doi:10.4018/978-1-5225-1735-1.ch002

Kowalsky, M. (2020). School Librarian Experiences of Learning Management Implementation. In A. Tella (Ed.), *Handbook of Research on Digital Devices for Inclusivity and Engagement in Libraries* (pp. 160–184). IGI Global. https://doi.org/10.4018/978-1-5225-9034-7.ch008

Kumar, K. (2018). Library in Your Pocket Delivery of Instruction Service Through Library Mobile Apps: A World in Your Pocket. In S. Bhattacharyya & K. Patnaik (Eds.), *Changing the Scope of Library Instruction in the Digital Age* (pp. 228–249). Hershey, PA: IGI Global. doi:10.4018/978-1-5225-2802-9.ch009

Kwanya, T. (2018). Social Bookmarking in Digital Libraries: Intellectual Property Rights Implications. In A. Tella & T. Kwanya (Eds.), *Handbook of Research on Managing Intellectual Property in Digital Libraries* (pp. 1–18). Hershey, PA: IGI Global. doi:10.4018/978-1-5225-3093-0.ch001

Related References

Lapo, P., Makhmudov, G., & Rakhmatullaev, M. (2020). Internationalization of Library and Information Science Education in Tajikistan and Uzbekistan: Implications in Central Asia. In R. Alenzuela, H. Kim, & D. Baylen (Eds.), *Internationalization of Library and Information Science Education in the Asia-Pacific Region* (pp. 225–245). IGI Global. https://doi.org/10.4018/978-1-7998-2273-8.ch010

Lewis, J. K. (2018). Change Leadership Styles and Behaviors in Academic Libraries. In M. Khosrow-Pour, D.B.A. (Ed.), Encyclopedia of Information Science and Technology, Fourth Edition (pp. 5194-5203). Hershey, PA: IGI Global. doi:10.4018/978-1-5225-2255-3.ch451

Lillard, L. L. (2018). Is Interdisciplinary Collaboration in Academia an Elusive Dream?: Can the Institutional Barriers Be Broken Down? A Review of the Literature and the Case of Library Science. In M. Al-Suqri, A. Al-Kindi, S. AlKindi, & N. Saleem (Eds.), *Promoting Interdisciplinarity in Knowledge Generation and Problem Solving* (pp. 139–147). Hershey, PA: IGI Global. doi:10.4018/978-1-5225-3878-3. ch010

Liu, C., Dou, T., Zhou, H., Zhang, B., & Zhang, C. (2021). Library Service Innovation Based on New Information Technology: Taking the Interactive Experience Space "Tsinghua Impression" as an Example. *International Journal of Library and Information Services*, *10*(1), 71–81. https://doi.org/10.4018/IJLIS.2021010106

Long, X., & Yao, B. (2017). The Construction and Development of the Academic Digital Library of Chinese Ancient Collections. In L. Ruan, Q. Zhu, & Y. Ye (Eds.), *Academic Library Development and Administration in China* (pp. 126–135). Hershey, PA: IGI Global. doi:10.4018/978-1-5225-0550-1.ch008

Long, X., & Yao, B. (2020). The Construction and Development of the Academic Digital Library of Chinese Ancient Collections. In I. Management Association (Ed.), *Digital Libraries and Institutional Repositories: Breakthroughs in Research and Practice* (pp. 78-87). IGI Global. https://doi.org/10.4018/978-1-7998-2463-3.ch006

Lowe, M., & Reno, L. M. (2018). Academic Librarianship and Burnout. In *Examining the Emotional Dimensions of Academic Librarianship: Emerging Research and Opportunities* (pp. 72–89). Hershey, PA: IGI Global. doi:10.4018/978-1-5225-3761-8.ch005

Lowe, M., & Reno, L. M. (2018). Emotional Dimensions of Academic Librarianship. In *Examining the Emotional Dimensions of Academic Librarianship: Emerging Research and Opportunities* (pp. 54–71). Hershey, PA: IGI Global. doi:10.4018/978-1-5225-3761-8.ch004

Lowe, M., & Reno, L. M. (2018). Why Isn't This Being Studied? In *Examining the Emotional Dimensions of Academic Librarianship: Emerging Research and Opportunities* (pp. 90–108). Hershey, PA: IGI Global. doi:10.4018/978-1-5225-3761-8.ch006

Lowe, M., & Reno, L. M. (2018). Research Agenda: Research Ideas and Recommendations. In *Examining the Emotional Dimensions of Academic Librarianship: Emerging Research and Opportunities* (pp. 109–125). Hershey, PA: IGI Global. doi:10.4018/978-1-5225-3761-8.ch007

Luyombya, D., Kiyingi, G. W., & Naluwooza, M. (2018). The Nature and Utilisation of Archival Records Deposited in Makerere University Library, Uganda. In P. Ngulube (Ed.), *Handbook of Research on Heritage Management and Preservation* (pp. 96–113). Hershey, PA: IGI Global. doi:10.4018/978-1-5225-3137-1.ch005

Ma, W. Y. (2022). Supporting Indigenous Education From a Distance: Adjusting Strategies to Maintain Access to a Rare Library Collection During a Global Crisis. In P. Pangelinan & T. McVey (Eds.), *Learning and Reconciliation Through Indigenous Education in Oceania* (pp. 197–209). IGI Global. https://doi.org/10.4018/978-1-7998-7736-3.ch012

Mabe, M., & Ashley, E. A. (2017). The Natural Role of the Public Library. In *The Developing Role of Public Libraries in Emergency Management: Emerging Research and Opportunities* (pp. 25–43). Hershey, PA: IGI Global. doi:10.4018/978-1-5225-2196-9.ch003

Mabe, M., & Ashley, E. A. (2017). I'm Trained, Now What? In *The Developing Role of Public Libraries in Emergency Management: Emerging Research and Opportunities* (pp. 87–95). Hershey, PA: IGI Global. doi:10.4018/978-1-5225-2196-9.ch007

Mabe, M., & Ashley, E. A. (2017). Emergency Preparation for the Library and Librarian. In *The Developing Role of Public Libraries in Emergency Management: Emerging Research and Opportunities* (pp. 61–78). Hershey, PA: IGI Global. doi:10.4018/978-1-5225-2196-9.ch005

Mabe, M., & Ashley, E. A. (2017). The CCPL Model. In *The Developing Role of Public Libraries in Emergency Management: Emerging Research and Opportunities* (pp. 15–24). Hershey, PA: IGI Global. doi:10.4018/978-1-5225-2196-9.ch002

Mabe, M., & Ashley, E. A. (2017). The Local Command Structure and How the Library Fits. In *In The Developing Role of Public Libraries in Emergency Management: Emerging Research and Opportunities* (pp. 44–60). Hershey, PA: IGI Global. doi:10.4018/978-1-5225-2196-9.ch004

Related References

Mafube, M. A., & Keakopa, S. M. (2019). Customer Services at the Library Archives of the National University of Lesotho. In P. Ngulube (Ed.), *Handbook of Research on Advocacy, Promotion, and Public Programming for Memory Institutions* (pp. 62–76). IGI Global. doi:10.4018/978-1-5225-7429-3.ch004

Majumdar, S. (2022). Community Engagement Through Extension and Outreach Activities: Scope of a College Library. In M. Taher (Ed.), *Handbook of Research on the Role of Libraries, Archives, and Museums in Achieving Civic Engagement and Social Justice in Smart Cities* (pp. 121–138). IGI Global. https://doi.org/10.4018/978-1-7998-8363-0.ch006

Mangone, E. (2022). The Difficult Joining of Theory and Empirical Research: Strengths and Weaknesses of Digital Research Methods. In G. Punziano & A. Delli Paoli (Eds.), *Handbook of Research on Advanced Research Methodologies for a Digital Society* (pp. 11–23). IGI Global. https://doi.org/10.4018/978-1-7998-8473-6.ch002

Manzoor, A. (2018). Social Media: A Librarian's Tool for Instant and Direct Interaction With Library Users. In R. Bhardwaj (Ed.), *Digitizing the Modern Library and the Transition From Print to Electronic* (pp. 112–128). Hershey, PA: IGI Global. doi:10.4018/978-1-5225-2119-8.ch005

Maringanti, H. (2018). A Decision Making Paradigm for Software Development in Libraries. In L. Costello & M. Powers (Eds.), *Developing In-House Digital Tools in Library Spaces* (pp. 59–75). Hershey, PA: IGI Global. doi:10.4018/978-1-5225-2676-6.ch003

Markman, K. M., Ferrarini, M., & Deschenes, A. H. (2018). User Testing and Iterative Design in the Academic Library: A Case Study. In R. Roscoe, S. Craig, & I. Douglas (Eds.), *End-User Considerations in Educational Technology Design* (pp. 160–183). Hershey, PA: IGI Global. doi:10.4018/978-1-5225-2639-1.ch008

Marrazzo, F. (2022). Doing Research With Online Platforms: An Emerging Issue Network. In G. Punziano & A. Delli Paoli (Eds.), *Handbook of Research on Advanced Research Methodologies for a Digital Society* (pp. 65–86). IGI Global. https://doi.org/10.4018/978-1-7998-8473-6.ch006

Mertens, D. (2022). Designing Mixed Methods Studies to Contribute to Social, Economic, and Environmental Justice: Implications for Library and Information Sciences. In P. Ngulube (Ed.), *Handbook of Research on Mixed Methods Research in Information Science* (pp. 173–189). IGI Global. https://doi.org/10.4018/978-1-7998-8844-4.ch009

Moahi, K. H. (2020). The Research Process and Indigenous Epistemologies. In P. Ngulube (Ed.), *Handbook of Research on Connecting Research Methods for Information Science Research* (pp. 245–265). IGI Global. https://doi.org/10.4018/978-1-7998-1471-9.ch013

Mohapatra, N. (2021). Webrarian: A Librarian on the Web. In C. Chisita, R. Enakrire, O. Durodolu, V. Tsabedze, & J. Ngoaketsi (Eds.), *Handbook of Research on Records and Information Management Strategies for Enhanced Knowledge Coordination* (pp. 458–470). IGI Global. https://doi.org/10.4018/978-1-7998-6618-3.ch027

Munatsi, R. (2020). National Research and Knowledge Systems: Role of Libraries. In C. Chisita (Ed.), *Cooperation and Collaboration Initiatives for Libraries and Related Institutions* (pp. 273–293). IGI Global. https://doi.org/10.4018/978-1-7998-0043-9.ch014

Musimbi, W. L., & Mutuku, P. K. (2019). The Future of LIS and Media Training in the Global Era: Challenges and Prospects. In C. Chisita & A. Rusero (Eds.), *Exploring the Relationship Between Media, Libraries, and Archives* (pp. 82–101). IGI Global. doi:10.4018/978-1-5225-5840-8.ch006

Mwanzu, A. (2019). Economics of Resource Sharing via Library Consortia. In C. Chisita & A. Rusero (Eds.), *Exploring the Relationship Between Media, Libraries, and Archives* (pp. 19–34). IGI Global. https://doi.org/10.4018/978-1-5225-5840-8.ch002

Na, L. (2017). Library and Information Science Education and Graduate Programs in Academic Libraries. In L. Ruan, Q. Zhu, & Y. Ye (Eds.), *Academic Library Development and Administration in China* (pp. 218–229). Hershey, PA: IGI Global. doi:10.4018/978-1-5225-0550-1.ch013

Nagarkar, S. P. (2017). Biomedical Librarianship in the Post-Genomic Era. In S. Ram (Ed.), *Library and Information Services for Bioinformatics Education and Research* (pp. 1–17). Hershey, PA: IGI Global. doi:10.4018/978-1-5225-1871-6.ch001

Natarajan, M. (2017). Exploring Knowledge Sharing over Social Media. In R. Chugh (Ed.), *Harnessing Social Media as a Knowledge Management Tool* (pp. 55–73). Hershey, PA: IGI Global. doi:10.4018/978-1-5225-0495-5.ch003

Nazir, T. (2017). Preservation Initiatives in E-Environment to Protect Information Assets. In T. Ashraf & N. Kumar (Eds.), *Interdisciplinary Digital Preservation Tools and Technologies* (pp. 193–208). Hershey, PA: IGI Global. doi:10.4018/978-1-5225-1653-8.ch010

Ngulube, P. (2017). Embedding Indigenous Knowledge in Library and Information Science Education in Anglophone Eastern and Southern Africa. In P. Ngulube (Ed.), *Handbook of Research on Social, Cultural, and Educational Considerations of Indigenous Knowledge in Developing Countries* (pp. 92–115). Hershey, PA: IGI Global. doi:10.4018/978-1-5225-0838-0.ch006

Ngulube, P. (2022). Using Simple and Complex Mixed Methods Research Designs to Understand Research in Information Science. In P. Ngulube (Ed.), *Handbook of Research on Mixed Methods Research in Information Science* (pp. 20–46). IGI Global. doi:10.4018/978-1-7998-8844-4.ch002

Nicolajsen, H. W., Sorensen, F., & Scupola, A. (2018). User Involvement in Service Innovation Processes. In M. Khosrow-Pour (Ed.), *Optimizing Current Practices in E-Services and Mobile Applications* (pp. 42–61). Hershey, PA: IGI Global. doi:10.4018/978-1-5225-5026-6.ch003

Ocholla, D. N. (2022). A Research Dashboard for Aligning Research Components in Research Proposals, Theses, and Dissertations in Library and Information Science. In P. Ngulube (Ed.), *Handbook of Research on Mixed Methods Research in Information Science* (pp. 629–640). IGI Global. https://doi.org/10.4018/978-1-7998-8844-4.ch029

Ochonogor, W. C., & Okite-Amughoro, F. A. (2018). Building an Effective Digital Library in a University Teaching Hospital (UTH) in Nigeria. In A. Tella & T. Kwanya (Eds.), *Handbook of Research on Managing Intellectual Property in Digital Libraries* (pp. 184–204). Hershey, PA: IGI Global. doi:10.4018/978-1-5225-3093-0.ch010

Okada, D. (2020). 10,000 Newly Certified Librarians, 100 Secure Jobs. In R. Alenzuela, H. Kim, & D. Baylen (Eds.), *Internationalization of Library and Information Science Education in the Asia-Pacific Region* (pp. 78–101). IGI Global. https://doi.org/10.4018/978-1-7998-2273-8.ch004

Oladapo, Y. O. (2018). Open Access to Knowledge and Challenges in Digital Libraries. In A. Tella & T. Kwanya (Eds.), *Handbook of Research on Managing Intellectual Property in Digital Libraries* (pp. 260–291). Hershey, PA: IGI Global. doi:10.4018/978-1-5225-3093-0.ch014

Oladokun, O., & Zulu, S. F. (2017). Document Description and Coding as Key Elements in Knowledge, Records, and Information Management. In P. Jain & N. Mnjama (Eds.), *Managing Knowledge Resources and Records in Modern Organizations* (pp. 179–197). Hershey, PA: IGI Global. doi:10.4018/978-1-5225-1965-2.ch011

Olubodun, O. J., & Oye, P. O. (2019). Library: A Tool for Information Dissemination and Creating Awareness in Conflict-Induced Situations. In E. Nyam & F. Idoko (Eds.), *Examining the Social and Economic Impacts of Conflict-Induced Migration* (pp. 55–63). IGI Global. https://doi.org/10.4018/978-1-5225-7615-0.ch003

Omeluzor, S. U., Abayomi, I., & Gbemi-Ogunleye, P. (2018). Contemporary Media for Library Users' Instruction in Academic Libraries in South-West Nigeria: Contemporary Library Instruction in the Digital Age. In S. Bhattacharyya & K. Patnaik (Eds.), *Changing the Scope of Library Instruction in the Digital Age* (pp. 162–185). Hershey, PA: IGI Global. doi:10.4018/978-1-5225-2802-9.ch007

Onwuchekwa, E. O. (2020). Library Signage and Information Graphics: A Communication Tool for Library Users. In A. Tella (Ed.), *Handbook of Research on Digital Devices for Inclusivity and Engagement in Libraries* (pp. 231–237). IGI Global. https://doi.org/10.4018/978-1-5225-9034-7.ch011

Onyancha, O. B. (2020). Informetrics Research Methods Outlined. In P. Ngulube (Ed.), *Handbook of Research on Connecting Research Methods for Information Science Research* (pp. 320–348). IGI Global. https://doi.org/10.4018/978-1-7998-1471-9.ch017

Oshilalu, A. H., & Ogochukwu, E. T. (2017). Modeling a Software for Library and Information Centers. *International Journal of Library and Information Services*, 6(2), 1–10. doi:10.4018/IJLIS.2017070101

Oswal, S. K. (2017). Institutional, Legal, and Attitudinal Barriers to the Accessibility of University Digital Libraries: Implications for Retention of Disabled Students. In H. Alphin Jr, J. Lavine, & R. Chan (Eds.), *Disability and Equity in Higher Education Accessibility* (pp. 223–241). Hershey, PA: IGI Global. doi:10.4018/978-1-5225-2665-0.ch010

Oukrich, J., & Bouikhalene, B. (2017). A Survey of Users' Satisfaction in the University Library by Using a Pareto Analysis and the Automatic Classification Methods. *International Journal of Library and Information Services*, 6(1), 17–36. doi:10.4018/IJLIS.2017010102

Oyelude, A. A., & Oluwaniyi, S. A. (2020). Managing Future Library Services for the Medical Sciences: A Pharmacy Library Experience. In N. Osuigwe (Ed.), *Managing and Adapting Library Information Services for Future Users* (pp. 200–220). IGI Global. https://doi.org/10.4018/978-1-7998-1116-9.ch012

Related References

Özel, N. (2018). Developing Visual Literacy Skills Through Library Instructions. In V. Osinska & G. Osinski (Eds.), *Information Visualization Techniques in the Social Sciences and Humanities* (pp. 32–48). Hershey, PA: IGI Global. doi:10.4018/978-1-5225-4990-1.ch003

Paganelli, A. L., & Paganelli, A. L. (2021). Blockchain and the Research Libraries: Expanding Interlibrary Loan and Protecting Privacy. In D. Gunter (Ed.), *Transforming Scholarly Publishing With Blockchain Technologies and AI* (pp. 232–250). IGI Global. https://doi.org/10.4018/978-1-7998-5589-7.ch012

Patel, D., & Thakur, D. (2017). Managing Open Access (OA) Scholarly Information Resources in a University. In A. Munigal (Ed.), *Scholarly Communication and the Publish or Perish Pressures of Academia* (pp. 224–255). Hershey, PA: IGI Global. doi:10.4018/978-1-5225-1697-2.ch011

Patnaik, K. R. (2018). Crafting a Framework for Copyright Literacy and Licensed Content: A Case Study at an Advanced Management Education and Research Library. In S. Bhattacharyya & K. Patnaik (Eds.), *Changing the Scope of Library Instruction in the Digital Age* (pp. 136–160). Hershey, PA: IGI Global. doi:10.4018/978-1-5225-2802-9.ch006

Paynter, K. (2017). Elementary Library Media Specialists' Roles in the Implementation of the Common Core State Standards. In M. Grassetti & S. Brookby (Eds.), *Advancing Next-Generation Teacher Education through Digital Tools and Applications* (pp. 262–283). Hershey, PA: IGI Global. doi:10.4018/978-1-5225-0965-3.ch014

Perry, S. C., & Waggoner, J. (2018). Processes for User-Centered Design and Development: The Omeka Curator Dashboard Project. In L. Costello & M. Powers (Eds.), *Developing In-House Digital Tools in Library Spaces* (pp. 37–58). Hershey, PA: IGI Global. doi:10.4018/978-1-5225-2676-6.ch002

Perumalsamy, R., & Kannan, S. P. (2019). User Information Needs in the Public Libraries in India. In S. Thanuskodi (Ed.), *Literacy Skill Development for Library Science Professionals* (pp. 25–53). IGI Global. https://doi.org/10.4018/978-1-5225-7125-4.ch002

Phuritsabam, B., & Devi, A. B. (2017). Information Seeking Behavior of Medical Scientists at Jawaharlal Nehru Institute of Medical Science: A Study. In S. Ram (Ed.), *Library and Information Services for Bioinformatics Education and Research* (pp. 177–187). Hershey, PA: IGI Global. doi:10.4018/978-1-5225-1871-6.ch010

Quadri, R. F., & Sodiq, O. A. (2018). Managing Intellectual Property in Digital Libraries: The Roles of Digital Librarians. In A. Tella & T. Kwanya (Eds.), *Handbook of Research on Managing Intellectual Property in Digital Libraries* (pp. 337–355). Hershey, PA: IGI Global. doi:10.4018/978-1-5225-3093-0.ch017

Quintana, A. J. (2021). Ensuring Research Integrity. In K. Elufiede & C. Barker Stucky (Eds.), *Strategies and Tactics for Multidisciplinary Writing* (pp. 192–201). IGI Global. https://doi.org/10.4018/978-1-7998-4477-8.ch015

Qutab, S., Adil, S. A., Gardner, L. A., & Ullah, F. S. (2022). The Role of Libraries, Archives, and Museums for Metaliteracy in Smart Cities: Implications, Challenges, and Opportunities. In M. Taher (Ed.), *Handbook of Research on the Role of Libraries, Archives, and Museums in Achieving Civic Engagement and Social Justice in Smart Cities* (pp. 355–375). IGI Global. https://doi.org/10.4018/978-1-7998-8363-0.ch019

Raj, S. K., & De, K. (2020). Electronic Resource Management and Digitisation: Library System of the University of Calcutta. In A. Kaushik, A. Kumar, & P. Biswas (Eds.), *Handbook of Research on Emerging Trends and Technologies in Library and Information Science* (pp. 231–265). IGI Global. https://doi.org/10.4018/978-1-5225-9825-1.ch017

Ram, S. (2017). Library Services for Bioinformatics: Establishing Synergy Data Information and Knowledge. In S. Ram (Ed.), *Library and Information Services for Bioinformatics Education and Research* (pp. 18–33). Hershey, PA: IGI Global. doi:10.4018/978-1-5225-1871-6.ch002

Rao, M. (2017). Use of Institutional Repository for Information Dissemination and Knowledge Management. In B. Gunjal (Ed.), *Managing Knowledge and Scholarly Assets in Academic Libraries* (pp. 156–173). Hershey, PA: IGI Global. doi:10.4018/978-1-5225-1741-2.ch007

Rao, Y., & Zhang, Y. (2017). The Construction and Development of Academic Library Digital Special Subject Databases. In L. Ruan, Q. Zhu, & Y. Ye (Eds.), *Academic Library Development and Administration in China* (pp. 163–183). Hershey, PA: IGI Global. doi:10.4018/978-1-5225-0550-1.ch010

Rao, Y., & Zhang, Y. (2020). The Construction and Development of Academic Library Digital Special Subject Databases. In I. Management Association (Ed.), *Digital Libraries and Institutional Repositories: Breakthroughs in Research and Practice* (pp. 24-44). IGI Global. https://doi.org/10.4018/978-1-7998-2463-3.ch002

Razip, S. N., Kadir, S. F., Saim, S. N., Dolhan, F. N., Jarmil, N., Salleh, N. H., & Rajin, G. (2017). Predicting Users' Intention towards Using Library Self-Issue and Return Systems. In N. Suki (Ed.), *Handbook of Research on Leveraging Consumer Psychology for Effective Customer Engagement* (pp. 102–115). Hershey, PA: IGI Global. doi:10.4018/978-1-5225-0746-8.ch007

Rothwell, S. L. (2018). Librarians and Instructional Design Challenges: Concepts, Examples, and a Flexible Design Framework. In S. Bhattacharyya & K. Patnaik (Eds.), *Changing the Scope of Library Instruction in the Digital Age* (pp. 24–59). Hershey, PA: IGI Global. doi:10.4018/978-1-5225-2802-9.ch002

Roy, L., & Frydman, A. (2018). Community Outreach. In M. Khosrow-Pour, D.B.A. (Ed.), Encyclopedia of Information Science and Technology, Fourth Edition (pp. 6685-6694). Hershey, PA: IGI Global. doi:10.4018/978-1-5225-2255-3.ch579

Rutto, D., & Yudah, O. (2018). E-Books in University Libraries in Kenya: Trends, Usage, and Intellectual Property Issues. In A. Tella & T. Kwanya (Eds.), *Handbook of Research on Managing Intellectual Property in Digital Libraries* (pp. 120–141). Hershey, PA: IGI Global. doi:10.4018/978-1-5225-3093-0.ch007

Sabharwal, A. (2017). The Transformative Role of Institutional Repositories in Academic Knowledge Management. In B. Gunjal (Ed.), *Managing Knowledge and Scholarly Assets in Academic Libraries* (pp. 127–155). Hershey, PA: IGI Global. doi:10.4018/978-1-5225-1741-2.ch006

Sadiku, S. A., Kpakiko, M. M., & Tsafe, A. G. (2018). Institutional Digital Repository and the Challenges of Global Visibility in Nigeria. In A. Tella & T. Kwanya (Eds.), *Handbook of Research on Managing Intellectual Property in Digital Libraries* (pp. 356–376). Hershey, PA: IGI Global. doi:10.4018/978-1-5225-3093-0.ch018

Sahu, M. K. (2018). Web-Scale Discovery Service in Academic Library Environment: A Birds Eye View. *International Journal of Library and Information Services*, 7(1), 1–14. doi:10.4018/IJLIS.2018010101

Salim, F., Saigar, B., Armoham, P. K., Gobalakrishnan, S., Jap, M. Y., & Lim, N. A. (2017). Students' Information-Seeking Intention in Academic Digital Libraries. In N. Suki (Ed.), *Handbook of Research on Leveraging Consumer Psychology for Effective Customer Engagement* (pp. 259–273). Hershey, PA: IGI Global. doi:10.4018/978-1-5225-0746-8.ch017

Saroja, G. (2017). Changing Face of Scholarly Communication and Its Impact on Library and Information Centres. In A. Munigal (Ed.), *Scholarly Communication and the Publish or Perish Pressures of Academia* (pp. 100–117). Hershey, PA: IGI Global. doi:10.4018/978-1-5225-1697-2.ch006

Sauti, L. (2020). Social Media and Library Collaboration: Analysis of Government Libraries (Kaguvi Building). In C. Chisita (Ed.), *Cooperation and Collaboration Initiatives for Libraries and Related Institutions* (pp. 312–334). IGI Global. https://doi.org/10.4018/978-1-7998-0043-9.ch016

Schuster, D. W. (2017). Selection Process for Free Open Source Software. In E. Iglesias (Ed.), *Library Technology Funding, Planning, and Deployment* (pp. 55–71). Hershey, PA: IGI Global. doi:10.4018/978-1-5225-1735-1.ch004

Seagraves, K., & Weyand, L. (2021). From Bake-Alongs to Tech Talks: How One Public Library System Pivoted to Virtual Programming. In B. Holland (Ed.), *Handbook of Research on Library Response to the COVID-19 Pandemic* (pp. 447-480). IGI Global. https://doi.org/10.4018/978-1-7998-6449-3.ch023

Segaetsho, T. (2018). Environmental Consideration in the Preservation of Paper Materials in Heritage Institutions in the East and Southern African Region. In P. Ngulube (Ed.), *Handbook of Research on Heritage Management and Preservation* (pp. 183–212). Hershey, PA: IGI Global. doi:10.4018/978-1-5225-3137-1.ch010

Shakhsi, L. (2017). Cataloging Images in Library, Archive, and Museum. In T. Ashraf & N. Kumar (Eds.), *Interdisciplinary Digital Preservation Tools and Technologies* (pp. 119–141). Hershey, PA: IGI Global. doi:10.4018/978-1-5225-1653-8.ch007

Sharma, C. (2017). Digital Initiatives of the Indian Council of World Affairs' Library. In T. Ashraf & N. Kumar (Eds.), *Interdisciplinary Digital Preservation Tools and Technologies* (pp. 231–241). Hershey, PA: IGI Global. doi:10.4018/978-1-5225-1653-8.ch012

Shook, R. (2022). Achieving Balance Through Fundamentals of Digital Librarianship. In P. Pangelinan & T. McVey (Eds.), *Learning and Reconciliation Through Indigenous Education in Oceania* (pp. 185–196). IGI Global. https://doi.org/10.4018/978-1-7998-7736-3.ch011

Shukla, P., & Das, C. (2020). Plagiarism: The Role of Librarian and Teachers in Combating It. In J. Jesubright & P. Saravanan (Eds.), *Innovations in the Designing and Marketing of Information Services* (pp. 148–158). IGI Global. https://doi.org/10.4018/978-1-7998-1482-5.ch011

Siddaiah, D. K. (2018). Commonwealth Professional Fellowship: A Gateway for the Strategic Development of Libraries in India. In R. Bhardwaj (Ed.), *Digitizing the Modern Library and the Transition From Print to Electronic* (pp. 270–286). Hershey, PA: IGI Global. doi:10.4018/978-1-5225-2119-8.ch012

Related References

Silvana de Rosa, A. (2018). Mission, Tools, and Ongoing Developments in the So.Re. Com. "A.S. de Rosa" @-library. In M. Khosrow-Pour, D.B.A. (Ed.), Encyclopedia of Information Science and Technology, Fourth Edition (pp. 5237-5251). Hershey, PA: IGI Global. https://doi.org/ doi:10.4018/978-1-5225-2255-3.ch455

Smolenski, N., Kostic, M., & Sofronijevic, A. M. (2018). Intrapreneurship and Enterprise 2.0 as Grounds for Developing In-House Digital Tools for Handling METS/ALTO Files at the University Library Belgrade. In L. Costello & M. Powers (Eds.), *Developing In-House Digital Tools in Library Spaces* (pp. 92–116). Hershey, PA: IGI Global. doi:10.4018/978-1-5225-2676-6.ch005

Sochay, L., & Junus, R. (2017). From Summon to SearchPlus: The RFP Process for a Discovery Tool at the MSU Libraries. In E. Iglesias (Ed.), *Library Technology Funding, Planning, and Deployment* (pp. 72–98). Hershey, PA: IGI Global. doi:10.4018/978-1-5225-1735-1.ch005

Soliudeen, M. J. (2021). The Relevance of Feedback Mechanisms to Library Databases in Academic Libraries. In A. Maake, B. Maake, & F. Awuor (Eds.), *Digital Solutions and the Case for Africa's Sustainable Development* (pp. 116–130). IGI Global. doi:10.4018/978-1-7998-2967-6.ch008

Sonawane, C. S. (2018). Library Catalogue in the Internet Age. In R. Bhardwaj (Ed.), *Digitizing the Modern Library and the Transition From Print to Electronic* (pp. 204–223). Hershey, PA: IGI Global. doi:10.4018/978-1-5225-2119-8.ch009

Sorokhaibam, S. D., & Mathabela, N. N. (2017). Information Needs and Assessment of Bioinformatics Students at the University of Swaziland: Librarian View. In S. Ram (Ed.), *Library and Information Services for Bioinformatics Education and Research* (pp. 188–198). IGI Global. https://doi.org/10.4018/978-1-5225-1871-6.ch011

Staley, C., Kenyon, R. S., & Marcovitz, D. M. (2018). Embedded Services: Going Beyond the Field of Dreams Model for Online Programs. In D. Polly, M. Putman, T. Petty, & A. Good (Eds.), *Innovative Practices in Teacher Preparation and Graduate-Level Teacher Education Programs* (pp. 368–381). Hershey, PA: IGI Global. doi:10.4018/978-1-5225-3068-8.ch020

Stevenson, C. N. (2020). Data Speaks: Use of Poems and Photography in Qualitative Research. In M. Baran & J. Jones (Eds.), *Applied Social Science Approaches to Mixed Methods Research* (pp. 119–144). IGI Global. doi:10.4018/978-1-7998-1025-4.ch006

Stewart, M. C., Atilano, M., & Arnold, C. L. (2017). Improving Customer Relations with Social Listening: A Case Study of an American Academic Library. *International Journal of Customer Relationship Marketing and Management*, 8(1), 49–63. doi:10.4018/IJCRMM.2017010104

Sukula, S. K., & Bhardwaj, R. K. (2018). An Extensive Discussion on Transition of Libraries: The Panoramic View of Library Resources, Services, and Evolved Librarianship. In R. Bhardwaj (Ed.), *Digitizing the Modern Library and the Transition From Print to Electronic* (pp. 255–269). Hershey, PA: IGI Global. doi:10.4018/978-1-5225-2119-8.ch011

Surendran, B., & Kumar, K. (2020). Implementing Information Literacy Skills and Soft Skills for Better Use of Library Resources and Services. In S. Thanuskodi (Ed.), *Handbook of Research on Digital Content Management and Development in Modern Libraries* (pp. 214–224). IGI Global. doi:10.4018/978-1-7998-2201-1.ch012

Suresh, M., & Ravi, S. (2020). Online Database Use by Science Research Scholars of Alagappa University, Karaikudi: A Study. In S. Thanuskodi (Ed.), *Handbook of Research on Digital Content Management and Development in Modern Libraries* (pp. 86-102). IGI Global. https://doi.org/10.4018/978-1-7998-2201-1.ch006

Tella, A., & Babatunde, B. J. (2017). Determinants of Continuance Intention of Facebook Usage Among Library and Information Science Female Undergraduates in Selected Nigerian Universities. *International Journal of E-Adoption*, 9(2), 59–76. doi:10.4018/IJEA.2017070104

Tella, A., Okojie, V., & Olaniyi, O. T. (2018). Social Bookmarking Tools and Digital Libraries. In A. Tella & T. Kwanya (Eds.), *Handbook of Research on Managing Intellectual Property in Digital Libraries* (pp. 396–409). Hershey, PA: IGI Global. doi:10.4018/978-1-5225-3093-0.ch020

Thobane, M. S., & Jansen van Rensburg, S. K. (2022). Transforming Methods for Research With Indigenous Communities: An African Social Sciences Perspective. In P. Ngulube (Ed.), *Handbook of Research on Mixed Methods Research in Information Science* (pp. 190–203). IGI Global. doi:10.4018/978-1-7998-8844-4.ch010

Thull, J. J. (2018). Librarians and the Evolving Research Needs of Distance Students. In I. Oncioiu (Ed.), *Ethics and Decision-Making for Sustainable Business Practices* (pp. 203–216). Hershey, PA: IGI Global. doi:10.4018/978-1-5225-3773-1.ch012

Titilope, A. O. (2017). Ethical Issues in Library and Information Science Profession in Nigeria: An Appraisal. *International Journal of Library and Information Services*, 6(2), 11–22. doi:10.4018/IJLIS.2017070102

Tutu, J. M. (2018). Intellectual Property Challenges in Digital Library Environments. In A. Tella & T. Kwanya (Eds.), *Handbook of Research on Managing Intellectual Property in Digital Libraries* (pp. 225–240). Hershey, PA: IGI Global. doi:10.4018/978-1-5225-3093-0.ch012

Related References

Udo-Anyanwu, A. J., & Alor, A. R. (2020). Library Associations, Leadership, and Programmes: IFLA, AfLIA, and NLA. In N. Osuigwe (Ed.), *Managing and Adapting Library Information Services for Future Users* (pp. 89–102). IGI Global. https://doi.org/10.4018/978-1-7998-1116-9.ch006

Wallace, D., & Hemment, M. (2018). Enabling Scholarship in the Digital Age: A Case for Libraries Creating Value at HBS. In S. Bhattacharyya & K. Patnaik (Eds.), *Changing the Scope of Library Instruction in the Digital Age* (pp. 86–117). Hershey, PA: IGI Global. doi:10.4018/978-1-5225-2802-9.ch004

Wang, W., & Wei, Z. (2021). Tongwei County Library: Practices of Social Cooperation in Grassroots Libraries in Western China. *International Journal of Library and Information Services, 10*(1), 48–60. https://doi.org/10.4018/IJLIS.2021010104

Wani, Z. A., Zainab, T., & Hussain, S. (2018). Web 2.0 From Evolution to Revolutionary Impact in Library and Information Centers. In M. Khosrow-Pour, D.B.A. (Ed.), Encyclopedia of Information Science and Technology, Fourth Edition (pp. 5262-5271). Hershey, PA: IGI Global. https://doi.org/ doi:10.4018/978-1-5225-2255-3.ch457

Watkins, K. E., Nicolaides, A., & Marsick, V. J. (2021). Action Research Approaches. In V. Wang (Ed.), *Promoting Qualitative Research Methods for Critical Reflection and Change* (pp. 119–139). IGI Global. https://doi.org/10.4018/978-1-7998-7600-7.ch007

Weiss, A. P. (2018). Massive Digital Libraries (MDLs). In M. Khosrow-Pour, D.B.A. (Ed.), Encyclopedia of Information Science and Technology, Fourth Edition (pp. 5226-5236). Hershey, PA: IGI Global. https://doi.org/ doi:10.4018/978-1-5225-2255-3.ch454

Wu, S. K., Bess, M., & Price, B. R. (2018). Digitizing Library Outreach: Leveraging Bluetooth Beacons and Mobile Applications to Expand Library Outreach. In R. Bhardwaj (Ed.), *Digitizing the Modern Library and the Transition From Print to Electronic* (pp. 193–203). Hershey, PA: IGI Global. doi:10.4018/978-1-5225-2119-8.ch008

Wulff, E. (2018). Evaluation of Digital Collections and Political Visibility of the Library. In R. Bhardwaj (Ed.), *Digitizing the Modern Library and the Transition From Print to Electronic* (pp. 64–89). Hershey, PA: IGI Global. doi:10.4018/978-1-5225-2119-8.ch003

Wulff, E. (2019). Research Data Access and Management in National Libraries. In R. Bhardwaj & P. Banks (Eds.), *Research Data Access and Management in Modern Libraries* (pp. 1–28). IGI Global. https://doi.org/10.4018/978-1-5225-8437-7.ch001

Xiao, L., & Liu, Y. (2017). Development of Innovative User Services. In L. Ruan, Q. Zhu, & Y. Ye (Eds.), *Academic Library Development and Administration in China* (pp. 56–73). Hershey, PA: IGI Global. doi:10.4018/978-1-5225-0550-1.ch004

Xin, X., & Wu, X. (2017). The Practice of Outreach Services in Chinese Special Libraries. In L. Ruan, Q. Zhu, & Y. Ye (Eds.), *Academic Library Development and Administration in China* (pp. 74–89). Hershey, PA: IGI Global. doi:10.4018/978-1-5225-0550-1.ch005

Yao, X., Zhu, Q., & Liu, J. (2017). The China Academic Library and Information System (CALIS). In L. Ruan, Q. Zhu, & Y. Ye (Eds.), *Academic Library Development and Administration in China* (pp. 1–19). Hershey, PA: IGI Global. doi:10.4018/978-1-5225-0550-1.ch001

Yin, Q., Yingying, W., Yan, Z., & Xiaojia, M. (2017). Resource Sharing and Mutually Beneficial Cooperation: A Look at the New United Model in Public and College Libraries. In L. Ruan, Q. Zhu, & Y. Ye (Eds.), *Academic Library Development and Administration in China* (pp. 334–352). Hershey, PA: IGI Global. doi:10.4018/978-1-5225-0550-1.ch019

Yuhua, F. (2018). Computer Information Library Clusters. In M. Khosrow-Pour, D.B.A. (Ed.), Encyclopedia of Information Science and Technology, Fourth Edition (pp. 4399-4403). Hershey, PA: IGI Global. doi:10.4018/978-1-5225-2255-3.ch382

Yusuf, F., & Owolabi, S. E. (2018). Open Access to Knowledge and Challenges in Digital Libraries: Nigeria's Peculiarity. In A. Tella & T. Kwanya (Eds.), *Handbook of Research on Managing Intellectual Property in Digital Libraries* (pp. 241–259). Hershey, PA: IGI Global. doi:10.4018/978-1-5225-3093-0.ch013

Zhang, Q., Zhang, C., & Zhang, Z. (2021). Open Data Services in the Library: Case Study of the Shanghai Library. *International Journal of Library and Information Services*, *10*(1), 1–17. https://doi.org/10.4018/IJLIS.2021010101

Zhang, W., Zou, W., & Qiu, X. (2019). A Unique Development Road of Urban Public Libraries of China: Practice and Exploration of Pudong Library. *International Journal of Library and Information Services*, *8*(2), 51–71. https://doi.org/10.4018/IJLIS.2019070104

Zhu, S., & Shi, W. (2017). A Bibliometric Analysis of Research and Services in Chinese Academic Libraries. In L. Ruan, Q. Zhu, & Y. Ye (Eds.), *Academic Library Development and Administration in China* (pp. 253–262). Hershey, PA: IGI Global. doi:10.4018/978-1-5225-0550-1.ch015

About the Contributors

Guillermo A. Francia III received his Ph.D. in Computer Science from New Mexico Tech. Before joining Jacksonville State University (JSU), he was the chairman of the Computer Science department at Kansas Wesleyan University. In 1996, Dr. Francia received one of the five national awards for Innovators in Higher Education from Microsoft Corporation. His research interests include embedded and industrial control systems security, automotive security, machine learning, and unmanned aerial vehicle security. He is a two-time recipient of a Fulbright award (UK, 2017 and Malta, 2007) and is the 2018 winner of the National CyberWatch Center Innovations in Cybersecurity Education award. He has successfully managed research projects with funds well over $2.5M from the National Science Foundation, Department of Defense, Department of Energy, and National Security Agency. He held Distinguished Professor and Director positions at JSU prior to joining the University of West Florida (UWF). In 2019, he received an appointment as Commissioner of the Computing Accreditation Commission of ABET. Currently, Dr. Francia is serving as Faculty Scholar and Professor at the Center for Cybersecurity.

Jeffrey S. Zanzig received both his Bachelor's and Master's of Business Administration degrees from Jacksonville State University. He also holds a Master's of Accounting from the University of Alabama at Birmingham, a Master's of Science in Computer Systems and Software Design from Jacksonville State University, and a Ph.D. in Accounting from the University of Mississippi. His professional designations include: Certified Public Accountant, Certified Internal Auditor, Certified Management Accountant, and Certified in Financial Management. He has authored a variety of articles in accounting and auditing and received the 2006 Max Block Distinguished Article Award for Informed Comment from the New York State Society of Certified Public Accountants. Dr. Zanzig is also affiliated with the Center for Information Security and Assurance at Jacksonville State University.

* * *

Eman El-Sheikh is Associate Vice President and Professor of Computer Science at the University of West Florida, where she leads the Center for Cybersecurity. Dr. El-Sheikh has extensive expertise in cybersecurity education, research and workforce development. She received several awards related to cybersecurity education and diversity, and was recognized among the 2020 Women Leaders in Cybersecurity by Security Magazine. Dr. El-Sheikh leads several national and regional initiatives, including the National CAE Cybersecurity Workforce Development Program and the Southeast Regional Hub for the National Centers of Academic Excellence in Cybersecurity. Eman received over $11 million in funding from the NSA, NSF and other organizations for cybersecurity education, workforce development and capacity building. She launched the Cybersecurity for All® Program to enhance competencies and hands-on skills for evolving cybersecurity work roles, which was recognized among the 2020 Innovations in Cybersecurity Education. Dr. El-Sheikh teaches and conducts research related to the development and evaluation of Artificial Intelligence and Machine Learning for cybersecurity. She has published several books, including most recently, Computer and Network Security Essentials by Springer Publishing, over 75 peer-reviewed articles and given over 100 invited talks and presentations. Eman also co-founded the Women in Cybersecurity Florida Affiliate.

Adamkolo Mohammed Ibrahim received his MSc degree in Development Communication from Universiti Putra Malaysia (UPM) in 2017 and had his first degree, BA Mass Communication from the University of Maiduguri in 2007. Currently, he is pursuing a PhD at Bayero University, Kano. Also, he teaches Mass Communication Diploma on a part-time basis at Yobe State University, Damaturu, and he is the Coordinator of the Mass Communication Diploma programme at Yobe State University. He has a total of over 60 publications (including journal articles, book chapters, conference papers and a couple of books). Since 2013, Adamkolo has received several merit awards including the award he received in 2018 from Publons, as Top Reviewer, for being among the top 1% of global peer reviewers in Psychiatry/Psychology of communication. Since 2014, Malam Adamkolo has been reviewing for several academic research journals including Computers in Human Behaviour (CHB) and Children and Youth Services Review (CYSR) both published by Elsevier, as well as Journal of Systems and Information Technology (JSIT) which is published by Emerald. Since 2014, Adamkolo has peer-reviewed not less than 60 academic research papers.

Bukar Jamri (PhD) is a Senior Lecturer at the Department of Sociology and Anthropology, Yobe State University. He is also the Deputy Vice-Chancellor, Administrative Services of the university.

Kátia Lemos is a PhD in Accounting by University of Santiago de Compostela, Spain and a Professor at the Department of Accounting and Taxation School of Management Institute Polytechnic of Cávado and Ave, Portugal.

Nkholedzeni Sidney Netshakhuma is Deputy Director of Records and Archives at the University of Mpumalanga in South Africa. Before this position, He worked for the South Africa Public Service for 12 years as Deputy Manager Information and Records Management, SANParks as the records manager, and the African National Congress as the archivists. He holds a BA (History and Political Studies), BTECH (Archival Studies), BPHIL (Honours) Information and Knowledge Management, Post Diploma in Records and Archives Management, Postgraduate Diploma in Heritage and Museum Studies, Advance Certificate in Records and Archives Management, Masters of Information Science from the University of South Africa and he recently completed a doctoral programme in archives and records management at UNISA. He served as the Advisory committee member of UNISA Centre for Applied Communication (Records and Archives Management), He is currently a Deputy Chairperson of the South Africa Higher Education Records Management Forum, He also served as the advisor (Reference Group for the Mpumalanga Records Management Forum.

Miloslava Plachkinova is an Assistant Professor of Information Security and Assurance at Kennesaw State University. Her research focuses on information security, cybercrime, and policy implications. Dr. Plachkinova's work has been published in journals such as Information Systems Frontiers, Journal of Information Systems Education, Journal of Information Technology Theory and Application, and Journal of Cyber Forensics and Advanced Threat Investigations. She is a Certified Information Systems Security Professional (CISSP), Certified Information Security Manager (CISM), Certified in Risk and Information Systems Control (CRISC), and a Project Management Professional (PMP®).

Sara Serra is a PhD in Accounting by University of Minho, Portugal and Professor at the Department of Accounting and Taxation School of Management Institute Polytechnic of Cávado and Ave.

David Thornton received his Ph.D. in Computer Science in 2008 from Auburn University. Currently, he serves as a Professor in the Mathematical, Computing, and Information Sciences Department at Jacksonville State University, where he developed the game development concentration for computer science majors. He has served as lead instructor in two GenCyber information awareness camps for instilling cyber-security awareness in secondary education curriculum. He has developed multiple web-based gamification tools for use in learning management systems, which are in use in over 30 high schools and universities across 7 different countries. He has worked with his colleagues on DoD-NSA funded research, workshops, and games promoting cybersecurity awareness.

Heidi Tribunella is a Clinical Professor of accounting at the University of Rochester.

Thomas Tribunella is an accounting professor at the State University of New York at Oswego.

Abubakar Zakari (BSc) is an Assistant Lecturer at the Department of General Studies, Federal Polytechnic, Damaturu, Yobe State, Nigeria.

Index

Recommended Reference Books

IGI Global's reference books can now be purchased from three unique pricing formats:
Print Only, E-Book Only, or Print + E-Book.
Shipping fees may apply.

www.igi-global.com

Premier Reference Source

Intelligence and Law Enforcement in the 21st Century

ISBN: 9781799879046
EISBN: 9781799879060
© 2021; 253 pp.
List Price: US$ 225

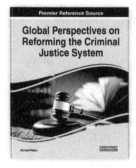

Premier Reference Source

Global Perspectives on Reforming the Criminal Justice System

ISBN: 9781799868842
EISBN: 9781799868866
© 2021; 380 pp.
List Price: US$ 195

Research Insights

Combating the Exploitation of Children in Cyberspace
Emerging Research and Opportunities

ISBN: 9781799823605
EISBN: 9781799823629
© 2021; 165 pp.
List Price: US$ 160

Premier Reference Source

Real-Time and Retrospective Analyses of Cyber Security

ISBN: 9781799839798
EISBN: 9781799839804
© 2021; 267 pp.
List Price: US$ 195

Premier Reference Source

NATO and the Future of European and Asian Security

ISBN: 9781799871187
EISBN: 9781799871200
© 2021; 331 pp.
List Price: US$ 195

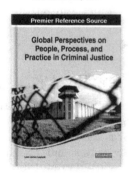

Premier Reference Source

Global Perspectives on People, Process, and Practice in Criminal Justice

ISBN: 9781799866466
EISBN: 9781799866480
© 2021; 282 pp.
List Price: US$ 195

Do you want to stay current on the latest research trends, product announcements, news, and special offers?
Join IGI Global's mailing list to receive customized recommendations, exclusive discounts, and more.
Sign up at: **www.igi-global.com/newsletters.**

Publisher of Timely, Peer-Reviewed Inclusive Research Since 1988

IGI Global
PUBLISHER of TIMELY KNOWLEDGE

www.igi-global.com   ✉ Sign up at www.igi-global.com/newsletters   f facebook.com/igiglobal   t twitter.com/igiglobal

Ensure Quality Research is Introduced to the Academic Community

Become an Evaluator for IGI Global Authored Book Projects

Premier Reference Source

Stabilizing Currency and Preserving Economic Sovereignty Using the Grondona System

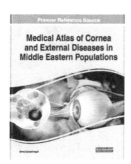

Premier Reference Source

Medical Atlas of Cornea and External Diseases in Middle Eastern Populations

Premier Reference Source

Examining Biophilia and Societal Indifference to Environmental Protection

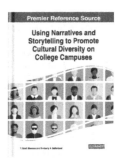

Premier Reference Source

Using Narratives and Storytelling to Promote Cultural Diversity on College Campuses

The overall success of an authored book project is dependent on quality and timely manuscript evaluations.

Applications and Inquiries may be sent to:
development@igi-global.com

Applicants must have a doctorate (or equivalent degree) as well as publishing, research, and reviewing experience. Authored Book Evaluators are appointed for one-year terms and are expected to complete at least three evaluations per term. Upon successful completion of this term, evaluators can be considered for an additional term.

If you have a colleague that may be interested in this opportunity, we encourage you to share this information with them.

Increase Your Manuscript's Chance of Acceptance
IGI Global Author Services

Learn More or Get Started Here:
www.igi-global.com/editorial-service-partners/

Copy Editing & Proofreading

Professional, native English language copy editors improve your manuscript's grammar, spelling, punctuation, terminology, semantics, consistency, flow, formatting, and more.

Scientific & Scholarly Editing

A Ph.D. level review for qualities such as originality and significance, interest to researchers, level of methodology and analysis, coverage of literature, organization, quality of writing, and strengths and weaknesses.

Figure, Table, Chart & Equation Conversions

Work with IGI Global's graphic designers before submission to enhance and design all figures and charts to IGI Global's specific standards for clarity.

- Professional Service

- Quality Guarantee & Certificate

- Timeliness

- Affordable Pricing

What Makes IGI Global Author Services Stand Apart?

Services/Offerings	IGI Global Author Services	Editage	Enago
Turnaround Time of Projects	3-5 Business Days	6-7 Busines Days	6-7 Busines Days
Pricing	Fraction of our Competitors' Cost	Up to 2x Higher	Up to 3x Higher

For Questions, Contact IGI Global's Customer Service Team at cust@igi-global.com or 717-533-8845

IGI Global
PUBLISHER of TIMELY KNOWLEDGE
www.igi-global.com

6,600+ E-BOOKS.
ADVANCED RESEARCH.
INCLUSIVE & ACCESSIBLE.

IGI Global e-Book Collection

- **Flexible Purchasing Options** (Perpetual, Subscription, EBA, etc.)
- Multi-Year Agreements with **No Price Increases** Guaranteed
- **No Additional Charge** for Multi-User Licensing
- No Maintenance, Hosting, or Archiving Fees
- Transformative **Open Access Options** Available

*Request More Information, or Recommend the IGI Global
e-Book Collection to Your Institution's Librarian*

Among Titles Included in the IGI Global e-Book Collection

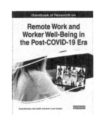

**Research Anthology on
Racial Equity, Identity,
and Privilege (3 Vols.)**
EISBN: 9781668445082
Price: US$ 895

**Handbook of Research
on Remote Work and
Worker Well-Being in
the Post-COVID-19 Era**
EISBN: 9781799867562
Price: US$ 265

**Research Anthology
on Big Data Analytics,
Architectures, and
Applications (4 Vols.)**
EISBN: 9781668436639
Price: US$ 1,950

**Handbook of Research
on Challenging Deficit
Thinking for Exceptional
Education Improvement**
EISBN: 9781799888628
Price: US$ 265

Acquire & Open

When your library acquires an IGI Global e-Book and/or e-Journal Collection, your faculty's
published work will be considered for immediate conversion to Open Access *(CC BY License)*, at
no additional cost to the library or its faculty *(cost only applies to the e-Collection content being
acquired)*, through our popular **Transformative Open Access (Read & Publish) Initiative**.

**For More Information or to Request a Free Trial, Contact IGI Global's e-Collections
Team:** eresources@igi-global.com | 1-866-342-6657 ext. 100 | 717-533-8845 ext. 100

Printed in the United States
by Baker & Taylor Publisher Services